NEW DIRECTIONS IN CYPRIOT ARCHAEOLOGY

NEW DIRECTIONS IN CYPRIOT ARCHAEOLOGY

EDITED BY

Catherine Kearns and Sturt W. Manning

CORNELL UNIVERSITY PRESS
Ithaca and London

Publication of this book has been aided by a grant from the
von Bothmer Publication Fund of the Archaeological
Institute of America.

First published 2019 by Cornell University Press

Printed in the United States of America

Library of Congress Cataloging-in-Publication Data

Names: Kearns, Catherine, editor. | Manning, Sturt W.,
    editor.
Title: New directions in Cypriot archaeology / edited by
    Catherine Kearns and Sturt W. Manning.
Description: Ithaca [New York] : Cornell University Press,
    2019. | Edited versions of some of the papers presented
    at a conference that took place at Cornell University,
    April 10–12, 2014. | Includes bibliographical references
    and index.
Identifiers: LCCN 2018035594 (print) | LCCN
    2018036462 (ebook) | ISBN 9781501732706 (pdf) |
    ISBN 9781501732713 (epub/mobi) | ISBN 9781501732690 |
    ISBN 9781501732690 (cloth: alk. paper)
Subjects: LCSH: Antiquities, Prehistoric—Cyprus. |
    Cyprus—Antiquities. | Bronze age—Cyprus. |
    Excavations (Archaeology)—Cyprus. | Archaeology and
    history—Cyprus.
Classification: LCC GN855.C93 (ebook) |
    LCC GN855.C93 N48 2019 (print) | DDC 939/.37—dc23
LC record available at https://lccn.loc.gov/2018035594

Contents

Contributors

Georgia Marina Andreou, Postdoctoral Fellow, Joukowsky Institute for Archaeology, Brown University

Stella Diakou, Postdoctoral Fellow, Department of History and Archaeology, University of Cyprus

Maria Dikomitou-Eliadou, Postdoctoral Fellow, Department of History and Archaeology, University of Cyprus

David Frankel, Professor Emeritus of Archaeology and History, La Trobe University

Artemis Georgiou, Marie Curie Research Fellow, Department of History and Archaeology, University of Cyprus

Catherine Kearns, Assistant Professor of Classics, University of Chicago

Sturt W. Manning, Goldwin Smith Professor of Classical Archaeology, Cornell University

Eilis Monahan, PhD Candidate, Department of Near Eastern Studies, Cornell University

Charalambos Paraskeva, Postdoctoral Fellow, Department of History and Archaeology, University of Cyprus

Anna Satraki, Archaeological Field Officer, Department of Antiquities of Cyprus

Matthew Spigelman, ACME Heritage Consultants, Partner

NEW DIRECTIONS IN CYPRIOT ARCHAEOLOGY

Introduction

New Directions in Method and Theory

CATHERINE KEARNS AND STURT W. MANNING

The title of this volume offers an echo of one published in 1975 stemming from a conference at Brock University in October 1971: *The Archaeology of Cyprus: Recent Developments* (Robertson 1975). That volume appeared barely a year after the Turkish invasion of Cyprus and the division of the island that remains over four decades later as we write. Its publication also occurred right as the "new" (processual) archaeology and related intellectual trends were sweeping the wider field of archaeology (e.g., Binford 1977; see also Trigger 2006: 386–443). Yet in keeping with the dominant modes of classical Mediterranean archaeology (cf. Renfrew 1980; Snodgrass 1985), such intellectual concerns, with a few honorable exceptions, took a considerable time to penetrate into Cypriot archaeology, where work largely continued to operate within the traditions of culture history (Knapp 2013: 21–24). The papers in the Robertson volume offer a view into a relatively conservative field, and although some presented then-recent fieldwork, the contributors focused largely on issues of evidentiary categories, boundaries of material culture (some from a distinctly art historical orientation), and normative historical questions and thus tended to avoid contemporary approaches to theory and method. A brief review in the *Journal of Near Eastern Studies* summarized the contents and concluded:

> The picture of the Island drawn from this collection of essays, though somewhat sketchy, gives some idea as to the current level of knowledge and opens avenues for further research. (Adelman 1978)

Much has changed in the decades since. *Force majeure* ended fieldwork in the north, including both active projects at many of the main archaeological sites on the island (e.g., Athienou *Bamboulari tis Koukounninas*, Ayia Irini, Ayios Epiktitos *Vrysi*, Enkomi, Lapithos, Morphou *Toumba tou Skourou*, Phlamoudhi, Salamis, and Soloi; see Figure I.1) as well as future work at any of the other northern loci identified through previous studies (e.g., Catling 1962).

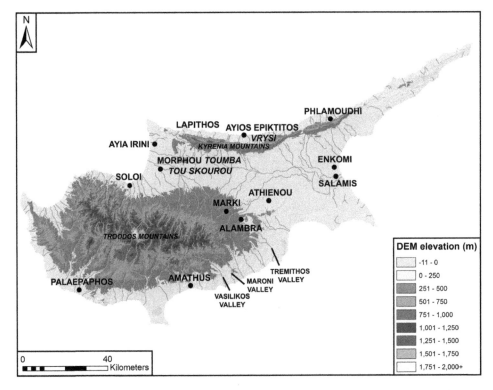

Figure I.1: List of sites and regions mentioned in text. Created by C. Kearns; basemap provided by the Geological Survey Department of Cyprus.

Subsequently, scholars began to focus on the understudied southern portions of the island, with a number of modern "scientific" or "processually informed" projects joining the long culture-historical tradition and bringing forth discoveries of a rich and long human presence on Cyprus over the last twelve thousand years. Several scholars have published accounts that summarize or review existing work for various periods or offer syntheses and agendas (see Karageorghis 1982; 1985; 1998; Stanley Price 1979; Knapp *et al.* 1994; Steel 2004; Pilides 2008; Knapp 2008; 2013: 23–25; Webb 2018—with Knapp 2008 and 2013 being the most recent and comprehensive syntheses of the prehistoric and protohistoric periods).

More than four decades later, where does the field of Cypriot archaeology stand? How different does it seem compared to the state of affairs five, four, even two decades ago? How does it connect to broader currents of methodological and theoretical change in the discipline of archaeology and its cognate fields? There have been a number of books collecting highlights of Cypriot archaeology and its materials (e.g., Karageorghis 1982; 2002; Hadjisavvas 2010) and numerous volumes from conferences on Cypriot archaeology that address various topics or themes (apart from the enormous number of edited conference volumes—and many other publications—by Vassos Karageorghis and colleagues, for which see https://www.ucy.ac.cy/aru/docu ments/Projects/Karagiorgis_CV_en.pdf); we cite just five such examples: Peltenburg

1982; 1989; Swiny *et al.* 1997; Iacovou 2004; Cadogan *et al.* 2012). These include also the several iterations of the Postgraduate Cypriot Archaeology Conference (e.g., Matthäus *et al.* 2015). We lack, however, a synthetic perspective on our current milieu and its salient methodological and theoretical trends. The field of the twenty-first century is now bolstered by digital techniques, for example, ranging from remote sensing and geographic information systems (GIS; e.g., Fall *et al.* 2012; Given *et al.* 2013; Lysandrou and Agapiou 2016; Andreou *et al.* 2017) to three-dimensional modeling and recording instrumentation (e.g., Demesticha *et al.* 2014). We also see the widespread use of scientific methods for analyzing bones, plant materials, ceramics, metals, lithics, and a variety of environmental data (e.g., Knapp and Cherry 1994; Webb *et al.* 2009; Frankel and Webb 2012; Kaniewski *et al.* 2013; Leon 2016), which are increasingly employed as the basis of reconstructing timeframes (e.g., Manning 2013; Peltenburg *et al.* 2013). Improved survey approaches and the integration of geophysical methods are both elucidating settlement areas and structures and guiding targeted excavations (e.g., Urban *et al.* 2014; Manning *et al.* 2014; Sneddon 2015). Scholars now pursue the spatial analysis of the human environment (Fisher 2009a; 2009b) with an awareness of how environments and landscapes are perceived and shaped by humans in a long, entangled, recursive relationship (e.g., Given *et al.* 2013; Kearns 2017).

They are also starting actively and widely to engage with archaeological theory in order to move beyond material categories and to explore issues such as identity and embodiment (Mina *et al.* 2016) or materiality (Given 2013; Knapp 2018). In shifting away from the model of the "great dig," we continue to see the construction of evidentiary foundations comprising numerous detailed and interdisciplinary archaeological excavations and surveys often set within regional contexts (e.g. Kassianidou 2004). Previously marginal or liminal subjects and zones, from the countryside and its inhabitants to the maritime sphere, have increasingly become foci and directed objects of investigation and theory (e.g., Rautman 2000; Given 2004; Toumazou *et al.* 2011; Andreou 2016; Andreou *et al.* 2017; Knapp and Demesticha 2017). Consequently, our field progressively recognizes the profound yet complicated patterns of diachronic, internal trajectories at local, regional, or island-wide scales within Cyprus (e.g., Merrillees 1971; Manning and DeMita 1997; Hein 2009; Peltenburg and Iacovou 2012; Webb and Frankel 2013). These approaches have engendered a recent turn to "Cyprocentric" studies (e.g., Iacovou 2007) as well as work on extra-island networks of trade, diplomacy, and cultural exchange (e.g., Knapp 2008; Leidwanger 2013; Knapp and Demesticha 2017). What ties all of these and other trends together, and how are they made manifest through current research on the island? Perhaps more importantly, where are these new directions taking us?

Three registers of twenty-first century archaeology on Cyprus seem particularly prominent and form the core of the recent research and perspectives presented within this volume. The first entails the reworking of established chronologies, regional patterns, typologies, and histories, as David Frankel explores in this volume. The urge to go back to traditional narratives and refine them as new data are produced and new techniques become available has always characterized Cypriot research, and current developments are no exception. Yet with an increasingly diverse array of methods provided by the digital explosion in archaeology, we are seeing long-held chronologies wobble on the basis of never-before-seen occupational horizons (particularly in early prehistory; see Manning 2014) and quantitative methods of analysis (e.g., Manning 2013; Peltenburg *et al.* 2013). Regions and topics that have typically sat outside normative boundaries appear and engage our attention through the integration of satellite imagery, geomorphological reconnaissance, and field survey (e.g., Given and Knapp 2003; Fall *et al.* 2012; Iacovou 2012; Zomeni 2012; Given *et al.* 2013; Caraher *et al.* 2014; Kearns 2016; Papantoniou and Vionis 2017). One uniting feature of these studies is spatial analysis, which has become a ubiquitous presence in twenty-first-century fieldwork, from topographical surveys with global positioning systems, to GIS-based statistical analyses of sites, to the mapping of intra-site artifact concentrations. In addition, the relatively low-cost availability of techniques such as composition and isotopic analysis has expanded research questions that were much more constrained to traditional artifact studies decades ago, such as those related to materials characterization, paleoenvironmental change, mobility, and diet.

Given the accessibility of scientific methods and frameworks, we are also seeing a new generation of archaeologists specializing in archaeometric techniques in addition to mastering the cultural histories of periods and categories of evidence. Across Cyprus, local and international field projects now include students trained in spatial analysis, petrography and composition analysis, geophysics and remote sensing, zooarchaeology and palaeobotany, and artifact studies, such as the Palaepaphos Urban Landscapes Project (Iacovou 2008b), echoing trends seen across the wider discipline (Chapman and Wylie 2015). Increasingly, it is recognized that archaeology is an exciting and challenging inter- and cross-disciplinary enterprise involving the coordination of diverse research teams (e.g., Pollard and Bray 2007). Questions, data, interpretations, and answers merge into a dynamic, intertwined, and recursive process. Integration of method and theoretical debate is indeed a current focus (e.g., Hodder 2012b), and rather than rely on external specialists only, archaeological projects on Cyprus have started to celebrate the inclusion of students and young scholars who know how to navigate digital databases and mobile technology, lab rooms, and archives as well as how to combine debates from across the humanities and social sciences. These interdisciplinary movements become clear in many of the papers represented in this volume. While the contributions illustrate the wide array of expertise encouraged (and indeed demanded) by the digital era, they simultaneously bring younger scholars together through a shared fluency in innovative techniques, international networks, and collaborative projects.

If some current work is challenging established constructs of archaeological knowledge and historical narratives through new methodological developments and research designs, a third register pertains to the application of the most recent archaeological interest in landscape, social practice, and agency in order to investigate perennially important topics related to complexity and sociopolitical change (e.g., Meskell 2005; Hodder 2012a; Ingold 2013). Rather than privilege top-down models of power and authority and impose them on archaeological remains, contemporary projects seek to push groupings of materials like ceramics, architecture, and landscapes to the fore, interrogating their interactions and relationships with economic, social, and political practices (e.g., Given 2004; Fisher 2009a; Mina *et al.* 2016). While arguably not a paradigmatic shift in the field, these insights on asymmetrically situated objects and places are undoubtedly reconfiguring how many archaeologists are starting to think about and critically examine the fragmentary material record without preconceived assumptions of power, authority, economy, or culture. These diverse theoretical frameworks are poised to ask how materials and landscapes conditioned the formation of social complexities, the growth of inequalities, or the making of regional and interregional connections.

We contend that these are exciting times for Cypriot archaeology, which point to future tracks that weave together diverse methods and frameworks in order both to ask new questions and to reformulate older, enduring ones. The combination of archaeometry and new finds in the identification of Alashiya as Cyprus during the protohistoric Bronze Age has, for example, brought text and material culture together after decades of debate (Knapp 2008: 306–316, 335–341; Peltenburg 2012; Knapp 2013: 432–447). The breakdown of the Bronze to Iron Age transition in diachronic studies that take on both periods is another prime example of how important this up-and-coming work is (Iacovou 2008a; Satraki 2012). There are, of course, many persistent traits of Cypriot archaeology: our fascination with its insularity and what that means for the development from villages to polities, our curiosity with its paradoxical placement between east and west, and our acknowledgment that in the wider field, Cyprus often occupies an enigmatic, elusive position. If anything, current work shows the possibilities of innovation in applying advancing techniques to these enduring interests. The papers included here rally around these directions by taking up registers of twenty-first-century trends for some of the most important questions in Cypriot archaeology: the transition to the complexity of the Late Bronze Age, the nature of political economies of copper and trade, and the growth of Iron Age settlements following the breakdown of protohistoric systems.

Outline of the Volume

It was with these concerns, questions, and interests in mind that we organized a conference at Cornell University in the spring of 2014 in order to explore self-reflexively "new directions in Cypriot archaeology." In our effort to sample a wide range of current research, yet also to acknowledge pioneering work still at initial stages, we invited early career scholars, both graduate students and postdoctoral fellows, from Cyprus, Israel, and the United States to showcase the concerns that they are examining through their training in the twenty-first century. This international underpinning further emphasized the inclusive and collaborative nature of the island's archaeology. Given the leading position of prehistoric studies at the vanguard of Cypriot research, the overwhelming focus of the contributions was the Bronze Age and its internal complexities, with papers on the Neolithic and Iron Age periods acting as bookends. We certainly do not deny the important advances happening in the studies of later historical periods (e.g., Rautman *et al.* 2003; Caraher *et al.* 2014; Leidwanger 2014; Demesticha *et al.* 2014; Papantoniou and Vionis 2017), but we found that anchoring the contributions around the Bronze Age and its preceding and succeeding transitions provided a cohesive foundation with which to question the contours of Cypriot archaeology. Our keynote speaker, David Frankel, whose chapter opens this volume, afforded a long-term intimacy with the state of the field and the scholarly authority to point our discussions toward the future, keeping in mind the rich complexities of making, producing, and publishing archaeological materials and interpretations in a Cypriot, and wider Mediterranean, context.

From the start, our goal included the publication of the contributions, in order to disseminate this new research to a broader audience interested in Cyprus, the eastern Mediterranean, and the state of Mediterranean archaeological research more widely. Of the original thirteen papers delivered, ten are included in this edited volume. Each chapter serves to highlight some of the varied approaches that a new(er) generation of scholars is taking to the island's pasts and the methodologies it is refining. The chapters also raise questions about the broader connections between Cypriot studies and the diffuse field of archaeology in the face of advancing techniques, trending theoretical tools and concepts, and shifting epistemological concerns.

As an entryway to the following chapters on specific articulations of materials and power in prehistoric practices, David Frankel steps back to consider diversity and variability in Early and Middle Bronze Age Cyprus through the methodology of ceramic analysis in his opening essay (Keynote). Frankel highlights the transformations of society on both temporal and spatial scales through differences and variations within and between a wide variety of assemblages, while at the same time calling on us to acknowledge the complexities of our scholarly apparatus and the epistemological stakes rooted in explanations of varied patterns through the established constructs of Cypriot archaeology. From the site to the region, and from small bowl to large cemetery, Frankel adeptly traces these variations and illuminates the problems that occur when correlating major formal or structural patterns without also addressing internal, contingent ones at varying scales. In doing so, he calls for a hermeneutics of Bronze Age archaeology that pays as much attention to the diversity of the ancient materials as to our constructs of period and site, our categories of evidence, and our choices of interpretive or explanatory scale.

Our first part, "The Context and Matter of Prehistory," takes its cue from expanding interest over the last two decades in the island's prehistories. Undoubtedly, research on prehistoric to protohistoric periods has dominated the field (e.g., Stanley Price 1979; Steel 2004; Knapp 2013). Increasingly, work has filled in gaps in chronology, material culture, and lived spaces, which has helped elucidate the ebbs and flows of social change that preceded the explosion of highly complex structures during the later phases of the Middle Bronze Age (see e.g., Knapp 1990; 2013; Manning 1993; Peltenburg 1996; Swiny 2001; Bolger 2003; Iacovou 2008a). Recent studies at Neolithic, Chalcolithic, and Bronze Age sites have helped to clarify mobile and increasingly sedentary agropastoral communities in terms of their production and consumption strategies, their technologies, and their social and ritual practices. Various examples of exciting and provocative work in recent years have focused on establishing and contextualizing the early occupations of the island (e.g., Peltenburg 2003; Knapp 2013: 43–119; Simmons and DiBenedetto 2014; Ammerman and Davis 2013–2014) and integrating environmental histories (e.g., Butzer and

Harris 2007; Harris 2012; Kearns 2013). Others have considered animal and plant resources as well as human bioarchaeology (e.g., Croft 1991; Hansen 1991; Yerkes 2000; Harper and Fox 2008), changing relationships with mainland cultures, and modes of influence and connectivity (e.g., Knapp 2008; Bachhuber 2014).

Some of the most persistent questions for prehistory concern its chronology, as Charalambos Paraskeva shows in his work on absolute dating models (Chapter 1). As more data from prehistoric sites become available, scholars have been eager to understand their temporal positioning vis-à-vis major shifts in material culture and relationships with Mediterranean neighbors. Appropriate analysis requires detailed and robust methodological work on radiocarbon data and their statistical modeling as well as attention to data quality. Paraskeva's research simultaneously opens up this often hidden statistical machinery and highlights the utility of methodological precision and rigorous data management for interpreting chronological timeframes of fragmentary archaeological evidence. Through his discussion of both the technical language of radiometric analysis and the prehistoric evidence from Cyprus, Paraskeva deliberates on important questions about the challenges of recognizing dissimilarities between eras and the mechanisms driving social change.

Maria Dikomitou-Eliadou takes up the pragmatic importance of filling gaps with new methodological techniques in the register of ceramic composition analysis through her work in petrography (Chapter 2). While petrography has been a facet of composition analysis in archaeology for decades (Braekmans and Degryse 2017: 233–234), few scholars have explored its potential on Cypriot material, and Dikomitou-Eliadou's analysis of ceramics from the Early and Middle Bronze Age contexts of Marki and Alambra exemplifies the power of this technique for understanding prehistoric production technologies. Building on her earlier work (e.g., Dikomitou-Eliadou 2013) by including evidence from the site of Alambra, she reveals different strategies related to modes of production between local styles and imported ones and their continuity throughout the period, attesting to enduring yet socially constructed technological choices. Dikomitou-Eliadou also addresses the benefits and challenges of petrographic analysis on ceramics, especially as they relate to sampling and analytic strategies. In providing an archaeometric lens on the traditional study of ceramic fabrics, this work emphasizes the importance of reflexive methodologies for explanations that rely on this ubiquitous class of archaeological evidence.

In the last chapter of this part, Sturt Manning pauses to revisit earlier paradigms and to assess prevailing theories on the rise of prehistoric complexity during the third to earlier second millennia BCE through a careful dissection of concepts like ecological and climatic marginality and the secondary products revolution. The matters at stake here consist of the prosaic categories of economic growth: climate conditions, barley and wheat yields, and population. The full suite of twenty-first-century advancements in interdisciplinary archaeology is at work in this synthesis: paleoclimatic analyses and spatial visualization, demographic and agricultural economic modeling, social theory on power and emergent sociopolitical inequalities, and insights from political ecology. Manning argues for a "stealth" revolution in agropastoral production associated with technological control of dryland farming that took root quickly, offering a critique on existing narratives of environmental history and social change as well as advocating for an integrated methodological approach to Bronze Age transitions.

In the next part, "Bronze Age Complexities," three papers hone in on the state of the field of later Bronze Age studies on Cyprus, marked by dynamic investigations of identity and entanglement (e.g., Knapp 2008), complexity and authority (e.g., Keswani 1996; Peltenburg 1996; Fisher 2009a; 2009b), and urbanism (e.g., Brown 2013; Manning *et al.* 2014), among others. These analyses also take their cue from central questions in the discipline: the nature of authority and political economy in the transition to the Late Bronze Age, for example, or the position of Cyprus (Alashiya) in major interregional networks of gift exchange and trade (e.g., Muhly 1996; Goren *et al.* 2003; Monroe 2009; Broodbank 2013: 407–409). Moving from Early to Late Bronze Age assemblages, the authors interrogate commonly held assumptions about the mechanisms driving economic growth, settlement patterns, and social power. At stake in the papers presented here, which each take multidisciplinary approaches to Bronze Age complexity, is the repositioning of our common categories of material culture—built environments, resources and materials, and crafted objects—as elements of dynamic, diverse systems emerging out of new landscape practices, new architectural forms, and new historical relationships.

Eilis Monahan and Matthew Spigelman, in their study of Middle Bronze Age fortresses, challenge several assumptions that these architectonics emerged as a direct response to the state control of copper supply across Cyprus, principally directed at Enkomi (Chapter 4). Rather, Monahan and Spigelman situate these fortresses within a wider field of changes in material culture, landscape, and trade and ask altogether different questions of the social lives of built environments vis-à-vis the *chaîne opératoire* (e.g., Lemonnier 1986) of copper production. Given their appearance during a formative period before the height of the Late Bronze Age, how might these fortresses have conditioned the rise of new authorities? In conceptualizing the materiality of fortresses and not just their economic rationale through the theoretical work of writers like Bruno Latour and Manuel DeLanda, Monahan and Spigelman bring the study of these less understood built spaces in Cypriot prehistory within the fold of contemporary philosophical and archaeological interest in the efficacy of objects and places in social worlds.

Our current understandings of Bronze Age political economies tend to impose too much of a separation between elite and non-elite involvement in the production, distribution, and consumption of commodities, as Georgia Marina Andreou argues in her examination of Late Bronze Age market practices (Chapter 5). Utilizing concepts of "gray economics" drawn from modern studies of globalization and the socioeconomic structure of world markets, Andreou challenges the straightforward conception that Cypriot elites manipulated, controlled, and used mechanisms like the metals industry for their own aggrandizement, while the non-elite masses, often those living in smaller settlements and tied to practices like land and animal management, had little agency of their own. How might we enrich this picture to explore archaeological evidence for the informal production and consumption practices that do not conform to state or hierarchical models of economic growth and settlement structure? Through her original spatial analysis of Late Bronze Age evidence from across the south of the island combined with sustained engagement with modern economic theory, Andreou highlights the possibilities of interstitial, small-scale economic agency during a period where macroeconomic processes and patterns have too often taken center stage.

Taking a different angle to the transition to increased socioeconomic complexity during the Late Bronze Age, Artemis Georgiou throws the spotlight on the Paphos region, which has traditionally sat somewhat enigmatically to the side of better-known narratives of protohistoric polity formation, like Enkomi (Chapter 6). Georgiou provides evidence for the early development of the site of Palaepaphos and its surrounding settlements through her skilled analysis of material remains and their spatial distribution in the local geomorphological setting. She argues for a dynamic shift in the regional importance of the site as it oriented itself toward emerging maritime networks. As a result, she raises methodological and conceptual questions about our foundation narratives for Late Bronze Age urban centers, especially those whose impressive monumental remains, such as the Sanctuary of Aphrodite, often overshadow their earliest instantiations. Attending to these questions entails both the rigorous study of ceramic styles and chronologies as well as a novel multiscalar approach to land use and settlement patterns.

As archaeology has embraced and engaged the study of ancient and historical landscapes over the last few decades, approaches to the spatiality of life on Cyprus have become more theoretically and methodologically diverse. They feature prominently in our final part, "Diachronic Landscapes." The GIS and digital revolution, integrated with a suite of remote sensing, geophysics, and mapping techniques, has brought new interpretive challenges to the use of archaeological data in investigations of artifact distributions and settlement patterns, social structures, and human-environment relationships more broadly (e.g., Given *et al.* 2013; Caraher *et al.* 2014; Andreou 2016). The long history of survey work, aerial photography, and geology on the island has intermittently fostered the examination of regional histories, and much of the exciting work happening now attends to the diachronic makeup of Cypriot terrains and seascapes, especially between the Bronze and Iron Ages (e.g., Iacovou 2004; Zomeni 2012). Following on from Georgiou's chapter, the last three essays center on the difficult patterning of Iron Age landscapes in tension with Bronze Age precedents, each foregrounding varied methodological approaches.

Anna Satraki's paper on the survey and excavation evidence from the Tremithos Valley in southeastern Cyprus (Chapter 7) highlights the possibilities of longitudinal landscape analysis by integrating topographical GIS maps with the historical survey data of Catling (1962) from the 1950s. Satraki frames her study of interrelationships between settlements in the Tremithos Valley around the important Middle Bronze Age site of Alambra and questions the instrumentality of that settlement for the valley's histories. How central was Alambra to the development of local politics and social structure through time, and how does the later site of Idalion, one of the prominent polities of the Iron Age, relate to this regional Bronze Age past? Through her background in the political iconography and objects of the Iron Age *basileus* institution (Satraki 2012), she is able to zoom out from the material relationships of the center to explore the interconnections between surrounding settlements and the formation of authorities, economies, and cultural identity. In doing so, she reconstructs the landscapes of the Tremithos area as dynamic and active in the development of major settlements like Alambra and Idalion using a culture-historical perspective.

Stella Diakou exposes some of the limitations of the modern study of ancient landscapes by tackling the complex problems of reconstructing archaeological places and histories from archived maps, field reports, personal journals, and collected remains (Chapter 8). For the Lapithos region near the Kyrenia coast of Cyprus, the locations of early twentieth-century archaeological investigations of Cypro-Geometric and Cypro-Archaic cemeteries have become unknown. While materials from Lapithos have long sat in storage in the University of Pennsylvania Museum of Archaeology and Anthropology, high rates of urban development in the region and the inaccessibility of sites for archaeological fieldwork have obscured information on the whereabouts of the original excavations. Through her work in piecing together maps and journal entries on the whereabouts of excavated tombs and materials, Diakou reconstructs the Iron Age mortuary landscapes of Lapithos. In exemplifying the power of combining detailed archival study with digital spatial analysis, Diakou is able to examine the development of these cemeteries and their interrelationship with settlements and previous activity in this important coastal region. In doing so, she builds up a narrative of diachronic landscape change and problematizes the regional categorization of first-millennium BCE political and social orders.

Scholars exploring these Iron Age developments have traditionally focused on polities known from epigraphic, historical, or archaeological evidence from urban centers. Catherine Kearns approaches the topic of landscape development from the opposite direction: can we understand the formation of Iron Age polities and their constituent economic and social changes from the perspective of land use and place-making practices far outside urban polities (Chapter 9)? In her paper, Kearns highlights the importance of investigating the ancient environments of Cyprus through the application of integrated scientific and archaeological methods, such as stable isotope analysis and surface survey, in order to examine how communities were relating to shifting environmental conditions. By analyzing archaeological survey data from the Vasilikos and Maroni valleys outside of the polity of Amathus in tandem with these scientific data, Kearns is able to theorize heterogeneous landscape practices that help complement biases towards urban histories. Attending to the dynamic recursivity of environmental and social change of this region also invites further inquiry into what exactly constitutes presumed "favorable" climates of historic progress.

New Directions

The papers of this volume suggest a road map for critical analysis of twenty-first-century directions in the domain of Cypriot archaeology (and further afield) and engage with frameworks ranging from culture-historical to post-processual and "new materialist" modes of theoretical engagement. They tack between persistent historiographical questions and novel, integrated analyses that combine techniques from an expanding array of scientific investigations in order to measure and model diverse bodies of evidence. It is our contention that these new directions do not cleave current methodological or theoretical interests from those of the last century but rather retool them to serve existing and original data in new ways. They also underscore a community of discourses happening on the island rather than a single unified front (*sensu* Hodder 2012b: 3). We thus encourage in this volume not one new direction, a single trajectory of scholarship that underlies an insular or unilinear plan of discovery, but new directions, instrumentalized via engagement with inter-disciplinary research, and with historically situated local and international modes of training and a growing yet varying awareness of trends across the humanities and social sciences.

Acknowledgments

We would like to thank Jeffrey Leon for his help in organizing the 2014 conference and editing various stages of papers as well as all of the contributors, who made the original conference so exciting and who had to negotiate a long publication schedule. Bethany Wasik of Cornell University Press graciously offered diligent help with the editing and review process for the publication, and we thank the two anonymous reviewers for their important and invaluable critiques and suggestions. Support for the conference came from the Department of Classics at Cornell University, and we are grateful to the Archaeological Institute of America for supporting this publication with a subvention grant.

References

Adelman, C.M. 1978. Book review of *The Archaeology of Cyprus: Recent Developments*, Noel Robertson (ed.). *Journal of Near Eastern Studies* 37: 76.

Ammerman, A.J. and T. Davis. (eds.) 2013–2014. Island Archaeology and the Origins of Seafaring in the Eastern Mediterranean. Proceedings of the Wenner Gren Workshop held at Reggio Calabria on October 19–21, 2012. *Eurasian Prehistory* Vols. 10–11. Oxford: Oxbow.

Andreou, G.M. 2016. Understanding the rural landscape of Late Bronze Age Cyprus: A diachronic perspective from the Vasilikos Valley. *Journal of Mediterranean Archaeology* 29.2: 143–172.

Andreou, G.M., R. Opitz, S.W. Manning, K.D. Fisher, D.A. Sewell, A. Georgiou, and T. Urban. 2017. Integrated methods for understanding and monitoring the loss of coastal archaeological sites: The case of Tochni-Lakkia, south-central Cyprus. *Journal of Archaeological Science*: Reports 12: 197–208.

Bachhuber, C. 2014. The Anatolian context of Philia material culture in Cyprus. In A.B. Knapp and P. van Dommelen (eds.), *The Cambridge Prehistory of the Bronze and Iron Age Mediterranean*, 139–156. New York: Cambridge University Press.

Binford, L.R. (ed.) 1977. *For Theory Building in Archaeology*. New York: Academic Press.

Bolger, D. 2003. *Gender in Ancient Cyprus: Narratives of Social Change on a Mediterranean Island*. Walnut Creek: Altamira Press.

Braekmans, D. and P. Degryse. 2017. Petrography: Optical microscopy. In A.M.W. Hunt (ed.), *The Oxford Handbook of Archaeological Ceramic Analysis*, 233–265. Oxford: Oxford University Press.

Broodbank, C. 2013. *The Making of the Middle Sea: A History of the Mediterranean from the Beginning to the Emergence of the Classical World*. London: Thames and Hudson Ltd.

Brown, M. 2013. Waterways and the political geography of southeast Cyprus in the second millennium BCE. *Annual of the British School at Athens* 108: 121–136.

Butzer, K.W. and S.E. Harris. 2007. Geoarchaeological approaches to the environmental history of Cyprus: Explication and critical evaluation. *Journal of Archaeological Science* 34: 1932–52.

Cadogan, G., M. Iacovou, K. Kopaka and J. Whitley. (eds.) 2012. Parallel Lives: Ancient Island Societies in Crete and Cyprus. Proceedings of the Conference in Nicosia Organized by the British School at Athens, the University of Crete and the University of Cyprus in November-December 2006. London: The British School at Athens.

Caraher, W.R., R.S. Moore and D.K. Pettegrew. 2014. Pyla Koutsopetria I: Archaeological Survey of an Ancient Coastal Town. *American Schools of Oriental Research Archaeological Reports* 21. Boston: American Schools of Oriental Research.

Catling, H. 1962. Patterns of settlement in Bronze Age Cyprus. *Opuscula Atheniensia* 4: 129–169.

Chapman, R. and A. Wylie. (eds.) 2015. *Material Evidence: Learning from Archaeological Practice.* New York: Routledge.

Croft, P. 1991. Man and beast in Chalcolithic Cyprus. *Bulletin of the American Schools of Oriental Research* 282–283: 63–79.

Demesticha, S., D. Skarlatos and A. Neophytou. 2014. The 4th-century BCE shipwreck at Mazotos, Cyprus: New techniques and methodologies in the 3D mapping of shipwreck excavations. *Journal of Field Archaeology* 39.2: 134–150.

Dikomitou-Eliadou, M. 2013. Interactive communities at the dawn of the Cypriot Bronze Age: An interdisciplinary approach to Philia phase ceramic variability. In A.B. Knapp, J.M. Webb and A. McCarthy (eds.), *J.R.B. Stewart—An Archaeological Legacy*, 22–32. *Studies in Mediterranean Archaeology* 139. Uppsala, Sweden: Åströms Förlag.

Fall, P.L., S.E. Falconer, C.S. Galletti, T. Shirmang, E. Ridder and J. Klinge. 2012. Long-term agrarian landscapes in the Troodos foothills, Cyprus. *Journal of Archaeological Science* 39: 2335–2347.

Fisher, K.D. 2009a. Placing social interaction: An integrative approach to analyzing past built environments. *Journal of Anthropological Archaeology* 28: 439–457.

Fisher, K.D. 2009b. Elite place-making and social interaction in the Late Cypriot Bronze Age. *Journal of Mediterranean Archaeology* 22.2: 183–209.

Frankel, D. and J. Webb. 2012. Pottery production and distribution in prehistoric Bronze Age Cyprus: An application of pXRF analysis. *Journal of Archaeological Science* 39: 1380–1387.

Given, M. 2004. *The Archaeology of the Colonized.* London: Routledge.

Given, M. and A.B. Knapp. (eds.) 2003. *The Sydney Cyprus Survey Project: Social Approaches to Regional Archaeological Survey.* Los Angeles: Cotsen Institute, University of California, Los Angeles.

Given, M., A.B. Knapp, J. Noller, L. Sollars & V. Kassianidou. (eds.) 2013. Landscape and Interaction: The Troodos Archaeological and Environmental Survey Project, Cyprus. Volume I: Methodology, Analysis and Interpretation. *Levant Supplementary Series* 14. London: Council for British Research in the Levant.

Goren, Y., S. Bunimovitz, I. Finkelstein and N. Na'aman. 2003. The location of Alashiya: New evidence from petrographic investigation of Alashiyan tablets from El-Amarna and Ugarit. *American Journal of Archaeology* 107: 233–255.

Hadjisavvas, S. (ed.) 2010. *Cyprus: Crossroads of Civilizations.* Nicosia: Republic of Cyprus.

Hansen, J. 1991. Palaeoethnobotany in Cyprus: Recent research. In J.M. Renfrew (ed.), *New Light on Early Farming: Recent Developments in Palaeoethnobotany*, 225–236. Edinburgh: Edinburgh University Press.

Harper, N. and S.C. Fox. 2008. Recent research in Cypriot bioarchaeology. *Bioarchaeology of the Near East* 2: 1–38.

Harris, S.E. 2012. Cyprus as a degraded landscape or resilient environment in the wake of colonial intrusion. *Proceedings of the National Academy of Sciences of the United States of America* 109: 3670–3675.

Hein, I. (ed.) 2009. *The Formation of Cyprus in the 2nd Millennium B.C. Studies in Regionalism During the Middle and Late Bronze Ages.* Vienna: Verlag der Österreichischen Akademie der Wissenschaften.

Hodder, I. 2012a. *Entangled: An Archaeology of the Relationships Between Humans and Things.* Malden, MA: Wiley-Blackwell.

Hodder, I. 2012b. Introduction: Contemporary theoretical debate in archaeology. In I. Hodder (ed.), *Archaeological Theory Today*, 1–14. 2nd ed. Cambridge: Polity Press.

Iacovou, M. (ed.) 2004. *Archaeological Field Survey in Cyprus: Past History, Future Potentials. Proceedings of a Conference Held by the Archaeological Research Unit of the University of Cyprus, 1–2 December 2000.* London: The British School at Athens.

Iacovou, M. 2007. Advocating Cyprocentricism: An indigenous model for the emergence of state formation on Cyprus. In S.W. Crawford, A. Ben-Tor, J.P. Dessel, A. Mazar and J. Aviram (eds.), *"Up to the Gates of Ekron": Essays on the Archaeology and History of the Eastern Mediterranean in Honor of Seymour Gitin,* 461–475. Jerusalem: The W.F. Albright Institute of Archaeological Research.

Iacovou, M. 2008a. Cultural and political configurations in Iron Age Cyprus: The sequel to a protohistoric episode. *American Journal of Archaeology* 112: 625–657.

Iacovou, M. 2008b. The Palaepaphos Urban Landscape Project: Theoretical background and preliminary report 2006–2007. *Report of the Department of Antiquities,* Cyprus: 263–289.

Iacovou, M. 2012. From regional gateway to Cypriot kingdom: Copper deposits and copper routes in the chora of Paphos. In V. Kassianidou and G. Papasavvas (eds.), *Eastern Mediterranean Metallurgy and Metalwork in the Second Millennium BC: A Conference in Honour of James D. Muhly, Nicosia, 10th–11th October 2009,* 56–67. Oxford: Oxbow Books.

Ingold, T. 2013. *Making: Anthropology, Archaeology, Art, and Architecture.* Abingdon: Routledge.

Kaniewski, D., E. Van Campo, J. Guiot, S. Le Burel, T. Otto, and C. Bateman. 2013. Environmental roots of the Late Bronze Age crisis. *PLoS ONE* 8(8): e71004. doi:10.1371/journal.pone.0071004 1–10.

Karageorghis, V. 1982. *Cyprus: From the Stone Age to the Romans.* London: Thames and Hudson.

Karageorghis, V. (ed.) 1985. *Archaeology in Cyprus 1960–1985.* Nicosia: Leventis Foundation.

Karageorghis, V. 1998. *Cypriote Archaeology Today: Achievements and Perspectives.* Glasgow: Department of Archaeology, University of Glasgow.

Karageorghis, V. 2002. *Early Cyprus: Crossroads of the Mediterranean.* Los Angeles: Getty Museum.

Kassianidou, V. 2004. Recording Cyprus' mining history through archaeological survey. In M. Iacovou (ed.), *Archaeological Field Survey in Cyprus: Past History, Future Potentials. Proceedings of a Conference Held by the Archaeological Research Unit of the University of Cyprus, 1–2 December 2000,* 95–104. London: British School at Athens.

Kearns, C. 2013. "On a clear day the Taurus Mountains hang like a cloud": On environmental thought in the archaeology of Cyprus. In A.B. Knapp, J.M. Webb and A. McCarthy (eds.), *J.R.B. Stewart—An Archaeological Legacy,* 121–132. Studies in Mediterranean Archaeology 139. Uppsala, Sweden: Åströms Förlag.

Kearns, C. 2016. Re-survey and spatial analysis of landscape developments during the first millennium BCE on Cyprus. *Antiquity* 353: DOI: https://doi.org/10.15184/aqy.2016.164

Kearns, C. 2017. Mediterranean archaeology and environmental histories in the spotlight of the Anthropocene. *History Compass* 15:e12371. https://doi.org/10.1111/hic3.12371

Keswani, P. 1996. Hierarchies, heterarchies, and urbanization processes: The view from Bronze Age Cyprus. *Journal of Mediterranean Archaeology* 9.2: 211–250.

Knapp, A.B. 1986. *Copper Production and Divine Protection: Archaeology, Ideology and Social Complexity on Bronze Age Cyprus. Studies in Mediterranean Archaeology PB 42.* Göteborg, Sweden: Paul Åströms Förlag.

Knapp, A.B. 1990. Production, location and integration in Bronze Age Cyprus. *Current Anthropology* 31: 147–176.

Knapp, A.B. 2008. *Prehistoric and Protohistoric Cyprus: Identity, Insularity, and Connectivity.* Oxford: Oxford University Press.

Knapp, A.B. 2013. *The Archaeology of Cyprus: From Earliest Prehistory Through the Bronze Age.* Cambridge: Cambridge University Press.

Knapp, A.B. 2018. The way things are . . . In A.R. Knodell and T.P. Leppard (eds.), *Regional Approaches to Society and Complexity,* 288–308. Monographs in Mediterranean Archaeology 15. Sheffield: Equinox Publishing.

Knapp, A.B. and J.F. Cherry. 1994. *Provenience Studies and Bronze Age Cyprus: Production, Exchange, and Politico-Economic Change.* Monographs in World Archaeology 21. Madison: Prehistory Press.

Knapp, A.B. and S. Demesticha. 2017. *Mediterranean Connections: Maritime Transport Containers and Seaborne Trade in the Bronze and Early Iron Ages.* London: Routledge.

Knapp, A.B. with S.O. Held and S.W. Manning. 1994. The prehistory of Cyprus: Problems and prospects. *Journal of World Prehistory* 8: 377–453.

Leidwanger, J. 2014. Integrating an empire: Maritime trade and agricultural supply in Roman Cyprus. *Skyllis* 13.1: 59–66.

Lemonnier, P. 1986. The study of material culture today: Toward an anthropology of technical systems. *Journal of Anthropological Archaeology* 5: 147–186.

Leon, J.F. 2016. More than "Counting Sheep": Isotopic Approaches to Minoan and Late Cypriot Wool Production Economies. Unpublished PhD dissertation, Cornell University.

Lysandrou, V. and A. Agapiou. 2016. Cities of the dead: Approaching the lost landscape of Hellenistic and Roman necropoleis of Cyprus. *Archaeological and Anthropological Sciences* 8.4: 867–877.

Manning, S.W. 1993. Prestige, distinction, and competition: The anatomy of socio-economic complexity in 4th–2nd millennium B.C.E. Cyprus. *Bulletin of the American School of Oriental Research* 292: 35–58.

Manning, S.W. 2013. Appendix: A new radiocarbon chronology for prehistoric and protohistoric Cyprus, ca. 11,000–1050 Cal BC. In A.B. Knapp, *The Archaeology of Cyprus: From Earliest Prehistory Through the Bronze Age*, 485–533. Cambridge: Cambridge University Press.

Manning, S.W. 2014. Temporal placement and context of Cypro-PPNA activity on Cyprus. *Eurasian Prehistory* 11.1–2: 9–28.

Manning, S.W., G.M. Andreou, K.D. Fisher, P. Gerard-Little, C. Kearns, J.F. Leon, D.A. Sewell and T.M. Urban. 2014. Becoming urban: Investigating the anatomy of the Late Bronze Age complex, Maroni, Cyprus. *Journal of Mediterranean Archaeology* 27.1: 3–32.

Manning, S.W. and F. DeMita. 1997. Cyprus, the Aegean and Maroni-Tsaroukkas. In D. Christou (ed.), *Cyprus and the Aegean in Antiquity*, 103–142. Nicosia: Department of Antiquities, Cyprus.

Matthäus, H., B. Morstadt and C. Vonhoff. (eds.) 2015. *PoCA (Postgraduate Cypriot Archaeology)* 2012. Newcastle: Cambridge Scholars Publishing.

Merrillees, R.S. 1971. The early history of Late Cypriote I. *Levant* 3: 56–79.

Meskell, L. (ed.) 2005. *Archaeologies of Materiality*. Malden, MA: Blackwell.

Mina, M., Triantaphyllou, S. and Y. Papadatos. (eds.) 2016. *An Archaeology of Prehistoric Bodies and Embodied Identities in the Eastern Mediterranean*. Oxford: Oxbow Books.

Monroe, C.M. 2009. *Scales of Fate. Trade, Tradition, and Transformation in the Eastern Mediterranean ca. 1350–1175 BCE*. Münster: Ugarit-Verlag.

Muhly, J.D. 1996. The significance of metals in the Late Bronze Age economy of Cyprus. In V. Karageorghis and D. Michaelides (eds.), *The Development of the Cypriot Economy: From the Prehistoric Period to the Present Day*, 45–59. Nicosia: Bank of Cyprus.

Papantoniou, G. and A.K. Vionis. 2017. Landscape archaeology and sacred space in the eastern Mediterranean: A glimpse from Cyprus. *Land* 6.2: 1–18.

Peltenburg, E. 1982. *Recent Developments in the Later Prehistory of Cyprus. Studies in Mediterranean Archaeology* PB 16. Göteborg, Sweden: Paul Åströms Förlag.

Peltenburg, E. 1996. From isolation to state formation in Cyprus, c. 3500–1500 BC. In V. Karageorghis and D. Michaelides (eds), *The Development of the Cypriot Economy from the Prehistoric Period to the Present Day*, 17–44. Nicosia: Bank of Cyprus.

Peltenburg, E. 2012. Text meets material in Late Bronze Age Cyprus. In A. Georgiou (ed.), *Cyprus: An Island Culture. Society and Social Relations from the Bronze Age to the Venetian Period*, 1–23. Oxford: Oxbow Books.

Peltenburg, E. (ed.) 1989. *Early Society in Cyprus*. Edinburgh: Edinburgh University Press.

Peltenburg, E. (ed.) 2003. The Colonisation and Settlement of Cyprus: Investigations at Kissonerga Mylouthkia, 1976–1996. *Studies in Mediterranean Archaeology* 70.4. Sävedalen: Paul Åströms Förlag.

Peltenburg, E., D. Frankel and C. Paraskeva. 2013. Radiocarbon. In E. Peltenburg (ed.), ARCANE. *Associated Regional Chronologies for the Ancient Near East and the Mediterranean*. Vol. II. Cyprus, 313–338. Turnhout: Brepols.

Peltenburg, E. and M. Iacovou. 2012. Crete and Cyprus: Contrasting political configurations. In G. Cadogan, M. Iacovou, K. Kopaka and J. Whitley (eds.), *Parallel Lives: Ancient Island Societies in Crete and Cyprus*. Proceedings of the Conference in Nicosia Organized by the British School at Athens, the University of Crete and the University of Cyprus in November–December 2006, 345–363. London: The British School at Athens.

Pilides, D. 2008. An outline of the history of archaeological research in Cyprus. In J. Smith (ed.), *Views from Phlamoudhi, Cyprus*, 15–24. Boston: American Schools of Oriental Research.

Pollard, A.M. and P. Bray. 2007. A bicycle made for two? The integration of scientific techniques into archaeological interpretation. *Annual Review of Anthropology* 36: 245–259.

Rautman, M. 2000. The busy countryside of Late Roman Cyprus. *Report of the Department of Antiquities*, Cyprus: 317–331.

Rautman, M., M.C. McClellan, L.V. Benson, S.C. Fox, M.D. Glascock, B. Gomez, H. Neff, W. O'Brien, and D.S. Reese. 2003. *A Cypriot Village of Late Antiquity: Kalavasos Kopetra in the Vasilikos Valley*. Supplementary Series 52. Portsmouth, R.I.: Journal of Roman Archaeology.

Renfrew, C. 1980. The great tradition versus the great divide: Archaeology as anthropology? *American Journal of Archaeology* 84: 287–298.

Robertson, N. (ed.) 1975. *The Archaeology of Cyprus: Recent Developments*. Park Ridge: Noyes Press.

Simmons, A.H. and K. DiBenedetto. 2014. *Stone Age Sailors: Paleolithic Seafaring in the Mediterranean*. Walnut Creek: Left Coast Press.

Sneddon, A. 2015. Revisiting Alambra Mouttes: Defining the spatial configuration and social relations of a prehistoric Bronze Age settlement in Cyprus. *Journal of Mediterranean Archaeology* 28.2: 141–170.

Snodgrass, A.M. 1985. The new archaeology and the classical archaeologist. *American Journal of Archaeology* 89: 31–37.

Stanley Price, N.P. 1979. *Early Prehistoric Settlement in Cyprus: A Review and Gazetteer of Sites, c. 6500–3000 B.C. British Archaeological Reports International Series 65.* Oxford: British Archaeological Reports.

Steel, L. 2004. *Cyprus before History: From the Earliest Settlers to the End of the Bronze Age*. London: Duckworth.

Swiny, S (ed.). 2001. *The Earliest Prehistory of Cyprus: From Colonization to Exploitation*. Boston: American Schools of Oriental Research.

Swiny, S., R.L. Hohlfelder and H. Wylde Swiny. (eds.) 1997. *Res Maritimae: Cyprus and the Eastern Mediterranean from Prehistory to Late Antiquity*. Proceedings of the Second International Symposium "Cities on the Sea," Nicosia, Cyprus, October 18–22, 1994. Atlanta: Scholars Press.

Toumazou, M.K., P.N. Kardulias, and D.B. Counts. (eds.) 2011. *Crossroads and Boundaries: The Archaeology of Past and Present in the Malloura Valley, Cyprus*. Boston: American Schools of Oriental Research.

Trigger, B.G. 2006. *A History of Archaeological Thought*. 2nd ed. Cambridge: Cambridge University Press.

Urban, T.M., J.F. Leon, S.W. Manning and K.D. Fisher. 2014. High resolution GPR mapping of Late Bronze Age architecture at Kalavasos-Ayios Dhimitrios, Cyprus. *Journal of Applied Geophysics* 107: 129–136.

Webb, J.M. and D. Frankel. 2013. Cultural regionalism and divergent social trajectories in Early Bronze Age Cyprus. *American Journal of Archaeology* 117: 59–81.

Webb, J.M., D. Frankel, P. Croft and C. McCartney. 2009. Excavations at Politiko Kokkinorotsos: A Chalcolithic hunting station in Cyprus. *Proceedings of the Prehistoric Society* 75: 189–237.

Yerkes, R.W. 2000. Ethnoarchaeology in central Cyprus: Interdisciplinary studies of ancient population and agriculture by the Athienou Archaeological Project. *Near Eastern Archaeology* 63: 20–34.

Zomeni, Z. 2012. Quaternary Marine Terraces on Cyprus: Constraints on Uplift and Pedogenesis, and the Geoarchaeology of Palaipafos. Unpublished Ph.D. Dissertation, Oregon State University, Eugene, OR.

Keynote

Exploring Diversity in Bronze Age Cyprus

DAVID FRANKEL

Introduction

On the outskirts of New Cuyama, a small Californian town some 60 kilometers north of Santa Barbara, a road sign summarizes geographical and historical information (Figure 0.1).

Each of the three dimensions (size, altitude, date) may be correlated with the others; they may even be causally related. But the simple sum of these values makes no sense. Obvious in this example, such integration of diverse measures and variables is often implicit and hidden within our approaches to describing and structuring the archaeological record. As pattern-seeking animals we group and connect evidence, simplifying inherent complexity in order to make sense of it. In doing so we not only select and emphasize but also link together various elements and in the process often lose sight of how different dimensions of material may follow dissonant trajectories, each with its own timing, tempo, rhythm, and amplitude.

In considering a theme of new directions for research, one critical challenge is the development of a more nuanced understanding of the constant tension between approaches that identify common trends and those that highlight diversity. Naturally, the constant acquisition (ideally publication) of new material, which is one of the characteristics of our discipline, can lead to significant adjustments to simpler models and the recognition of variability where none could be seen before. However, established structures can be so embedded in practice and understanding that incremental additions of evidence may be unconsciously squeezed or stretched to fit Procrustean systems of identification, classification, and explanation. It is always appropriate to bear in mind that archaeological sites of all kinds—indeed, the entire archaeological record—is at least as much a creation of the last century and a half of archaeological research as of the ancient people whose relics we investigate (Carver 2009; cf. Frankel 1993; 1998; 2012). Which areas are studied and which sites are recorded and excavated: the approach to documentation and the nature of the even-

Figure 0.1: Road sign, New Cuyama, California. Photo: David Frankel, 2000.

tual publication (if any) structure the evidence we have to work with and how it can be used. One task is to disentangle the complexities inherent in the archaeological record and our processes of analysis and to consider how different factors influence patterning, and hence explanation, on one hand, and how we should match types of explanation to scales of observation, on the other.

A conscious consideration of how our approaches to data and analysis may affect, if not preempt, explanation will therefore always be essential. With this in mind I will revisit some issues and reconsider how variability and variation at different scales—between objects, within sites, of site histories, through time, between sites, and across regions—can be affected by intrinsic cultural, technical, and depositional factors as well as by the analytical units we set up and use to group material.

Establishing Frameworks

An understanding of analytical units is an essential prerequisite for characterization and comparison of datasets. Although often combined or confused in practice, there are essentially two main ways in which units are constructed: those that depend largely on intrinsic characteristics of the material and those that are constructed on the basis of extrinsic evidence. The former can lead to self-fulfilling observations of internal homogeneity and external differentiation, creating false images of sharp divisions within and between sets of data (compare, for example, Frankel 1988a:

41–42). The scope or scale of analytical units also affects observations of the degree of variability within them. It is very likely that as the size of units increases, so does the degree of internal variability such that, for example, larger chronological units (periods) may display greater diversity than apparently more uniform material from shorter periods (Frankel 1991). Ideally, therefore, comparisons are best when analytical units are of the same size, duration, and nature.

Framing Time

We can blame Myres and Gjerstad for introducing and developing the chronological structures that frame so much of our discourse on the Cypriot Bronze Age (Frankel 1974: 2; Knapp 2013: 25). The tripartite model (and associated nomenclature) of Early/Middle/Late Bronze Age periods with finer—again tripartite—subdivisions that we have inherited fulfils a dual purpose, serving as often as not to date as well as to characterize material. Attempts to develop an alternative scheme, notably that argued for by Knapp (most recently, 2013: 26–29), provide, in essence, the same form of periodization where intrinsic attributes of individual artifacts or of assemblages both characterize temporal units and provide a relative date. However ideal, it is simply not possible at present to separate absolute dates from the sets of material to which they refer. Even when we have radiocarbon dates in stratigraphic context that have been subjected to sophisticated techniques of analysis (e.g., Manning 2013a; 2013b; 2014; Peltenburg *et al.* 2013a; Paraskeva in this volume), their meaning ultimately still relies on these intrinsically defined building blocks with their inherent assumptions and cultural/chronological assignments. One important issue here is how precise these assignments are.

Myres, importing the basic divisions of the Bronze Age to Cyprus, could only define three major periods. Gjerstad, making use of stratigraphic evidence alongside typological seriation, subdivided these to construct our familiar ninefold periodization (Gjerstad 1926; compare Myres 1926). In his magisterial *Corpus of Cypriot Antiquities*, Stewart (J.R. Stewart 1962; E. Stewart and Åström 1988; 1992; E. Stewart 1999; Webb and Frankel 2012) took chronological precision further, at least so far as available (mainly north coast cemetery) assemblages were concerned, with finer-scale divisions and sequences.

Recently, it has become increasingly clear that such a fine scale of definition cannot be applied more generally to other assemblages, especially those from other regions. In order to look at contemporary developments across the island, it is necessary to drop back to a coarser scale of analysis, grouping finer units into more reliably contemporary larger ones—for example using a sequence such as Philia, Early Cypriot (EC) I–II, EC III–Middle Cypriot (MC) I. The one advantage of Knapp's most recent alternative scheme of Prehistoric Bronze Age 1 and 2 is to simplify this somewhat clumsy terminology: its disadvantage is that, while now (Knapp 2013: Table 2) more closely mapped onto "traditional" periodization than in previous iterations (e.g., Knapp 2008: Table 1), it nevertheless still conflates sets of data that it is important to separate, such as Philia from EC I–II. Despite recognizing that the conventional Bronze Age subdivisions can lead to a unilinear approach to explanation, the renaming of periods does not avoid this problem—for example where the "Philia phase" is seen as entirely following, rather than significantly overlapping, the Late Chalcolithic (Knapp 2013: Table 2).

In contrast to the construction of temporal units based on intrinsic factors (such as pottery ware and style) are situations where extrinsic factors, independent of the constituent material, are used. The most obvious of these is stratigraphy. Of course the definition of layers, phases, or periods within sequences can still be based on a particular view of site formation (see further discussion below) and at times makes use of the artifacts in determining to which unit a particular deposit belongs. This categorization can lead to self-fulfilling models involving the forced linkage of variations in artifact assemblages with other aspects of site history, perhaps exaggerating the significance of some points of change. While there may be little option when confronted with the complexities and inadequacies inherent in all site formations, the imperative to construct or impose a site-wide sequence of necessity conflates events from different areas into simpler groups. It also dictates a coarser scale of analysis, so that disparate events are regarded as contemporaneous even where they may have occurred at different times. Site phases or layers that are seemingly short-lived are generally of far greater duration than any individual's life span.

Underpinning any system are the criteria used to define and differentiate periods of time and the implications for explanation as these become reified and inappropriately structure later analysis. As noted above, the coarser the scale of observation and analysis, the more the past will be seen as a form of punctuated equilibrium where internal variation is suppressed and external differences emphasized, imposing a strophic model of relatively rapid and significant points of change rather than one of slower, more gradual, incremental development.

Working with Space

Just as the precision and nature of temporal units affect our perceptions and explanations of change, approaches to spatial analysis affect our view of inter-site or interregional patterns and the nature of the boundaries between them (Kantner 2008). Different approaches are in evidence (Frankel 2009). Once again these analytical units can be defined in different ways, each with consequences for explanation, although here extrinsic definitions are more clear-cut and can be more readily expanded or contracted. The most common approach is to define regions on general administrative or topographical grounds (Catling 1962; Stanley Price 1979; Georgiou 2006; see also Satraki in this volume). Applied in its simplest form, this framework presupposes a meaningful relationship within and between these predefined, fixed geographical units and past behavior. The degree of variability within and variation between regions defined in this way will be, in part, a product of how closely these boundaries match social ones. Alternatively, plotting the distribution of types or of attributes (e.g., Frankel 1974) is more likely to reveal patterns of similarity and relationship and perhaps cultural boundary that may not correlate with physical features of the landscape.

Assemblage Definition

Just as equivalence of scale is essential if variability is being compared between analytical units defined in space or time, so too it must be sought in the many other dimensions of variation that affect the structure of the archaeological record. An obvious comparison can be made between material from single events, such as a single burial, and assemblages incorporating artifacts from less controlled contexts (ranging from multiple burials within a tomb to site or regional groups). These can differ considerably in date, duration, and type, with inherent implications for the degree of internal variability likely to be present. This variation affects the scale of observation and hence the explanation.

While cemetery material has the advantage of deliberate selection and deposition of sets of material, settlement assemblages as a rule do not. The most significant factors involved here can be broadly considered under the general rubric of "site formation processes" developing the approach outlined several decades ago by Schiffer (1976). Difficult though it may be, identifying the nature of deposits is crucial. Rarely, despite our best efforts to identify them, do any settlement assemblages represent specific activities or specific points of time. Most include material from a variety of sources and activities: they are inherently complex mixtures of older and newer material so that even the finest scale of stratigraphy does not imply fine chronological precision or primary behavioral relationships.

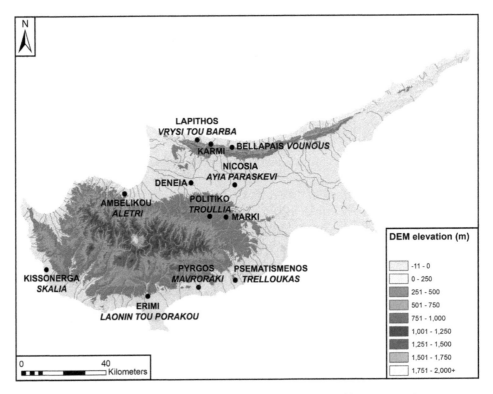

Figure 0.2: Map showing the location of sites mentioned in text. Created by C. Kearns; basemap provided by Geological Survey Department of Cyprus.

Digging and clearance during episodes of ancient refurbishing and construction may bring up old, long-buried items adding to the stock of everpresent residual material evident in all long-lasting sites, confusing simple associations and chronological attributions so familiar from textbook examples of stratigraphy and seriation, as seen, for example, at Marki (Frankel and Webb 2006a: 32, Text Figures 3.2, 4.57; see also Peltenburg *et al.* 2013b: Figure 1.2; Frankel *et al.* 2013: Figure 2.3) (Figures 0.2 and 0.3).

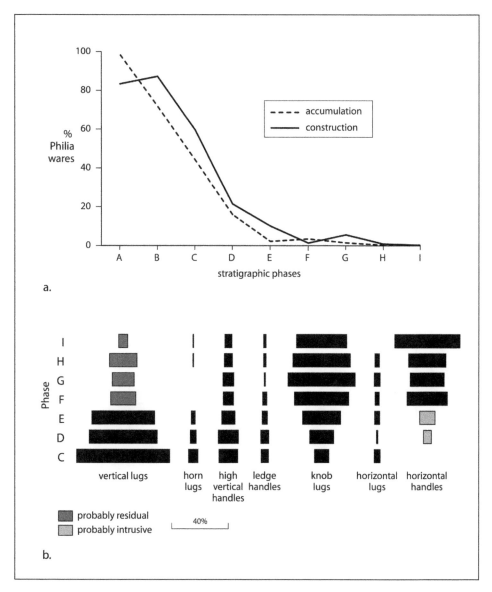

Figure 0.3: Monitoring and assessing residuality at Marki: (a) the occurrence of Philia sherds in post-Philia accumulations; (b) Interpretation of a seriation of small bowl attributes suggesting residuality and intrusion of sherdage (after Frankel and Webb 2006a: Text Figures 3.2 and 4.57).

In addition, it is important to recognize the functional or behavioral context of deposition (Webb 2006). Seldom, and generally only in circumstances of catastrophic destruction and abandonment, do we have inventories of items left in their context of use. A comparison of the proportional occurrence of artifact types between assemblages of different depositional type or integrity is valuable in its own right (Frankel and Webb 2006a: 153, Text Table 4.3) (Figure 0.4, Table 0.1).

Where comparisons of degrees of variability are the focus of attention, then equivalence of context, type of deposit, and temporal resolution are clearly even more necessary.

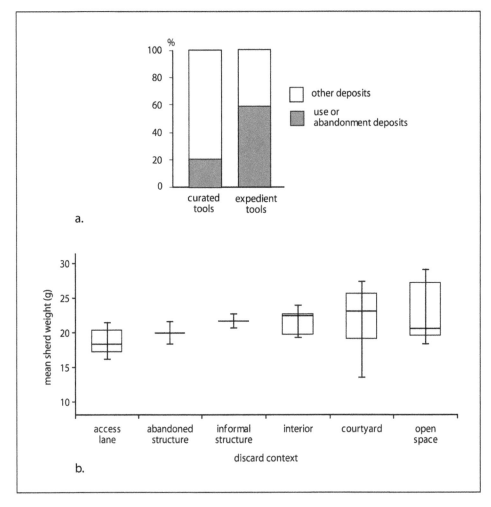

Figure 0.4: Variation in aspects of artifact occurrence in different depositional contexts at Marki *Alonia* (after Frankel and Webb 2012: Figures 3 and 6).

Table 0.1: Incidence of complete and near-complete vessels in three functional classes in various accumulation deposits in different spaces (data from Frankel and Webb 2006a: Text Table 4)

	Interior	Courtyard	Open space	Access	Informal structure	Passage	Total
Small bowl	47	7	11			1	51
Juglet	12						12
Cutaway-spouted jug	7						7
Serving	66	7	11			1	70
Jar	7		1				8
Amphora	2						2
Round-mouthed jug	4	1					5
Storage	13	1					14
Cooking pot	12	1	1				14
Spouted bowl	6						6
Pan	2						2
Preparation	20	1	1				22

Classification

Typology is inherently a normalizing process. Although necessary at one level, it can hide or suppress significant variability between sets of artifacts. By identifying—or inventing—types and by grouping artifacts into sets meaningful to us, we again set up boundaries that imply items within a field are all of a kind and distinct from those without. The choice of attributes selected, the weighting given to each, and the degree of difference regarded as significant are all involved to some extent in decision-making, and all therefore affect the scope and structure of types. While the core may be cohesive and uniform, there are always varieties and outliers whose differences are lost once assigned to and subsumed within a broader group. If we are concerned to identify the degree of variability within and between assemblages, the homogenizing effects of predefined types become problematic. Classification needs to walk the fine line between broader groupings that ignore variations and over-precise systems where the wood cannot be seen for the trees. Our task is to find appropriate scales or alternative approaches to analysis that address each particular circumstance or question (cf. Adams and Adams 1991; Read 2007).

A related question is the extent to which our types map onto those that were significant in the past. Of course general functional types must have been clearly recognized by their makers and users. So, too, might finer or more minor elements, although not all aspects or attributes need have been of emic significance, despite some natural degree of variation in the characterization of semantic domains reflecting the ways in which people classify artifact types (Kempton 1981). This is in part a question of how much variation was recognized by, accepted by, or sought after and the extent to which individuals or groups asserted difference or conformed to common patterns in order to mark relationships and identity. This may sometimes have been deliberate but could also have been an entirely unconscious aspect of social reproduction.

Explaining Ceramic Variability

The variation within and between artifact types or assemblages reflects numerous, often intertwined factors and systems. I will briefly discuss two of these with reference to pottery: scale/context of production and individual creativity/community expectations or demands.

Production

The degree of artifact standardization is often regarded as a key to assessing the mode of production and hence the broader social context. An underlying assumption here is that the more specialized the producers and context of production, the greater the degree of standardization and perhaps simplicity of products (see, for example, Arnold 1991; Costin 1991; Frankel 1991; London 1991; Longacre 1999; Frankel and Kewibu 2000). There are other considerations as well, however, including the frequency and scale of production events (Deal 1998: 165), the effects of skill, routine, and repetition as well as of community expectations (Rice 1991: 268–273; Longacre 1999: 44–45). The lack of ethnographic data on variability within individual or community production, combined with the difficulties of defining appropriate and comparable archaeological datasets, create difficulties for this approach.

While much Early and Middle Bronze Age pottery in Cyprus appears to conform to common types, there was clearly also a contemporary tendency toward individuality and the assertion of difference within the general tradition. One example of this is the variation within the small bowl assemblage from the cemeteries at Deneia (Frankel and Webb 2007: 101–103, 154; Webb and Frankel 2009). The fragmentary nature of the assemblage militates against reliable analysis of size and proportions, but comparative measurements can be made of attributes such as the thickness of the vessel walls. Figure 0.5 summarizes the measurements on a range of wares. It is clear that the Middle Bronze Age wares (Black Polished, Red Polished Black Top, Red Polished III, and Red Polished IV) have a greater degree of internal variability with regard to this particular attribute than Late Bronze Age Base Ring and White Slip wares.

This pattern fits well with the general understanding of an increase in mass production associated with the more formally structured communities that developed on Cyprus during the Late Bronze Age.

While matching expectations in this case, such measures are harder to apply in others, even where the context of deposition, and hence assemblage integrity, is

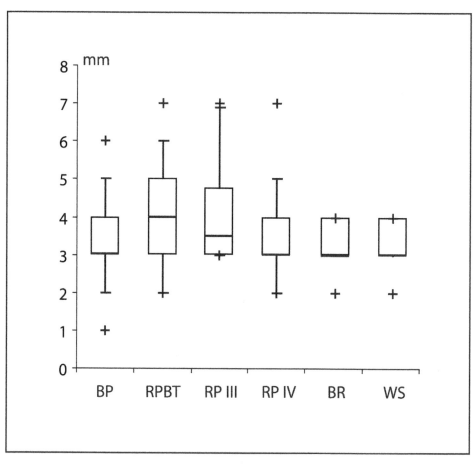

Figure 0.5: Box-and-whisker plots of wall thickness of small bowls from Deneia (after Frankel and Webb 2007: Text Figure 4.136). (BP=Black Polished, RPBT=Red Polished Black Top, RP III=Red Polished III, RP IV= Red Polished IV, BR=Base Ring, WS=White Slip).

relatively well controlled. Here we may compare the variation in proportions of Red Polished jugs from the EC I–II cemetery at Psematismenos *Trelloukkas* (Figure 0.6) and those from a MC potter's workshop at Ambelikou *Aletri* (Figure 0.7) (Georgiou *et al.* 2011; Webb and Frankel 2013a).

The latter probably represent a single kiln-load destroyed in a catastrophic event and are therefore not only exactly contemporaneous but also were probably made by the same artisan. The assemblage with lower integrity from Psematismenos *Trelloukas* is likely to have an inherently greater degree of heterogeneity than the single production episode at Ambelikou *Aletri* even if they were made in a similar mode of production and with a similar approach to standardization (Webb and Frankel 2013a: 217–218; Frankel and Webb 2014; Webb 2014; see also Frankel 1988b: 44–45).

Figure 0.6: A selection of Red Polished Mottled I–II jugs from Psematismenos *Trelloukkas*.

The coefficients of variation comparing the two assemblages do not, however, neatly conform to this expectation (Table 0.2).

Some of the proportions of the Psematismenos jugs were more uniform than those from Ambelikou—despite deriving from numerous tombs and therefore suggestive of a more mixed origin. Another complicating factor may well be at play, as it may be easier to control shape when forming flat-based vessels, such as those from Psematismenos, than round-based ones, as at Ambelikou, just as there appears to be a technical requirement for tighter control over the body shape of closed vessels than there is for open ones (Frankel 1988b). If so, then the variability in these two sets of jugs (one round-based, the other flat-based) cannot be directly compared in this way: diversity is a tricky beast to handle!

Figure 0.7: A selection of Red Polished III jugs from a single production episode at Ambelikou *Aletri*.

Table 0.2: Coefficients of variation in different attributes of Red Polished ware jugs at Ambelikou *Aletri* and Psematismenos *Trelloukkas*

	Total height	Body height	Height of maximum diameter	Diameter of body
a. Dimensions				
Psematismenos *Trelloukkas*				
Mean	380.84	351.00	186.67	325.83
StdD	64.48	52.89	33.09	57.16
CV	16.93	15.07	17.73	17.54

(*Continued*)

Table 0.2—*cont.*

	Total height	Body height	Height of maximum diameter	Diameter of body
Ambelikou *Aletri*				
Mean	318.32	149.51	76.55	150.91
StdD	54.80	27.10	15.29	27.97
CV	17.21	18.13	19.98	18.54
b. Proportions				
	BodyHt/Ht	HtMaxD/BodyHt	HtMaxD/BodyD	BodyHt/BodyD
Psematismenos *Trelloukkas*				
Mean	68.84	56.95	57.04	100.18
StDev	4.34	3.82	4.51	6.75
CV	6.30	6.71	7.91	6.74
Ambelikou *Aletri*				
Mean	47.50	50.95	50.73	99.54
StDev	3.26	4.71	3.81	5.14
CV	6.86	9.24	7.51	5.17

Creativity and Community

The overall uniformity of the Psematismenos *Trelloukas* assemblage, in fabric, color, clays, and shape, argues for local production, perhaps by a small number of potters. It also suggests that there was a very strong, perhaps an inter-generational, desire for conformity within a tightly maintained tradition. Community expectations at other sites may not have been so strict. The Ambelikou jugs, for example, not only display minor variation in size and proportions but also in added features such as knobs or relief modeling on the body and neck. This raises another issue, that of individual creativity and of assertive rather than general emblemic styles (Weissner 1983). Unlike the unpredictable (even if sought-after) mottling often found on the Red Polished Mottled ware at Psematismenos, the Ambelikou potter deliberately played with his or her products, adding the extra elements that meant that no two vessels were identical, even if they were of the same overall appearance. Community expectations and personal preferences may therefore have allowed greater freedom to the artisan at Ambelikou than they did to what appears to have been the more conformist community at Psematismenos.

The differences between the Ambelikou jugs are understated and subtle. A more obvious assertion of both individual variation and community identity is seen at Deneia. Thick, deep incision typifies the work of Deneia potters; it is one characteristic of a local aesthetic and technique that set their products apart from those of other places (Frankel and Webb 2007: 154; Webb 2009; 2010). But within this local tradition there is great variation. Although only a relatively small repertoire of incised geometric motifs was used, their selection and arrangement differ considerably from one vessel to another—so much so that no two bowls had the same specific appearance (Figure 0.8).

This strongly suggests, again, that there was a deliberate attempt to make these vessels different from one another: an assertion of individuality, here played out

Figure 0.8: A selection of incised Red Polished Black Top bowls from Deneia.

across assemblages of longer duration. At Deneia, therefore, we can see two counterpoised forces. One, identified as diversity at a regional level, promoted conformity to a strong local style, perhaps reflecting a broad social need to identify with and demonstrate a sense of belonging to a rapidly expanding community (Frankel and Webb 2007: 154–156; Webb 2010; Webb and Frankel 2009). The other, finer scale of diversity suggests that a more personal individuality was demonstrated at a different level, with potters apparently reluctant to repeat regular patterns and their customers pleased to have unique items.

A similar interplay between highly individualizing behavior and local site or regional scale techniques and style can be seen at EC I–II Bellapais *Vounous*. Here, as at Deneia, a specific local craft tradition developed within which both more complex forms and simpler, basic utilitarian shapes were produced. The former, especially, allowed opportunities for artisans to be inventive in creating complex, unusual vessels that can be thought of as having a special, probably ritual function and significance (Webb and Frankel 2010; Webb 2016). Some simpler shapes, most notably "tulip bowls" or drinking vessels, probably also had a particular role in social activities. These, too, demonstrate great variation in both incised and modeled decoration, signaling the individuality or social identity of those who used them (Figure 0.9).

We have, therefore, different degrees of variability possible with, or promoted by, social structures and negotiated relationships. These factors differed from one community or region to another and through time. Perhaps these aspects and the functions of vessels within social performances had at least as great effect on assemblage variability as the context, mode, and scale of production.

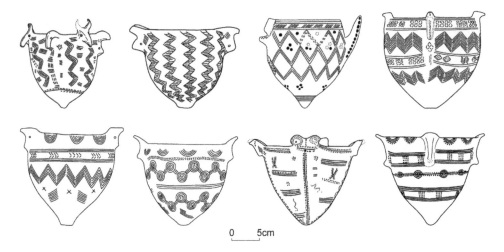

0   5cm

Figure 0.9: Examples of Early Cypriot I–II tulip bowls from *Vounous* and Karmi (after Webb and Frankel 2013b: Figure 4).

Time and Variability at a Regional Scale

Regional pottery styles at Psematismenos, Deneia, and Bellapais *Vounous* have already been alluded to. Each can be understood to represent a local variation of the broad general Red Polished ware tradition characteristic of the Early and Middle Bronze Age (Webb 2014; Dikomitou-Eliadou in this volume). But they should not be thought of as developing as the result of the same processes and stimuli. Nor need cultural or stylistic boundaries be the same in all periods. The degree of diversity within areas, or across the island as a whole, also varies. This may be due to a number of factors. Although elsewhere in the world attempts have been made to correlate the relative degree of diversity within regions with the size of population and related social patterning, with consequences for social cohesion and resilience (e.g., Nelson *et al.* 2011), no equivalent general processes can be identified within prehistoric Bronze Age Cyprus. Instead, we can argue for historically contingent and specific responses to different circumstances.

With the development of the Philia facies of the Early Bronze Age, a very wide-spread and homogeneous material culture can be identified (Webb and Frankel 1999). For at least some time this archaeological (and, we may argue, social) "culture" would have coexisted with the latest of the Late Chalcolithic communities. It is possible that some of the Philia material commonality served to mark cultural identity and to differentiate members of this group from other peoples: in other words, variability within the island was at least partly instrumental as well as an intrinsic characteristic. From a materialist perspective the artifacts themselves helped construct social patterns. Within one or two centuries the Late Chalcolithic became at least archaeologically invisible and only "Bronze Age" material appears in all parts of the island. Although the legacy of the older systems may be traceable in specific aspects of later material in particular regions (Bolger and Peltenburg 2014), in general an earlier broad dichotomy in overall lifeways gives way to a unified system: how we should understand this process of assimilation, integration, acculturation, or hybridization is a matter of considerable interest and debate (Knapp 2013: 264–277).

The widespread uniformity of Philia communities must have been maintained by regular interactions. The spread of Philia villages into new territory meant that the small size of new foundations would have required regular interaction with others to ensure the supply of necessities, including marriage partners. As settlements grew in size, these imperatives may have become less intense. Other factors, however, continued. It is most likely that longer-distance relationships were always underpinned by exchange systems that facilitated the flow of copper from source areas and the reciprocal distribution of goods such as finer pottery wares (Dikomitou 2010; 2013; 2014). The demand for copper beyond immediate quotidian uses can be attributed to opportunities to supply overseas markets within a broader eastern Mediterranean interaction sphere (Webb *et al.* 2006; Webb 2013; see also Knapp 2013). In this way, external factors contributed to internal patterns of interregional uniformity on the island.

About 2200 BCE, significant changes can be observed widely across the Near East, including the collapse of established exchange systems (for recent discussions, see Finné *et al.* 2011; Meller *et al.* 2015). The external demand for Cypriot copper dried up, removing one major incentive for the maintenance of a cohesive, integrated society. Archaeologically this is seen in a greater diversity of pottery types, styles, and technologies, which characterize the post-Philia, EC I–II period. Although generically similar in continuing the established tradition of Red Polished pottery, two major zones can at present be observed in that ware: one covering the center and central south coast and the other in the north. As typified by the assemblage from Psematismenos *Trelloukkas* (Georgiou *et al.* 2011), central and southern pottery is hard-fired, fairly coarse, and generally plain. North coast pottery, especially that from Bellapais *Vounous*, is, by contrast, finer, softer-fired, and marked by a related use of complex incised decoration and the introduction of complex shapes, as noted above. Although there was certainly contact between different areas, as evidenced by the distribution of particular vessels, this new division of the island into several identifiable ceramic zones signals different responses to changing circumstances. As suggested above, the Psematismenos potters emphasized conformity to social norms, suppressing variation. At Bellapais *Vounous*, different forces came into play. On the north coast the complexity of pottery and other activities can be connected to the assertion of authority, expressed through control of esoteric knowledge and ritual in the place of earlier economic power (Webb *et al.* 2009: 249–250; Webb and Frankel 2010; 2013b; Webb 2013; 2014).

Although Red Polished pottery displays less clear regional variation during the Middle Bronze Age, local variations are still evident (see Dikomitou-Eliadou in this volume), while other wares have particular distributions. North coast sites such as Lapithos *Vrysi tou Barba* and Bellapais *Vounous* now appear to have more in common with sites in the center, such as Nicosia *Ayia Paraskevi*, than they did during EC I–II. This may be attributed to a renewed demand for Cypriot copper, leading to an expansion of production and associated networks linking the northern foothills of the Troodos to coastal sites such as Lapithos. The distribution of White Painted wares provides

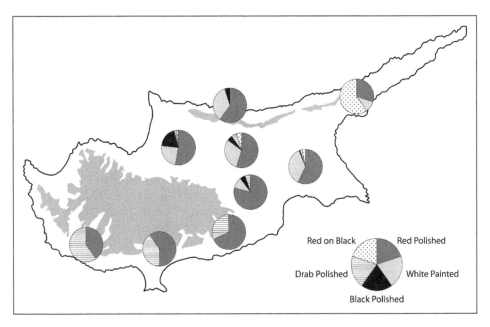

Figure 0.10: Schematic, notional distribution of major prehistoric Bronze Age wares (after Frankel 2009: Figure 2).

one signal of these connections: the way in which stylistic variation in this pottery has been assessed provides one example of how different approaches to measurement and analysis structure explanation—either favoring a simpler dichotomous model (Åström 1972) or a more complex series of interconnections (Frankel 1974). These are not necessarily exclusive alternatives. They might equally well be seen as observations at different scales, each exposing a different pattern and reflecting different processes.

At the same time, the proportions of other major wares show alternate patterns of relationship and connections (Figure 0.10).

In each case the challenge before us is to determine what our observations (all too often still dependent on very patchy and limited available evidence) mean. Within the broad distribution of major wares there are—or are likely to be—more subtle variations from one locality to another, reflecting various modes of technology and stylistic transfer and adoption or patterns of artifact exchange. Or, as can be argued at least in the case of the emergence of very distinctive types and styles at Deneia, a particular signaling of community identity and belonging developed during a period of rapid expansion and inward migration followed by greater homogeneity later (Webb 2010; 2014). We are still at a very early stage of research.

Settlement Structure and Function

Settlements are not all equivalent. It is only in the last decade that we are in a position to see some settlement variability as more sites begin to be excavated. These show differences in site location, access to resources, function, size, longevity, and history. Indeed, each individual site needs to be considered as an evolving series of settlements, avoiding the temptation to regard each as being the same throughout its history. As an example of change over time we may briefly look at Marki *Alonia*—if only because it is the one place where the particular area excavated allows for a relatively long history of development during the prehistoric Bronze Age to be traced in some detail, although even here creative assumptions must round out our story of significant architectural developments (Frankel and Webb 2006a; 2006b; 2012) (Figure 0.11).

Marki began as a part of the Philia expansion about 2400 BCE. Initially very small, it is likely to have been an outpost or outlier from a larger center such as Nicosia *Ayia Paraskevi* with the few families who lived there dependent on nearby villages to ensure survival. Most pottery and other manufactured goods would have had to be brought in from elsewhere and its inhabitants would have had a concept of their place in the world that was framed by these necessary links and connections. Our analysis of subsequent developments during some five hundred years of occupation is based on the recognition of a series of compounds that often included open courtyards as well as enclosed rooms. While some aspects of these compounds remained more or less the same over time, it is possible to trace a process of gradual replacement of an initially more open system, appropriate for a pioneer community, by new, non-communicating compounds of roughly equal size with almost fully enclosed courtyards and opposing orientations. As the village grew in size, these individual residential units became secure enough to meet their needs as economic entities, one result of the overall increase in population and the development of efficient and reliable production systems and inter-site relationships. It is, furthermore, possible to suggest an increasing desire by individual households to establish and maintain private ownership of buildings, land, and other resources. Interpersonal relationships within the village must have changed considerably as the population expanded and access between compounds became more restricted. In the early phases, with a handful of small households, people would have had regular face-to-face interaction with their neighbors. Later, Middle Bronze Age generations living in a larger, more densely inhabited space would have had fewer occasions for casual daily communication with fellow villagers beyond their immediate neighborhood. There was, therefore, an increase in interpersonal distance coincident with the development of more enclosed household and access systems, which may have led to new mechanisms of social cohesion and control. Finally, the last inhabitants lived in a different sector of the site, with the ruined houses of their ancestors nearby, providing a different environment imbued with memory.

Essentially, however, Marki was always a small agropastoral community with some engagement with copper production. While nearby Alambra may well have had a similar history and role, other villages were different. Although our view is skewed by the accident of excavation of two industrial areas with no architectural evidence of domestic housing, Ambelikou *Aletri* appears to have been a much more specialized village, producing both copper and pottery alongside a subsistence economy based on mixed farming. Set where it was to take advantage of a particular

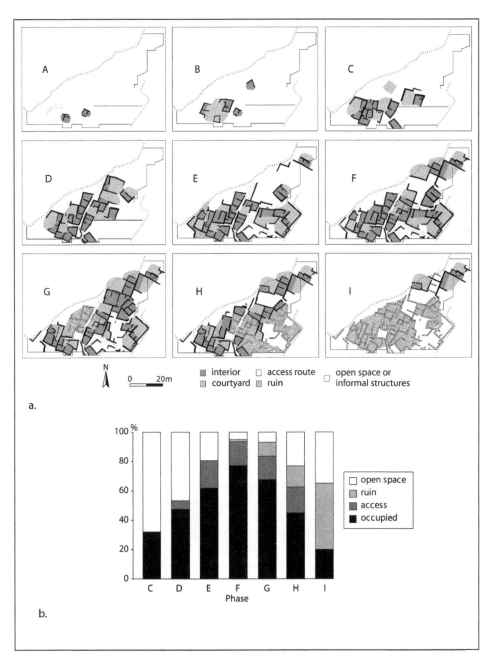

Figure 0.11: The changing nature of the built environment in the excavated area at Marki: (a) growth and decline in households and occupation; (b) the proportion of the area taken up by different types of space in successive phases (after Frankel and Webb 2012: Figure 10).

copper source, it was occupied for a far shorter time than Marki, reflecting the often unpredictable and episodic nature of mining settlements.

More recently excavated sites increasingly reveal internal variations, if not broader specialization, in a range of industrial activities (Bombardieri 2013; 2014; 2017). This is well illustrated at MC Erimi *Laonin tou Porakou* with evidence of purpose-built workshop complexes adjacent to domestic housing. These were dedicated to particular tasks and are perhaps indicative not only of spatial variation in architecture and functions but also of a degree of specialization in the organization of labor (Bombardieri 2013). Other Middle Cypriot sites also provide evidence of an increase during the first half of the second millennium BCE in task-specific areas and installations, seen in the industrial complex at Pyrgos *Mavrorachi* (Belgiorno 2004), the possible brewing facilities at Kissonerga *Skalia* (Crewe and Hill 2012), and the traces of copper working activities adjacent to domestic areas at Politiko *Troullia* (Fall *et al.* 2008).

We have no direct evidence from the villages associated with the Middle Bronze Age cemeteries at sites such as Nicosia *Ayia Paraskevi*, Deneia, and Lapithos *Vrysi tou Barba*. These developed into far larger places than Marki, Alambra, Ambelikou, and Politiko. The cemeteries at Deneia reveal a massive and rapid expansion during MC I–II (Frankel and Webb 2007; Webb and Frankel 2009)—perhaps a process not unrelated to the decline and final abandonment of sites like Alambra and Marki. The distinctive pottery styles developed at Deneia and discussed above may be seen as one response to this expansion and the associated integration of newcomers into the community. Deneia and Nicosia *Ayia Paraskevi* may always have been key points in the networks of connections linking the north coast to the copper-rich areas. Situated as they were near the agricultural resources of the Pediaos and Ovgos river systems, they were strategically placed to control the movement of goods, especially copper destined for dominant places such as Lapithos (Webb 2017a; Webb 2017b). If this model is correct, then these settlements would have been of a very different order of magnitude from specialized production or generalized agricultural villages, with attendant differences in many aspects of internal relationships and control. The social landscape of MC II–III Cyprus should be viewed as a complex of varied types of sites that are dynamically and continually evolving.

Aspects of Burial

The differences between settlements through time and in size and function are also evident in the nature of cemeteries and approaches to funeral ritual. One significant development is the trend from small to large chamber tombs. EC I–II tombs at both Psematismenos *Trelloukkas* and Bellapais *Vounous* are typically small, with a limited number of grave goods and often only a single body. At some sites such as Bellapais *Vounous* and Karmi there is some evidence that the remains—both of the dead and the associated goods—were removed to make way for new burials, although this does not seem to have occurred at Psematismenos. Relatively small tombs are also seen at some later cemeteries, but at Deneia, Nicosia *Ayia Paraskevi,* and Lapithos *Vrysi tou Barba*, far larger chambers were excavated. Older burials were left in them and new goods added to the stock of old. This different approach can be read as an indication of a different attitude, where tombs were constructed with an eye to the future, as repositories for successive burials linking one generation with the next and at the same time asserting individual or family rights to place and position in society. Such an explanation chimes with those suggested above regarding the assertion of identity through pottery.

Much of my discussion thus far has focused on pottery. Other manufactures have different stories to tell, different degrees and patterns of variation. In the case of metalwork this may appear in the context and nature of funerary deposition rather than through typology. Unlike pottery, there is little fine-scale variability in metal artifacts: certainly the techniques of manufacture of copper-base tools and utensils remained uniform across the island throughout the Early and Middle Bronze Age (Philip 1991). This in itself suggests a very conservative craft tradition, with no consumer demands for innovation.

Significant differences can, however, be identified in the use—more particularly the final use of items. The quantities and perhaps also the size of metal items placed in tombs varies considerably. Metal had different value or significance in different places, with the largest and most numerous finds at Lapithos *Vrysi tou Barba* (Webb 2017a; Webb 2017b). Some particular aspects also vary. For example, about one-fifth

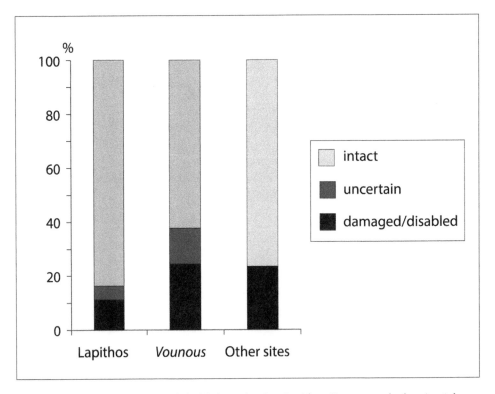

Figure 0.12: Incidence of intact and disabled spearheads at Lapithos, *Vounous*, and other sites (after Webb and Frankel 2015: Figure 4).

of spearheads and knives were deliberately disabled before being placed in tombs (Webb and Frankel 2015). While this custom was observed elsewhere, it was most common at Bellapais *Vounous* and notably less so at nearby Lapithos (Figure 0.12).

Could this be related to a move away from a focus on personal ownership toward accumulation and conspicuous consumption at Lapithos in the Middle Cypriot period? If disabled items signal an earlier intimate connection with individual adult males, then this may represent a shift, at this one site at least, toward a more communal or lineage-based notion of accumulation where metal items were retained in tombs but separated from skeletal remains and curated in groups and sets.

New Directions?

This brief review of issues, approaches, and explanations has, I hope, exposed some of the underlying concerns in considering variation and variability during the eight centuries or so of the Early and Middle Bronze Age. We are increasingly in a position to identify both of these, not only through the excavation of additional sites but also through a clearer understanding of the nature of the archaeological record and the appropriate types of questions we can ask or models we can build. These must take account of in-built or imposed limitations of scale, precision, and integrity. The artificial archaeological entities or units of analysis through which the past is perceived may also differ both in their constituent elements and in their degree of uniformity or homogeneity, while the material evidence has many different facets that reflect functional, historical, economic, and social patterns. Each needs to be considered separately to allow later integration, rather than assuming correlations between them.

Scale is of critical importance to explanation, determining whether we see gradual or sudden change, diffuse or sharp boundaries, close or distant relationships, or uniform or disparate systems. No single scale is, however, superior. Each brings a different aspect of material into focus. It is a major challenge to find the right types of explanation for both smaller and larger patterns and to connect these into a cohesive overall understanding.

It used to be more common to make reference to a peculiar Cypriot character: perhaps the modern equivalent is to talk in terms of identity. This may be seen as a question of the extent to which the island should be considered as a single system. This may be appropriate at one broad scale, but it does not necessarily apply at finer levels, or in the same way at different times. While there is a degree of commonality in the long-lasting traditions that we refer to as the prehistoric Bronze Age, we can, increasingly, also see diversity in both time and space. It was a varied and complex place—so that not all people lived in the same Bronze Age. As we begin more clearly to identify which elements regions and times have in common and which differentiate between them, we can begin to recognize processes or contingent circumstances that mediate the tensions between countervailing forces that encourage variety and innovation on the one hand and adherence to tradition or provide incentives for uniformity on the other.

Much new research is often tightly focused and specific, as diverse as prehistoric Bronze Age Cyprus itself. Broader understanding of the period and new directions for research will need not only a self-conscious regard for the nature of the archaeological record and its constructs but also clear frameworks for integrating often disparate analyses to address questions of social process and historical contingency as we explore the inherent diversity of the period.

References

Adams W.Y., and E.W. Adams. 1991. *Archaeological Typology and Practical Reality: A Dialectical Approach to Artifact Classification and Sorting.* Cambridge: Cambridge University Press.

Arnold, P.J. 1991. Dimensional standardization and production scale in Mesoamerican ceramics. *Latin American Antiquity* 2: 363–370.

Åström, P. 1972. *The Middle Cypriote Bronze Age. The Swedish Cyprus Expedition IV 1B.* Lund, Sweden: The Swedish Cyprus Expedition.

Belgiorno, M.-R. 2004. *Pyrgos Mavroraki: Advanced Technology in Bronze Age Cyprus.* Nicosia: Nicosia Archaeological Museum.

Bolger, D., and E. Peltenburg. 2014. Material and social transformations in 3rd millennium BCE Cyprus: Evidence of ceramics. In J.M. Webb (ed.), *Structure, Measurement, and Meaning: Studies on Prehistoric Cyprus in Honour of David Frankel,* 187–198. Studies in Mediterranean Archaeology 143. Uppsala, Sweden: Åströms Förlag.

Bombardieri, L. 2013. The development and organisation of labour strategies in prehistoric Cyprus: The evidence from Erimi Laonin tou Porakou. In A.B. Knapp, J.M. Webb and A. McCarthy (eds.), *J.R.B. Stewart: An Archaeological Legacy,* 91–102. Studies in Mediterranean Archaeology 139. Uppsala, Sweden: Åströms Förlag.

Bombardieri, L. 2014. The second face of identity: Processes and symbols of community affiliation in Middle Bronze Age Cyprus. In J.M. Webb (ed.), *Structure, Measurement and Meaning: Studies on Prehistoric Cyprus in Honour of David Frankel,* 43–55. Studies in Mediterranean Archaeology 143. Uppsala, Sweden: Åströms Förlag.

Bombardieri, L. 2017. *Erimi Laonin tou Porakou: A Middle Bronze Age Community in Cyprus. Excavations 2008–2014.* Studies in Mediterranean Archaeology 145. Uppsala, Sweden: Astrom Editions.

Carver, M. 2009. *Archaeological Investigation.* London: Routledge.

Catling, H.W. 1962. Patterns of settlement in Bronze Age Cyprus. *Opuscula Atheniensia* 4: 129–169.

Costin, C.L. 1991. Craft specialisation: Issues in defining, documenting, and explaining the organization of production. In M.B. Schiffer (ed.), *Archaeological Method and Theory* 3: 1–56. Tucson: University of Arizona.

Crewe, L., and I. Hill. 2012. Finding beer in the archaeological record: A case study from Kissonerga-Skalia on Bronze Age Cyprus. *Levant* 44: 205–237.

Deal, M. 1998. *Pottery Ethnoarchaeology in the Central Maya Highlands.* Salt Lake City: University of Utah Press.

Dikomitou, M. 2010. A closer look at Red Polished Philia fabrics: Inquiring into ceramic uniformity in Cyprus, ca. 2500–2300 B.C. *The Old Potter's Almanack* 15: 1–6.

Dikomitou-Eliadou, M. 2013. Interactive communities at the dawn of the Cypriot Bronze Age: An interdisciplinary approach to Philia phase ceramic variability. In A.B. Knapp, J.M. Webb and A. McCarthy (eds.), *J.R.B. Stewart: An Archaeological Legacy,* 23–32. Studies in Mediterranean Archaeology 139. Uppsala, Sweden: Åströms Förlag.

Dikomitou-Eliadou, M. 2014. Rescaling perspectives: Local and island-wide ceramic production in Early and Middle Bronze Age Cyprus. In J.M. Webb (ed.), *Structure, Measurement and Meaning: Studies on Prehistoric Cyprus in Honour of David Frankel,* 199–211. Studies in Mediterranean Archaeology 143. Uppsala, Sweden: Åströms Förlag.

Fall, P.L., S.E. Falconer, M. Horowitz, J. Hunt, M.C. Metzger, and D. Ryter. 2008. Bronze Age settlement and landscape at Politiko-Troullia, 2005–2007. *Report of the Department of Antiquities,* Cyprus: 183–208.

Finné, M., K. Holmgren, H.S. Sundqvist, E. Weiberg, and M. Lindblom. 2011. Climate in the Eastern Mediterranean, and adjacent regions during the past 6000 years: A review. *Journal of Archaeological Science* 38: 3153–3173.

Frankel, D. 1974. *Middle Cypriot White Painted Pottery: An Analytical Study of the Decoration.* Studies in Mediterranean Archaeology 42. Göteborg, Sweden: Paul Åströms Förlag.

Frankel, D. 1988a. Characterising change in prehistoric sequences: A view from Australia. *Archaeology in Oceania* 23: 41–48.

Frankel, D. 1988b. Pottery production in prehistoric Bronze Age Cyprus: Assessing the problem. *Journal of Mediterranean Archaeology* 1.2: 27–55.

Frankel, D. 1991. Ceramic variability: Measurement and meaning. In J. Barlow, D. Bolger, and B. Kling (eds.), *Cypriot Ceramics: Reading the Prehistoric Record,* 241–252. University Museum Monograph 74. Philadelphia: University of Pennsylvania.

Frankel, D. 1993. The excavator: Creator or destroyer? *Antiquity* 67: 875–877.

Frankel, D. 1998. Constructing Marki Alonia: Reflections on method and authority in archaeological reporting. *Journal of Mediterranean Archaeology* 11.2: 242–256.

Frankel, D. 2009. What do we mean by "regionalism"? In I. Hein (ed.), *The Formation of Cyprus in the 2nd Millennium B.C. Studies in Regionalism during the Middle and Late Bronze Age,* 15–25. Denkschriften der Österreichischen Akademie der Wissenschaften. Contributions to the Chronology of the Eastern Mediterranean XX. Vienna: Österreichische Akadamie der Wissenschaften.

Frankel, D. 2012. "Strange places crammed with observation": Reporting the site. In J.M. Webb and D. Frankel (eds.), *SIMA After Fifty Years: Contributions to Mediterranean Archaeology,* 25–31. Studies in Mediterranean Archaeology 137. Lund, Sweden: Åströms Förlag.

Frankel, D., P. Keswani, D. Papaconstantinou, E. Peltenburg, and J.M. Webb. 2013. Stratigraphy in a non-tell archaeological environment. In E. Peltenburg (ed.), *ARCANE Associated Chronologies for the Ancient Near East and the Eastern Mediterranean,* Vol II Cyprus, 15–38. Turnhout, Belgium: Brepols.

Frankel, D., and V. Kewibu. 2000. Early Ceramic Period pottery from Murua (Site ODR), Gulf Province, Papua New Guinea. In A. Anderson and T. Murray (eds.), *Australian Archaeologist. Collected Papers in Honour of Jim Allen,* 279–290. Canberra: Coombs Academic.

Frankel, D., and J.M. Webb. 2006a. *Marki Alonia: An Early and Middle Bronze Age Settlement in Cyprus. Excavations 1995–2000.* Studies in Mediterranean Archaeology 123.2. Sävedalen, Sweden: Åströms Förlag.

Frankel, D., and J.M. Webb. 2006b. Neighbours: Negotiating space in a prehistoric village. *Antiquity* 80: 287–302.

Frankel, D., and J.M. Webb. 2007. *The Bronze Age Cemeteries at Deneia in Cyprus.* Studies in Mediterranean Archaeology 135. Sävedalen, Sweden: Åströms Förlag.

Frankel, D., and J.M. Webb. 2012. Household continuity and transformation in a prehistoric Cypriot village. In B.J. Parker and C.P. Foster (eds.), *New Perspectives on Household Archaeology,* 473–500. Winona Lake, IN: Eisenbrauns.

Frankel, D., and J.M. Webb. 2014. A potter's workshop from Middle Bronze Age Cyprus: New light on production context, scale and variability. *Antiquity* 88: 425–440.

Georgiou, G. 2006. Η Τοπογραφία της Ανθρώπινης Εγκατάστασης στην Κύπρο κατά την Πρώιμη και Μέση Χαλκοκρατία. Unpublished PhD dissertation, University of Cyprus.

Georgiou, G., J.M. Webb, and D. Frankel. 2011. *Psematismenos Trelloukkas: An Early Bronze Age Cemetery in Cyprus.* Nicosia: Department of Antiquities, Cyprus.

Gjerstad, E. 1926. *Studies on Prehistoric Cyprus.* Stockholm: Uppsala University.

Kantner, J. 2008. The archaeology of regions: From discrete analytical toolkit to ubiquitous spatial perspective. *Journal of Archaeological Research* 16: 37–81.

Kempton, W. 1981. *The Folk Classification of Ceramics: A Study of Cognitive Prototypes.* New York: Academic Press.

Knapp, A.B. 2008. *Prehistoric and Protohistoric Cyprus: Identity, Insularity, and Connectivity.* Oxford: Oxford University Press.

Knapp, A.B. 2013. *The Archaeology of Cyprus: From Earliest Prehistory through the Bronze Age.* New York: Cambridge University Press.

London, G.A. 1991. Standardization and variation in the work of craft specialists. In W.A. Longacre (ed.), *Ceramic Ethnoarchaeology,* 182–204. Tucson: University of Arizona Press.

Longacre, W.A. 1999. Standardization and specialization: What's the link? In J.A. Skibo and G.M. Feinman (eds.), *Pottery and People: A Dynamic Link,* 44–58. Salt Lake City: University of Utah.

Manning, S.W. 2013a. Appendix: A new radiocarbon chronology for prehistoric and protohistoric Cyprus, ca. 11,000–1050 CalBC. In A.B. Knapp, *The Archaeology of Cyprus: From Earliest Prehistory through the Bronze Age*, 485–533. New York: Cambridge University Press.

Manning, S.W. 2013b. Cyprus at 2200: Rethinking the chronology of the Early Cypriot Bronze Age. In A.B. Knapp, J.M. Webb, and A. McCarthy (eds.), *J.R.B. Stewart: An Archaeological Legacy*, 1–21. Studies in Mediterranean Archaeology 139. Uppsala, Sweden: Åströms Förlag.

Manning, S.W. 2014. Timings and gaps in the early history of Cyprus and its copper trade: What these might tell us. In J.M. Webb (ed.), *Structure, Measurement, and Meaning: Studies on Prehistoric Cyprus in Honour of David Frankel*, 23–41. Studies in Mediterranean Archaeology 143. Uppsala, Sweden: Åströms Förlag.

Meller, H., H.W. Arz, R. Jung, and R. Risch. (eds.) 2015. *2200 BC: A Climatic Breakdown as a Cause for the Collapse of the Old World? 7th Archaeological Conference of Central Germany October 23–26, 2014 in Halle (Saale)*. Tagungen des Landesmuseum für Vorgeschichte Halle 12. Halle, Germany: Landesmuseum für Vorgeschichte.

Myres, J.L. 1926. Review of E. Gjerstad, Studies on Prehistoric Cyprus. *Journal of Hellenic Studies* 46: 289–291.

Nelson, M.C., M. Hegmon, S.R. Kulow, M.A. Peeples, K.W. Kintigh, and A.P. Kinzig. 2011. Resisting diversity: A long-term archaeological study. *Ecology and Society* 16.1: 25 [online] URL: http://www.ecologyandsociety.org/vol16/iss1/art25/.

Peltenburg, E., D. Frankel, and C. Paraskeva. 2013a. Radiocarbon. In E. Peltenburg (ed.), *ARCANE Associated Chronologies for the Ancient Near East and the Eastern Mediterranean II*: Cyprus, 313–338. Turnhout, Belgium: Brepols.

Peltenburg, E., D. Frankel, and J.M. Webb. 2013b. Introduction. In E. Peltenburg (ed.), *ARCANE Associated Chronologies for the Ancient Near East and the Eastern Mediterranean II*: Cyprus, 1–13. Turnhout, Belgium: Brepols.

Philip, G. 1991. Cypriot bronzework in the Levantine world: Conservatism, innovation, and social change. *Journal of Mediterranean Archaeology* 4.1: 59–107.

Read, D.W. 2007. *Artifact Classification: A Conceptual and Methodological Approach*. Walnut Creek, CA: Left Coast.

Rice, P.M. 1991. Specialisation, standardisation, and diversity: A retrospective. In R.L. Bishop and F.W. Lange (eds.), *The Ceramic Legacy of Anna O. Shepard*, 257–279. Niwot: University Press of Colorado.

Schiffer, M.B. 1976. *Behavioral Archaeology*. New York: Academic Press.

Stanley Price, N.P. 1979. *Early Prehistoric Settlement in Cyprus: A Review and Gazetteer of Sites, c.6500–3000 B.C.* British Archaeological Reports International Series 65. Oxford: British Archaeological Reports.

Stewart, E. 1999. *Corpus of Cypriot Artefacts of the Early Bronze Age*. Part 3.1 by James R. Stewart. Studies in Mediterranean Archaeology 3.3. Jonsered, Sweden: Paul Åströms Förlag.

Stewart, E., and P. Åström. 1988. *Corpus of Cypriot Artefacts of the Early Bronze Age*. Part 1 by James R. Stewart. Studies in Mediterranean Archaeology 3.1. Göteborg, Sweden: Paul Åströms Förlag.

Stewart, E., and P. Åström. 1992. *Corpus of Cypriot Artefacts of the Early Bronze Age*. Part 2 by James R. Stewart. Studies in Mediterranean Archaeology 3.2. Jonsered, Sweden: Paul Åströms Förlag.

Stewart, J.R. 1962. The Early Cypriote Bronze Age. In P. Dikaios and J.R. Stewart, *The Stone Age and the Early Bronze Age in Cyprus*. Swedish Cyprus Expedition IV 1A, 205–401. Lund, Sweden: The Swedish Cyprus Expedition.

Webb, J.M. 2006. Material culture and the value of context: A case study from Marki, Cyprus. In D. Papaconstantinou (ed.), *Deconstructing Context: A Critical Approach to Archaeological Practice*, 98–119. Oxford: Oxbow Books.

Webb, J.M. 2009. Deneia: A Middle Cypriot site in its regional and historical context. In I. Hein (ed.), *The Formation of Cyprus in the 2nd Millennium B.C. Studies in Regionalism during the Middle and Late Bronze Age*, 27–37. Denkschriften der Österreichischen Akademie der Wissenschaften. Contributions to the Chronology of the Eastern Mediterranean XX: 15–25. Vienna: Österreichische Akademie der Wissenschaften.

Webb, J.M. 2010. The ceramic industry of Deneia: Crafting community and place in Middle Bronze Age Cyprus. In D. Bolger and L.C. Maguire (eds.), *The Development of Pre-State Communities in the Ancient Near East: Studies in Honour of Edgar Peltenburg*, 174–182. Oxford: Oxbow Books.

Webb, J.M. 2013. "The mantle of Vasilia": Have Stewart's views on the centrality of the copper trade in prehistoric Cyprus stood the test of time? In A.B. Knapp, J.M. Webb, and A. McCarthy (eds.), *J.R.B. Stewart—An Archaeological Legacy*, 59–71. Studies in Mediterranean Archaeology 139. Uppsala, Sweden: Åströms Förlag.

Webb, J.M. 2014. Pottery production and distribution in prehistoric Bronze Age Cyprus: The long road from measurement to meaning. In J.M. Webb (ed.), *Structure, Measurement, and Meaning: Studies on Prehistoric Cyprus in Honour of David Frankel*, 213–227. Studies in Mediterranean Archaeology 143. Uppsala, Sweden: Åströms Förlag.

Webb, J.M. 2016. Pots and people: An investigation of individual and collective identities in Early Bronze Age Cyprus. In M. Mina, S. Triantaphyllou, and Y. Papadatos (eds.), *Embodied Identities in the Prehistoric Eastern Mediterranean: Convergence of Theory and Practice*, Proceedings of a Conference on Cyprus, 10–12 April 2012, 55–62. Oxford: Oxbow Books.

Webb, J.M. 2017a. Lapithos revisited: a fresh look at a key Middle Bronze Age site in Cyprus. In G. Bourogiannis and C. Mühlenbock (eds), *Ancient Cyprus Today: Museum Collections and New Research*. Studies in Mediterranean Archaeology PB 184, 57–67. Uppsala, Sweden: Astrom Editions.

Webb, J.M. 2017b. Vounoi (Vounous) and Lapithos in the Early and Middle Bronze Age: a reappraisal of the central north coast of Cyprus in the light of fieldwork and research undertaken since 1974. In D. Pilides and M. Mina (eds), *Four Decades of Hiatus in Archaeological Research in Cyprus: Towards Restoring the Balance*, Kypriaka – Forschungen zum Antiken Zypern: Studies on Ancient Cyprus 2, 128–139. Wien.

Webb, J.M., and D. Frankel. 1999. Characterising the Philia facies. Material culture, chronology, and the origin of the Bronze Age in Cyprus. *American Journal of Archaeology* 103: 3–43.

Webb, J.M., and D. Frankel. 2009. Exploiting a damaged and diminishing resource: Survey, sampling, and society at Bronze Age Deneia in Cyprus. *Antiquity* 83: 54–68.

Webb, J.M., and D. Frankel. 2010. Social strategies, ritual, and cosmology in Early Bronze Age Cyprus: An investigation of burial data from the north coast. *Levant* 42: 185–209.

Webb, J.M., and D. Frankel. 2012. *Corpus of Cypriot Artefacts of the Early Bronze Age Part 4*, by James R. Stewart. Studies in Mediterranean Archaeology 3.4. Uppsala, Sweden: Åströms Förlag.

Webb, J.M., and D. Frankel. 2013a. *Ambelikou Aletri: Metallurgy and Pottery Production in Middle Bronze Age Cyprus*. Studies in Mediterranean Archaeology 138. Uppsala, Sweden: Åströms Förlag.

Webb, J.M., and D. Frankel. 2013b. Cultural regionalism and divergent social trajectories in Early Bronze Age Cyprus. *American Journal of Archaeology* 117: 59–81.

Webb, J.M., and D. Frankel. 2015. Coincident biographies: Bent and broken blades in Bronze Age Cyprus. In K. Harrell and J. Driessen (eds.), *Thravsma: Contextualising the Intentional Destruction of Objects in the Bronze Age Aegean and Cyprus*, 117–142. Louvain-la-Neuve, Belgium: Presses universitaires de Louvain.

Webb, J.M., D. Frankel, K.O. Eriksson, and J.B. Hennessy. 2009. *The Bronze Age Cemeteries at Karmi Palealona and Lapatsa in Cyprus*. Excavations by J.R.B. Stewart. Studies in Mediterranean Archaeology 136. Sävedalen, Sweden: Åströms Förlag.

Webb, J.M., D. Frankel, S. Stos, and N. Gale. 2006. Early Bronze Age metal trade in the Eastern Mediterranean. New compositional and lead isotope evidence from Cyprus. *Oxford Journal of Archaeology* 25: 261–288.

Weissner, P. 1983. Style and social information in Kalahari San projectile points. *American Antiquity* 48: 253–276.

PART I

The Context and Matter of Prehistory

1

The Middle Chalcolithic to Middle Bronze Age Chronology of Cyprus

Refinements and Reconstructions

CHARALAMBOS PARASKEVA

Introduction

Taking a step back and looking at the stories we weave about the past, one realizes that their most consistent element is that enigmatic essence holding together the fabric of reality, namely time. Inevitably this realization elevates time to one of the funda-mental building blocks of archaeological argumentation and *pari passu* the starting point of any inquiry into the past (Piggott 1959: 51). Following this line of reasoning, the present study endeavors first to examine critically recent efforts at elucidating the chronology of the Middle Chalcolithic to Middle Bronze Age in Cyprus. Second, it aims to reconstruct and to refine the chronology of the island for the abovementioned periods based on absolute dating evidence, Bayesian analysis, and new directions in post-analytical comparison of chronological models.

The Absolute Chronology of Prehistoric Cyprus: A Review of Recent Studies

Arguably, the onset of and ensuing enthusiasm over the third radiocarbon revolu-tion (Bayliss 2009: 126–127) has brought about a new level of self-awareness for archaeology as a discipline and in parallel has led to a profusion of studies attempt-ing to tackle difficult chronological issues (e.g., Manning *et al.* 2006; Bronk Ramsey *et al.* 2010; Manning 2014a). Indeed, it is now a commonplace observation that prior to the introduction of Bayesian analysis of radiocarbon dates, the majority of attempts at constructing chronological systems for prehistoric Cyprus had been utilizing relative data derived from comparative stratigraphy and ceramic seriation, whereas absolute dates were limited to the role of setting *termini* for periods or functioned as contributing arguments for the adoption or rejection of chronologi-cal schemata (Manning 2013a: 486; Peltenburg *et al.* 2013a: 7–9). The practice of using non-quantifiable relative dates for constructing chronologies in conjunction

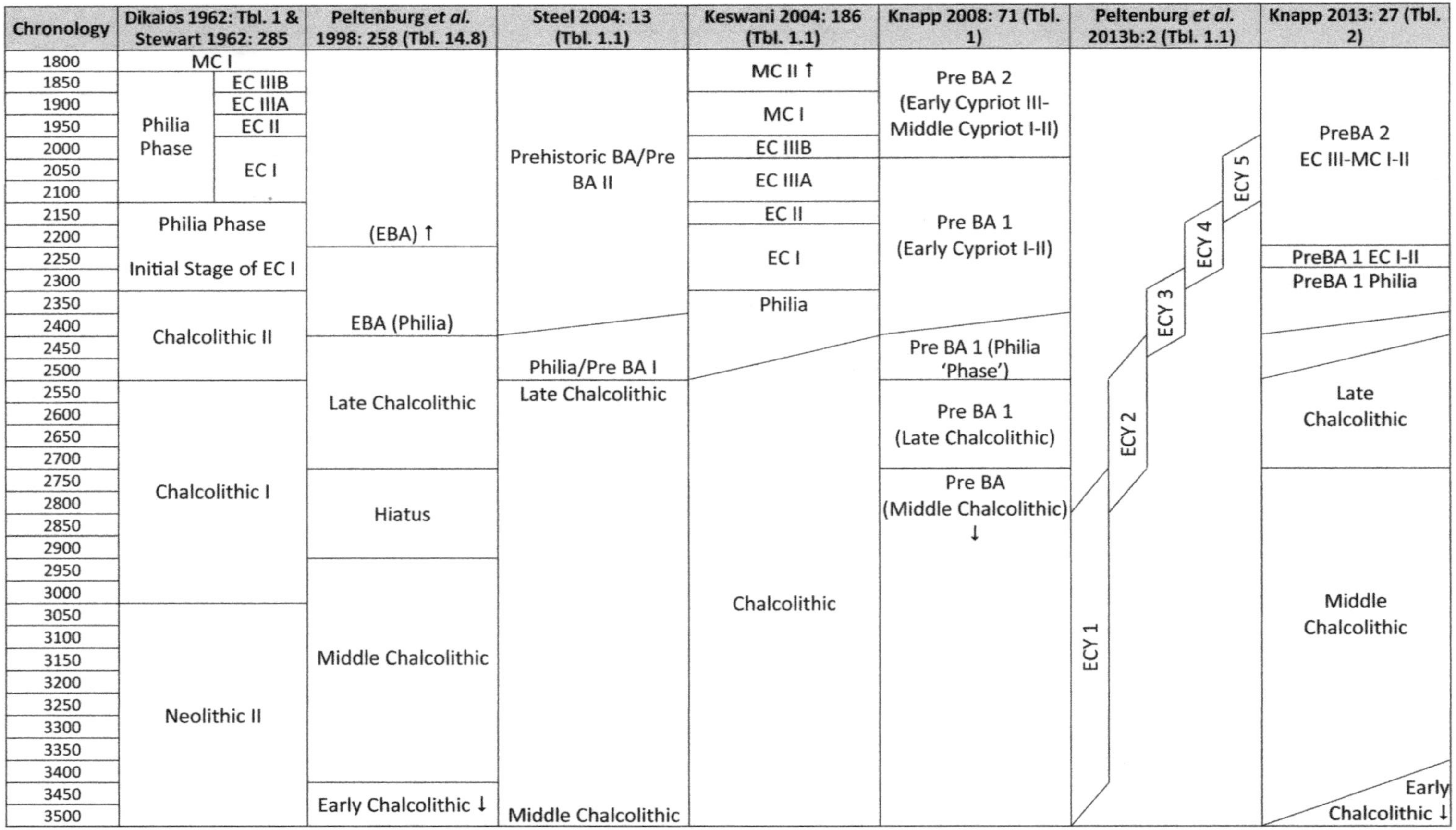

Figure 1.1: Selection of chronological systems for Middle Chalcolithic to Middle Bronze Age Cyprus.

Chronology	Dikaios 1962: Tbl. 1 & Stewart 1962: 285	Peltenburg et al. 1998: 258 (Tbl. 14.8)	Steel 2004: 13 (Tbl. 1.1)	Keswani 2004: 186 (Tbl. 1.1)	Knapp 2008: 71 (Tbl. 1)	Peltenburg et al. 2013b:2 (Tbl. 1.1)	Knapp 2013: 27 (Tbl. 2)
1800	MC I			MC II ↑			
1850	EC IIIB			MC I	Pre BA 2 (Early Cypriot III–Middle Cypriot I-II)		PreBA 2 EC III-MC I-II
1900	EC IIIA		Prehistoric BA/Pre BA II	MC I			
1950	EC II			EC IIIB			
2000	Philia Phase / EC I			EC IIIA			
2050	EC I			EC IIIA			
2100	EC I			EC II			
2150	(EBA) ↑			EC II			
2200	Philia Phase			EC II		ECY 5	
2250	Philia Phase	EBA (Philia)		EC I	Pre BA 1 (Early Cypriot I-II)		
2300	Initial Stage of EC I			EC I			PreBA 1 EC I-II
2350	Initial Stage of EC I		Philia/Pre BA I	Philia		ECY 4	PreBA 1 Philia
2400	Chalcolithic II			Philia			
2450	Chalcolithic II			Philia			
2500	Chalcolithic II	Late Chalcolithic	Late Chalcolithic	Chalcolithic	Pre BA 1 (Philia 'Phase')	ECY 3	Late Chalcolithic
2550	Chalcolithic I			Chalcolithic			
2600	Chalcolithic I			Chalcolithic		ECY 2	
2650	Chalcolithic I			Chalcolithic	Pre BA 1 (Late Chalcolithic)		
2700	Chalcolithic I			Chalcolithic			
2750	Chalcolithic I	Hiatus		Chalcolithic	Pre BA (Middle Chalcolithic) ↓	ECY 1	
2800	Chalcolithic I			Chalcolithic			
2850	Chalcolithic I			Chalcolithic			
2900	Chalcolithic I			Chalcolithic			
2950				Chalcolithic			
3000	Neolithic II	Middle Chalcolithic		Chalcolithic			Middle Chalcolithic
3050	Neolithic II			Chalcolithic			
3100	Neolithic II			Chalcolithic			
3150	Neolithic II			Chalcolithic			
3200	Neolithic II			Chalcolithic			
3250	Neolithic II			Chalcolithic			
3300	Neolithic II			Chalcolithic			
3350	Neolithic II			Chalcolithic			
3400	Neolithic II			Chalcolithic			
3450	Neolithic II	Early Chalcolithic ↓		Chalcolithic			
3500	Neolithic II	Middle Chalcolithic		Chalcolithic			Early Chalcolithic ↓

with competing theoretical positions of researchers resulted, on the one hand, in the development of incongruent chronological systems and conflicting periodization terminologies (Figure 1.1). On the other hand, it led to scholars avoiding the issue of temporal duration of social phenomena occurring on the island, particularly during transitional periods.

Nonetheless, as the rightmost part of Figure 1.1 illustrates, recent work is addressing these concerns, and that work has been propelled by the proliferation of absolute dates, the utilization of Bayesian analysis for data calibration, and the modeling of absolute chronometric data by several recent chronology studies (Manning 2013a; 2013b; 2014b; Peltenburg *et al.* 2013b; earlier studies include Held 1989: 211–284; Manning and Swiny 1994; Clarke 2007: 9–29). The use of similar sets of absolute dates and the application of comparable statistical treatment methods within a common Bayesian analytical framework has led to less speculation on the order and relationships of cultural eras and more convergence of the period boundary values across the proposed chronological systems. In addition, the process of constructing chronologies is now more transparent and testable. Despite these positive steps, caution must be raised, as the resulting chronological models from recent contributions should not be considered as finite and perfected but rather as exploratory in nature. In this light, a critical review of the studies cited above, and several issues related to modeling is timely and appropriate, albeit not with the aim of annulling results but rather of detecting areas for improvement and new directions for research.

If we start with issues that concern the radiocarbon data selected for incorporation in temporal models (note that OxCal terms, like Phase, Sequence, and so forth are used from here on with capitalization; for terminological clarification, see Bronk Ramsey 2009a; 2014), we observe that the studies under review typically assign samples in model Phases according to their original designation in equivalent cultural eras by the excavator of the site they derive from (Clarke 2007; Manning 2013a: 487, Sub Appendix I; 2013b: 15, Figure 10; 2014b: 221). Only in rare cases of problematic samples do the authors thoroughly examine the contextual information of the samples (Manning 2013a: 488; 2013b: 5–6; 2014b: 208–209). Further issues regarding data incorporation include the enforcement of excessively strict and inflexible criteria in the selection process (Peltenburg *et al.* 2013b: 313, 319; Manning 2013a: 487–488), the use of data from a single site for dating entire cultural periods (Peltenburg *et al.* 2013b: 334, Figure 9.14, 336–337), the use of original determination values that were later corrected for laboratory errors (Manning 2013a: 497, 499, 528; 2014b: 238), and the conflation of distinct cultural eras into single model Phases (Manning 2013a: 509–511, Figure A9). These practices can potentially alter the boundaries of modeled Phases by misattributing samples to the wrong phase. They can also lead to data exclusion when Outlier Analysis is performed or can cause erroneous calculations of the model Agreement Indices. Therefore, attention should shift to a closer examination of the contextual information of the data used for the construction of chronological systems.

Turning to model design, the principal issue observed specifically for the timeframe of this study concerns the deployment of models employing a single set of assumptions, which leads to avoidance of model quality index cross-comparisons.

For example, the team working in the ARCANE project employed a Sequential model, which produced very low Agreement Indices (Peltenburg *et al.* 2013b: 319, 333, Figure 9.13) and then reverted to a mixed Sequential-Overlapping model (Peltenburg *et al.* 2013b: 319, 332–338, Figures 9.14 and 9.15, Table 1) that due to software limitations does not produce Agreement Indices for comparisons. In another set of studies, Manning (2013a: 497–501; 2014b: 210–211) employed a Sequential model that was iterated eight and four times respectively, each time manually removing data that were in poor agreement with the model's last iteration. Even though some data are indeed reconsidered between the studies, the overall approach, despite producing Agreement Indices, does not compare models employing different sets of assumptions but rather the same model with different datasets. In turn, this practice is not considered to produce directly comparable results (Thulman *et al.* 2013), especially since Outlier Analysis was not employed due to software and hardware limitations (Manning 2013a: 496; 2014b: 209–210). Generally, the above approaches did not produce models of different underlying logical assumptions in order to determine by comparison the most robust model to adopt, which means that their results are awaiting validation. Furthermore, these studies represent the first exploratory attempts at employing Bayesian analysis in the study of chronology on the island; and to a certain extent it is understood that a degree of vagueness is inherent within the datasets.

One last issue with the modeling procedure has to do with model structure. More specifically, on several occasions scholars have attempted to incorporate site stratigraphy, namely nested models, within overarching models in order to elucidate the chronology of a region (Manning 2013a: 493, 510, Figure A9, 512, Figure A10, 514, Figure A11; 2013b: 15, Figure 10; 2014b: 221, Figure 2). Although it would be ideal to incorporate the stratigraphy of sites within models, at present this is problematic for two reasons:

a. When the stratigraphy of a long-lived site spans two or more Phases/ Sequences in the overarching model, where the latter represent distinct cultural eras, then that stratigraphy essentially becomes truncated, and the relationship between site phases becomes dependent on the boundaries of the overarching model rather than the boundaries of the individual site phases. Moreover, at present there is no mathematical calculation method nor programming instruction that allows the preservation of the stratigraphy of a site that breaks across two or more cultural phases. It is therefore considered difficult to create models that incorporate the stratigraphy of long-lived sites, when trying to elucidate the chronology of multiple cultural periods on a regional scale. Beyond improvements of the technical implementation of Bayesian analysis in the study of chronology, one possible avenue moving forward is the construction of site-specific models incorporating stratigraphy and their cross-comparison with overarching models to exhibit the relevance of long-lived sites to proposed chronological schemata (see for example the discussion in Manning 2014b: 212–215).

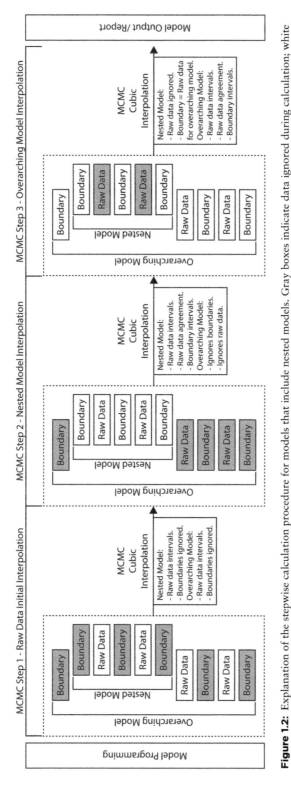

Figure 1.2: Explanation of the stepwise calculation procedure for models that include nested models. Gray boxes indicate data ignored during calculation; white boxes indicate data used during calculation.

b. When there is a nested model within an overarching one, the MCMC (Markov Chain Monte Carlo) algorithm employed in OxCal first processes the nested models and then the overarching model. Furthermore, due to the limitations of the Chronological Query Language, the samples included in the nested model are not reprocessed for the purposes of the overarching one, and only their Boundaries are considered (Bronk Ramsey 2001: 359), as the latter supersede the sample functions in the programming code (Figure 1.2).

This limitation can often be a complication, as Boundaries are not probability distributions based on actual raw data but calculated probability distributions based on the relationship of prior probabilities and sets of parameters initially assigned by the user (Bronk Ramsey 1995: 427; 2014). In order to observe the effect of nested model Boundaries to overarching model Boundaries, a small-scale experiment with simulated data was performed in OxCal 4.2.3, where an identical set of data was applied in two Sequential models, one of which used a nested model to represent the hypothetical stratigraphy of a site. Both models were iterated three times, each time lowering by one hundred years the dates of the samples included in the second overarching model Phase. The expected outcome for both models was that the lower Boundary of the first Phase of the overarching model would be lowered with each iteration but would remain approximately the same for both models. Contrary to expectations, the first Phase of the overarching model Boundary in the model using a nested model was consistently lower than the equivalent Boundary in the model using data without modifications (Figure 1.3).

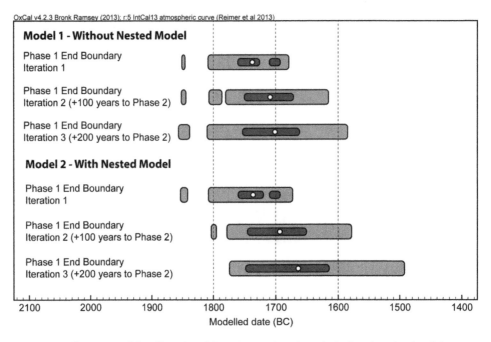

Figure 1.3: Illustration of the effect of model nesting on Phase boundaries based on simulated data.

This experiment suggests that when using nested models, there is a genuine risk of inserting nonexistent data into the overarching model, which can affect the calculation of its Boundaries and eventually alter the boundaries of the cultural eras that the latter model is attempting to trace. Therefore, nesting models within complex overarching models with a view of reconstructing the chronology of a region should be used with the utmost caution, and their results should be tested via simulations to measure and if possible to quantify the effects of model nesting.

To conclude this critical assessment of the latest contributions to prehistoric chronology, it is important to stress that despite their deficiencies, they indeed constitute an important departure from older practices and should therefore be considered as harbingers of a new era in chronology studies on Cyprus.

Data and Methodology

Prior to presenting the methodology of the study, I consider it useful to clarify that this paper is building on past work within the ARCANE project (Associated Regional Chronologies for the Ancient Near East; Peltenburg *et al.* 2013b), while essentially updating the data pool employed within my doctoral work. I therefore do not repeat here a lengthy discussion on the samples, their contexts and attribution to cultural periods, and the pre-modeling data quality analysis. Instead, this section focuses on the new data that have been found in relevant literature as well as on the methodology of the modeling phase.

Starting with the newly discovered radiocarbon data, a set of thirty-five samples from five sites is now integrated into the body of data used in the study, which raises the total number of samples for the Middle Chalcolithic to Middle Bronze Age timeframe to 149. More precisely, nine dates come from Politiko *Troullia* (Falconer and Fall 2013: 106, Table 1; Falconer *et al.* 2014: 7, Table 1), ten from Pyrgos *Mavrorachi* (Calderoni 2009: 190), seven from Erimi *Laonin tou Porakou* Cemetery (Sciré Calabrisotto *et al.* 2013: 476, Table 1), six from Lophou *Kolaouzou* (Sciré Calabrisotto *et al.* 2013: 477, Table 2), and three from Episkopi *Phaneromeni* (Fishman *et al.* 1977: 189; see map in Figure 1.4). It is useful to bear in mind that the above information is found mostly in preliminary publications, which do not offer a thorough presentation of site stratigraphy and therefore cannot be assessed in depth. Nevertheless, the new data have been examined in terms of content, sample material, and context, when information is available.

Looking at the new data *in toto*, we can observe at first that they temporally range from the Philia Culture Phase to the end of the Middle Bronze Age. It is particularly significant that there is at least one new Philia Culture Phase determination from the site of Pyrgos (Calderoni 2009: 190, no. 1538, 193), while the rest of the data mostly regard the ending of the Early Bronze Age and provide further data for the elucidation of the Middle Bronze Age on Cyprus. Contextually, the data from Politiko, Pyrgos, and Episkopi are associated with relatively mixed domestic and industrial contexts that are prone to disturbances due to formation processes, while the remainder of the data from Lophou and Erimi come from closed or disturbed mortuary contexts, namely sealed or looted tombs. In terms of dating techniques, the Politiko, Erimi, and Lophou samples are AMS-dated (Accelerator Mass Spectrometer; Sciré

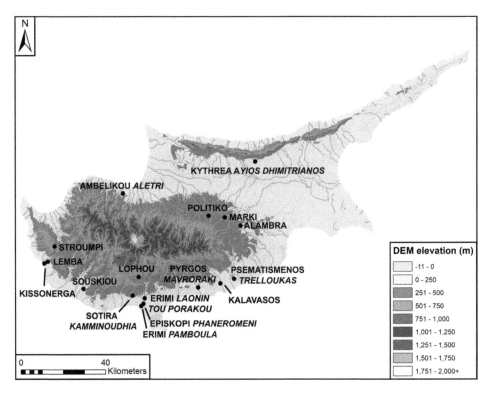

Figure 1.4: Map of the sites mentioned in text. Created by C. Kearns, basemap provided by the Geological Survey Department of Cyprus.

Calabrisotto *et al.* 2013: 474; Falconer *et al.* 2014: 4), while the samples from Pyrgos and Episkopi have been dated using LSC (Liquid Scintillation Counting; Fishman *et al.* 1977: 188; Calderoni 2009: 189). In terms of material, the samples can be divided into three groups, viz. long-lived charcoal samples, mid-lived human bone collagen samples, and short-lived seed samples. Using the above classification there are three charcoal and six seed samples from Politiko (Falconer *et al.* 2014: 7, Table 1), seven and six bone collagen samples from Erimi and Lophou, respectively (Sciré Calabrisotto *et al.* 2013: 476, Table 1, 477, Table 2) three charcoal samples from Episkopi (Fishman *et al.* 1977: 189), and finally one short-lived organic matter and nine charcoal/ash/burnt earth samples from Pyrgos (Calderoni 2009: 189–190).

Moving to a more detailed examination of the data, it is observed that the Politiko samples, even though they derive from two spatially distant locales (East and West) of the same Early to Middle Bronze Age settlement site, cluster well together and cover a relatively short span of time between ca. 2140–1875 BCE at the one-sigma confidence interval with sub-range likelihood probabilities above 10 percent. Furthermore, the statement that Politiko East Phase E1 and Politiko West Phase W2 and W1 are roughly contemporaneous (Falconer *et al.* 2014: 4) should be reconsidered. On the one hand, differences in the ceramic assemblages have already been noted

(Falconer *et al.* 2014: 4), while on the other hand, the radiocarbon data accentuate the latter differences by splitting into two distinct groups, when modeled in OxCal. One group is formed by the Politiko West Phases W1 to W3 and represents the Early Bronze Age–Middle Bronze Age I component of the site and another is formed by the Politiko East Phase E1 and embodies the Middle Bronze Age II–III. Beyond the subtle differences upon modeling, another factor that should be considered is the fact that all Politiko West samples are short-lived seeds, while all the Politiko East samples are carbonized pine wood; that is, they potentially carry an in-built age element. Based on this observation, it is highly probable that the Politiko East samples are elevating the calendric ranges of the associated E1 site phase, which in effect does not correspond to the archaeological reality. As a corollary to this, it is maintained that the E1 phase radiocarbon dates provide a good TPQ (*terminus post quem*) for the Middle Bronze Age on the site, partially contradict the argument for its contemporaneity with W1 to W2, and possibly provide evidence for settlement drift at the Early to Middle Bronze Age transition.

The next set of wood charcoal dates that are possibly affected by in-built age derive from Episkopi. These dates span between ca. 2200–1750 BCE, Early Bronze I to Middle Bronze III, which is considered a rather long and problematic span of time for a settlement site that is thought to be of Middle Bronze III and Late Bronze IA periods based on ceramic typology (Weinberg 1956; Swiny 1989: 14). In addition to this disparity, all the samples have been located inside deteriorating or collapsed domestic units (Fishman *et al.* 1977: 189), which inevitably signifies disturbance of the stratigraphy. Observing the depth of discovery and radiocarbon age of the samples in more detail, an inverse relationship is evident, where the samples from the deeper layers provide younger radiocarbon ages and vice versa. This stratigraphic inversion has been noticed in the past at the site of Kissonerga *Mosphilia* (Peltenburg 1998: 37, Figure 3.5; Peltenburg *et al.* 2013b: 324) and could possibly indicate collapse of a roof constructed from timbers predating the beginning of the domestic unit's lifetime. Unfortunately, the stratigraphy for Episkopi has not yet appeared in the literature (Peltenburg 1988: 261), so these hypotheses cannot be tested. Nonetheless, based on the material, limited contextual information, and calibrated ranges of the dates, samples P-2387 and P-2388 are considered to form a rather uncertain TPQ for the beginning of the Middle Bronze Age II. The early P-2386 date is designated as a probable outlier and can be conceived as either wood dating to the initial construction phase of the domestic unit before the beginning of Middle Bronze Age I or old wood reused for the construction or repair of the roof whose time of felling/collection dates to the Early Bronze Age.

The next pair of sites under examination are Erimi and Lophou, which have produced the first sets of radiocarbon samples from bone collagen for the specific timeframe of the present study. Data from Erimi derive from undisturbed tombs 228, 230, and 248 (Bombardieri 2009: 286–287; Sciré Calabrisotto *et al.* 2013: 476), while the data from Lophou derive from tombs 8, 15, 20, and 21, which are probably looted, as most tombs at this cemetery are reportedly "interfered with by clandestine digging or by recent bulldozing operations" (Sciré Calabrisotto *et al.* 2013: 477). In terms of relative dating, the Erimi cemetery is generally dated to the

Middle Bronze Age III to Late Bronze Age I (Bombardieri 2009: 287–288), with some tombs dating even earlier to Early Bronze Age III–Middle Bronze Age I–II (Sciré Calabrisotto *et al.* 2013: 476). The Lophou cemetery is dated between Early Bronze Age I and Middle Bronze Age III (Sciré Calabrisotto *et al.* 2013: 477). As the finds from each tomb are not yet published, the excavator's attribution of tombs to cultural periods is accepted, and the relevant radiocarbon data are allocated in the models based on these designations. Beyond the inherent difficulties regarding the use of bone collagen for radiocarbon dating (Hedges and van Klinken 1992; Fiedel *et al.* 2013; Zazzo *et al.* 2013), samples T228_3 and LT8_2 are *ab initio* rejected as extreme outliers, since they produced radiocarbon ages 1000–1500 years lower than the bottom margin of the timeframe explored in this study, while LT 8_2 is designated as a probable outlier for the same reason.

The last site providing radiocarbon data for this study is the Early to Middle Bronze Age site of Pyrgos. Ten dates spanning from the Philia Culture Phase to the end of Middle Bronze Age I upon calibration have been reported with limited contextual information (Calderoni 2009: 190) and loosely assigned to cultural phases by the excavator (Belgiorno *et al.* 2010). The validity of their attribution to cultural periods, however, is difficult to assess due to the scarcity of information on the stratigraphy and pottery typology of the site. Despite the above limitations, at least one sample described as charcoal, found in the central perforation of a Philia Culture Phase spindle whorl (Calderoni 2009: 193, sample 1538), can with some reservation be assigned to the Philia Culture Phase. Hesitation stems from the fact that the date carries a wide uncertainty value, which elongates its calibrated calendrical range from ca. 2855–2340 BCE and indicates laboratory issues with sample size or contaminants. Its importance, however, cannot be ignored, as it is the first site aside from Marki *Alonia* with absolute dating data contextually associated and temporally correlating well with the Philia Culture Phase, as the single date (GU-2167) from Kissonerga *Mosphilia* previously attributed to the Philia Culture Phase (Peltenburg 1998: 14, 20) has been reassigned to the Late Chalcolithic after assessment of the stratigraphy and associated material culture of the sample's context (Peltenburg *et al.* 2013b: 324). In addition to the above, the calibrated ranges for samples 1501, 1502, and 1504 may potentially represent the transition between Early Bronze Age III/Middle Bronze Age I to Middle Bronze Age II–III, as their calibrated ranges fall well within the boundaries of this transition, and at least sample 1502 lies contextually only 10 centimeters below the soil surface of the site (Calderoni 2009: 192), thus dating the uppermost (later) phases of the site. Finally, sample 1539 has been discarded as an extreme outlier, since it produced a radiocarbon age about a millennium earlier than any other sample and is also accompanied by a very wide two-hundred-year band of statistical uncertainty. Although this may indicate habitation on the site at a much earlier time, viz. the Early or Middle Chalcolithic, there is at present no material evidence to support this hypothesis.

Having presented the body of new data incorporated into the study, I now shift attention to the methodology employed in this study. The principal aim is not to trace the boundaries of individual site phases but to elucidate the boundaries of the overarching cultural periods by approximation and to the degree possible based on the available data. This decision implicitly involves a series of actions on the part of the researcher, which include the following and are addressed in the remainder of this section:

a. Conceptual division of the timeframe into logical management units, which correspond to cultural periods in the archaeological literature, mapping of the former units onto the latter periods, and attribution of the data to the relevant units.
b. Programming and execution of multiple models, which utilize identical initial datasets but employ different assumptions and parameters.
c. Parallel to the above, planning for a method to statistically assess data that present low agreement with the chronological models.

Beginning with the conceptual division of the timeframe into management units, I decided to employ a descriptive cultural-historical-inspired schema, although without adhering to the limitations of the Three Age System, such as the constraint of periods within strict, non-overlapping boundaries and their subdivision to evolutionary triplets. In other words, the terms employed are not meant to connote specific cultural periods or subdivisions of periods but rather serve as a bridge between the virtual grouping function of popular terminology of the past and their actual post-terminological function as conceptual vessels for inputting data. Table 1.1 below lists the names of the cultural phases utilized during modeling and explains their

Table 1.1: Concordance of terminology between the current study and prominent chronological systems in the archaeological literature of Cyprus

Current study	Steel 2004: 13, Table 1.1	Keswani 2004: 186, Table 1.1	Peltenburg *et al.* 2013b: 2, Table 1.1	Knapp 2013: 27, Table 2
Middle Chalcolithic	Equivalent to Middle Chalcolithic	Partly equivalent with Chalcolithic	Equivalent to ECY 1	Equivalent to Middle Chalcolithic
Late Chalcolithic	Equivalent to Late Chalcolithic	Partly equivalent with Chalcolithic	Equivalent to ECY 2	Equivalent to Late Chalcolithic
Philia Culture Phase	Equivalent to Philia/Pre-BA I	Equivalent to Philia	Equivalent to ECY 3	Equivalent to Pre-BA 1/Philia
Early Bronze Age I–III/Middle Bronze Age I (=EBA I–III/MBA I)	Partly equivalent to Pre-BA II	Equivalent to EC I, EC II, EC IIIA, EC IIIB, MC I	Equivalent to ECY 4, ECY 5	Equivalent to Pre-BA 1/EC I–II and partly equivalent to Pre-BA 2/EC III–MC I–II
Middle Bronze Age II–III (=MBA II–III)	Partly equivalent to Pre-BA II	Equivalent to MC II, MC III	N/A	Partly equivalent to Pre-BA 2/EC III–MC I–II and partly equivalent to Pro BA 1/MC III–LC I

relation as cultural concepts to terms already employed in other chronological systems, even if the temporal boundaries of the periods are not in agreement (see e.g., Frankel in this volume).

Concurrent with the construction of the conceptual template of the study, the totality of the data available was assigned into the abovementioned cultural periods. Table 1.2 below lists 149 samples representing the sum of available samples, relevant

Table 1.2: Data incorporated in the models of the present study divided by model Phases representing cultural eras. Data listed include site and site phase abbreviations, sample laboratory code, radiocarbon date in ^{14}C years BP and uncertainty. Samples excluded as extreme outliers, site abbreviations, and citations to the sources of information for all data are listed in the lower part of the table.

Middle Chalcolithic - 26 Samples	
KA 1 - BM-1833R, 5000, 170	KVP - P-2980, 4330, 80
KA 1 - BM-1836R, 4700, 310	KM 3B - BM-2526, 4690, 70
KMyl 3 - OxA-7463, 4710, 50	KM 3B - BM-2528, 4600, 60
KMyl 3 - OxA-7462, 4650, 50	KM 3B - OxA-2963, 4520, 80
KM 3A - AA-10497, 4605, 55	KM 3B - BM-2568, 4490, 50
LL 1 - BM-1543, 5000, 260	KM 3B - OxA-2962, 4370, 70
EP 2 - St-202, 4630, 80	KM 3B - OxA-2961, 4310, 75
EP 2 - St-203, 4540, 80	KM 3B - OxA-2162, 4300, 80
EP 2 - St-338, 4540, 80	KM 3B - OxA-2161, 4290, 80
KAD - Lu-1695, 4410, 60	KM 3B - GU-2968, 4240, 100
SA - OxA-20926, 4127, 31	KM 3B - GU-2168, 4210, 105
SL 1 - SUERC-18273, 4525, 35	KM 3B - GU-2426, 3880, 100
SL 1 - SUERC-18272, 4465, 35	LL 2 - BM-2278R, 4090, 120

Late Chalcolithic - 33 Samples	
PK - OZK-147, 4260, 60	SL 2 - SUERC-15048, 4195, 35
PK - OZK-140, 4220, 60	SL 2 - SUERC-15049, 4165, 35
PK - OZK-137, 4210, 60	SL 2 - SUERC-15044, 4130, 35
PK - OZK-142, 4210, 60	KM 4 - AA-10496, 4285, 60
PK - OZK-145, 4200, 60	KM 4 - GU-2537, 4020, 110
PK - OZK-139, 4190, 70	KM 4 - GU-2536, 4170, 80
PK - OZK-141, 4180, 70	KM 4 - GU-2155, 4250, 170
PK - OZK-144, 4180, 70	KM 4 - GU-2158, 4220, 75
PK - OZK-148, 4170, 60	KM 4 - OxA-2960, 4220, 70
PK - Wk-18983, 4151, 38	KM 4 - BM-2279R, 4180, 130
PK - OZK-138, 4090, 60	KM 4 - BM-2529, 4160, 50
PK - OZK-143, 4090, 60	KM 4 - BM-2527, 4130, 50
LL 3 - BM-1542, 3890, 50	KM 4 - GU-2535, 4070, 130
LL 3 - BM-1541A, 3970, 45	KM 4 - BM-2530, 3960, 80
LL 3 - BM-1541, 4000, 45	KM 4 - GU-2157, 3900, 50
LL 3 - BM-1354, 4050, 50	KM 4 - GU-2167, 3990, 50
LL 3 - BM-1353, 4090, 90	

Philia Culture Phase - 7 Samples	
MA A-B - Beta-138630, 3780, 30	MA A-B - OZB-161, 3886, 42
MA A-B - Beta-138629, 3780, 30	MA A-B - OZB-163, 3834, 42
MA A-B - Beta-100553, 3810, 50	PM - No. 1538, 4005, 130
MA A-B - OZB-162, 3892, 39	

Early Bronze Age I–III - Middle Bronze Age I - 45 Samples

SK 1-2 - OxA-3308, 3890, 90	PM - No. 1489, 3705, 55
SK 1-2 - OxA-3311, 3890, 100	PM - No. 1490, 3640, 55
SK 1-2 - OxA-3545, 3860, 75	PM - No. 1500, 3680, 50
SK 1-2 - OxA-3547, 3860, 80	PM - No. 1501, 3620, 50
SK 1-2 - OxA-3544, 3840, 75	PM - No. 1502, 3570, 50
SK 1-2 - OxA-3548, 3800, 75	PM - No. 1503, 3765, 55
SK 1-2 - OxA-3309, 3780, 90	PM - No. 1504, 3600, 70
SK 1-2 - OxA-3310, 3780, 90	PM - No. 1537, 3720, 55
SK 1-2 - OxA-3546, 3760, 75	MA E-F - OZA-334, 3550, 50
SK 1-2 - OxA-3312, 3690, 100	MA E-F - OZA-340, 3740, 40
MA C-D - OZA-338, 3770, 50	MA E-F - OZB-160, 3675, 118
MA C-D - Wk-166434, 3597, 39	MA E-F - OZA-279U, 3645, 95
MA C-D - OZA-344, 3770, 50	PT W - AA-94183, 3665, 38
MA C-D - OZA-339, 3720, 50	PT W - AA-101943, 3622, 44
MA C-D - OZA-337, 3670, 50	PT W - AA-94184, 3630, 38
MA C-D - OZA-336, 3650, 50	PT W - AA-101942, 3632, 45
MA C-D - OZA-342, 3700, 40	PT W - AA-94185, 3688, 38
ELP - Ch_us391, 3750, 30	PT W - AA-101941, 3650, 44
ELP - Ch_us392, 3795, 35	AA - Lu-1694, 3660, 55
LK - LT15_1, 3685, 40	AA - Lu-1726, 3630, 55
LK - LT15_2, 3685, 40	ELPC - T248_1, 3620, 40
LK - LT20_2, 3710, 45	ELPC - T248_2, 3570, 55
PTr - OxA-14952, 3709, 35	

Middle Bronze Age II–III - 17 Samples

AM - Beta-82994, 3610, 60	EPh - P-2387, 3620, 60
AM - ETH-210, 3500, 120	EPh - P-2388, 3520, 70
AM - ETH-206, 3440, 140	LK - LT21, 3445, 45
PT E - AA-101939, 3562, 44	LK - LT8_2, 3015, 75
PT E - AA-94182, 3600, 37	ELPC - T228_1, 3145, 30
PT E - AA-101940, 3661, 44	ELPC - T230_1_fa, 3500, 65
MA I-H - Beta-50757, 3460, 90	ELPC - T230_1_o, 3450, 55
MA I-H - Beta-50756, 3480, 80	ELPC - T230_2, 3240, 40
EPh - P-2386, 3720, 70	

Extreme outliers - 21 Samples

KM - GU-2967, 5540, 110	MA - OZA-345, 3730, 50
KM - GU-2966, 5620, 60	MA - OZB-159, 3764, 50
LL - BM-2280R, 5890, 120	MA - OZA-281U, 1038, 44
LL - HAR-6173, 4280, 100	MA - OZA-341, 2830, 40
SK - ETH-6659, 3445, 70	MA - OZA-343, 2750, 40
SK - ETH-6660, 2715, 65	ELP - Ch_us394, 1000, 35
SK - ETH-6661, 3100, 80	AM - Beta-82995, 3970, 90
SK - ETH-6662, 3225, 75	PM - No. 1539, 5170, 200
SK - ETH-6663, 3460, 60	ELPC - T228_3, 2140, 50
MA - OZA-280U, 4394, 58	LK - LT8_1, 2580, 60
MA - OZA-335, 330, 35	

Site abbreviations and references

KA: Kalavasos-*Ayious*	Burleigh *et al.* 1982b: 274; Bowman *et al.* 1990: 72, Table 2A; Todd 2004a: 218–219, Table 44
KMyl: Kissonerga-*Mylouthkia*	Peltenburg 2003: 259, Table 24.2

(*Continued*)

Table 1.2:—*cont.*

Site abbreviations and references	
LL: Lemba-*Lakkous*	Burleigh 1981: 21; Burleigh *et al.* 1982a: 238; Peltenburg 1982: 112, Table 1; Peltenburg 1985: 16, Table 2; Ambers *et al.* 1987: 68; Bowman *et al.* 1990: 72; Peltenburg 1991a: 10.
EP: Erimi-*Pamboula*	Östlund 1957: 496; Östlund 1959: 43; Dikaios 1962: 198
KAD: Kythrea-*Ayios Dhimitrianos*	Håkansson 1981: 402
SA: Stroumpi-*Ayios Andronikos*	Ammerman *et al.* 2009: 27
SL: Souskiou-*Laona*	Peltenburg *et al.* 2013b: 317, Table 9.1
KVP: Kalavasos-Village/Panagia Church	Hurst and Lawn 1984: 214; Todd 1986: 28, 183; Todd 2004b: 108
KM: Kissonerga-*Mosphilia*	Ambers *et al.* 1987: 68; Bowman *et al.* 1990: 72; Ambers *et al.* 1991: 60; Peltenburg 1991a: 10; Hedges *et al.* 1992: 351; Peltenburg 1998: 12–14, Table 2.3
PK: Politiko-*Kokkinorotsos*	Webb *et al.* 2009: 192, Table 1
MA: Marki-*Alonia*	Frankel and Webb 1996: 270, Table 4.5; Frankel and Webb 2006a: 37, Table 3.3
PM: Pyrgos-*Mavrorachi*	Calderoni 2009: 190
SK: Sotira-*Kaminoudhia*	Swiny 1986: 41; Hedges *et al.* 1993: 321; Manning and Swiny 1994: 157, Table 1, 158, Table 2
PTr: Psematismenos-*Trelloukkas*	Manning and Sewell 2006: 67-68
ELP: Erimi-*Laonin tou Porakou*	Sciré Calabrisotto *et al.* 2012: 479, Table 1
PT: Politiko-*Troullia*	Falconer *et al.* 2014: 7, Table 1
LK: Lophou-*Kolaouzou*	Sciré Calabrisotto *et al.* 2013: 477, Table 2
AA: Ambelikou-*Aletri*	Håkansson 1981: 402
ELPC: Erimi-*Laonin tou Porakou* Cemetery	Sciré Calabrisotto *et al.* 2013: 476, Table 1
AM: Alambra-*Mouttes*	Coleman 1992a: 286; Coleman 1992b: 225; Coleman *et al.* 1996: 339, Table 29
EPh: Episkopi-*Phaneromeni*	Fishman *et al.* 1977: 189

* Alphanumeric characters following the site abbreviation represent site phases or other subdivisions of the site data pool into discrete temporal entities.

and known to the author, of which 128 are further allocated to cultural periods for modeling, while 21 (14.1%) are rejected as extreme outliers based on the outlier determination process advanced in the study and explained later in this section. It is noted that the main reason for designation of extreme outliers are the errors associated with laboratory procedures.

Following data allocation is the modeling stage, which demands the selection of a software package for the analysis and then construction of chronological models based on sets of prior assumptions incorporated to the latter as core structure and added parameters. OxCal 4.2.3 was the software package selected for its analytical abilities in computing complex Bayesian probabilistic models

(Bronk Ramsey 2009a; 2014), the utilization of the most recent calibration curve (IntCal13; Reimer *et al*. 2013), and the depth of model parameterization it allows. In terms of core structure and common parameterization, I decided to run two models based on different underlying logical assumptions, to integrate the 128 samples selected as suitable for modeling into the overarching model Phases by assuming that they are free-floating data without constraints or grouping functions and to avoid nesting models that represent site stratigraphy for the reasons explained in the previous section. Also, Outlier Analysis was performed for eliminating suspect data according to the outlier determination process proposed later in this section, while the basic models were iterated at least once for removal of the abovementioned outlying data. Finally, an After function and a 0.25 outlier probability value was assigned to the entire dataset of Sotira *Kaminoudhia* to counteract the effects of in-built age and wide uncertainty affecting these samples (see Peltenburg *et al*. 2013b: 328). Regarding the latter choice, it is noted that, while it is *a posteriori* recognized that the Charcoal Plus outlier model would potentially be a more suitable instrument for examining these dates (Dee and Bronk Ramsey 2014), at the time the research for this paper was being conducted, it had not yet become available. Based on the above parameters and limitations the following models were programmed and executed:

Model 1: Contiguous Uniform Phases model bounded by simple Boundaries (Bronk Ramsey 2009a: 349, Figure 6), viz. it expects that there are probably short transitional periods between the cultural phases, but no gaps or significant overlaps. It also employs a General Outlier Analysis model for 28 samples (Bronk Ramsey 2009b: 1028).

Model 1+: Identical to the above, but with 18 samples removed as the previous Outlier Analysis indicated they are likely Outliers. The Outlier command is still attached to 5 samples to allow their inclusion by model averaging (Bronk Ramsey 2009b: 1042, Figure 9c).

Model 2: Overlapping Uniform Phases model bounded by simple Boundaries (Bronk Ramsey 2009a: 349, Figure 6), viz. it expects that there are probably significant overlaps between cultural phases, but no gaps. It also employs a General Outlier Analysis model for 28 samples (Bronk Ramsey 2009b: 1028).

Model 2+: Identical to the above, but with 18 samples removed as the previous. Outlier Analysis indicated they are definite Outliers. The Outlier command is still attached to 6 samples to allow their inclusion by model averaging (Bronk Ramsey 2009b: 1042, Figure 9c).

Execution of the above models was successful, as all models ran at least twice and converged to their results after 6–8 million MCMC iterations, without reporting any issues or presenting irregular results.

At this point, one may wonder why Outlier Analysis was not performed on all data, which is recommended for models for which there are samples that may or may not relate to the timing of the phase being dated (Bronk Ramsey 2009b: 1024).

The answer to the above is that Outlier Analysis may indeed be a very useful tool for assessing whether the samples fit the models but is also a highly demanding tool in terms of computational power (see the identical situation in Manning 2013a: 496). Given that OxCal currently is a 32-bit software performing calculations on a single core, it becomes impossible for a large and complex model to finish running. An experimental version of Model 1 with Outlier Analysis enabled for all samples was attempted but was stopped after nearly six days and 60 million MCMC iterations, as the model was converging and progressing very slowly. In that order, an outlier determination method needed to be developed, with the aim of bridging the gap between arbitrary manual rejection and statistical rejection via Outlier Analysis in OxCal. Similar subjective methods for data evaluation have already been proposed by Manning (2013a: 490, Figure A2, 497–500; 2014b: 209–210) but are considered unsuitable for the purposes of this study for two reasons:

a. Setting arbitrary and extensive limits to discover extreme outliers (Manning 2013a: 490, Figure A2) does not consider the temporal length of cultural periods; in other words it does not scale appropriately. A 1000-calendar-year-wide band around a moving average of calibrated data may be a suitable instrument for detecting extreme outliers for long periods, such as the Neolithic or the Middle Chalcolithic, but fails to detect such outliers for shorter periods, such as the Philia Culture Phase, the Early Bronze Age, and even the Late Chalcolithic.

b. Excluding dates based solely on their Agreement Index to the model (Manning 2013a: 497–500; 2014b: 209–210) is not advised, as the index is directly influenced by the core structure and underlying assumptions of the model and not the factual relationship between the samples grouped within a Phase. Effectively, if the model structure changes or if constraints and functions are used, the Agreement Index also shifts. Furthermore, this tends to affect mostly data lying at the edge of phases, which can potentially result in the rejection of data that are useful for detecting the duration of transitions or overlaps between cultural periods.

In order to more effectively contend with the above issues, I employed a novel approach to outlying data. The basic assumption of the method is that relative dating chronological periods may be wrong but are not importantly wrong, so that the boundaries for the cultural periods need refinement and not total revision. Correspondingly, the boundaries proposed by the most prominent chronological systems were merged to produce the minimum and maximum duration of each period (Peltenburg 1998: 258, Table 14.8; Steel 2004: 13, Table 1.1; Knapp 2008: 71, Table 1; 2013: 27, Table 2; Manning 2013a: 521, Table A2; Peltenburg et al. 2013a: 2, Table 1.1). Following this, a variable distance or extension zone was established by halving the maximum duration of each archaeological period, which was then attached at both ends of the cultural period under examination. The only exception is the Middle Bronze Age II–III Phase, which was given an extension period at its lower boundary equal to the maximum duration of the concomitant cultural period due to the less well-defined character of the Middle Bronze Age to Late Bronze Age transition. In the next step, the calibrated date ranges were plotted against these cultural period boundaries with their extension zones to assess the data for fitness. The evaluation system set forth generated the following ranges:

- Ranges with 50 percent or more of their cumulative probabilities lying within the already established period durations were considered safe and were not subjected to Outlier Analysis during modeling.
- Ranges with 50 percent or more of their cumulative probabilities lying within the 50 percent of the extension zone close to a cultural period's upper or lower boundary were considered as probable outliers and assigned a 0.25 probability value in the Outlier Analysis during modeling. If the Outlier Analysis exhibited a high agreement to the prior probability assigned, the date was discarded prior to model re-run.
- Ranges with 50 percent or more of their cumulative probabilities lying above the 50 percent of the extension zone close to a cultural period's upper or lower boundary but within the extension zone boundaries were considered as highly probable outliers and assigned a 0.5 probability value in the Outlier Analysis during modeling. If the Outlier Analysis exhibited a high agreement to the prior probability assigned, the date was discarded prior to model re-run.
- Ranges with 50 percent or more of their cumulative probabilities lying beyond the extension zones of the cultural periods were considered as extreme outliers and were manually removed prior to any modeling (Bronk Ramsey 1995: 425; 2009b: 1024–1025).

The practical application of the proposed outlier detection process resulted to the designation of three samples as extreme outliers and twenty-eight samples as probable or highly probable outliers (Figure 1.5).

One final query that needs to be addressed before presenting the results of models regards the conscious choice of not using the prevalent type of Sequential Uniform Phases model (see applications by Manning 2013a; 2013b; 2014b; Peltenburg *et al.* 2013b: 319, 333, Figure 9.13) as a third alternative model type for comparative purposes. To tackle this issue, it is necessary to state that a wide and in-depth experiment employing twenty-eight models of various structure (Contiguous, Overlapping, Sequential; Bronk Ramsey 2014) and boundary (Simple and Trapezoidal) types has already been performed within my doctoral thesis; as the results of that study are not the topic of the present paper, they are not repeated here. However, based on the experience gained and the similarity of the present approach to the above, it is safe to exclude Sequential Uniform Phases models, as the latter are unsuitable for modeling the relative cultural periods of this timeframe. The principal issue with these types of models is that they presuppose the existence of gaps between the periods being modeled, while the cultural periods in question and the archaeological reality of Cyprus portray either direct succession or in certain cases overlap of the cultural periods. This reality is also reflected in the post-analysis of the doctoral thesis, where I visually demonstrated that Sequential models underperform

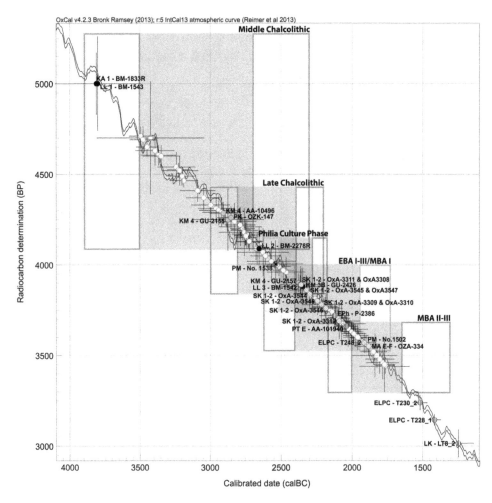

Figure 1.5: Cross-plotting of calibrated date ranges and cultural period ranges with respective upper and lower extension zones. Outlying date ranges are named and coded as follows: black dots = Middle Chalcolithic; light grey dots = Late Chalcolithic; dark gray and black checkered dots = Philia Culture Phase; dotted white dots = EBA I–III/MBA I; striped white dots = MBA II–III. Extreme outliers omitted, as they extend beyond the x-axis margins.

in relation to Contiguous and Overlapping models when the exact same initial data set is employed, while they only become equally or more successful when data can be rejected based on low Agreement Indices. However, in the latter case the Sequential models tend to function in a procrustean manner by rejecting nearly four times more data than Contiguous and Overlapping models in order to produce equal or slightly better Model and Overall Agreement Indices. Ultimately, these tests prove that Sequential models are more inflexible and less robust and thus less suitable for answering the questions posed in this study. Consequent to this, Sequential models have not been employed.

Results and Discussion

As noted above, the execution of the initial and re-run models was successful and did not produce errors or aberrant results in the repeat runs of each model. Additionally, the initial run of models provided the necessary statistical evidence for the rejection of eighteen dates as certain outliers, which resulted in greater clarity regarding the boundaries of cultural periods in the re-run models. Table 1.3 summarizes the results for the ranges and boundaries of each cultural period by model at one-sigma distance, while Figure 1.6 illustrates the four models and the non-modeled calibrated ranges (Model 0) for comparative purposes.

Before discussing the results of the models, it becomes critical to assess model fitness and robustness in terms of Model and Overall Agreement Indices and in conjunction with the Rejection Rate after the application of Outlier Analysis. The initial models, viz. Models 1 and 2, have produced expectedly low and borderline unacceptable values (Bronk Ramsey 1995: 428; 2009a: 357) in the range of 55.4–73.2 for A_{model} and 52.2–57.3 for $A_{overall}$. Contrary to the above, the re-run models, viz.

Table 1.3: Maximum/starting and minimum/ending one-sigma values of the Upper Boundary, Ranges and Lower Boundary for each cultural period in the four Models processed in the study. Values in plain font indicate good concentration of cumulative probabilities from more than two samples, while values in **bold** indicate poor concentration of cumulative probabilities (<10%) from three or fewer samples.

Cultural period	Modeled elements	Model 1		Model 1+		Model 2		Model 2+	
		Start	End	Start	End	Start	End	Start	End
Middle Chalcolithic	Upper Boundary	3550	3435	3545	3435	3570	3445	3555	3440
	Ranges	3525	2800	3500	2820	3555	2715	3500	2775
	Lower Boundary	2845	2790	2850	2795	2850	2705	2860	2750
Late Chalcolithic	Upper Boundary	2845	2790	2850	2795	2920	2795	2915	2805
	Ranges	2810	2440	2810	2510	**2905/**2815	2505/**2450**	**2890/**2820	2510
	Lower Boundary	2545	2450	2555	2480	2560	2465	2560	2480
Philia Culture Phase	Upper Boundary	2545	2450	2555	2480	2460	2280	2450	2275
	Ranges	2485	2190	2505	2190/**2165**	2370	2200	2365	2200
	Lower Boundary	2210	2150	2205	2135	2270	2150	2270	2160
EBA I–III/MBA I	Upper Boundary	2210	2150	2205	2135	2235	2145	2195	2090
	Ranges	2180	1955	2175	1955	**2210/**2185	1940	2165	1970
	Lower Boundary	2005	1950	1995	1940	2005	1930	2025	1950
MBA II–III	Upper Boundary	2005	1950	1995	1940	2060	1935	2000	1900
	Ranges	1990	1800	1965	1800	2025	1770/**1755**	1970	1800
	Lower Boundary	1865	1740	1860	1740	1865	1690	1870	1740

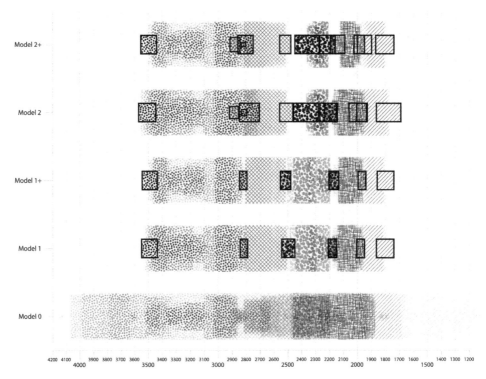

Figure 1.6: Cross-plotting of the four Contiguous and Overlapping models (Models 1, 1+, 2, 2+) against the non-modeled ranges (Model 0). Only one-sigma ranges are plotted. Cultural periods pattern codes are as follows: small dots = Middle Chalcolithic (USGS20 Scrubs pattern); diamond hatches = Late Chalcolithic; mezzotint dots = Philia Culture Phase; burlap = EBA I–III/MBA I; diagonal lines = MBA II–III. Calibrated sub-ranges for each sample, either modeled or non-modeled, is represented as a rectangle. The opacity of all sub-ranges is set to 15 percent to allow the visual representation of sub-range probabilities concentration, while the y-axis width of each rectangle represents the cumulative posterior probability of each modeled sub-range or the cumulative likelihood for each non-modeled sub-range. The maximum y-axis width equals a probability of 68.2 percent (one-sigma distance) and all rectangle widths scale according to the afore. OxCal-calculated Boundaries are marked by black stroked rectangles filled with patterns according to the cultural period they represent. Boundary widths follow the same guidelines as the widths for the above sub-ranges, although the maximum width has been halved in the illustration for clarity purposes.

Models 1+ and 2+, have produced very good Agreement Index values, while keeping the Rejection Rate constant at 14 percent of the initial data set. More specifically, the A_{model} is 126.4 for Model 1+ and 114.5 for Model 2+, while $A_{overall}$ is 118.7 for Model 1+ and 96.6 for Model 2+ (Figure 1.7).

Based on the above results it appears that Model 1+ fits the data for the Middle Chalcolithic to Middle Bronze Age better than any of the other models, so the final proposition for cultural period boundaries should weigh in more the results of this model. Nevertheless, as the archaeological reality illustrates (Model 0), there appears to be some overlap in the transitions between the Middle to Late Chalcolithic, and the EBA I–III/MBA I and MBA II–III, where the Overlapping Models 2 and 2+ may be a better guide for elucidating the boundaries of these periods.

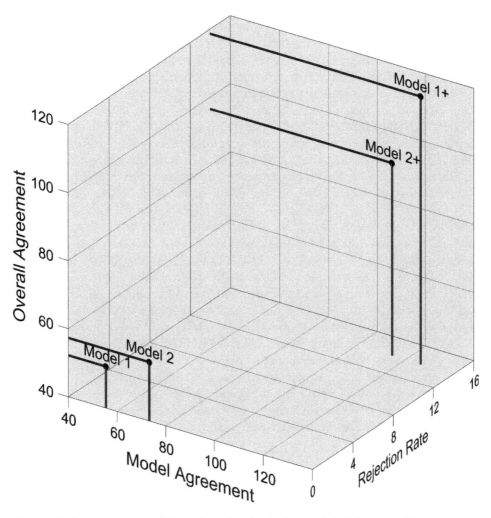

Figure 1.7: Cross-comparison of the quality indices for the four Models of the study. All axes represent percentages.

Taking into account both the results of the models and the post-analytical comparison of Agreement Indices, it becomes feasible to commence discussion on the definition of boundaries for the cultural periods under examination. With regard to boundaries, it is noted *a priori* that the Boundaries calculated by OxCal are a more precise but not necessarily a more accurate approximation for the dating of the relevant cultural periods. Hence, the OxCal calculated Boundaries will be considered in this discussion as fuzzy elements that contribute to the decrease of precision, instead of accurate calculations of the real cultural period boundaries.

Starting with the Middle Chalcolithic, it is observed that all models are in good agreement in regard to the upper boundary and beginning of modeled period ranges, which set the former boundary between 3550/3525 and 3500 BCE. On the other hand, the lower boundary of the period is a more contested matter, as the modeled ranges endings fluctuate between 2800 and 2715 BCE, while the calculated lower boundaries for the period extend from 2850 to 2700 BCE. The issue needs to be assessed in combination with the Late Chalcolithic upper boundary, as it also falls within the same general time span with modeled ranges spanning between 2905 and 2810 BCE and calculated upper boundaries between 2920 and 2800 BCE. Although confusing, this situation essentially portrays a very real archaeological situation, namely the different rates of change between geographically distant sites. Looking at the matter in more detail, it appears that at the sites of Politiko *Kokkinorotsos* and Souskiou *Laona* the material culture and specifically the pottery shifts to the characteristic Late Chalcolithic monochrome tradition earlier than at Kissonerga *Mosphilia* and the Ktima Lowland sites (Webb *et al.* 2009: 205; Bolger and Webb 2013: 45–46). Placing these events in time, it appears that Politiko and Souskiou shift to Late Chalcolithic traditions around 2900 to 2850 BCE, while Kissonerga adheres to Middle Chalcolithic traditions up to about 2850 to 2800 BCE. Also, Lemba enters the scene around 2800 BCE, at a time when the Ktima Lowland sites slowly complete their transition to Late Chalcolithic between 2800 and 2750 BCE. This complex situation cannot be properly addressed by using singular chronological systems but at present is reconciled by accepting an upper boundary for the Late Chalcolithic between 2900 and 2850/2800 BCE and a lower boundary for the Middle Chalcolithic spanning from 2850 to 2750 BCE, thus allowing a quite wide 50- to 150-year overlap between the two periods.

Contrary to the above situation, the Late Chalcolithic to Philia Culture Phase transition seems to have been more rapid and abrupt. The lowest of modeled calibrated ranges for the Late Chalcolithic across all models vary between 2510 and 2440 BCE, albeit values after 2480 BCE concentrate very limited posterior probabilities (<10%), while the lower boundaries for the period are calculated to be somewhere between 2555 and 2450 BCE. Parallel to the above the upper boundaries for the Philia Culture Phase range from 2555 to 2275 BCE, while the earliest modeled ranges lie between 2505 and 2365 BCE. Looking at the calibrated, non-modeled data it appears that there indeed exists significant overlap between at least three radiocarbon samples of the Late Chalcolithic (GU-2157 and BM-2530 from Kissonerga and BM-1353 from Lemba; BM-2530 is a long-lived charcoal sample and is not further discussed here, as it overlaps with both periods) and three more of the Philia Culture Phase, as illustrated in Figure 1.8.

This overlap, however, is by all probabilities not the product of cultural continuity, hybridization, or interaction post-dating the arrival of migrant populations at the very beginning of the Philia Culture Phase but rather the effect of a long plateau on the calibration curve between ca. 2450 and 2300 BCE, which essentially allows any sample with a radiocarbon age lower than 3950 BP and an uncertainty of ±40 years and above to overlap with the Philia Culture Phase. Outlier Analysis performed on the two most outlying samples, viz. GU-2157 and BM-1353, confirms their status as definite outliers in both Model 1 (58/25 and 65/25, respectively) and Model 2 (64/25 and 71/25, respectively). These numbers represent the posterior probability of the samples being outliers; that is, they are

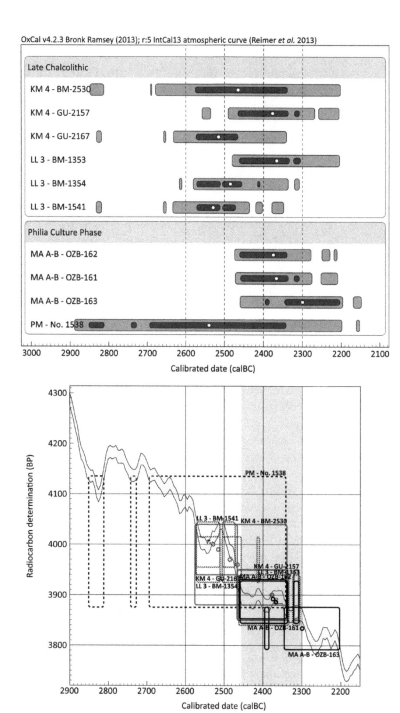

Figure 1.8: Multiplot (above) and curve plot (below) of the most significant overlapping, non-modeled ranges from radiocarbon samples of the Late Chalcolithic and Philia Culture Phase. The multiplot presents one- (dark gray) and two-sigma (light gray) ranges, as well as the mean of each range (white dot). The curve plot presents the ranges at one sigma and are colored according to the site they derive from, while their mean is illustrated as a hollow circle coded according to site. Site codes are as follows: dashed outline = Pyrgos *Mavrorachi*; diagonally hashed outline = Lemba *Lakkous*; gray outline = Kissonerga *Mosphilia*; black outline = Marki *Alonia*. A significant calibration curve plateau spanning the lower part of the Late Chalcolithic to Philia Culture Phase transition is indicated by the light gray band in the curve plot.

probabilities suggesting the designation of the samples to the Outlier group given the rest of the data, which contrasts their prior probability, the probability that a sample may fall into a particular group before data collection (see Bronk Ramsey 2014). Contextually GU-2157 lies within a well-stratified sequence and is overlain by older dates (Peltenburg 1998: 37, Figure 3.5), while BM-1353 was found alongside an older date (BM-1354) in a disturbed stratigraphy without indications of Philia Culture Phase cultural material (Peltenburg 1985: 115). These associations, in conjunction with the results of the Outlier Analysis above, suggest that the samples in question should be considered problematic and possibly affected by laboratory issues. As far as cultural period boundaries are concerned, it is maintained here that the Late Chalcolithic ends abruptly sometime between 2510 and 2480 BCE, while the onset of the Philia Culture Phase is more controversial due to the lack of evidence from settlements at the beginning of this period. Marki *Alonia* is admittedly a second- or third-generation site (Frankel and Webb 2006b: 290), while the single date from Pyrgos is affected by issues discussed above. Based on currently available data, such as the modeled radiocarbon dates from Models 1 and 1+, the mortuary data on the life span of Philia Marki populations (Frankel and Webb 2006a: 310), and the Marki *Alonia* starting boundaries, the beginning of the Philia Culture Phase can tentatively be placed around 2510/2480 BCE, while the earliest Marki boundaries are thought to provide the lower end of the starting boundary for this cultural period, placing it around 2450 BCE and allowing a 30- to 60-year period for the completion of the sociocultural transformations observed at the start of this period.

Another rapid transition can be observed between the Philia Culture Phase and the EBA I–III/MBA I. The chronology of the above periods benefits from the existence of well-stratified high-precision data from short-lived materials, and these result in increased accuracy in the designation of cultural period boundaries. Thus, the ending of the Philia Culture Phase can be securely placed between 2210/2205 and 2190 BCE, while the onset of the EBA I–III/MBA I spans from 2210/2205 to 2185/2175 BCE. The swiftness of this transition portrays a punctuated social transformation expressed through changes in the material culture and demography of the island. The stimuli for this development are still not well understood or well documented, but Manning (2013b: 17) has recently proposed that the end of the Philia Culture Phase may be causally linked to a series of social changes in the Mediterranean, such as the collapse of the Great Caravan Route in the Aegean and Anatolia and the termination of the Urban Phase (EB II–III) in the Levant. At present due to lack of evidence the causality clause of the argument is questioned, but the synchronicity of the abovementioned events to the end of the Philia Culture Phase is indeed corroborated.

Turning to the EBA I–III/MBA I to MBA II–III transition, it is noticed by looking at the non-modeled ranges of Model 0 (Figure 6) that there is considerable overlap between the two eras, which means that Models 2 and 2+ are undoubtedly more suitable instruments for estimating the boundaries of the above periods. According to these models the lower part of the EBA I–III/MBA I ranges stop around 1970 to 1940 BCE, while the calculated lower boundaries oscillate between 2025 and

1950/1930 BCE. At the same time the ranges of the MBA II–III start around 2025 to 1970 BCE, while the calculated upper boundaries vary from 2060 to 1935/1900 BCE. Taking into account that the samples forming the period boundaries derive from geographically distant sites, and that changes during this transition do not probably occur contemporaneously, it is expected that the periods will present large temporal overlaps that in turn represent the diverse sociocultural paths followed by the different regions or even sites on the island, as in the case of the transition from the Middle to the Late Chalcolithic. Based on the above, the lower boundary for EBA I–III/MBA I is set between 2025 and 1950/1930 BCE, while the upper boundary of the MBA II–III ranges from 2060 to 1970/1935 BCE, which allows a period of nearly a century for the gradual changes occurring between the earlier and middle part of the Bronze Age on the island.

One final point of discussion regards the end boundary for the MBA II–III, which essentially represents the Middle Bronze Age in Cyprus. Unfortunately, the nonexistence of radiocarbon data from the lower part of the MBA II–III does not allow the construction of a reliable enough model for the ending part of the sequence (Manning 2014b: 214). This assertion gains support from the lower calculated boundaries for the period, which range in all models from c. 1870/1860 to 1740/1690 BCE. This boundary, however, may indeed represent a TPQ for the earlier part of the period, rather than the actual ending of the entire period. In a relevant study, Merrillees (2002: 6), based on the earliest and latest appearance of White Painted Pendent Line Style pottery at several sites in Egypt, Anatolia, the Levant, and the Aegean, proposed that MC III should be placed between 1750 and 1650 BCE. Recently this conclusion has been supported by Manning (2014b: 214–215), albeit not based on actual radiocarbon data but on a set of justified TPQ/TAQ functions that push the boundaries for the ending of the Middle Bronze Age to 1690–1650 BCE. Based on the lowest values produced by the models in this study and the conclusions by Merrillees and Manning, the lower boundary of the MBA II–III is cautiously set between 1740 and 1690/1650 BCE.

To summarize and conclude the discussion on the dating of cultural periods, the following starting and ending boundaries are proposed for each period based on the currently available data. These boundaries are considered to improve the precision of the chronology put forward in the ARCANE project (Peltenburg *et al.* 2013b: 338, Table 9.3) and compare favorably with chronological systems proposed elsewhere (Manning 2013a: 521, Table A2; 2013b: 14, Table 1; 2014b: 215). Modifications to previous studies concern the Middle to Late Chalcolithic transition, where the upper boundary for the Late Chalcolithic is raised by 50–100 years for reasons already explained in the text; as well as the upper and lower boundaries of the Philia Culture Phase, which are raised and lowered by approximately fifty years each to accommodate the new data from Pyrgos *Mavrorachi* and to counteract the effect of the long-lived Sotira *Kaminoudhia* charcoal samples. Finally, the inter-studies convergence of results serves as a verification of the robustness of the methods employed and as a testament to the potential of absolute data in constructing a more realistic chronological system for prehistoric Cyprus.

Table 1.4: Summary of the proposed starting and ending boundaries for the cultural periods under consideration in this study

	Start	End
Middle Chalcolithic	3550/3525–3500 BCE	2850–2750 BCE
Late Chalcolithic	2900–2850/2800 BCE	2510–2480 BCE
Philia Culture Phase	2510/2480–2450 BCE	2210/2205–2190 BCE
EBA I–III/MBA I	2210/2205–2185/2175 BCE	2025–1950/1930 BCE
MBA II–III	2060–1970/1935 BCE	1740–1690/1650 BCE

Future Prospects

Any study with a view to improving our collective knowledge of the past is a *de facto* candidate for discovering previously unknown or overlooked issues, which inadvertently raise new questions. Such issues have indeed been encountered by the present study, which circumstance leads to the necessity of devoting the last section to presenting them and suggesting possible routes for moving forward.

A first issue arose during the conceptual design phase of the study and has to do with the very concept of an era. Until very recently all chronology studies and most of the sociocultural history narratives in Cyprus regarded the virtual subdivisions of the island's prehistory as contingent one to another, which resulted in constraining them into clearly defined, non-overlapping timeslots. While it is acknowledged on numerous occasions in the literature that the succession of eras is a gradual process, rather than an instantaneous event, this admission is rarely transferred into discussions of the chronological duration of these processes (e.g., Frankel 2000: 181; 2005; Peltenburg 1991b: 32; 1996: 18). As a corollary to this, discussions on the social change mechanisms set in motion during transitions between eras are scarce, while attention is usually focused on exposing and emphasizing material culture differences of any two adjoining cultural periods. It is hoped that the advent of studies discussing absolute data and chronological models will gradually reveal that the existing black box approach to chronology is no longer tenable, thus leading to refinement of the terminology utilized, improvement of the research practices employed, and adoption of novel concepts emphasizing the fuzzy elements already embedded in the archaeological reality (e.g., Manning 2013a; Knapp 2013; Bolger and Peltenburg 2014).

Beyond concepts, the study also came across data scarcity and quality issues, which are noted in several parts of the text. It is not my intention to reiterate the issues beleaguering the data pool here but instead to suggest that the acquisition of more and higher-quality short-lived radiocarbon data from secure and preferably sealed archaeological contexts will not only lead to better accuracy and precision in the definition of chronological boundaries for the cultural periods in question but also probably give rise to regional chronologies illustrating more vividly the varied and complex processes of social change within and between periods.

A final set of issues encountered in this study involves the technical implementation of its methodology. Starting with model structure, it is noticed that the utilization of singular sets of assumptions does not correctly illustrate archaeological reality, as cultural eras occupying a certain timeframe can overlap, abut, or present gaps between the elements. Based on this, it is expected that there will be further advances in the Bayesian mathematical formulae underlying the entire approach, which will allow the employment of mixed-mode models. Furthermore, model nesting, as employed in software packages today, has numerous uses, but is inadequately representing real-life situations, such as site stratigraphy breaking across two or more cultural periods. This is a more complex issue, as it requires a redesign of the approach to apply mathematical formulae in a layered manner rather than a stepped-linear one. However, the evolution of these structures will allow the parallel execution of specific site stratigraphic models and regional cross-site models and may indeed benefit archaeology by providing better tools for exploring the element of time.

Endnote

This paper was prepared in early 2014 and serves as a reflection of the views held by the author at the time. Since the production of this paper, the author has significantly shifted his positions, especially regarding the Late Chalcolithic to Philia Culture Phase transition. Also, the CQL code for OxCal models, the modeled and non-modeled calibrated datasets, and the full illustrations for the models are not reproduced in the paper due to space limitations but are available upon request.

References

Ambers, J., K. Matthews, and S. Bowman. 1987. British Museum natural radiocarbon measurements XIX. *Radiocarbon* 29.1: 61–77.

Ambers, J., K. Matthews, and S. Bowman. 1991. British Museum natural radiocarbon measurements XXII. *Radiocarbon* 33.1: 51–68.

Ammerman, A., P. Flourentzos, and J. Noller. 2009. Excavation at the site of Pigi-Agios Andronikos in Stroumpi (Pafos). *Report of the Department of Antiquities, Cyprus*: 17–38.

Bayliss, A. 2009. Rolling out revolution: Using radiocarbon dating in archaeology. *Radiocarbon* 51.1: 123–147.

Belgiorno, M.R., D. Fossataro, and O. Menozzi. 2010. Project: Pyrgos (Limassol) and Its Territory: Preliminary Report of the 2010 Archaeological Investigations. Sacrofano, IT: Associazione Culturale Armonia, Cypriot Italian Project on Pyrgos-Mavroraki Conservation. Internet Edition: http://www.pyrgos-mavroraki.net/pyrgos-mavroraki _g000010.pdf.

Bolger, D., and J.M. Webb. 2013. Ceramics. In E. Peltenburg (ed.), *ARCANE Associated Regional Chronologies for the Ancient Near East II: Cyprus*, 39–127. Turnhout: Brepols.

Bolger, D., and E.J. Peltenburg. 2014. Material and social transformations in 3rd millennium Cyprus: Evidence of ceramics. In J.M. Webb (ed.), *Structure, Measurement and Meaning, Studies on Prehistoric Cyprus in Honour of David Frankel*, 187–197. Studies in Mediterranean Archaeology 143. Uppsala, Sweden: Åströms Förlag.

Bombardieri, L. 2009. The MBA–LBA I period in the Kourion region: New evidences from Erimi-Laonin tou Porakou (Lemesos, Cyprus). *Antiguo Oriente: Cuadernos del Centro de Estudios de Historia del Antiguo Oriente* 7: 281–300.

Bronk Ramsey, C. 1995. Radiocarbon calibration and analysis of stratigraphy: The OxCal program. *Radiocarbon* 37.2: 425–430.

Bronk Ramsey, C. 2001. Development of the radiocarbon program OxCal. *Radiocarbon* 43.2: 355–363.

Bronk Ramsey, C. 2009a. Bayesian analysis of radiocarbon dates. *Radiocarbon* 51.1: 337–360.

Bronk Ramsey, C. 2009b. Dealing with outliers and offsets in radiocarbon dating. *Radiocarbon* 51.3: 1023–1045.

Bronk Ramsey, C. 2014. *OxCal 4.2 Manual* [Digital Resource]. Oxford: Oxford Radiocarbon Accelerator Unit. Internet Edition: https://c14.arch.ox.ac.uk/oxcalhelp/hlp_contents.html.

Bronk Ramsey, C., M.W. Dee, J.M. Rowland, T.F.G. Higham, S.A. Harris, F. Brock, A. Quiles, E.M. Wild, E.S. Marcus, and A.J. Shortland. 2010. Radiocarbon-based chronology for Dynastic Egypt. *Science* 328.5985: 1554–1557.

Bowman, S.G.E., J.C. Ambers, and M.N. Leese. 1990. Re-evaluation of British Museum radiocarbon dates issued between 1980 and 1984. *Radiocarbon* 32.1: 59–79.

Burleigh, R. 1981. Radiocarbon dates for Lemba. In J. Reade (ed.), *Chalcolithic Cyprus and Western Asia*, 21. British Museum, Occasional Paper 20. London: British Museum.

Burleigh, R., K. Matthews, and J. Ambers. 1982a. British Museum natural radiocarbon measurements XIV. *Radiocarbon* 24.3: 229–261.

Burleigh, R., K. Matthews, and J. Ambers. 1982b. British Museum natural radiocarbon measurements XV. *Radiocarbon* 24.3: 262–290.

Calderoni, G. 2009. Diagrammi di calibrazione per le età C-14 convenzionali misurate per il sito di Pyrgos-Mavroraki, Cipro. In M.R. Belgiorno (ed.), *Cipro all'Inizio dell'Età del Bronzo, Realtà Sconosciute della Communita Industriale di Pyrgos/Mavroraki*, 188–193. Rome: Gangemi Editore.

Clarke, J.T. 2007. Chronology and terminology. In J.T. Clarke, C. McCartney and A. Wasse (eds.), *On the Margins of Southwest Asia: Cyprus During the 6th to 4th Millennia BC*, 9–29. Oxford: Oxbow Books.

Coleman, J.E. 1992a. Greece, the Aegean and Cyprus. In R. Ehrich (ed.), *Chronologies in Old World Archaeology* 1, 247–288. Chicago: University of Chicago Press.

Coleman, J.E. 1992b. Greece, the Aegean and Cyprus. In R. Ehrich (ed.), *Chronologies in Old World Archaeology* 2, 203–229. Chicago: University of Chicago Press.

Coleman, J.E., J.A. Barlow, M.K. Mogelonsky, and K.W. Schaar. 1996. *Alambra: A Middle Bronze Age Settlement in Cyprus. Archaeological Investigations by Cornell University 1974–1985*. Studies in Mediterranean Archaeology 118. Jonsered, Sweden: Paul Åströms Förlag.

Dee M.W., and C. Bronk Ramsey. 2014. High-precision Bayesian modeling of samples susceptible to inbuilt age. *Radiocarbon* 56.1: 83–94.

Dikaios, P. 1962. The Stone Age. In E. Gjerstad, O. Vessberg and J. Lindros (eds.), *Swedish Cyprus Expedition* Vol. IV, 1A, 1–204. Lund, Sweden: The Swedish Cyprus Expedition.

Falconer, S.E., and P.L. Fall. 2013. Household and community behavior at Bronze Age Politiko-Troullia, Cyprus. *Journal of Field Archaeology* 38.2: 101–119.

Falconer, S.E., E.M. Monahan, and P.L. Fall. 2014. A stone plank figure from Politiko-Troullia, Cyprus: Potential implications for inferring Bronze Age communal behavior. *Bulletin of the American Schools of Oriental Research* 371: 3–16.

Fiedel, S.J., J.R. Southon, R.E. Taylor, Y.V. Kuzmin, M. Street, T.F.G. Higham, J. Van der Plicht, M.-J. Nadeau, and S. Nawalade-Chavan. 2013. Assessment of interlaboratory pretreatment protocols by radiocarbon dating an elk bone found below Laacher See tephra at Miesenheim IV (Rhineland, Germany). *Radiocarbon* 55.2–3: 1443–1453.

Fishman, B., H. Forbes, and B. Lawn. 1977. University of Pennsylvania radiocarbon dates XIX. *Radiocarbon* 19.2: 188–228.

Frankel, D. 2000. Migration and ethnicity in prehistoric Cyprus: Technology as Habitus. *European Journal of Archaeology* 3: 167–187.

Frankel, D. 2005. Becoming Bronze Age: Acculturation and enculturation in third millennium. In J. Clarke (ed.), *Archaeological Perspectives on the Transmission and Transformation of Culture in the Eastern Mediterranean*, 18–24. Levant Supplementary Series 2. Oxford: Oxbow Books.

Frankel, D., and J.M. Webb. 1996. *Marki Alonia: An Early and Middle Bronze Age Town in Cyprus, Excavations 1990–1994*. Studies in Mediterranean Archaeology 123.1. Jonsered, Sweden: Paul Åströms Förlag.

Frankel, D., and J.M. Webb. 2006a. *Marki Alonia: An Early and Middle Bronze Age Settlement in Cyprus, Excavations 1995–2000*. Studies in Mediterranean Archaeology 123.2. Sävedalen, Sweden: Paul Åströms Förlag.

Frankel, D., and J.M. Webb. 2006b. Neighbours: Negotiating space in a prehistoric village. *Antiquity* 80: 287–302.

Håkansson, S. 1981. University of Lund radiocarbon dates XIV. *Radiocarbon* 23.3: 384–403.

Hedges, R.E.M., and J. Van Klinken. 1992. A review of current approaches in the pretreatment of bone for radiocarbon dating by AMS. *Radiocarbon* 34.3: 279–291.

Hedges, R.E.M., R.A. Housley, C. Bronk Ramsey, and G J.V. Klinken. 1992. Radiocarbon dates from the Oxford AMS system: Archaeometry datelist 15. *Archaeometry* 34.2: 337–357.

Hedges, R.E.M., R.A. Housley, C. Bronk Ramsey, and G J.V. Klinken. 1993. Radiocarbon dates from the Oxford AMS system: Archaeometry datelist 17. *Archaeometry* 35.2: 305–326.

Held, S.O. 1989. Early Prehistoric Island Archaeology in Cyprus: Configurations of Formative Culture Growth from the Pleistocene/Holocene Boundary to the mid-3rd Millennium B.C. Unpublished PhD dissertation, University College London, Institute of Archaeology.

Hurst, B.J., and B. Lawn. 1984. University of Pennsylvania radiocarbon dates XXII. *Radiocarbon* 26.2: 212–240.

Keswani, P.S. 2004. *Mortuary Ritual and Society in Bronze Age Cyprus*. Monographs in Mediterranean Archaeology 9. London: Equinox.

Knapp, A.B. 2008. *Prehistoric and Protohistoric Cyprus: Identity, Insularity, and Connectivity*. Oxford: Oxford University Press.

Knapp, A.B. 2013. *The Archaeology of Cyprus: From Earliest Prehistory through the Bronze Age*. Cambridge: Cambridge University Press.

Manning, S.W. 2013a. Appendix: A new radiocarbon chronology for Prehistoric and Protohistoric Cyprus, ca. 11,000–1050 cal BC. In A.B. Knapp, *The Archaeology of Cyprus: From Earliest Prehistory through the Bronze Age*, 485–533. Cambridge: Cambridge University Press.

Manning, S.W. 2013b. Cyprus at 2200 BC: Rethinking the chronology of the Cypriot Early Bronze Age. In A.B. Knapp, J.M. Webb and A. McCarthy (eds.), *J.R.B. Stewart: An Archaeological Legacy*, 1–21. Studies in Mediterranean Archaeology 139. Uppsala, Sweden: Åströms Förlag.

Manning, S.W. 2014a. *A Test of Time and a Test of Time Revisited: The Volcano of Thera and the Chronology and History of the Aegean and East Mediterranean in the Mid-Second Millennium BC*. Oxford: Oxbow Books.

Manning, S.W. 2014b. A radiocarbon-based chronology for the Chalcolithic through Middle Bronze Age of Cyprus (as of AD 2102). In F. Höflmayer and R. Eichmann (eds.), *Egypt and the Southern Levant during the Early Bronze Age: C14, Chronology, Connections*. Proceedings of a Workshop Held in Berlin, 14th–16th September 2011, 207–240. Orient-Abteilung des Deutschen Archäologischen Instituts, Orient-Archäologie 31. Rahden, Westfalen: Verlag Marie Leidorf GmbH.

Manning, S.W., and D. Sewell. 2006. Psematismenos Trelloukkas Project, Cyprus. *Council for British Research in the Levant Bulletin* 1: 66–68.

Manning, S.W., and S. Swiny. 1994. Sotira Kamminoudhia and the chronology of the Early Bronze Age in Cyprus. *Oxford Journal of Archaeology* 13: 149–172.

Manning, S.W., C. Bronk Ramsey, W. Kutschera, T. Higham, B. Kromer, P. Steier, and E. Wild. 2006. Chronology for the Aegean Late Bronze Age. *Science* 312: 565–569.

Merrillees, R.S. 2002. The relative and absolute chronology of the Cypriote White Painted pendent line style. *Bulletin of the American Schools of Oriental Research* 326: 1–9.

Östlund, H.G. 1957. Stockholm natural radiocarbon measurements I. *Science*, New Series 126/3272: 493–497.

Östlund, H.G. 1959. Stockholm natural radiocarbon measurements II. *American Journal of Science*, Radiocarbon Supplement 1: 35–44.

Peltenburg, E. 1982. *Recent Developments in the Later Prehistory of Cyprus*. Studies in Mediterranean Archaeology PB 16. Göteborg, Sweden: Paul Åströms Förlag.

Peltenburg, E. 1988. Notices of books. Review of S. Swiny, P.T. Craddock and R.F. Tylecote, *Episkopi Phaneromeni, The Kent State University expedition to Episkopi Phaneromeni* 2, Studies in Mediterranean Archaeology 74.2 (Göteborg, Sweden: Paul Åströms Förlag, 1986). *The Journal of Hellenic Studies* 108: 261.

Peltenburg, E. 1991a. Towards a definition of the Late Chalcolithic in Cyprus: The monochrome pottery debate. In J.A. Barlow, D.I. Bolger and B. Kling (eds.), *Cypriot Ceramics: Reading the Prehistoric Record*, 9–20. University Museum Symposium Series 2, University Museum Monograph 74. Philadelphia: University Museum.

Peltenburg, E. 1991b. Kissonerga-Mosphilia: A major Chalcolithic site in Cyprus. *Bulletin of the American Schools of Oriental Research* 282/283: 17–36.

Peltenburg, E. 1996. From isolation to state formation in Cyprus, c. 3500–1500 BC. In V. Karageorghis, and D. Michaelides (eds.), *The Development of the Cypriot Economy*, 17–43. Nicosia: Bank of Cyprus.

Peltenburg, E. (ed.) 1985. *Excavations at Lemba-Lakkous, 1976–1983, Lemba Archaeological Project 1.* Studies in Mediterranean Archaeology 70.1. Göteborg, Sweden: Paul Åströms Förlag.

Peltenburg, E. (ed.) 1998. *Excavations at Kissonerga-Mosphilia 1979–1992. Lemba Archaeological Project 2, 1A.* Studies in Mediterranean Archaeology 70.2. Jonsered, Sweden: Paul Åströms Förlag

Peltenburg, E. (ed.) 2003. *The Colonisation and Settlement of Cyprus: Investigations at Kissonerga-Mylouthkia, 1976–1996.* Lemba Archaeological Project 3, 1. Studies in Mediterranean Archaeology 70.4. Sävedalen, Sweden: Paul Åströms Förlag.

Peltenburg, E., D. Frankel, and J.M. Webb. 2013a Introduction. In E. Peltenburg (ed.), *ARCANE Associated Regional Chronologies for the Ancient Near East II: Cyprus*, 1–13. Turnhout: Brepols Publishers.

Peltenburg, E., D. Frankel, and C. Paraskeva. 2013b. Radiocarbon. In E. Peltenburg (ed.), *ARCANE Associated Regional Chronologies for the Ancient Near East II: Cyprus*, 313–338. Turnhout: Brepols Publishers.

Piggott, S. 1959. *Approach to Archaeology.* Cambridge, MA: Harvard University Press.

Reimer, P.J., E. Bard, A. Bayliss, J.W. Beck, P.G. Blackwell, C. Bronk Ramsey, P.M. Grootes, T.P. Guilderson, H. Haflidason, I. Hajdas, C. Hattž, T.J. Heaton, D.L. Hoffmann, A.G. Hogg, K.A. Hughen, K.F. Kaiser, B. Kromer, S.W. Manning, M. Niu, R.W. Reimer, D.A. Richards, E.M. Scott, J.R. Southon, R.A. Staff, C.S.M. Turney, and J. Van der Plicht. 2013. IntCal13 and Marine13 radiocarbon age calibration curves 0–50,000 years cal BP. *Radiocarbon* 55.4: 1869–1887.

Sciré Calabrisotto, C.S., M.E. Fedi, L. Caforio, and L. Bombardieri. 2012. Erimi-Laonin tou Porakou (Limassol, Cyprus): Radiocarbon analyses of the Bronze Age cemetery and workshop complex. *Radiocarbon* 54.3–4: 475–482.

Sciré Calabrisotto, C.S., M.E. Fedi, L. Caforio, L. Bombardieri, and P.A. Mando. 2013. Collagen quality indicators for radiocarbon dating of bones: New data on Bronze Age Cyprus. *Radiocarbon* 55.2–3: 472–480.

Steel, L. 2004. *Cyprus before History: From the Earliest Settlers to the End of the Bronze Age.* London: Duckworth.

Stewart, J.R.B. 1962. The Early Cypriote Bronze Age. In E. Gjerstad, O. Vessberg, and J. Lindros (eds.), *Swedish Cyprus Expedition* Vol. 4, part 1A: 205–401. Lund, Sweden: The Swedish Cyprus Expedition.

Swiny, S. 1986. The Philia culture and its foreign relations. In V. Karageorghis (ed.), *Acts of the International Symposium "Cyprus between the Orient and the Occident," Nicosia, 8–14 September 1985*, 29–44. Nicosia: Republic of Cyprus, Ministry of Communications & Works, Department of Antiquities.

Swiny, S. 1989. From round house to duplex: A reassessment of prehistoric Bronze Age Cypriot society. In E. Peltenburg (ed.), *Early Society in Cyprus*, 14–31. Edinburgh: University of Edinburgh Press.

Thulman, D., F. Riede, and C. Bronk Ramsey. 2013. *Use of the AModel index to compare different models.* OxCal Google Group. Menlo Park, CA: Google. Archived Edition: https://groups.google.com/forum/#!topic/oxcal/XAQu8DYJcis.

Todd, I.A. 1986. *The Bronze Age Cemetery in Kalavasos Village, Vasilikos Valley Project 1.* Studies in Mediterranean Archaeology 71.1. Göteborg, Sweden: Paul Åströms Förlag.

Todd, I.A. 2004a. *Excavations at Kalavasos-Ayious, Vasilikos Valley Project 8.* Studies in Mediterranean Archaeology 71.8. Sävedalen, Sweden: Paul Åströms Förlag.

Todd, I.A. 2004b. *Vasilikos Valley Project 9: The Field Survey of the Vasilikos Valley.* Vol 1. Studies in Mediterranean Archaeology 71.9. Sävedalen, Sweden: Paul Åströms Förlag.

Webb, J.M., D. Frankel, P. Croft, and C. McCartney. 2009. Excavations at Politiko Kokkinorotsos: A Chalcolithic hunting station in Cyprus. *Proceedings of the Prehistoric Society* 75: 189–237.

Weinberg, S.S. 1956. Exploring the Early Bronze Age in Cyprus. *Archaeology* 9.2: 112–121.

Zazzo, A., M. Lebon, L. Chiotti, C. Comby, E. Delqué-Koli&ccaron, R. Nespoulet, and I. Reiche. 2013. Can we use calcined bones for radiocarbon dating the Paleolithic? *Radiocarbon* 55.2–3: 1409–1421.

2

The Fabric Next Door

A Comparative Study of Pottery Technology and Composition at the Early and Middle Bronze Age Settlements of Marki *Alonia* and Alambra *Mouttes*

MARIA DIKOMITOU-ELIADOU

Introduction

Both Red Polished and Red Polished Coarse ware pottery samples from Marki *Alonia* (Webb 1994; Frankel and Webb 1996; 2006; Dikomitou 2012; Dikomitou-Eliadou 2013; 2014) and Red Polished pottery from Alambra *Mouttes* (Barlow 1989; 1991; 1996a; 1996b; Barlow and Idziak 1989; Barlow and Vaughan 1992; Weisman 1996) have been the subject of compositional and technological studies in recent years. These studies provide an important opportunity to compare ceramic fabrics from these two Early and Middle Bronze Age sites in order to determine the degree of similarity and difference in their composition and production technology. Marki *Alonia* and Alambra *Mouttes* are neighboring, roughly contemporary settlement sites located in the northern foothills of the Troodos mountain range in central Cyprus (Figure 2.1).

Marki was founded around 2400 BCE and continued to be occupied for approximately seven hundred years (Frankel and Webb 2006: 35) (Figure 2). Systematic excavations by La Trobe University from 1992 to 2000 have revealed a vibrant settlement with a maximum estimated population of four hundred inhabitants (Frankel and Webb 2001: 120–122; 2006: 309–310). The more limited excavations undertaken by Cornell University at Alambra from 1974 to 1985 were not able to establish the full life span of the settlement, nor its maximum size. The area excavated (Area A) was inhabited much later during the Early Cypriot (hereafter EC) III/Middle Cypriot (hereafter MC) I period and had a shorter life span of "a single habitation episode" or approximately one hundred years, from about 1900 to 1800 BCE (Coleman *et al.* 1996: 17, 327, 334–335). The partial excavation, however, of other areas of the settlement and of a number of tombs at Alambra clearly indicates that the settlement was occupied from at least Early Cypriot (EC) II, and, like Marki, was abandoned in Middle Cypriot (MC) II (Coleman *et al.* 1996: 17–18, 327, 338; Frankel and Webb 2006: 308). Renewed excavations by the Queensland Alambra

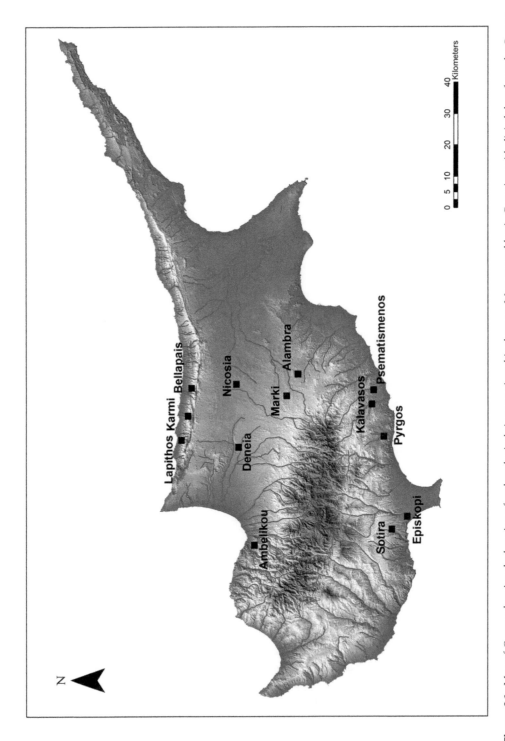

Figure 2.1: Map of Cyprus showing the location of archaeological sites mentioned in the text. Map created by A. Georgiou with digital data from the Cyprus Geological Survey Department, Republic of Cyprus.

Archaeological Mission will undoubtedly shed more light on the history of the settlement (see Sneddon 2015).

Marki and Alambra share many characteristics due to their contemporaneity and location in the same geographic and geological area of Cyprus and had a common material culture and economy. Excavations at these two neighboring communities provide an important opportunity to compare various aspects of pottery production and to assess technological uniformity or variability in pottery production at the local level in central Cyprus.

Petrographic analysis of almost two hundred Red Polished and Red Polished Coarse ware samples from all the occupation strata of the settlement at Marki *Alonia* has recently been undertaken using optical polarizing microscopy (Dikomitou-Eliadou 2013; 2014; Dikomitou 2012). It is important that these results should now be compared with available data deriving from the wider area surrounding the settlement. Earlier analyses of Red Polished ware pottery from Alambra by Barlow and her collaborators (Barlow 1989; 1991; 1996a; 1996b; Barlow and Idziak 1989; Weisman 1996) provide an excellent opportunity to assess whether technological choices in pottery production recorded at Marki were also documented at Alambra and to achieve a more comprehensive understanding of pottery production in this region of Cyprus. For the purposes of this paper, discussion will focus on the analytical study of ceramic fabrics from EC III to MC II strata at Marki, as these phases of occupation are contemporaneous with those excavated at Alambra. The Red Polished pottery from these phases at Marki mainly falls into the Red Polished III group—a subdivision that carries chronological, typological, technological, and geographical connotations (Barlow 1989: 51). Likewise, more than 99 percent of the entire pottery assemblage from Alambra is of Red Polished III (Barlow 1989: 54; Barlow and Coleman 1982).

The ceramic thin sections from Alambra were prepared many years ago by Barlow and her colleagues and are unfortunately no longer available. This study therefore compares the analytical results from Red Polished and Red Polished Coarse pottery samples from Marki *Alonia* with accounts of the pottery samples from Alambra *Mouttes* published in scientific journals and edited volumes (Barlow 1989; 1991; Barlow and Idziak 1989) and the site excavation monograph (Coleman *et al.* 1996; Barlow 1996a; 1996b; Weisman 1996). It serves as a small tribute to the Cornell University team and particularly to Barlow, who initiated one of the first systematic, analytical studies of Red Polished pottery.

In what follows, the petrographic data deriving from the analysis of pottery samples from Marki and Alambra are presented and used as the basis for a comparative discussion of technological patterns in pottery production at these two contemporary and neighboring settlements. Moving beyond such localized inter-site technological comparisons, the final section of this study addresses the mechanisms of pottery production and distribution in Early and Middle Bronze Age Cyprus more broadly.

Red Polished Ware Pottery From Alambra *Mouttes* and Marki *Alonia*: The Story So Far

Red Polished and Red Polished Coarse were the predominant pottery wares in use across Cyprus during the Early and Middle Bronze Age. Previous attempts to classify these wares and identify chronological and regional variations were beset with a number of problems, including a lack of detailed analysis and theoretical justification as well as a scarcity of well-stratified material (Sandwith 1877; Myres and Ohnefalsch-Richter 1899; Myres 1914; Gjerstad 1926; Åström 1957; Stewart 1962). Moreover, as more data became available, increasing evidence for regional variants prevented the use of a single classification system across the island.

Red Polished Pottery from Alambra *Mouttes*

In her study of the pottery assemblage from Alambra *Mouttes*, Barlow tried to address the incommensurability of preexisting classification systems and to divide the more than one hundred thousand sherds of Red Polished ware into meaningful technological groups (Barlow and Idziak 1989: 66). This work exposed the difficulties encountered when using Stewart's (1962) classification system for EC and MC wares, which was based almost entirely on material excavated at sites on the north coast of Cyprus and turned out to have little applicability beyond this region (Barlow and Idziak 1989: 66; Barlow 1996a: 237).

Barlow distinguished between the use of calcareous and non-calcareous fabrics at Alambra, arguing that the technological and compositional characterization of pottery could assist in the recognition of regional patterns in pottery production (Barlow and Idziak 1989: 75; Barlow and Vaughan 1992: 9; 1999: 15–16; Barlow 1996a: 237). Stewart (1962: 212) himself acknowledged that discussions about the technological attributes of pottery were still absent from Cypriot ceramic studies. Referring to his own classification system, he admitted that, except for pottery from his own excavations at Bellapais *Vounous,* information about fabrics was almost entirely lacking, making normal ceramic classification impossible (Stewart 1962: 212).

With these issues in mind, Barlow embarked on the first systematic analytical study of ancient pottery from Cyprus, employing a combination of techniques for the compositional and technological characterization of Red Polished, Black Polished, and White Painted ware samples from the lowest levels of the excavated units at Alambra (Barlow and Idziak 1989: 68). In doing so, she shifted the research focus from typology and style to the definition and categorization of ceramic fabrics, the raw materials selected for pottery production, and the techniques and successive stages for the processing of fabrics, including pot building, firing, and decoration, always in accordance with ceramic shapes and resulting styles. The methods that she employed were ceramic petrography and energy-dispersive scanning electron microscopy (Barlow and Idziak 1989: 68). Finally, in order to gain a broader view of the identified calcareous and non-calcareous clay groups, she used drops of a 10 percent solution of hydrochloric acid on the freshly exposed surfaces of 502 sherds in order to distinguish those made with highly calcareous clays from those that, even though macroscopically indistinguishable, were made with wholly non-calcareous clays (Barlow and Idziak 1989: 68).

Table 2.1 summarizes the main clay groups that Barlow and her collaborators distinguished, groups on which they developed their subsequent arguments. They identified two principal groups. The first calcareous one originated in sedimentary deposits (Table 2.1: Group A).

Table 2.1: Summary of the compositional, typological, and other technological characteristics of Red Polished and Red Polished Coarse fabric groups from Alambra and Marki

Alambra (Barlow and colleagues)		Marki (Dikomitou-Eliadou)	
Group	Fabric description	Group	Fabric description
A	Wholly calcareous	XII	Very fine, calcareous fabric; infrequent inclusions include calcite grains, micritic limestone fragments, and quartz grains. In fine fraction some mica laths were also identified. Softness of fabric paste.
B1	Wholly non-calcareous with igneous components	IV	Coarse, non-calcareous, igneous fabric with gabbro and diabase fragments, quartz, amphibole and altered pyroxene grains. Heavily altered components. Pyroxene and altered pyroxene dominant mineral.
		VIII	Coarse, non-calcareous, igneous fabric with quartz grains, gabbro and diabase fragments, pyroxene, amphibole plagioclase feldspar, and olivine grains.
		X	Fine, non-calcareous fabric, very homogeneous. Monocrystalline quartz and plagioclasse feldspar grains, and pyroxene and altered pyroxene grains, mostly in fine fraction.
B2	Calcareous with combination of igneous and sedimentary components	II	Coarse, calcareous fabric, coexistence of sedimentary and igneous inclusions as well as the distinct presence of microfossils within the micritic limestone fragments
		VI	Coarse, calcareous fabric with micritic clay, presence of micritic limestone fragments and calcite-filled microfossils. Calciferous material coexists with igneous inclusions, such as basalt and diabase fragments and plagioclase feldspar and pyroxene grains.
		VII	Fine, calcareous fabric with dominant presence of microfossils and more infrequently, some fragments of basalt and pyroxene grains and even rarer, some clinopyroxene and plagioclase feldspar grains
		IX	Fine, calcareous fabric. Frequent monocrystalline quartz, small fragments, almost in fine fraction of micritic limestone, and olivine, calcite, pyroxene, plagioclase feldspar grains and diabase fragments. Presence of voids, replacing organic matter that burned out during firing.

They further separated the second into two sub-groups: the first being wholly non-calcareous, containing only volcanic inclusions (Table 2.1: Group B1), and the second containing both sedimentary and igneous components (Table 2.1: Group B2) (Barlow and Idziak 1989: 68; Barlow 1996a: 248–254). From a typological point of view, Group A included finer Red Polished, Red Polished Black-topped, Black Polished, and White Painted ware samples, while Group B comprised coarser Red Polished utilitarian pottery (Barlow and Idziak 1989: 71; Barlow 1996a: 240–242).

Alambra Group A is characterized by soft, low-fired, buff-colored or pinkish fabrics made with calcareous clay, which reacted to Barlow's dilute solution of hydrochloric acid test. The fabrics included in Group A contain aplastic inclusions that are usually sparse but may be more numerous in larger vessels and show traces of organic material (Barlow 1994: 45). The surface of the vessels, which are normally small in size and include mainly juglets and small bowls, is covered with a moderately thick to thick lustrous slip that is red or, in the case of black-topped vessels, black at the rim, and for open vessels, also black in the interior (Barlow 1994: 45). The decoration on these vessels includes incised geometric motives filled with a white paste and occasional plastic attachments (Barlow 1994: 45).

Group B, which includes samples from both the calcareous and non-calcareous sub-groups, can be distinguished macroscopically, during hand sorting, by the density of visible inclusions in their clay matrix (Barlow and Idziak 1989: 71). This larger compositional group is comprised mostly of Red Polished and Red Polished Coarse fabrics, including small and large bowls, jugs and juglets, medium-sized amphorae, cooking pots and griddles (Barlow and Idziak 1989: 71, Table 1).

In addition to the analytical work conducted by Barlow and Idziak (1989) and Barlow (1996a; 1996b), Weisman (1996) studied several samples of Red Polished, Red Polished Coarse, Red Polished black-topped, Black Polished, and White Painted wares from Alambra. Like Barlow, Weisman argued that the Alambra fabrics could be divided into two major groups derived from two different kinds of geological deposits: weathered volcanic rocks and calcareous marine sediments (Weisman 1996: 468). Within these two broad groups, Weisman (1996: 470) recognized two different varieties of calcareous sedimentary material, one containing foraminiferous limestone and microfossil foraminifera filled with recrystallized calcite and the other with primarily open, unaltered foraminifera. This distinction between the calciferous fabrics with "open" and "closed" foraminifera allowed him to conclude that the heavily calciferous groups derived from two distinct marine, and thus geological, environments (Weisman 1996: 470).

From a typological perspective, Weisman observed that open foraminifera are the dominant constituent in the finer Red Polished Group A, which includes Red Polished black-topped and Black Polished wares, and that they are virtually absent from the coarser Red Polished ware vessels of Group B (Weisman 1996: 470). Finally, Weisman (1996: 470–473) made the following observations regarding the relationship between vessel type and fabric. First, Red Polished fabrics of Barlow's Group A are mixtures of material from both kinds of calcareous sedimentary sources with a lesser amount of volcanic material. Second, Red Polished fabrics in Barlow's Group B are made only with calcareous sediment containing limestone and calcite-filled foraminifera mixed with a variety of volcanic inclusions, meaning that Red Polished Group B contains no open foraminifera. Third, the composition of bowls in Group B1 is characterized by a dominance of volcanic and metamorphic minerals and rock fragments, while the composition of jugs and jars of Group B2 is distinguished by a higher concentration of calcareous components. And finally, cooking pots are made with raw material derived from volcanic terrain, and the mineralogy of the parent rocks is different from that used for Red Polished bowls, jugs, and jars of Group B.

Red Polished Pottery from Marki *Alonia*

A first attempt to analyze Red Polished pottery from Marki was made by a group led by Summerhayes with the employment of electron microprobe analysis (Summerhayes *et al.* 1996). As at Alambra, these first results indicated that Red Polished pottery at Marki can be divided into two major groupings: a fine, highly calcareous variety and a coarser pottery with lower proportions of calcium (Summerhayes *et al.* 1996: 178). These roughly corresponded compositionally to the two Alambra pottery groups, A and B (Table 2.1). What differentiates the Marki from the Alambra analytical study is the argument that these compositional divisions of Red Polished pottery are not as clear-cut as Barlow had suggested and particularly that the association between composition and shape is not straightforward. Summerhayes *et al.* argued that within the broad Red Polished ceramic series, the collection of raw materials is more arbitrary, governed by both the physical characteristics of such materials and the techniques employed in pottery production, making typo-compositional classifications of Red Polished pottery extremely difficult to determine with confidence (Summerhayes *et al.* 1996: 180).

In terms of the provenance of Red Polished pottery from Marki, Summerhayes *et al.* concluded that the majority was made locally. All mineral inclusions identified in the Marki samples can be found in the nearby volcanic and intrusives (Summerhayes *et al.* 1996: 179). Barlow and her collaborators, more reserved in their conclusions, avoided assigning a definitive provenance to the Red Polished pottery from Alambra. On the contrary, Barlow argued that "it is not possible to identify a ware, fabric or shape that originates specifically in Alambra" (Barlow 1996a: 265). Moreover, while there are some recorded morphological characteristics of Red Polished juglets and small bowls that could be linked with local production, there is an overall homogeneity in pottery techniques across the island (Barlow 1996a: 265).

Red Polished Fabrics from Marki under Compositional Investigation: Methodology and Analytical Results

The excavations at Marki *Alonia* (Frankel and Webb 1996; 2006) offer a unique opportunity to study technological change in ceramic production at a single settlement over a period of almost seven hundred years, from its foundation during the Philia cultural phase (ca. 2400–2200 BCE, Frankel and Webb 2006: 35) to its abandonment in MC II (2000–1700 BCE, Frankel and Webb 2006: 35) (Figure 2.2). Moreover, the systematic and detailed recording of the Marki diagnostic assemblage by Frankel and Webb (1996; 2006) provides an abundant and readily accessible dataset for a technological study of the pottery from the site, combining descriptive data with analytical assessments.

Red Polished tableware and storage vessels and Red Polished Coarse ware cooking pots and pans were selected from all periods of occupation at Marki and subjected to a detailed technological assessment in order to determine the selection and processing of raw materials and the techniques of building and firing. Fragments of mealing bins (semi-permanent oval or circular basins used for food processing),

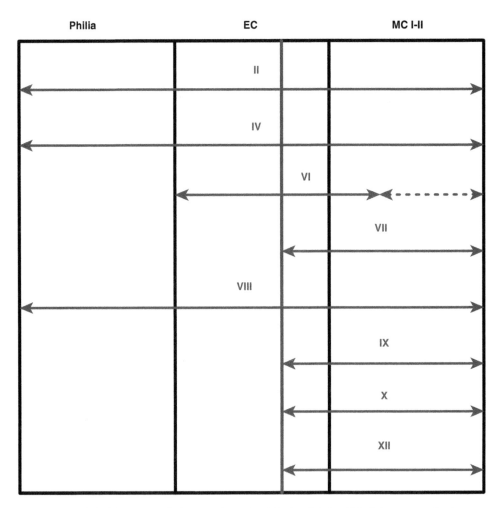

Figure 2.2: All the fabrics identified among the Red Polished and Red Polished Coarse samples from Marki and their chronological span, according to the occupational phases in which the samples were recovered. See also Dikomitou-Eliadou 2014: 203, Tables 1 and 2.

loom weights, and hobs (hearth accessories for supporting cooking pots above the fire) were also included in the analyzed samples as these are very likely to have been made locally. In addition, soil samples from clay deposits near Marki were collected with the aim of comparing and potentially associating the ceramic fabrics with the local geological context. This methodology offered the prospect of distinguishing local and imported fabrics and assessing the relationship between shapes and fabrics.

The methods employed for the analytical assessment of Early and Middle Bronze Age pottery from Marki *Alonia* were ceramic petrography and energy dispersive X-ray fluorescence spectrometry (Dikomitou 2012). This methodology shares many similarities with that applied by Barlow in the 1980s and 1990s for the study of Early and Middle Bronze Age pottery from Alambra *Mouttes*.

In the broader analytical study, the Red Polished and Red Polished Coarse ware samples from Marki were found to consist of thirteen fabric groups in total (Dikomitou 2012; Dikomitou-Eliadou 2013; 2014). Among these groups, which range in date from the Philia phase of the EC period to MC II, eight fabrics appear to have been principally employed between EC III and MC II (Figure 2.2), the chronological spectrum of a fabric defined here as the occupational phase or phases during which it was in use. The fabrics of interest in this context are Fabrics II, IV, VI, VII, VIII, IX, X, and XII (Figure 2.2, Table 2.1). These are the eight Red Polished and Red Polished Coarse pottery fabrics utilized at Marki, roughly contemporaneous with the pottery from Alambra studied by Barlow and her collaborators. Whereas some fabrics, such as II and VI, seem to have been in use throughout the life span of the settlement of Marki, others, namely VII, IX, X, and XII, were introduced in occupational Phase F, or from EC III onwards. Fabric IV was in use from the earliest periods of the settlement, while the production of Fabric VIII seems to have begun in the earlier periods and intensified during EC III.

Table 2.1 presents the general mineralogical profile of each of the eight ceramic fabrics and the attempts to correlate them with the two broad clay groups identified at Alambra by Barlow. The Marki sample is dominated by fabrics rich in igneous materials, forming the basis of two of the coarse fabrics, Fabric IV (Figure 2.3) and Fabric VIII (Figure 2.4). These appear to have been used alongside Fabrics II (Figure 2.5) and VI (Figure 2.6), which are composed of sedimentary materials. Igneous materials are also present in the finer fabrics (Figures 2.7–2.10).

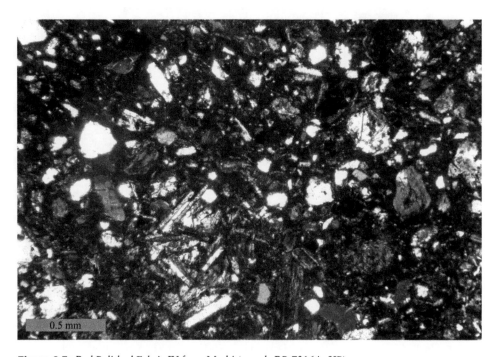

Figure 2.3: Red Polished Fabric IV from Marki (sample RP-7316 in XP).

Figure 2.4: Red Polished Fabric VIII from Marki (sample RP-13007 in XP).

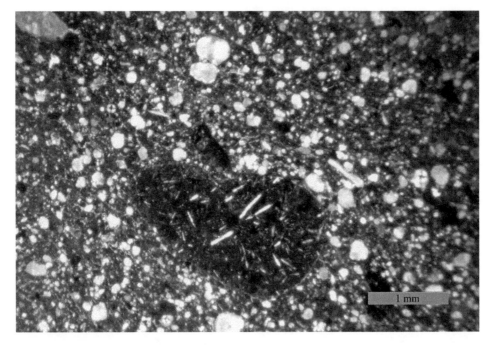

Figure 2.5: Red Polished Fabric II from Marki (sample RP-12361 in XP). Some calcite-filled foraminifera are visible.

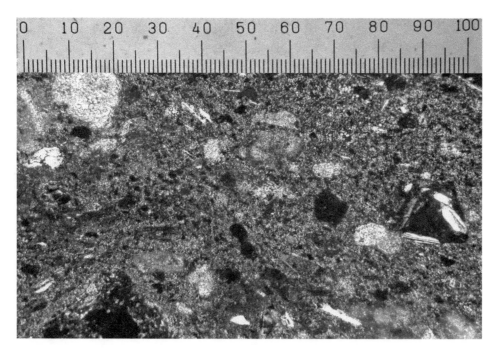

Figure 2.6: Red Polished Fabric VI from Marki (sample RP-14262 in PPL). Some calcite-filled foraminifera are visible.

The presence of igneous materials in seven of the identified fabrics (Fabrics II, IV, VI, VII, VIII, IX, and X), in the form of basalt, gabbro, and diabase fragments as well as olivine, pyroxene, altered pyroxene, amphibole, and plagioclase grains, indicates that the raw materials for their production came from areas around the circumference of the Troodos mountain range (Constantinou 2002; Gass 1960).

Statistical manipulation of the elemental data that were generated with the employment of energy dispersive X-ray fluorescence spectrometry further confirmed these mineralogical groupings (Figure 2.11A and 2.11B).

Fabrics II (Figure 2.5), IV (Figure 2.3), and VIII (Figure 2.4) were used indiscriminately for the production of a number of different vessel types, including small open vessels, large open and closed vessels, pans, and mealing bins. Cooking pots were made exclusively with the non-calcareous Fabrics IV and VIII. Fabric IV was the predominant fabric for the production of cooking pots from the foundation of Marki until approximately EC III, when it was gradually replaced by Fabric VIII. Hob and loom-weight fragments were all made with Fabric VI, a local alluvial clay, also represented among the collected soil samples and suitable for these types of sun-dried artifacts. Of the remaining fabrics, Fabrics VII (Figure 2.7) and IX (Figure 2.8) were used for different types of Red Polished tableware, including small and large bowls and jars and jugs. On the other hand, Fabric X (Figure 2.9) is mainly associated with small bowls and Fabric XII (Figure 2.10) with small bowls and juglets.

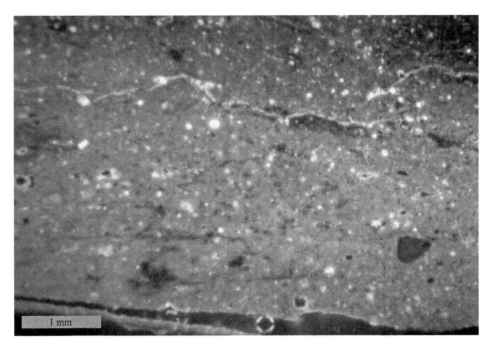

Figure 2.7: Red Polished Fabric VII from Marki (sample RP-12359 in XP).

Figure 2.8: Red Polished Fabric IX from Marki (sample RP-7359 in XP).

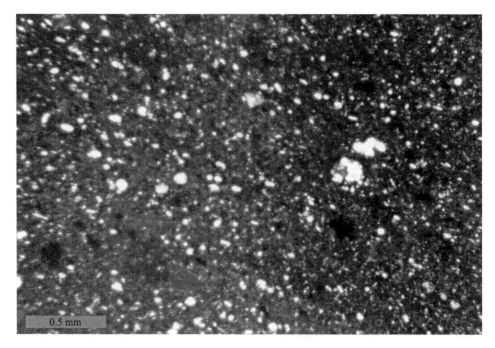

Figure 2.9: Red Polished Fabric X from Marki (sample RP-7208 in XP).

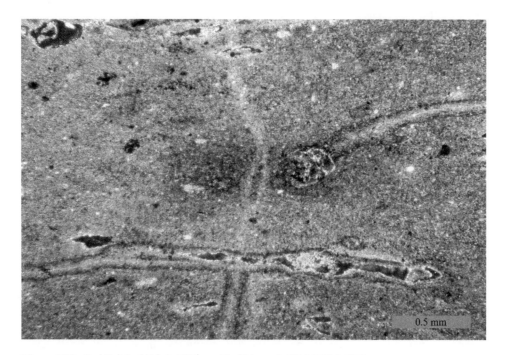

Figure 2.10: Red Polished Fabric XII from Marki (sample RP-14053 in XP).

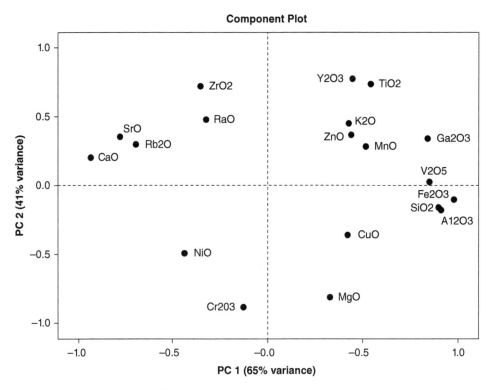

Figure 2.11A: PCA component plot based on the energy-dispersive X-ray fluorescence spectrometry dataset.

Overall, it can be argued that most fabrics were used for the production of a range of vessel types, while only cooking pots were made exclusively of specific fabrics. In other words, with the notable exception of cooking pots, there appears to be little correlation between specific vessel types and fabrics.

While the large number of fabrics in use at Marki is related to the long life span of the settlement, there are indications of technological changes in ceramic production over time. As the raw materials for the majority of these fabrics can be associated with the nearby Troodos terrane, at the northern border of which Marki is located, it would appear that most of these ceramic fabrics were either locally produced or distributed from elsewhere within the central region of the island. The typology and surface treatment of vessels in each fabric provide a useful additional means of determining for many if not all defined fabrics whether they are local to Marki or imported. Notably, the inclusion of mealing bin samples of Fabrics II and IV and both hob and loom-weight samples of Fabric VI confirms the local character of these three fabrics (see also Dikomitou-Eliadou 2014: Table 2). Overall, it seems that the community at Marki was producing utilitarian pottery and other ceramic artifacts related to everyday domestic activities using the full range of locally available fabrics. With respect to these vessel and object types, there is no strict correspondence between fabrics and specific shapes.

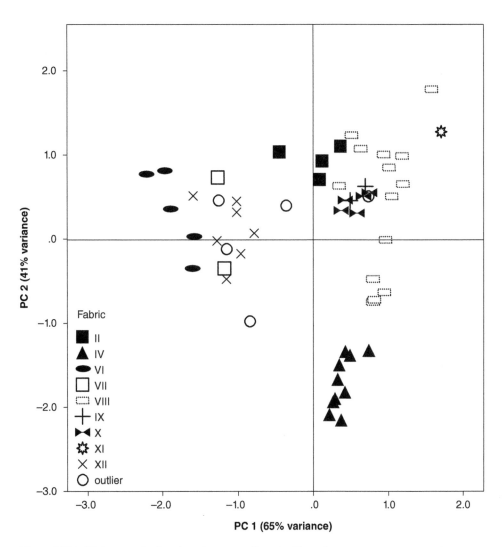

Figure 2.11B: PCA scatterplot based on the energy-dispersive X-ray fluorescence spectrometry dataset. Samples are labeled according to the fabric group to which they have been allocated with the employment of ceramic petrography.

Similar to Alambra (see Weisman 1996: 470), the Marki calcareous fabrics can be distinguished between those containing microfossils filled with recrystallized calcite and foraminiferous limestone (Fabrics II and VI) and those with open, unaltered microfossils (Fabric VII, in some cases Fabric XII and some outlier samples). As Weisman (1996: 468, 470) has already argued, these different types of microfossils indicate that the corresponding raw materials originated in different geological environments. The Alambra Group B fabric with the calcite-filled microfossils and foraminiferous limestone must have derived from the same local environment as the Marki Fabrics II and VI, as did the calcareous soil samples. On the other hand, the calcareous ceramic fabrics with the open, unaltered microfossils (Alambra Group A and Marki Fabrics VII and XII) could be imports.

Petrographic study of the local Fabrics II, IV and VI, as well as of Fabric VIII, does not indicate any detailed processing of the clays before the building of the pots. The size and distribution of the inclusions, for example, are analogous to those of analyzed soil samples. Furthermore, the presence of clay striations in one of the alluvial soil samples indicates the natural mixing of clays as part of the alluvial blend. Similar striations found in the samples of Fabrics II and VI may therefore be regarded as the result of natural processes rather than an artificial mixing of different clays.

Fabrics VII (Figure 2.7), IX (Figure 2.8), X (Figure 2.9), and XII (Figure 2.10) are finer in texture than Fabrics II, IV, VI, and VIII and contain a smaller number of inclusions, predominantly in fine fraction. These finer fabrics all date to the later periods of the settlement, to EC III and MC I–II (see Dikomitou-Eliadou 2014: 203, Table 1). It seems that from the EC III period onwards, craftspeople attempted to use finer clays and/or to more thoroughly process the clays used to produce Red Polished ware, for both calcareous and non-calcareous fabrics.

Fabric X is particularly interesting from both a technological perspective and with respect to the evolution of Red Polished ware during the EC III and MC I–II periods. This fabric is linked in the Marki sample with a series of Red Polished bowls, which are very similar mineralogically (Figure 2.9), chemically (Figures 2.11A and 2.11B), and typologically. The samples of Fabric X come from the latest phases of the settlement (Phases F to I), suggesting an increasing technological standardization from EC III onwards. Their compositional and typological consistency further suggest that these bowls are imports from another production center or that potters at Marki systematically used the same raw materials, fabric recipe, and vessel building techniques and a mode of production dependent on a more standardized operational sequence.

The other large Red Polished ware compositional group worth considering is Fabric XII (Figure 2.10). In contrast to Fabric X, which is very homogeneous both compositionally and morphologically, the samples of Fabric XII form a heterogeneous group encompassing elementally (Figures 2.11A and 2.11B) and stylistically different vessels. What unites these vessels into one compositional group is the systematic use of highly calcareous, well-processed, and/or carefully selected clays. All Fabric XII samples are, also, small bowls and juglets, and the majority have incised decoration, their soft, plastic clays and minimal inclusions being well suited to this decorative technique. While the technological similarity of this group appears clear, the energy-dispersive X-ray fluorescence analysis and the statistical manipulation of the elemental dataset (Figures 2.11A and 2.11B) clearly indicate that Fabric XII consists of chemically dissimilar vessels, indicating the use of different raw material resources and possibly different production centers.

Incised Red Polished pottery is also found in a coarser version, made with less calcareous clays. This variant seems to belong to a different ceramic tradition than the one used for the production of the finer and more carefully decorated vessels of Fabric XII. The cruder execution of the incised motifs on these samples primarily relates to the coarser nature of the clays that belong chiefly to Fabrics II and IX. Fabric II (Figure 2.5) contains large igneous inclusions, which obstruct the smooth and uninterrupted flow of the incising tool. On the other hand, Fabric IX (Figure 2.8) is calcareous but not as soft or fine, and consequently not as plastic, as calcareous Fabrics VII and XII and some of the outliers. Fabrics II and IX may have been local or regional alternatives for the production of incised pottery at Marki. A local origin for Fabric II, in particular, is indicated by its use both for this coarser type of incised Red Polished ware and utilitarian vessels such as pans and mealing bins.

A final observation relates to the Red Polished black-topped vessels in the sample, all of which are made with a fine fabric very similar to that used for Red Polished incised vessels of Fabric XII. The mineralogical and chemical variability among the Red Polished black-topped samples—one was found to be made with Fabric VII, another with Fabric XII, with the remainder classified as outliers during the petrographic study—indicates that these were imported to Marki from various production centers. This sub-variety of Red Polished ware is believed to have been produced mainly in the north and center of the island (Frankel and Webb 2006: 139), suggesting that both wider regional and extra-regional contacts were firmly in place from at least EC III.

Local and Non-Local Pottery at Marki and Alambra: A Closer Look

Being neighboring sites, Alambra and Marki are likely to have shared many technological and stylistic characteristics in pottery production, distribution, and use. Both settlements are located at the interface between the sedimentary deposits of the central lowlands and the igneous formations of the Troodos Ophiolite complex (Gass 1960; Coleman 1985: 125; Frankel and Webb 1996). Northeast of Marki, the Alykos River traverses these different geological series, collecting and depositing a large variety of rock particles and soils. This alluvial mélange was and still is easily accessible along the extent of the river. Similarly, the two watercourses in the immediate vicinity of Alambra, namely the Ammos stream, which originates to the southwest, and the Kalamoudhia stream, which originates in the area of the pillow lavas, traverse and carry with them the same raw materials (Coleman 1985: 128, Figure 2). This mélange of sedimentary and igneous materials is visible in Marki Fabrics II, VI, VII, and IX and the fabrics of Alambra Group B2 (Table 2.1).

Barlow and Idziak (1989: 73) argued for a selective use of fabrics closely related to the functional role of pottery at Alambra. In their study, Red Polished ware liquid containers of Group B2 (Table 2.1), for example, were made with volcanic clays containing significant proportions of calcareous material, while entirely non-calcareous Group B1 (Table 2.1) fabrics were used for cooking pots. On the other hand, Red Polished pottery of Group A, made with well-levigated, wholly calcareous fabrics, is primarily comprised of small incised vessels (Barlow and Idziak 1989: 74). Similar technological choices broadly governed the selection of raw materials at Marki, even though it should be stated that these typo-compositional associations were never strict. Local Fabrics II, IV, VI, and VIII at Marki were used for a variety of shapes, including pans, medium and large jars, and large and small bowls. Utilitarian vessels associated with domestic activities, such as food processing, were made with both calcareous and non-calcareous clays. This may be contrasted with the more standardized imported pottery, which would appear to derive from a different mode of production, as seen in vessels made with Fabrics X and XII.

Particular attention was paid by Webb and Frankel to cooking pots, a category of pottery that required a high degree of technological sophistication in order to meet functional requirements, including thermal shock resistance, conduction of heat, and mechanical strength (see Webb 1994: 18–19; Frankel and Webb 1996: 166–171; 2006: 100–101, 133–137). More recent analytical work (Dikomitou 2012; Dikomitou-Eliadou 2014) on cooking pots from Marki has confirmed these observations and has shown, as noted above, that cooking pots at Marki were exclusively made with Fabrics IV and VIII. Fabric IV was used for the production of cooking pots until EC III, when Fabric VIII gradually prevailed. This raises additional questions about raw material exploitation and the relationship between cooking pot fabrics and dietary habits and suggests a possible change in the organization of pottery production at Marki in EC III.

In the case of Alambra, Weisman noted that cooking pot fabrics could be distinguished from the other igneous fabrics of Group B1, as they derived from raw materials from volcanic terrain and were also substantially different from those used for the Red Polished bowls, jugs, and jars of Group B2 (Weisman 1996: 472; see also Barlow 1996: 261). Two different cooking pot fabrics were recorded at Alambra (Weisman 1996: 462–463, catalogues 11–12). Both present mineralogical similarities with the Marki cooking pot fabrics. The different recording system used in petrographic analysis and the loss of the Alambra thin sections, however, prevent a thorough comparison of the samples from the two settlements.

Another observation that supports the argument for technological changes in pottery production in EC III relates to Red Polished ware bowls, which from EC III onward became both more common and more standardized in form and fabric (Frankel and Webb 2006: 105, 149–150). The bowl samples of Fabric X in particular, as already noted, form a very homogeneous cluster, both typologically and compositionally. Similar observations were made by Weisman (1996: 471) and Barlow (Barlow and Idziak 1989; Barlow 1996a; 1996b) regarding the use of a finer, igneous fabric for the production of both small and large Red Polished bowls at Alambra. Weisman suggested that some of these reached Alambra from "outside the local radius" (Weisman 1996: 464, catalogue 15). The description of the fabric of these imported small bowls at Alambra suggests strong similarities with Fabric X at Marki. While the exact provenance of these vessels remains unclear, their igneous character leaves little doubt that they were produced within the central region.

The non-local character of these small, plain Red Polished bowls adds to our understanding of the range of vessels that circulated between sites and regions. It is clear that they included simpler pottery forms in addition to elaborately decorated vessels. This finding accords well with the increasing standardization in ceramic production evident more broadly in EC III and with the greater inter-site typological uniformity observed during this period.

More broadly, an island-wide convention can be observed in the use of thoroughly processed or naturally fine inclusion-free clays for the production of Red Polished incised pottery. The selection of these fine calcareous clays was evidently associated with the physical properties of the resulting fabric, the plasticity and fineness of which facilitated the execution of elaborately incised motifs. The presence of an early Red Polished sample (RP-3609) in Fabric XII at Marki suggests that this ceramic tradition has its roots in EC I, if not earlier, and became more widespread for the production of Red Polished III incised pots in EC III. Indeed, highly calcareous fabrics were first used for the production of vessels with incised decoration during the Philia phase (Dikomitou 2012; Dikomitou-Eliadou 2013). It would appear, then, to have been a longstanding tradition, which is likely to have evolved initially in the north of the island (Webb and Frankel 2013a: 72).

In considering the entire sample of finely incised Red Polished vessels from Marki, many differing fabrics are evident. In addition to incised Red Polished vessels made with Fabric XII, one finely incised jug (RP-4864) is of Fabric VII, while an elaborately incised bowl (RP-12372) is classified as an outlier, presenting no compositional similarities with any of the recorded fabrics. This fabric variability suggests that incised Red Polished pottery was reaching Marki from more than one production center. At least one of these centers seems to have been located on the north coast, as the decorative motifs on Red Polished III gourd juglet RP-7256 suggest (Webb, personal communication), while the igneous components in RP-4864, made with Fabric VII, suggest that finely incised Red Polished pottery was also made in the central region of the island.

It seems that Red Polished pottery production at both Marki and Alambra operated at several levels, one characterizing local production aimed at serving community needs with little attention paid to sophistication, while finer pottery produced with overt surface preparation and decoration was being made in more specialized contexts and circulating between settlements. The presence of finer, wholly calcareous Red Polished pottery at Marki and Alambra, made with Fabric XII/Group A, is certainly indicative of inter-regional networks of distribution. On the other hand, the fine and coarser ceramic artifacts found at both sites, made with fabrics characterized by igneous components, represent more restricted local and intra-regional networks.

Refocusing Perspectives on Red Polished Pottery

Red Polished ware pottery has been studied for the past century, and scholars have constructed many variant inferences over the years regarding the mode and organization of ceramic production and distribution, with implications for understanding the degree of complexity and social organization of Early and Middle Cypriot communities. A recent article by Webb illustrates meticulously how numerous studies have contributed to this "evolving story" (Webb 2014: 213).

Frankel and Webb, both individually and together, have addressed the scale and context of ceramic production in Early and Middle Bronze Age Cyprus (e.g., Frankel 1994; 1991; 1988; 1974a; 1974b; Frankel and Webb 2001; 2012; 2014; Webb and

Frankel 2013a; 2013b; Webb 2014). Frankel's (1981: 96–97) initial argument for local, small-scale production units has recently been revised in favor of a "model of elementary specialization" (Frankel and Webb 2001). Population estimates during the lifetime of the settlement at Marki combined with estimated household pottery discard/replacement rates suggest that individual households were unlikely to have produced their own pottery, as replacement requirements fall below a level of economic efficiency (Frankel and Webb 2001: 126; Webb 2014: 216–217). Instead, it may have been more efficient for a small number of local "potting households" to engage in part-time manufacture and exchange (Frankel and Webb 2001: 126). This "model of elementary specialization" may explain the degree of compositional variability among the local Marki sample as well as the relatively low degree of standardization. Local potters at Marki appear to have primarily produced simple shapes suited for everyday domestic and other utilitarian tasks.

The pottery workshop excavated by Dikaios at Ambelikou *Aletri* in 1942 but only recently published (Webb and Frankel 2013b; Frankel and Webb 2014) has both confirmed the existence of pottery workshops outside the household environment and provided a picture of a specialized (or semi-specialized) pottery workshop from Middle Bronze Age Cyprus. While there is no other evidence deriving from production *loci* in Early and Middle Bronze Age Cyprus, which might allow us to compare workshops operating at different scales of production, that is for local, regional and interregional distribution networks, the Red Polished pottery itself allows some further observations on production and distribution.

As in the case of Alambra and Marki, the petrographic study of Red Polished pottery from Sotira *Kaminoudhia*, Episkopi *Phaneromeni A* and Episkopi *Phaneromeni G*, Kalavasos *Panayia Church* and Kalavasos *Cinema Area*, and Nicosia *Ayia Paraskevi* (Barlow and Vaughan 1992; 1999, and recent re-examination by the author) has indicated that the majority of vessels were made using raw materials found within the immediate vicinity of each settlement. Vaughan has argued that local potters exploited calcareous and igneous clays, from both residual and alluvial sources (Vaughan n.d.), with particular material properties (e.g., porosity, permeability, strength, toughness, thermal shock resistance, fineness, color) guiding the choice of raw material (Vaughan n.d.). As at Alambra and Marki, however, there is no evidence to suggest that individual fabrics were used exclusively for the production of specific pottery types.

Concerning the compositional study of Red Polished pottery from the center and south of Cyprus, it is important to consider two factors. The first is what appears to have been a widely shared knowledge of production technology; second is the access to similar types of clays in the northern and southern foothills of the Troodos, carried by rivers that flow through similar, if not identical, geological formations (Barlow and Vaughan 1996). From a methodological standpoint, these factors confirm that the mineralogical study of Red Polished pottery, or any other kind of Cypriot pottery, cannot solely be used as a solution for addressing issues of provenance. On the contrary, such studies require a combination of compositional techniques, together with the kind of detailed typological and stylistic analyses on which every archaeometric study of pottery should be founded.

In central and southern Cyprus, it is now clear that during the EC I and II phases, Red Polished ware production involved a hard-fired, dark, gritty fabric, which dominates the utilitarian assemblage at each site (Georgiou *et al.* 2011: 282). This model of local production for the majority of vessel types clearly continued in both regions in EC III and into the MC period, as indicated by intra-site typological and compositional consistency and the sheer quantity of vessels at each site (Georgiou *et al.* 2011; Eccleston *et al.* 2011; Frankel and Webb 2012; Dikomitou-Eliadou 2013; 2014).

The imported pottery at Marki and Alambra reflects, as already noted, a considerable degree of interaction between these settlements and other regions of the island, both to the north and the south. Fabric variability among the non-local Red Polished vessels, comprising at least Fabrics VII, X, and XII at Marki and many outlier samples, indicates that imports came from numerous different production centers. From EC III onwards, there is increasing evidence for an island-wide tradition in operation for the production of Red Polished III pottery (Webb 2014: 220), which suggests of changing systems of interaction. The technological changes observed in the Marki sample in this transitional period, especially the refinement of fabrics and the growing degree of typological and compositional standardization, should be considered in relation to population increase at the settlement (Frankel and Webb 2001: 120) and stronger inter-community and inter-regional interaction manifested by the island-wide Red Polished III tradition.

Both in terms of technology and organization, it appears that Early and Middle Bronze Age pottery production operated in at least two modes. Ceramic production at Marki and Alambra belonged to a more modest mode, perhaps typical for most villages in central and south Cyprus, being very different from practices represented by the imported pottery at the two settlements. These differing modes of production and distribution seem to have existed from the beginning of the Bronze Age (Webb and Frankel 2013a; Dikomitou-Eliadou 2013; 2014; Webb 2014), and reflect the evolving systems of interaction within and between EC and MC communities.

The classification, analysis, and interpretation of ceramic fabrics are not easy tasks, and they are heavily dependent on the type of analytical method, the experience and perspective of the researcher, and the sampling strategy. A new direction in the study of Red Polished pottery could focus more methodically and systematically on the differing modes of ceramic production outlined in this paper, trying to compare and illustrate them in technological and compositional terms, using archaeometry and ethnographic parallels from the island's more recent past to enhance our understanding of Early and Middle Bronze Age Cyprus.

Acknowledgments

It was an honor for me to contribute to *New Directions in Cypriot Archaeology*, and I am extremely grateful to Sturt Manning, Catherine Kearns, and Jeffrey Leon for their invitation and warm hospitality at Cornell during the days of the conference and for their support and patience during the preparation of the publication of the conference proceedings. Special thanks are due especially to Catherine Kearns for her manifold comments and suggestions on an earlier version of this paper and to the two anonymous reviewers for their comments. I would also like to express my everlasting gratitude to David Frankel and Jennifer M. Webb for giving me the permission to study ceramic samples from their excavations at Marki *Alonia* and most significantly for their continuous support and generous advice. I would like to warmly thank Jennifer M. Webb in particular for reviewing an earlier version of this paper and for dedicating time and effort to revise the language and comment on the arguments proposed. Also, I thank my colleague and friend Artemis Georgiou for preparing Figure 2.1 for me in ArcGIS. Finally, I would like to express my overdue thank you to Jane Barlow and Sarah J. Vaughan for sending me their published and unpublished work on Red Polished pottery and those surviving ceramic thin sections.

References

Åström, P. 1957. *The Middle Cypriote Bronze Age*. Lund, Sweden: Hakan Ohlssons Boktryckeri.

Barlow, J.A. 1989. Red Polished ware: Toward clarifying the categories. *Report of the Department of Antiquities, Cyprus*: 51–58.

Barlow, J.A. 1991. New light on Red Polished ware. In Barlow, J.A., D.L. Bolger, and B. Kling (eds.), *Cypriot Ceramics: Reading the Prehistoric Record*, 51–58. University Museum Monograph 74. University Museum Symposium series, Vol. 2. Pennsylvania: The A.G. Leventis Foundation and the University Museum of Archaeology and Anthropology, University of Pennsylvania.

Barlow, J.A. 1994. Notes on decoration of Red Polished ware. *Report of the Department of Antiquities, Cyprus*: 45–50.

Barlow, J.A. 1996a. Chapter F: Pottery. In J.E. Coleman, J.A. Barlow, M.K. Mogelonsky, and K.W. Schaar, *Alambra: A Middle Bronze Age Settlement in Cyprus. Archaeological Investigations by Cornell University 1974–1985*, 237–323. Studies in Mediterranean Archaeology 118. Jonsered, Sweden: Paul Åströms Förlag.

Barlow, J.A. 1996b. Appendix 6: Technical studies of Alambra pottery. In J.E. Coleman, J.A. Barlow, M.K. Mogelonsky, and K.W. Schaar, *Alambra: A Middle Bronze Age Settlement in Cyprus. Archaeological Investigations by Cornell University 1974–1985*, 437–446. Studies in Mediterranean Archaeology 118. Jonsered, Sweden: Paul Åströms Förlag.

Barlow, J.A., and J.E. Coleman. 1982. Alambra and the earliest phases of the Cypriot Bronze Age. *Report of the Department of Antiquities, Cyprus*, 71–79.

Barlow, J.A., and P. Idziak. 1989. Selective use of clays at a Middle Bronze Age site in Cyprus. *Archaeometry* 31: 66–76.

Barlow, J.A., and S.J. Vaughan. 1992. Cypriot Red Polished ware: A regional study in materials and technology. In P. Åström (ed.), *Acta Cypria: Acts of an International Congress on Cypriot Archaeology Held in Göteborg on 22–24 August 1991*, part 3, 6–22. Jonsered, Sweden: Paul Åströms Förlag.

Barlow, J.A., and S.J. Vaughan. 1996. Geology and pottery at seven sites in Cyprus. Paper given at annual meeting of American Schools of Oriental Research, New Orleans, November 24, 1996.

Barlow, J.A., and S.J. Vaughan. 1999. Breaking into Cypriot pottery: Recent insights into Red Polished ware. In P. Betancourt, V. Karageorghis, R. Laffineur, and W.D. Niemeier (eds.), *Meletemata: Studies in Aegean Archaeology*, 15–20. Vol. 1. AEGAEUM 20. Liège, Belgium: Université de Liège.

Coleman, J.E. 1985. Investigations at Alambra, 1974–1984. In V. Karageorghis (ed.), *Archaeology in Cyprus, 1960–1985*, 125–142. Nicosia: A.G. Leventis Foundation.

Coleman, J.E., J.A. Barlow, M.K. Mogelonsky, and K.W. Schaar. 1996. *Alambra: A Middle Bronze Age settlement in Cyprus. Archaeological Investigations by Cornell University, 1974–1985*. Studies in Mediterranean Archaeology 118. Jonsered, Sweden: Paul Åströms Förlag.

Constantinou, G. 2002. *Η γεωλογία της Κύπρου*. Nicosia: Department of Geological Surveys, Ministry of Agriculture, Natural Resources and Environment, Republic of Cyprus.

Dikomitou, M. 2012. Ceramic Production, Distribution and Social Interaction. An Analytical Approach to the Study of Early and Middle Bronze Age Pottery from Cyprus. Unpublished PhD dissertation, University College London, Institute of Archaeology.

Dikomitou-Eliadou, M. 2013. Interactive communities at the dawn of the Cypriot Bronze Age: An interdisciplinary approach to Philia phase ceramic variability. In A.B. Knapp, J.M. Webb, and A. McCarthy (eds.), *J.R.B. Stewart: An Archaeological Legacy*, 23–31. Studies in Mediterranean Archaeology 139. Uppsala, Sweden: Åströms Förlag.

Dikomitou-Eliadou, M. 2014. Rescaling perspectives: Local and island-wide ceramic production in Early and Middle Bronze Age Cyprus. In J.M. Webb (ed.), *Structure, Measurement, and Meaning: Studies on Prehistoric Cyprus in Honour of David Frankel*, 199–211. Studies in Mediterranean Archaeology 143. Uppsala: Åströms Förlag.

Eccleston, M.A.J., D. Frankel, and J.M. Webb. 2011. XRF analysis of pottery. In G. Georgiou, J.M. Webb, and D. Frankel, *Psematismenos-Trelloukas: An Early Bronze Age Cemetery in Cyprus*, 259–277. Nicosia: Department of Antiquities, Cyprus.

Frankel, D. 1974a. *Middle Cypriot White Painted Pottery: An Analytical Study of the Decoration*. Studies in Mediterranean Archaeology 42. Göteborg, Sweden: Paul Åströms Förlag.

Frankel, D. 1974b. Inter-site relationships in the Middle Bronze Age of Cyprus. *World Archaeology* 6: 190–208.

Frankel, D. 1981. Uniformity and variation in a Cypriot ceramic tradition: Two approaches. *Levant* 13: 88–106.

Frankel, D. 1988. Pottery production in prehistoric Bronze Age Cyprus: Assessing the problem. *Journal of Mediterranean Archaeology* 1.2: 27–55.

Frankel, D. 1991. Ceramic variability: Measurement and meaning. In J.A. Barlow, D.L. Bolger, and B. Kling (eds.), *Cypriot Ceramics: Reading the Prehistoric Record*, 241–252. University Museum Monograph 74, University Museum Symposium series, Vol. 2. Pennsylvania: The A.G. Leventis Foundation and the University Museum of Archaeology and Anthropology, University of Pennsylvania

Frankel, D. 1994. Colour variation on prehistoric Cypriot Red Polished pottery. *Journal of Field Archaeology* 21.2: 205–219.

Frankel, D., and J.M. Webb. 1996. *Marki Alonia: An Early and Middle Bronze Age Town in Cyprus: Excavations 1990–1994*. Studies in Mediterranean Archaeology 123.1. Jonsered, Sweden: Paul Åströms Förlag.

Frankel, D., and J.M. Webb. 2001. Population, households, and ceramic consumption in a prehistoric Cypriot village. *Journal of Field Archaeology* 28.1–2: 115–129.

Frankel, D., and J.M. Webb. 2006. *Marki Alonia: An Early and Middle Bronze Age Settlement in Cyprus. Excavations 1995–2000*. Studies in Mediterranean Archaeology 123.2. Sävedalen, Sweden: Paul Åströms Förlag.

Frankel, D., and J.M. Webb. 2012. Pottery production and distribution in prehistoric Bronze Age Cyprus: An application of pXRF analysis. *Journal of Archaeological Science* 39: 1380–1387.

Frankel, D., and J.M. Webb. 2014. A potter's workshop from Middle Bronze Age Cyprus: New light on production context, scale and variability. *Antiquity* 88: 425–440.

Gass, I.G. 1960. *The Geology and Mineral Resources of the Dhali Area*. Memoir no. 4. Nicosia: Geology Survey Department Cyprus.

Georgiou, G., J.M. Webb, and D. Frankel. 2011. *Psematismenos-Trelloukas: An Early Bronze Age Cemetery in Cyprus*. Nicosia: Department of Antiquities, Cyprus.

Gjerstad, E. 1926. *Studies on Prehistoric Cyprus*. Uppsala, Sweden: Uppsala Universitets Arsskrift.

Myres, J.L. 1914. *Handbook of the Cesnola Collection of Antiquities from Cyprus*. New York: Metropolitan Museum of Art.

Myres, J.L., and M. Ohnefalsch-Richter. 1899. *A Catalogue of the Cyprus Museum with a Chronicle of Excavations Undertaken since the British Occupation and Introductory Notes on Cypriote Archaeology*. Oxford: Clarendon Press.

Sandwith, T.B. 1877. On the different styles of pottery found in ancient tombs in the island of Cyprus. *Archaeologia* 45: 127–142.

Sneddon, A. 2015. Revisiting Alambra: Defining the spatial configuration and social relations of a prehistoric Bronze Age settlement in Cyprus. *Journal of Mediterranean Archaeology* 28.2: 141–170.

Stewart, J.R. 1962. The Early Cypriote Bronze Age. In P. Dikaios and J.R. Stewart, *The Swedish Cyprus Expedition—The Stone Age and the Early Bronze Age in Cyprus*, Vol. IV, part 1A, 205–300. Lund, Sweden: Håkan Ohlssons Boktrycheri.

Summerhayes, G.R., D. Frankel, and J.M. Webb. 1996. Electron microprobe analysis of pottery. In D. Frankel and J.M. Webb, *Marki Alonia: An Early and Middle Bronze Age Town in Cyprus: Excavations 1990–1994*, 175–180. Studies in Mediterranean Archaeology 123.1. Jonsered, Sweden: Paul Åströms Förlag.

Vaughan, S. n.d. A regional study of the materials and technology of Cypriot Red Polished ware: A petrographic assessment. Unpublished report.

Webb, J.M. 1994. Techniques of pottery manufacture at Marki Alonia. *Archaeologia Cypria* 3: 12–21.

Webb, J.M. 2014. Pottery production and distribution in prehistoric Bronze Age Cyprus: The long road from measurement to meaning. In J.M. Webb (ed.), *Structure, Measurement, and Meaning: Studies on Prehistoric Cyprus in Honour of David Frankel*, 213–227. Studies in Mediterranean Archaeology 143. Uppsala, Sweden: Åströms Förlag.

Webb, J.M., and D. Frankel. 2013a. Cultural regionalism and divergent social trajectories in Early Bronze Age Cyprus. *American Journal of Archaeology* 117: 59–81.

Webb, J.M., and D. Frankel. 2013b. *Ambelikou Aletri: Metallurgy and Pottery Production in Middle Bronze Age Cyprus*. Studies in Mediterranean Archaeology 138. Uppsala, Sweden: Åströms Förlag.

Weisman, R.M. 1996. Appendix 7: Petrographic analyses of pottery from Alambra. In J.E. Coleman, J.A. Barlow, M.K. Mogelonsky, and K.W. Schaar, *Alambra: A Middle Bronze Age settlement in Cyprus. Archaeological Investigations by Cornell University 1974–1985*, 447–473. Studies in Mediterranean Archaeology 118. Jonsered, Sweden: Paul Åströms Förlag.

3

Environment and Sociopolitical Complexity on Prehistoric Cyprus

Observations, Trajectories, and Sketch

STURT W. MANNING

Introduction

This study resumes discussions in earlier work, in particular Manning (1993). That paper considered especially the role and impacts of the so-called secondary products revolution and prestige goods in creating a context for the development of socio-economic complexity on Cyprus. Among others, Bolger (2003: 8–9) fairly critiqued aspects and—apart from criticizing what she identified as an inherent androcentric bias—in particular complained that

> we are left to puzzle over the identity of elite and non-elites. Who, in particular, created the necessary "agricultural surplus" that "allowed their support and sponsorship of specialized production"? Who, in economic and political terms, benefitted from those new productive strategies? (Bolger 2003: 8)

And, although "probably not the result that Manning intended," Bolger goes on to argue that there is a

> general assumption that "big events" function as "prime movers" in prehistory and "in conjunction with a "gender neutral" narrative of the past . . . [this leads to] essential views. . . [and] an unmediated view of the past in which men played prominent and instrumental roles in the transformation of societies from simple egalitarian villages to complex urban polities, while women . . . contributed only marginally to those developments. (Bolger 2003: 9)

So: who did what and how/why? This concern segues directly with another recurring issue or explanatory problem in all such discussions of the development of socio-political complexity from early prehistory onwards, namely: how and why one (or more) group(s), those who become the subsequent "elite," were allowed to claim or to negotiate or to establish power successfully over others. In other words, why did some, a majority, give up rights and autonomy to a minority (see Gamble 1986: 41)? Resistance and negotiation are always possible (Scott 1985), and all power relations are relations of autonomy and dependence (Giddens 1979: 93). Thus, what circumstances led a substantive number in a society to decide to recognize, and so confer, authority? Once power (and hierarchy) is established, then it is usually argued that the ultimate basis for ongoing power is the recognized duality of both threat and protection from the potential and real exercise of force (broadly defined). But why make the initial choice, especially within a fluid "prior" context, where, although perhaps somewhat stronger, the would-be elite did not hold any monopoly on force, nor an acknowledged status? It is also a context where other groups could simply move away as an alternative, since Cyprus lacks the strong topographic and environmental "caging" or circumscription constraints on agricultural land of some special-case instances like the Nile Valley in Egypt or the key river-irrigation circumstances of Mesopotamia, the Indus, or the valleys of Peru (Carneiro 1970). Indeed, Peltenburg (1993: 9, quote from abstract) argued that just such a logic applied across the two thousand years of the Chalcolithic on Cyprus, with "recurrent community fissioning caused by resistance to attempts by subgroups to extend power." What changed?

Or are we asking the wrong questions? Scholars have long observed that potential power resources within societies can tend to be either more corporate or more exclusionary (Renfrew 1974) and that complex societies tend to divide into more group-oriented versus more individualizing forms (Blanton *et al.* 1996) or more hierarchical versus more heterarchical types. But increasingly, we recognize aspects of both of these poles as in fact present in most cases depending on perspective (Yoffee 2005). Thus, as argued by Blanton and Fargher (2016), it may be more productive to explain cooperation. The arguments of Reemtsma (2012) seem relevant: trust (and the associated perceived benefits), not violence or coercion, forms the ultimate source of lasting power (as Kissinger likewise observes: "Any system of world order, to be sustainable, must be accepted as just—not only by leaders, but also by citizens" [2014: 8]). Thus, how did some groups engender trust and permission and provide opportunity and benefits without creating self-defeating opposition and resistance?

To offer some contribution to these discussions, I wish to elaborate a little further on the steps of socioeconomic transformation in Cyprus from the third to second millennia BCE and to address which group(s) were involved, and why, and thus try at least partly to address some past explanatory weaknesses. In particular, I want to consider the who, and why, concerning the advent and impact of the secondary products agropastoral revolution on Cyprus. I argue that this great transformation in human history had a particular potential and could form a basis for subsequent social, political, and economic trajectories in semi-arid contexts like Cyprus. I continue to employ a largely gender-neutral lens but note and accept that in nearly all cases the secondary products revolution (in its various forms) initiated or coalesced entanglements (see Hodder 2011) that engendered radical and long-lasting changes in, among other things, gender roles (e.g., Hodder 1990; Bolger 2003: 38–39, 106)— while observing critique, complications, and varying scenarios (Bolger 2010: 508).

Blessed or Marginal?

Most of lower-elevation Cyprus—where many of the known major prehistoric and historic sites are located—is semi-arid to arid, and drought is a real threat (e.g., Christodoulou 1959: 28; see map in Figure 3.1).

Christodoulou (1959: 51), for example, discusses how serious drought in 1902 led to substantial emigration, and droughts (or extreme heat/dryness) are a feature of Cypriot history (e.g., Stewart 1908: 38; Hill 1940: 13; Harris 2007; Iacovou 2013: 19–21; Kaniewski *et al.* 2013; Griggs *et al.* 2014). Iacovou concludes that "the island's many and different landscapes were *marginal . . .*" (2013: 21, emphasis added). This situation and the challenges of marked inter-annual variability in climate are evident from instrumental meteorological records (see below), from reconstructions both for the island and the wider eastern Mediterranean region over the past couple of centuries to nine hundred years (Griggs *et al.* 2014; Touchan *et al.* 2014; Cook *et al.* 2016), and from reviews of historical and other information for Cyprus (e.g., Kypris 1996) and the wider Mediterranean (e.g., Horden and Purcell 2000). In pre-modern (pre-irrigation) times much of lower elevation Cyprus and especially the central area (broadly the Mesaoria Plain or central lowlands) fall into the range of what is termed dry land farming where water availability is a challenge (Christodoulou 1959: 21, 28, 122)—despite much of this area forming the "granary of Cyprus," the main zones on the island where cereals are grown (Christodoulou 1959: 127, 205, Figures 64, 66).

Figures 3.2–3.4 show the average distribution of annual rainfall across the eastern Mediterranean, and then specifically for Cyprus, for the years 1960–1990. There is no agreed definition, but the lowland areas of Cyprus typically fall into the categories of semi-arid or arid (FAO 2004: ch. 2; FAO 1987; Bruggeman *et al.* 2015: Figure 1; http://environ.chemeng.ntua.gr/AquastressCS/Default.aspx?t=288—accessed 10 September 2016). Most lowland areas not fortunate to be close to one of the perennial rivers were thus "marginal."

At the same time, it is important to consider exactly what *marginal* means in such a semi-arid context. In themselves, the terms *semi-arid* and *arid* are but *average* descriptions. In mere subsistence terms the key issue is that in arid and semi-arid circumstances years with below-average rainfall may well be heading toward, or fall below, the usual useful productive thresholds for some of the likely dry land farming subsistence crops, especially wheat and barley. There are other critical natural risks for cereal farmers in addition, like locust plagues, which were a feature of early modern to recent Cyprus (Jennings 1988; Christodoulou 1959: 125). Similarly, as in a study considering southeast China (Stige *et al.* 2007), we might anticipate some correlation of locust plagues with drought years, which would only worsen circumstances for farmers. In wider terms beyond just mere subsistence, however, the reality is that in the other more average or above average years production likely ranged from OK to good, and the land could be regarded as productive. It was not all bad—just sometimes.

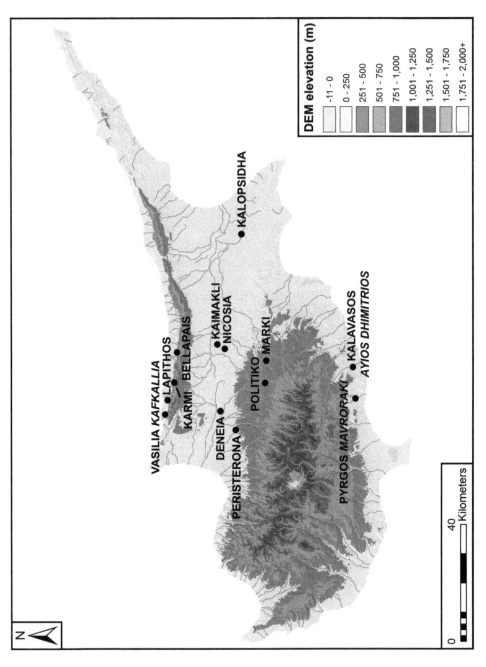

Figure 3.1: Sites mentioned in text. Created by C. Kearns; basemap provided by the Geological Survey Department of Cyprus.

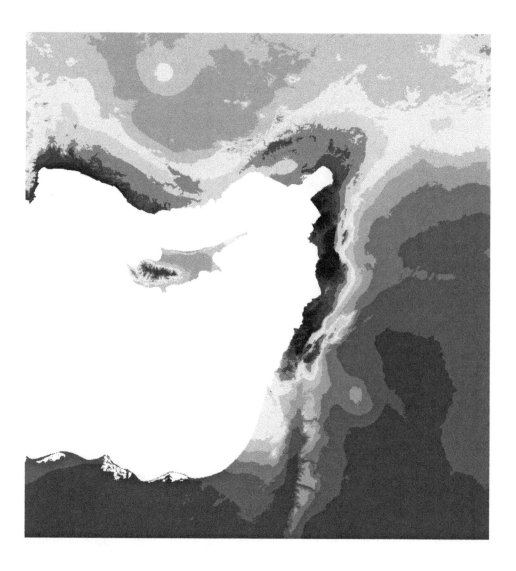

Average Precipitation in mm (1960-1990)

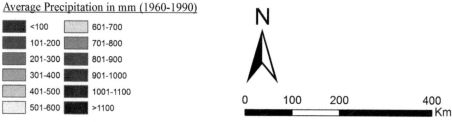

<100	601-700
101-200	701-800
201-300	801-900
301-400	901-1000
401-500	1001-1100
501-600	>1100

N

0   100   200   400
                              Km

Figure 3.2: East Mediterranean maritime region average precipitation map, 1960–1990, derived from data from the WorldClim website (http://worldclim.org/current) employing the interpolation methods between the different stations across the island described at http://worldclim.org/methods1, derived from Hijmans *et al.* (2005).

Average Precipitation in mm (1960-1990)

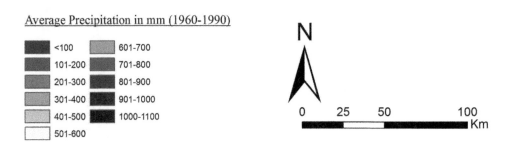

Figure 3.3: Cyprus average precipitation map 1960–1990 derived from data from the WorldClim website (http://worldclim.org/current) employing the interpolation methods between the different stations across the island described at http://worldclim.org/methods1, derived from Hijmans *et al.* (2005). Average precipitation shown in 100mm increments.

Indeed, there is the irony that the land of Cyprus was also referred to as blessed in scattered ancient sources (Plin. *HN* 5.35.129), which spurred Iacovou's (2013: 19–21) discussion of whether Cyprus had a blessed or a marginal environment (see also Kearns in this volume). As Iacovou's (2013: Figures 1–2) maps illustrate (on these maps and their construction, see Zomeni *et al.* 2014), there are relatively plentiful areas of acceptable to fertile soil on the island, and ancient and historical sources indicate at various times at least that Cyprus was not only self-sufficient in grain, etc. (Strab. 14.6.5) but even an exporter (e.g., Andoc. 20–21; Bakirtzis 1995; Michaelides 1996: 142, 146–147). This contradictory "marginality"—sometimes OK/good, sometimes bad/disaster—is captured in the first line of the description of Cyprus as a source of "corn" (cereals) by Hill (1940: 173), referring to the Ptolemaic period:

> Its corn was always—at least when it was not itself the victim of drought—available for less fortunate states; just as during the famine years 330–326 in Greece Athens was helped by private traders in Cyprus . . . so Euergetes I was able to buy corn in Cyprus . . . when Egypt was suffering from drought.

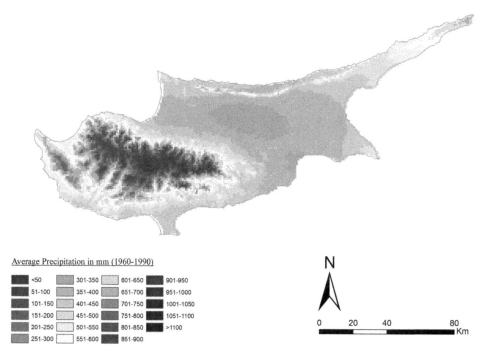

Figure 3.4: Cyprus average precipitation map 1960–1990 derived from data from the WorldClim website (http://worldclim.org/current) employing the interpolation methods between the different stations across the island described at http://worldclim.org/methods1, derived from Hijmans *et al.* (2005). Average precipitation shown in 50mm increments.

Thus we may regard marginal Cyprus as to an extent limited by its environmental context, as Iacovou (2013: 19–24) argues, but also as potentially offering an opportunity, at least sometimes.

Dryland Farming—Issues and Feeding People

To explore further the contradictions in dryland farming we can consider Wilkinson's (2004) detailed investigations in northern Syria. He observed that the minimum threshold for "viable dry farming"—in the absence of irrigation or other special water source—was an annual rainfall of somewhere around or between 200–300 mm. This limit does not mean that barley especially cannot grow with less than 200 mm of rainfall per annum but that the yields rapidly decline (Wilkinson 2004: Table 3.1). Further, although total annual rainfall variation does correlate with yield even for barley in semi-arid to arid areas (like Syria; see Mona 1986), it is the timing and distribution of the rainfall that is as, or more, important (Hadjichristodoulou 1982), and thus marked variations in total yield occur on an inter-annual timescale (Ceccarelli *et al.* 2007). Hence, as Wilkinson (2004: Table 3.1) summarizes, the real danger in the marginal zones (e.g., zones 3–5 in his table, covering 350–250 mm, 200–250 mm, and sub-200 mm average annual rainfall) is that in these zones there is real drought and "no harvest" respectively

36 percent of years (or around 1 in 3 years), 46 percent of years (or nearly 1 in 2 years), or 64 percent of years (or nearly 2 in 3 years).

The potential to feed people is similarly dynamic. Various estimates for average or minimum cereal consumption in the ancient Mediterranean region (whether stated as allowing for assumed age composition of the population or just an average) produce values of 212 kg wheat (so about 254 kg barley, at a ratio of 1:1.2) or 230 kg of grain or 250 kg of cereals per person per year (Foxhall and Forbes 1982; Garnsey 1988: 104; Wilkinson 2004: Table 7.1) and stated ancient ration statements are in fact more generous (Foxhall and Forbes 1982: 51–62, 60). Bishaw (2004: 90) observes that modern average consumption of bread wheat in the West Africa and North Africa (WANA) area, including Syria, remains very high at 170 kg per person per year—if the barley ratio was applied, this would become about 204 kg per person per year.

Wilkinson (2004: Table 3.1) reports barley yields in the 250–350 mm average annual rainfall zone 2 at on average 885 kg per hectare (and only 1 in 100 years failure), 576 kg/ha for the zone 3 at under 250–350 mm but >250 mm (and 1 in 3 years failure), and 480 kg/ha for zone 4 with 200–250 mm (and 1 in 2 years failure) and a mere 359 kg/ha for zone 5 and <200 mm rainfall on average per year (and more than 1 in 2 years failure). We can expect something similar or perhaps less (with no modern fertilizers or modern plow technology or irrigation) in pre-modern times in Cyprus in comparable rainfall zones (and not dissimilar estimates are made for pre-modern Greece and especially drier areas like Attica: see Garnsey 1988: 95). Bissa (2009: 174–175), referring to the Roman writer Columella, observes likely even more modest pre-modern barley yields—425–530 kg/ha—and it is a reasonable argument that these may better represent typical ancient circumstances. For early to mid-twentieth-century CE Cyprus (with ca. 3 donums = 1 acre and employing the British Imperial measures for barley and wheat and not US values), Christodoulou (1959: 128) reports 3.7 bushels per donum for barley in a bad year (about 702 kg/ha) and the best average he reports corresponds to 1557 kg/ha. Wheat is the lower-yielding (if more valuable) crop, which in 1947–1948 (a very poor year) produced on average 2.8 bushels per donum (about 598 kg/ha) and in the worst year on record in 1951 averaged 2.1 bushels per donum (about 448 kg/ha; Christodoulou 1959: 125–126). The best average yield Christodoulou (1959: 125) reports for wheat is equivalent to 1111 kg/ha. Note the large range—to which I will return.

Before calculating people from available food supply, we must remember that some of any harvest is required for seed for the following year. Wilkinson allows for 50 kg (2004: Table 7.1), and this is very much a minimum, since it seems likely that broadcast sowing, versus a seeding plow, was employed in prehistoric Cyprus. Broadcast sowing, while requiring low labor input, is relatively inefficient in contrast with the very capital- and labor-intensive methods including the seeding plow linked with irrigated fields known for example from ancient Mesopotamia (Potts 1997: 78–84). In modern circumstances for rain-fed broadcast sowing and plow use, 150 kg/ha of seed is recommended in Ethiopia and 120–150 kg/ha of seed in Syria

(Bishaw 2004: 44, 110–111), and observed practice varies widely but from above 100 kg/ha (Bishaw 2004: Tables 2.5, 3.10, 3.11)—the actual optimum in Syria for wheat is stated as 110 kg/ha for wheat and 100 kg/ha for barley (Bishaw 2004: 110). This is about double the Wilkinson estimate. And of course, a sustainable model would include at least a seed reserve to tide over a bad year, so let us consider at least 100–200 kg for total seed.

Therefore, putting the above information together, in a bad year 1 ha of barley would have supported about two people versus at least five in a good year—a big difference; likewise in a bad year, 1 ha of wheat could support around one person, but maybe four or five persons in a good year—again, note the big difference. (I note that the above heuristic discussion has focused solely on cereals. Of course there were other important aspects of diet and of the rural economy, such as olive oil—for Late Bronze Age, LBA, Cyprus: see e.g., Keswani 2015. I focus on cereals here for reasons of space, however, and as they likely formed the key subsistence resource.)

Traditional agriculture usually employed alternative fallow years. Wilkinson allowed for 2 ha to support one person over time including bad years (2004: Table 7.1) in areas with yields of at least 300 kg/ha, so in such a situation even a modest three-hundred-person agricultural village requires some 600 ha of farmland, or all land within a 1.4-km radius (see Wilkinson 2004: Table 7.1). In most realities, given less than completely available and favorable geography around any given settlement and slightly more conservative seed allowances, the requirement is in fact for a somewhat larger total land area and thus radius of exploitation and, in turn, greater maximum travel distances/times for the farming inhabitants.

These subsistence data combine to suggest that Cyprus is able to support only a relatively low population density on average and is not a context that is generally suitable for significant intensification. It is toward the opposite of the geographic circumscription scenario outlined by Carneiro (1970) or the essentially similar social and spatial "caging" logic employed by Mann (1986). Applied to Cyprus as a whole, it instead suggests relatively low population density in most areas *on average*. This was certainly the case in the early modern period. Iacovou (2013: 21) reports island-wide population densities from Christodoulou (1959: 51) that work out as ca. 20 and ca. 59.5 persons per square kilometer in 1881 and 1958, respectively. In the 1950s the percentage of Cyprus used as arable land (irrigated and non-irrigated) for crops (like cereals, etc.) or as pasture amounted to about 57 percent of the total (Christodoulou 1959: 108—that is categories 4 and 5 in total as a percent of the total categories of land use quantified in the table). If we regard this as roughly the land that can potentially support (via cereal component) a traditional population, then the 1881 and 1958 population densities versus farm/pasture land are about 35 to 104 persons per square kilometer, or 2.83 to 0.96 ha per person. Other historical estimates for the pre-modern population of Cyprus are few and of various and differing quality (Papadopoullos 1965: 16–77) but are broadly in line with the scale offered by the 1881 census under the British mandate. In the period with reports, 1490–1878 CE, most are in a range between about 100,000–200,000 total population with just a few higher estimates (e.g., 250,000 in 1600 or 259,782 in 1876;

Papadopoullos 1965: 37, 75), and these high estimates seem clearly suspect or mere guesses. The majority of the apparently better-informed estimates range from the lower to mid-100,000s to a few, for example from the high point of the Venetian period to just before the Ottoman Conquest, of around 200,000 (Papadopoullos 1965: 18–19). Papadopoullos gives these ca. 200,000 population estimates relative credence, but one must suspect a slight bias as he wishes to emphasize an upward demographic trend under Venetian rule "reversed by the catastrophic effects of the Ottoman conquest" (1965: 19). Nonetheless, if we take the lowest somewhat credible figure (106,000 in 1490) to a rough maximum of 200,000, we have an estimate of 2.6 to 5 ha of "arable and pasture" land per person on the island. This is a low-density population. Most estimates made on various criteria for the Bronze Age population of areas or sites on Cyprus achieve figures that are consonant with such a relatively low population by region (e.g., South 2014).

Diversity and Non-Diversity behind Averages

The overall low population density has several origins, but two seem obvious: (a) the limited areas of the island having fertile soil (e.g., Iacovou 2013: Figure 2), and (b) marginal rainfall, given the absence of perennial rivers in most areas. Here the marginal aspect in terms of subsistence needs to be stressed and explored. Even a low-population density in a low-yield environment is no good for survival if there are in fact relatively regular failed harvests, as in some of the areas in Wilkinson's study (zones 3–5) and as we may assume for some of central Cyprus where average annual rainfall is ≤300 mm to 350 mm (Figures 3.3–3.4). Although of course climate varies over time, and we currently lack a high-resolution climate-precipitation reconstruction for Cyprus and region before the second millennium CE (e.g., Cook *et al.* 2016), there is no reason to believe that the climate of Cyprus was substantially different in general from the range known from the past few hundred years in the period back through the third millennium BCE following the shift to more arid conditions in the mid-Holocene (e.g., Roberts *et al.* 2011; Brayshaw *et al.* 2011; Robinson *et al.* 2006). The limited historical information also suggests a broadly similar climate regime (Kypris 1996). Figure 3.5 shows the recorded rainfall for Cyprus as a whole (average) and for three meteorological stations from central Cyprus (Politiko, Peristerona, and Nicosia).

In general, there is a degree of coherence: good and bad years are often in common, and the two longer central Cyprus datasets, Nicosia and Peristerona, have a correlation of 0.73 for the common years 1926–1990. Overall, there is marked variation. Some very poor years for all stations with data stand out, like 1902, 1932, 1973, and 2008, and there are other years where all the available data indicate noticeably reduced rainfall: 1927, 1941, 1951, 1959, 1968, 1970, 1972, 1982, and 1986.

Of these stations, the area around Peristerona is clearly especially marginal: 18.8 percent of years in the record 1926–2010 received less than 200 mm of rainfall and thus could be considered as extremely marginal or poor for cereal prospects (equivalent in those years to Wilkinson 2004, zone 5). But, of course, not all land is equal. To take the Peristerona case, the village and some of the nearby farmland is

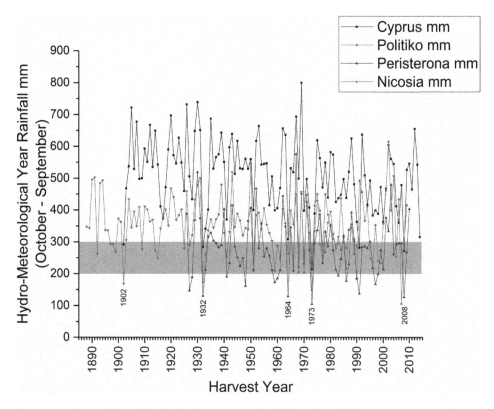

Figure 3.5: Recorded precipitation by hydro-meteorological year for all of Cyprus (average) and for three central Cyprus stations (Politiko, Peristerona, and Nicosia). Data from the Department of Meteorology, Cyprus.

near the Peristerona River, and even though this river is not perennial, the land near the river will thus have enjoyed in effect some irrigation and will have been more productive. It is the land away from the river that is really marginal. Such "marginal" land will vary from land that sits away from river water but still comprises fertile soil, which if there is rain can be productive, versus land that has soil but not soil that would be characterized as fertile and is very marginal—for example, contrast the two maps of soil versus fertile soil for Cyprus in Iacovou (2013: Figures 1–2).

Much more important in human terms, however, are consecutive years of very poor rainfall. These will challenge the usual traditional farming and recorded historical strategy of trying to store sufficient grain, seed, and other products (e.g., olive oil) to overcome the risk of one bad year (e.g., Forbes 1989: 93–94; Christakis 1999; Halstead 2014: 162; Keswani 2015: 6; Manning 2018). In these years the co-occurrence of some other problem, like locust plague, would then have been disastrous. Figure 3.6 shows the data from Figure 3.5 for the period where we have two or more stations available; we see that instances of two or more consecutive years for two or more stations (or one station and the Cyprus average) receiving less than 301 mm of rainfall occur over sixteen hydro-meteorological years, or 18.8 percent of the time.

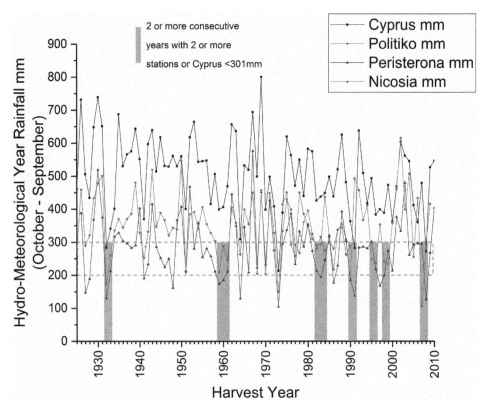

Figure 3.6: Recorded precipitation by hydro-meteorological year for all of Cyprus (average) and for three central Cyprus stations (Politiko, Peristerona, and Nicosia) for the years 1926–2010 where the data available from two+ stations or one station and the Cyprus average showed two or more consecutive years with less than 301 mm annual (hydro-meteorological year) rainfall. Data from the Department of Meteorology, Cyprus.

However, the real crisis stress of course occurs only in the second and subsequent years of these groups, when stores have run out. Second or subsequent consecutive years of two or more stations (or Cyprus average) receiving less than 301 mm of rainfall occurred in 9 of the 85 years in the record, or 10.6 percent of the time. This is not common—an important point—but does form a regular systemic risk. Kypris (1996: 121–122) refers to two historical cases from Cyprus, one from the nineteenth-century CE where, of 76 years for which there is information, 27.6 percent are described as bad or very bad (versus 53.9% good or very good and 18.4% average), and another from the early sixteenth-century CE where, of 11 years, 36 percent are listed as bad (versus 54% good and 10% average). While this evidence is relative and subjective, it nonetheless indicates a longer-term pattern of highly variable conditions with a substantive percentage as bad or unfavorable consonant both with the twentieth- to twenty-first-century instrumental data and the multi-century precipitation proxies from tree rings (Griggs *et al.* 2014; Touchan *et al.* 2014; Cook *et al.* 2016).

Access to more land in the same area does not solve the basic problem or risk of being left with no economic or survivable harvest in a given bad year in a marginal area—other "bad year" economics strategies are required to survive (see Halstead and O'Shea 1989). In semi-arid areas trading and/or using mobile animal holdings is one common strategy. Another obvious approach, but typically only once there already is social complexity and hierarchy and so on, is large-scale, beyond-household storage for durable crop products in the form of, for example, granaries that can tide a population over in bad years and be a bank and source of wealth in general. Storage within family or residential groups, such as might include trying to cover a bad year and need for seed, is evident in Early Cypriot–Middle Cypriot (EC–MC) Cyprus, but there is nothing that looks at all like a centralized or larger granary or storage facility (Knapp 2013a: 27; Tsipopoulou and South 2012: 219), and, generally, such infrastructure is the product of, not the cause of, the development of socioeconomic complexity.

In the absence of infrastructure and easy coping mechanisms beyond a one-year "bad year" window, we must assume that subsistence farmers tried to avoid too-marginal land—territory where serious risk was more than unusual or rare. There were no overriding demographic or other pressures on Cyprus during the Early Bronze Age (EBA) to Middle Bronze Age (MBA). Instead, the population will have occupied loci allowing farming of the fertile soils around drainages with low risks of lost harvests (equivalents to Wilkinson's 2004, zones 1 and 2 with 0 to 1% of years with no harvest). Maps of known prehistoric settlements largely show this for Cyprus in general (e.g., Catling 1962; Georgiou 2006) or for particular areas intensively surveyed (e.g., Given and Knapp 2003), with the richly studied EBA to MBA village of Marki *Alonia* (Frankel and Webb 1996; 2006) close to the Alykos River offering a perfect central Cyprus example. Thus, ironically, a discussion of the marginal nature of much of Cyprus in agricultural terms in fact concludes that given no other pressures or prompts, it is likely that a relatively modest population occupies a variety of the largely non-marginal (or as little marginal as possible) loci. The areas supported by the major rivers, like the Alykos-Gialias-Pedieos river system, will have been natural foci (e.g., Brown 2013). Both archaeology and history attest to this focused-density approach—leading to an overall low density of people across the island. It follows that most such settlements, in the absence of other factors, will be relatively modest conforming to the lowest-cost (in social and economic terms) small relatively egalitarian agricultural villages as typical of non-core or marginal areas of much of the Old World. Knapp (2013a: 27, 39) in fact argues that Cypriot settlements in general were at, and remained at, this sort of level through his PreBA period (until the end of MC II in the conventional chronology)—that is, through to the eighteenth-century BCE—although there are reasons to critique aspects of this characterization (see below; and see postscript).

Beginnings of Power and the Stealth Revolution

A semi-arid to arid marginal agricultural setting alone (I am not here discussing possible proximity or access to value resources like metals that may at certain times have been key to an engagement of various groups on Cyprus with the wider world) none-theless offers some options to spread risk or to create surplus. Wilkinson's (2004) study in fact indicates two likely and relevant answers. The first solution to such marginal circumstances is a paired strategy of pastoralism (e.g., Wilkinson 2004: 7; Wossink 2009). Pastoralism is of course a feature of pre-modern Cyprus also (Harris 2012) and has been highlighted as a key power resource and potential in the ancient Near East through exploitation of the (large) marginal zones (Porter 2012). The second way that more marginal land (including too-marginal land)—at least for nec-essarily risk-adverse subsistence farmers—can be exploited is when large (wealthy) landowners with capital expand into these areas and can afford "to absorb some of the risk of crop failure in order to recoup a profit during wet years. This risk is unac-ceptable to subsistence farmers in a traditional economy who must minimize risk by guaranteeing a certain minimal yield each year" (Wilkinson 2004: 41). This situa-tion is likely highly relevant to the development of prehistoric marginal cases, like Cyprus (or, for that matter, northern Syria), and is perhaps a fundamental but often not sufficiently appreciated component of the so-called secondary products revolu-tion (Sherratt 1981; 1983; see also for discussion Greenfield 2010; Marciniak 2011) and subsequent processes. I will return to this. But there is an alternative perspective to consider first.

Knapp (2013a: 39) argues that although there was some social evolution in prehistoric Cyprus through the MBA as well as some changes in the quantity and quality of grave goods and perhaps veneration of ancestors and/or negotiation of social identities, it was all very modest, with no evidence of settlement hier-archies and "no indication . . . that these practices resulted in the institutional-ization of social inequalities." He accepts that "most scholars who have studied Bronze Age Cyprus at any serious level would probably agree that the involvement of PreBA élites in social and material exchanges within and beyond the island led to changes in social organization and structure" and that "such élites may have assumed a focal position in PreBA society" (indeed, Knapp 2013b: 344–347 argues this). Yet he is firm that dramatic change—"a quantum leap in all aspects of mate-rial and social practices"—only occurs with the onset of the ProBA (so the end of MC-start Late Cypriot [LC] I period from ca. 1750–1700 BCE). Knapp (2013a: 39; Iacovou 2013 cites approvingly at 23) also observes that "certain social and environmental constraints may set ceilings on socio-political intensification," rather implying that EBA–MBA Cyprus operated under such a ceiling (Knapp's gradual evolution period) but that somehow it was shattered at the start of LBA revolution moment. But how does one get from the gradualist model to the efflorescence? Knapp (2013a: 38–39) stresses that "it is essential to investigate Cypriot prehis-tory in terms of internal developments and change. . . . Even so, the discontinuities seen in the Cypriot archaeological record equally demand that we consider internal developments within the context of the wider eastern Mediterranean worlds." If there is a single special factor, Knapp (2013a: 39) points to copper and adopts the premise that "growing demand from both within and beyond the island . . . must have resulted in increased production of copper." He states that "this intensified level of copper production to meet 'ceremonial demand' during the PreBA may well have set the stage for the transformation in copper production and exchange that is apparent at the onset of the ProBA."

I believe, however, that a couple of central issues are missing or incorrectly emphasized in Knapp's assessment. Knapp (2013a: 39) suggests that we now know enough about his PreBA (EBA–MBA) to make valid island-wide and general assessments and conclusions, writing: "Unlike the situation . . . 25 years ago, today we have the final publications of three PreBA 2 sites and several cemeteries. . . . From all this new evidence, it is clear that. . . ." However, I disagree (see also previously Manning 1993; 2014). What we know about several key areas and sites in the north of the island remains, sadly, extremely limited. Yet these areas/sites are likely pivotal during the EBA to early MBA (Webb and Frankel 2013a) (and see postscript). (One must also note that a likely key south coast site, Pyrgos *Mavrorachi*, exists, but its inappropriate and inadequate excavation and publication make it all but unknowable for respectable scholarship—noted also in Knapp 2013a: 23, 28.)

I give just two critical examples. First, we know next to nothing really—tip of the iceberg—about the *huge* and metal-rich cemetery of Vasilia *Kafkallia* (see Keswani 2004: 38, 56; 2005: 348) with its seemingly highly impressive chamber tombs of "extraordinary construction" (Keswani 2004: 56). Here one suspects—despite the lack of research since 1974—just the sort of apex site that Knapp asserts does not exist (see also Webb and Frankel 2013a: 60). The Bellapais *Vounous* tombs we do know about, but remembering we lack others as well as the contemporary settlement they represent, offer another prominent warning light. Webb and Frankel (2010: 200–202) observe and then comment (201) that "the apparently exclusive role played by *Vounous* in the development of . . . iconography in ECI and II is remarkable" (although see Knox 2013), and such a role—and the concentration of special ideologically imbued objects and entailed practices at the site (consider just for example the Vounous Bowl; see Steel 2013) might very likely indicate a (to us missing) focal site with specialists at work as part of a more complex ideological social structure.

Knapp (2013a: 27) himself is of course alert to the problem but chooses to downplay it: "Whilst there now seems little doubt that divergent social trajectories were at work in northern and central/southern regions of the island (Webb and Frankel 2013a), the material and ritual elaboration evident at northern sites such as *Vounous* was instrumental in *establishing a new social order, not an entrenched social hierarchy*" (emphasis added). Indeed the difference may be the unstated distinction between a "new social order" and "an entrenched social hierarchy." Less than a page later Knapp (2013a: 28) notes the marked mortuary elaboration and its increasing scale over the course of the PreBA and raises the likely themes of ancestor veneration and the negotiation of social identities, but he regards the critical change as only at the very end of the period (that is MC II–III), while admitting these may illustrate "the *potential* for the institutionalization of social inequalities."

But in fact, the evidence may be differently parsed to place emphasis and foundational shifts earlier. The EC–MC transition sees a fundamental shift to extramural collective burials, probably linked with the advent of plow agriculture and a focus on land, ancestors, and group identity (Keswani 2005: 348–349, 361–362), and there is significant, differential, and escalating elaboration in funerary practices during the EC (e.g., *Vounous*; see Keswani 2005: 363–370) and a "marked increase in ostentation occurring at the outset of the MC I period," at which juncture "mortuary consumption . . . escalated significantly" (e.g. Lapithos: Keswani 2005: 355, 392). Keswani (2005: 392) observes that the external contact and trade that would become so pivotal later (MC III–LC I) starts in this same late EC/early MC period (also Knapp 2013b: 307–311). Yes, Keswani (2005: 392) argues that such imports "were probably too rare to have formed essential components of Cypriot prestige symbolism for much of the EC-MC periods," supporting Knapp's argument to push structural change to late MC, but we must remember that we almost certainly lack much original evidence (e.g., because of the robbing of the Vasilia tombs). In addition, following the usual logic of prestige goods, in the early period of contact and rare exchange—when such objects are actually most socially powerful, transformational, wondrous, biography-encapsulating entities versus mere commodities (as Knapp 2013a: 21 summarizes)—there is also no inflationary and controlling logic for their removal from circulation via burial (or other forms of conspicuous consumption), rather than their continued conspicuous possession, display, and transfer above ground. Hence, this is very much a case where rare evidence in the archaeological record does not necessarily correlate with any lack of great contemporary significance—rather the reverse.

The very visible change by late MC to the start of the LC is of course both a step-change and highly significant as Knapp (2013a) argues. As Monahan and Spigelman in this volume also claim, innovations and creations in the built environment (notably, the "forts") during this in-between period shaped the better-known LBA social and political entities that followed on Cyprus. At the same time, however, I would argue that this transformation (and likely in part as response/stimulation from external influence and interest: Manning 2014: 29–31) reflects the already established and now formalized and routine structures and systems of a hierarchically organized society entering a sociopolitical form we might label as an early complex polity (Smith 2003) that was thus capable of such radical (but coherent and organized) restructuring—versus the transformational stage that enabled this and created the potential. It is this transformational stage that seems to lie earlier around the time the plow starts being central to Cypriot agriculture, and it is lost in Knapp's (2013a) synthesis. Thus, while the "forts" are, as Monahan and Spigelman argue in this volume, not products of an existing early state (or similar entity) as conceived by Peltenburg (1996), they also are not generated from a vacuum. Rather, they are solutions (reached in common or rapidly emulated, whether entirely locally or with external inspiration) capable of conception and delivery from societies where there is already sufficient hierarchy, which implies recognized leadership roles and scale to permit the organization of substantial and sustained labor required for such a monumental building project. Leaders proposing, enabling, and carrying out such society-enveloping and monumental schemes may achieve significant further authority (along the lines of Spencer 1993), and the places (and associations) and new lifeways, once made, themselves shape future developments (Fisher 2009).

Even if a reader is sympathetic of Knapp's (2013a) more minimalist assessment, we nevertheless reach a basic question. Where did the labor and time come from to obtain (mine) and process and craft all the (increasing over time) copper artifacts in the EC–MC tombs that have, despite everything, been archaeologically recovered (see Keswani 2005)? (From early MC at least, we know of some industrial workshop complexes involving mining, pottery, and other "specialized production": Knapp 2013a: 23; 2013b: 298–307; Webb and Frankel 2013b; Keswani 2005: 385–391.) Where did the time and labor come from to build and (in some cases) decorate or mark the elaborate tomb complexes of EC–MC and to craft all of the sophisticated ceramic and other non-metal objects archaeologically recovered, let alone those not recovered (Keswani 2004: 37–83; 2005; Webb *et al.* 2009; Knapp 2013b: 298–303, 311–343)? Knapp (2013b: 311) recognizes this issue: "All these factors . . . required new and different levels of communication, a new social infrastructure that involved the emergence of social alliances as well as socially differentiated groups or individuals. . . ." There must be specialists involved, and for that we have to imagine societies, at least at some of the larger or focal loci, with people who are not merely subsistence farmers but are engaged in other roles supported or financed by an underlying agricultural surplus created by others.

The plausible answer offered by scholarship is a step-change development of the agropastoral economy via development (or articulation) of a Cypriot version of the secondary products revolution (Knapp 1990; 2013b: 303–306; Manning 1993), which in turn seems to correlate with, and to explain, the shift to extramural burial and a range of new mortuary practices (and, we assume, social rituals). Additionally, we see a clear focus toward the importance of ancestors and a recognized legitimate past and social narrative (as much discussed and recognized in a range of contexts once landholding becomes important: e.g., Chapman 1981) during the EBA on Cyprus (Keswani 2005: 349; Webb and Frankel 2010). But let us return to our discussion of marginal environments and slightly rethink the secondary products revolution on Cyprus and especially the plow.

The advent of a capital-possessing group (class) who could afford to develop and maintain the equipment and infrastructure (e.g., oxen and the plow) and their impact in prehistory has been much discussed. The recognized importance of the plow and oxen—and the place of cattle as ideologically powerful symbols from this time—is evident even from the available body of coroplastic art and other representations from the EC–MC period itself (e.g., Morris 1985: 275, 278–279, 285–286; Keswani 2005: 349–350; Webb and Frankel 2010; Steel 2013). One of the key ideas holds that in the same time unit as non-plow (hand-hoe or similar) agriculture, the plow agriculturalist can cultivate a much greater area of land even if in per-unit terms less intensively—and thus in overall net terms produce a much larger harvest and so surplus (in a reasonable to good year). Overall this is a major "intensification" of agricultural production. But a problem has been to understand how "society" allowed this plow-developing group to take over new and extra land. Did they take otherwise valued and productive land by some form of coercion (as e.g., Gilman 1981)? Or was it land outside the previous usual or needed walking/exploitation range or a previously un-owned "outfield" (e.g., Bintliff 1982)?

While all models are possible, perhaps a missing key to this topic in discussions for the semi-arid east Mediterranean is that much of the land taken on by the new plow agriculturalists was in fact likely marginal land—land effectively not valued before, or difficult to exploit manually (clayey), or only considered at most as rough seasonal grazing territory. A conflict scenario involving existing owned and farmed land around villages could thus be largely avoided. And if this new, marginal land was now plow-farmed (providing some form of effective tillage)—which is the most effective and efficient way to employ available precipitation in semi-arid contexts for barley production (and we could generalize to all cereals)—versus no tillage or mere cereal-fallow rotation (López and Arrúe 1997), then in fact it would also offer better post-harvest grazing in a potential symbiotic model that brought fertilizer to these fields. (Manuring strategies can improve the use of available water for crops and are perhaps relevant in some archaeological cases in semi-arid areas, but the study of Styring *et al.* (2016) highlights that discriminating the relative role of manuring versus other constraints requires careful investigation.) Therefore, a mixed plow-and-pastoralist strategy might even be actively pursued and supported by the same groups who would also likely support and finance the labor behind the development and then use of the necessary workshop/processing facilities to deal with both larger harvests and large-scale animal secondary products.

Once this new agropastoralist model began (especially plow agriculture), it would have been revolutionary, even if its outsize impact was probably entirely unforeseen at the outset. The capital-holding plow group—non-subsistence—could afford the (for instance) 10–20 percent of crop failures for the impressive returns available from the 80–90 percent of OK-to-more-successful years (using the Peristerona poor rainfall/harvest occurrences discussed above as the example). Moreover, there was the prospect of a few very successful years—noting the big differences in yields between worst versus best years in the Christodoulou figures discussed earlier—when extraordinary efforts and practices (e.g., special feasts) might be possible or financed. An entire new beyond subsistence (surplus) agricultural sector now almost immediately existed—but without really "taking" from anyone else, instead adding to the scale of the economy—capable of creating capital for some of an entirely new order of magnitude and requiring infrastructure (e.g., equipment, additional storage, and transport—and larger pithoi are noted from the MC period, see Pilides 1996: 107) and indeed offering benefits and reasons to give trust to others in the society (who ally themselves with plow groups as associates and followers). Expanded pastoralism in marginal land formerly outside ownership/control would also likely cause few ructions but could again create large potential returns. In turn, and similarly, as a capital-based class emerged with access to and control of labor, other outfield crops requiring capital to set up and significant time to yield a return (as much as twenty-five years to reach measureable productivity in the case of olive trees, see Keswani 2015: 9) as well as labor and skill to care for and harvest and process, like olives and vines, could be developed toward an "industrial" scale (as seems the case subsequently at LBA Kalavasos *Ayios Dhimitrios*, see Keswani 2015). These could provide both an important, storable, and transportable resource that could form part of a regional staple finance model for the controlling elite, and the basis for producing crafted goods (perfumed olive oil, wine, etc.) suitable for engaging with and participating in the east Mediterranean trade world (this in addition to Cyprus' copper). This new agropastoral economy in turn at once required labor and so formed the basis for regular or periodic employment of numbers of the less well-off in unequal social debt/bond relationships. These created larger, beyond-immediate-family socioeconomic groups and the potential building blocks of wider status and power over time for the capable and ambitious. This revolution could in turn fuel much more of the already accepted forms of social display and competition; in turn, the consequent competitive and inflationary pressures of such escalating prestige goods/display systems (as is evident for EC–MC Cyprus, see Keswani 2005) would produce and require new categories leading to step-change potentials. This revolution would have been relatively rapid and would then have taken on a life and dynamic of its own. The requirements of the new extensive and intensive plow-agricultural model called for social solutions to the entailed needs for more and different types of labor and work pattern, which, in many cases around the world, led among other things to new divisions between males and females and thus radically different social structures (Bolger 2003: 38–39, 193). Overall, it was likely a key transition episode as Cyprus moved along a spectrum toward "tighter" social forms (see Gelfand *et al.* 2011).

In this way we may imagine a secondary products–based "stealth" revolution on Cyprus: largely uncontested *when it began* but fundamental in impact and quickly so. Rather than having to imagine a dramatic and binary revolutionary moment of conflict in which a few individuals acquired plows and the wherewithal and then "took" the outfield, one can instead imagine the rather more prosaic scenario above based initially on the natural differences to be found within any society. Some families (or social units), who through past social standing or fortune or strategy will have owned or had the right to use some of the favorable near-river land and over time will likely have been relatively more successful versus the average in the given community, will have had the opportunity to build some form of regular surplus and thus further create and support a favorable and central social, economic, and political position for themselves (following the sorts of arguments and logic of e.g., Hayden 1995; Dietler and Hayden 2001). Due to differing people, some more capable and some not, and differing social groups being fortunate to have successive leading figures who are more capable, circumstances would lead to some of those social groups having greater resources and potential simply through such natural social evolution applied in a less-than-perfect agrarian setting where some land and contexts are better than others. Some of these modest capital-holding groups then, because of an ambitious family leader or some other reason, took up extensive plow agriculture when the technology was, or became, available in their vicinity. The consequences—as a developing structure becomes practice over time—quickly reshaped the entire society and wider social world.

In particular, once established, the new larger plow-land areas and likely expanded areas of long-term fixed viticulture and arboriculture required (a new) ongoing security of ownership, especially since these larger areas would now be bringing previously more separated social groups into closer proximity. More than before, there was now value to defend, value to move (transport/trade to store and then to market or use-venue), or value to try to take, and so we might anticipate a rise in the potential for, or real occurrences of, violence—and the increase in occurrences of burned destructions in the MC and the appearance of the "forts" marking and surveilling territory (see Monahan and Spigelman in this volume) and the occurrences of weapons and other indications of warfare including mass burials during the MC and especially in the MC III–LC I period (e.g., Knapp 1986: 38) plausibly follow. All these processes, once started and both fueled and required by the developed secondary products revolution, offered further avenues and competitive necessities—and resources to engage (e.g., in trade within and beyond the island) for distinction, building status, and reinforcing hierarchy.

The Next Steps?

What was the prompt? Connection with the "Anatolian Trade Network" (Şahoğlu 2005) seems the obvious answer and context, and the only debate is exactly how much this was one-way (from Anatolia and via migration) or two-way, with movement of people and influences and technology and animals like cattle into Cyprus, but also significant stimulation of ambitious local Cypriot leaders and groups to engage and so transform (Knapp 2013b: 264–277; Manning 2014: 24–25; Crewe 2015—all with further references to what is now a large literature). But rather than consider origins, let us consider outcomes. Here it is interesting and important to reflect on the timeframe and circumstances, as I have suggested (Manning 2014).

The Philia facies stage when this kick-start began is likely dated within the period from the mid-third-millennium BCE to ca. 2200 BCE (Manning 2013; Paraskeva in this volume) and particularly involves the northwest to north of the island (Webb and Frankel 1999; 2013a). But, as elsewhere in the region and especially in marginal areas, there is then a likely significant challenge on Cyprus, forced by a shift to drier climate conditions around and in the couple of centuries following 2200 BCE/4200 BP, as much discussed for the Near East–east Mediterranean region (see generally papers in Meller *et al.* 2015; Weiss 2014)—with some indications in representational art on Cyprus that could be interpreted in support of such a scenario (Manning 2014: 27 and citations). There is perhaps reason to speculate that some areas of the north coast of the island (like around *Vounous*) already spurred and associated with the Philia developments would be better off both in agricultural terms precisely at such times (slightly better and more reliable rainfall) and could become foci (Manning 2014: 24–29). The (all we really have) mortuary record would indicate that *Vounous* saw significant and escalating ideological elaboration through the EC period, culminating in the cattle (or bucrania), plow, and society representations usually placed late in EC to early in MC or ca. 2000 BCE. From this same time around 2000 BCE, noting especially the rich tombs at Lapithos on the north coast, there was a "marked increase in ostentation occurring at the outset of the MC I period," during which "mortuary consumption . . . escalated significantly" (Keswani 2005: 355, 392) and external contacts picked up. In addition, concurrently, the plank figurines appear in what seem usually to be exclusive mortuary contexts (north coast, like *Vounous* and

Lapithos, but also elsewhere). The nature and decoration of the figurines suggest specific associations or identities or status in a number of cases, and several have indications of elaborate and perhaps distinctive textile decoration (Knapp 2013b: 339–343; Knox 2012; Talalay and Cullen 2002), indicating both the existence of, and an association with, another now-developed aspect of the secondary products revolution, one involving significant labor allocation (or control). While some of the figurines are sexed, others are not, or merge associations, and so instead these objects might better be interpreted as representing and delineating an emerging elite (both male and female members) and its identity, associations, ancestry, and reproduction (see Knapp 2013b: 340–342 and references).

The subsequent revolution that forms the "take-off" explosion of MC III–LC I likely begins by or from the mid-/late eighteenth century BCE (Manning 2014; Knapp 2013a: 29). While no good new dating evidence is yet available from Cyprus itself, the dating framework that can be derived from the wider Near East–east Mediterranean now even more firmly supports this approximate date range for Cyprus. The case for the Middle Chronology (or the eight years lower Low-Middle Chronology) for Mesopotamia has become more clearly required (Manning *et al.* 2016; de Jong 2013), as has the compatible need for a substantial raising of the date of the end of the MBA in the Levant (Höflmayer *et al.* 2016a; 2016b—but cf. Ben-Tor 2018), as well as a rethinking of the chronology of Avaris (Tell el-Dabᵉa: Manning 2014: 29–31; Manning *et al.* 2014; Höflmayer 2018; Aston 2018), linked in turn with the ever stronger evidence for the compatible "high" chronology for the start of the Aegean LBA (Manning *et al.* 2014). Where does this leave us? There is only maybe 150–250 years, or less, from *Vounous* to the MC III–LC I revolution.

This period of time is not long. It is *not* a gradualist situation, where things supposedly develop slowly and inexorably via some inevitable social evolutionary process over a millennium or more. Thus, although Cherry's (1983) punctuated evolution critique (regarding Early Minoan Crete) prompted Knapp's analysis (see Knapp 2013a: 21), I think we must contrast the Cretan versus Cypriot cases. The Cretan Prepalatial stretches out over a millennium or more. There is no single process. Cherry (2010: 112) observes that "when we refer (often somewhat cavalierly) to 'the prepalatial period,' we should remember that this now refers to a vast span of some 1,200 years, far too long to constitute an era about which any meaningful generalizations are possible." The temporal length of time relevant to the Cypriot case, outlined above, is much shorter and more equivalent to the length of time of the few centuries at the end of the Prepalatial era on Crete that Cherry identified for rapid, revolutionary change, versus some long gradualist process. The Cypriot case is the sort of sustained (a few centuries) but contained (*only* a few centuries) timescale whereby, once fueled by the secondary products revolution, cycles of increasingly intense sociopolitical competition—manifested for us in the prestige competition we see in the mortuary record—could as repeated performances of roles and rituals create ongoing and then permanent routinized associations for prominent persons, families, and groups over time and in space (e.g., specific tombs and mortuary areas as well as specific houses or public spaces). The intensive secondary products revolution agricultural model is both observed (e.g., Ember 1983: 291–293) and argued

(Ember 1983: 293–296) to lead to population increase—it both requires more labor (and thus children) and the increased sedentism (especially of females, as observed for intensive agricultural societies) leads to higher fertility rates (decreased birth spacing, see Ember 1983; Bolger 2003: 38–39). Perhaps the most important outcome of the secondary products revolution on Cyprus was that this population-increasing engine fueled an under-appreciated demographic explosion across the EC–MC period. Georgiou (2006) counts 44 ECI–II sites (Knapp's PreBA 1) but 345 EC III–MC II (Knapp's PreBA 2) sites (see also Knapp 2013b: 278). (Note: as recognized by Georgiou, some earlier surveys, like the Vasilikos Valley Project, failed to recognize EC; thus there may be some missing EC sites or some inflation of MC sites.) Using the chronology in Knapp (2013a: Table 1), this change occurs over a maximum period of 2250–1700 BCE (550 years) and a minimum period of 2000–1750 BCE (250 years)—if we take the middle of the range, then this is almost an eightfold increase over around 400 years, or just very slightly over a 0.5% increase every year. Of course not all of the sites identified are the same, but there are many more large sites during the MC, so actually the underlying population growth over this period is likely to be much more than eightfold, even while remaining entirely within the range achieved by growing populations in history (Sallares 1991: 86, 89–90, 134). Such rapid population growth is very possible, but usually only when expanding into a vacuum versus an area that is already filled (given prevailing technology, society, and economy). Thus we can assume that most of this agricultural village expansion was into previously unoccupied land. In contrast, moving through this period, as the landscape did fill, issues of territory, relationships, and alliances/enmities with neighboring communities become relevant (and are partly visible through analysis of designs and signaling found on ceramics: see Frankel 1974), and indeed become the building blocks for larger and more complex social, political, and economic units. For the first time on Cyprus they comprise a constraint or "caging" that at some point will encourage or even necessitate social transformation (including archaeologically visible traits such as place- and territory-making/-marking and, probably, increased group intersections, including warfare).

Larger population groups clearly form at several locations during the MC (Georgiou 2006). The large "complex" of MBA sites in the Vasilikos Valley is one such manifestation (Todd 2013: 90–91). The central plain, and the Alykos-Gialias-Pedieos river area especially, become foci in addition now, and—when the climate is not unfavorable—this granary of Cyprus region is capable of supporting greater extensive intensification than anywhere else on the island, and especially if managed investment and labor started to be directed by an emerging elite into water management infrastructure (wells, irrigation channels, terracing).

In particular, during MC I–II, generally considered a ca. 200-year period overall, the staggeringly large cemeteries at Deneia (Frankel and Webb 2007) are suggested to have received originally as many as 9,000–20,000 adult burials (highlighted by Knapp 2013a: 26). Even working on relatively conservative demographic assumptions for the pre-modern period of the sort behind well-known and likely minimalist estimates of for example Broodbank (1989) for the Cyclades, this implies contemporary populations of around 1100–2500 adults, with perhaps another 40 percent after

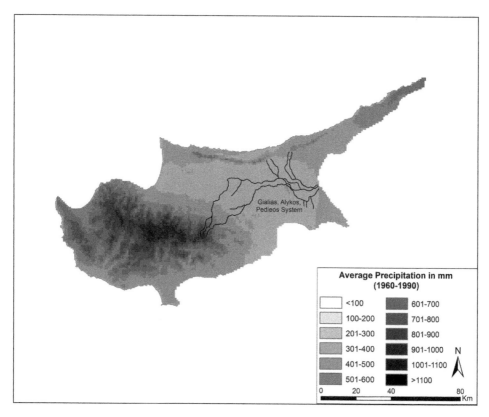

Figure 3.7: Cyprus average precipitation map 1960–1990 derived from data from the WorldClim website supplying global climate data, employing the interpolation methods between the different stations across the island, see http://worldclim.org/methods1, derived from Hijmans *et al.* (2005). Average precipitation shown in 50mm increments. The main watercourses/rivers on the island and the Alykos-Gialias-Pedeios river system are highlighted.

allowing for children. Not all this burying population necessarily lived in the same village, but a connected social community of this size is well beyond the scale of the usual small-scale, relatively egalitarian agricultural villages and the practicalities of communication, even allowing for the existence of supra-household social groupings and coordinating units such as "clans" and "phratries," based both on theory and observation (Johnson 1978; 1982; Manning 1993: 43, 50–51n7; Bernardini 1996).

Aggregation of population creates the opportunity, circumstances, and needs for more complex social integration and forms (Birch 2013; Kowalewski 2013). We must assume that a much more elaborate social universe and infrastructure was in operation, in particular in order to mitigate and overcome scalar stress, with more and intensified use of material culture symbols (Steel 2013: 57) and likely with additional hierarchy involving various individuals and small groups playing leading or coordinating, and thus prominent, roles (well) beyond mere family and kinship. As the scale of the community grew, opportunities were therefore present for the ambitious and capable to articulate and exploit the available "emergent properties" (adapting Yoffee 2005: 201–204). The would-be successful and sustained leaders of groups (whether merely within or at the apex of the overall community) in such a dynamic, pre-institutionalized situation will be those who can build and maintain recognized social centrality (Roscoe 1993). Usually this is achieved through regular performance and reinforcing of the social, economic, and political benefits to followers and to the group as a whole—through achieving trust. Holding or organizing feasts or other similar events (including funerals) that benefit both individuals and the group and create, reproduce, and affirm ties, beliefs, obligations and identities in turn affords and produces power and status both locally and within wider social networks (e.g., Hayden 2001). It is at such arenas where symbols—such as the increasingly elaborate material culture and various exotics known (and thus first acquired) across the EC–MC period (Keswani's 2005 "ceremonial" metal, ceramic, and other objects) and especially from EC III–MC II—are deployed, as status is displayed, negotiated, recognized, and reproduced. In the absence of failure or untoward circumstances, the routinized performance of such prominent roles over time becomes a natural state of affairs and the basis for ascribed or institutionalized power.

Conclusions

In what can be at most a very partial sketch, I have suggested that the semi-arid context of Cyprus provided a rich opportunity for the Cypriot development of a secondary products revolution (especially focusing on plow agriculture) into marginal land—to the benefit of, and supporting, an elite—without causing the social resistance that could otherwise undermine attempts by (more ambitious or successful) subgroups to so expand their base. This initiative derived out of the influences, personnel, and infrastructures present during the combined external (Anatolia-Cyprus) and internal (wider Cyprus to Philia centers and likely especially Vasilia and perhaps an as yet missing Morphou Bay center) dynamic system and cycle of contact and exchange during the period of the Anatolian Trade Network–Philia facies. Initial evolutionary trajectories were, however, likely compromised and constricted by the impacts of the more arid and cooler 2200 BCE/4200 BP climate episode on Cyprus, which would have had the effect of making some of the marginal zones (in central Cyprus especially) now too marginal. These circumstances likely focused population on the slightly more favorable areas and on those areas with additional resources (including for example maritime contact and resources), such as parts of the north coast (Manning 2014: 27–29) but also areas elsewhere on the island in the south and west. There may have been some migration into these more favorable areas, further promoting demographic nucleation or at least concentration and so greater social interaction and scale in these relatively constricted regions. The elaborate and symbolically complex social world evident from the mortuary assemblages at EC *Vounous* offers a window into these dynamic processes in one area (developing the discussion of Webb and Frankel 2010). These processes of concentration and nucleation likely created several more separate social universes in different areas of the island. This situation can partly explain the regionalism evident in the material culture of the EC period (Webb and Frankel 2013a) and, in turn, also will have afforded opportunities for (or promoted) forms of social, political, and economic leadership and so centralization within these centers in order to maintain group cohesion and efficiency. Fission away from the favorable centers would likely have been a less attractive option during the arid phase at the end of the third millennium BCE.

When climate-environment circumstances improved at the start of the second millennium BCE (as generally around the east Mediterranean), the now-established agropastoralist society of Cyprus expanded rapidly into most of the arable land of the island—engaging opportunity and relieving likely scalar stress in the late EC core settlements. It was a largely empty landscape and an opportunity for ambitious families and groups. We may assume that these communities brought the social organization and values of their ancestral home core centers. But population growth and the rapid filling up of the (relatively small) arable Cypriot landscape will quickly have required new networked social relationships within and between communities creating supra-community organization and an entire new order of magnitude of potential.

Several much larger communities developed by late EC and MC I–II, some undoubtedly involving significant social complexity and hierarchy. Of course, I recognize that we currently lack an excavated example—it is my hypothesis at this time that they did exist and will one day be recognized, whether in the north, like the settlement that went with the Lapithos tombs, or the settlements indicated around *Vounous* and Karmi, or those in the central plain like around the Deneia area, or around Nicosia *Ayia Paraskevi* (Georgiou 2013; Pilides 2014: 158), Kaimakli, and other loci near Nicosia (Webb 2012: 55), or in the east (like Kalopsidha; see Crewe 2010; Webb 2012), or in the south, such as within the Vasilikos Valley MC complex, or indeed elsewhere. The value of additional prestige constituents beyond the existing local EC–MC ceremonial sphere, that is of external contacts and access to exclusive exotica and esoteric knowledge, will have sharply increased among the Cypriot elites as these processes escalated from EC III–MC II, likely leading to further development of the copper resources of the island to support such external trade (and other specialist crafted products like textiles and oils/perfumes). This in turn will have brought more external notice and interest to Cyprus and its resources—especially copper.

The development of networks of larger populations across the island may almost by itself, as much as any new focus on contact and trade with the southeast Mediterranean and influences therefrom, have led to a switch in focus away from the north coast toward the much greater potential of the arable areas in the east (Alykos-Gialias-Pedieos system, Larnaca area) and the northwest in the Morphou Bay area and in the southern river valleys by the late MC period. In turn, larger communities and groups of communities both created proximate interaction potentials and synergies but also likely more self-sufficient, self-identifying social formations—"limited and exclusive in their social and territorial coverage" (Mann 1986: 39)—which therefore became more "bounded" with concerns to define and control land and strategic resources and routes in a way that was largely irrelevant earlier (the marginal was now engaged and used). This social caging in a context of neighbors and a landscape in, say, eastern Cyprus that was not naturally geographically segmented prompted new innovations like the "forts" to signal and mark. These buildings, through the very process of their creation (the initiative, organizing the labor, and then the process of making) and then their monumental, visible, and ever-present existence in the landscape, shape, select for and escalate further social and political changes within increasingly "caged" or bounded social worlds (emerging early complex polities; see Monahan and Spigelman in this volume). In sum, rather than evolution and then a final revolution to the Protohistoric Bronze Age (MC III–LC I) (as Knapp 2013a), I see instead several escalating cycles of revolution and challenge (in particular the couple-of-centuries-long 2200 BCE/4200 BP island- and region-impacting arid event) across the EC–MC period that created several larger, coalesced, emergent groupings by MC II pregnant with possibilities when Cyprus significantly intersected with the exponentially much larger and metals-hungry world of the east Mediterranean from the eighteenth century BCE (Manning 2014: 29–31).

Acknowledgments

I thank Georgia Andreou for her assistance and skill in producing Figures 3.2–3.4 and 3.7. I thank Georgia Andreou, Katie Kearns, and Bernard Knapp for their helpful and very prompt comments on an earlier draft. I thank the volume's two referees for their very helpful and constructive comments.

Postscript

It is not possible to account for or to discuss all the relevant literature appearing since this paper was submitted. However, one paper appearing as this volume was in proof, needs to be highlighted. Webb (2018), written after and in fact aware of the current chapter, offers an important, if undeniably maximalist, assessment of the EBA-MBA period and with a focus on the north coast and the special (geospatially associated) and precocious developments there, and so supports and further elaborates aspects of some of the arguments and themes presented in this chapter.

References

Ancient Authors:

Andocides, *On His Return*
Pliny, *Natural History*
Strabo, *Geography*

Aston, D. 2018. How early (and how late) can Khyan really be: An essay based on "conventional archaeological methods." In I. Forstner-Müller and N. Moeller (eds.), *The Hyksos Ruler Khyan and the Early Second Intermediate Period in Egypt: Problems and Priorities of Current Research*, 15–56. Ergänzungshefte zu den Jahresheften des Österreichischen Archäologischen Institutes 17. Vienna: Austrian Archaeological Institute.

Bakirtzis, C. 1995. The role of Cyprus in the grain supply of Constantinople in the early Christian period. In V. Karageorghis and D. Michaelides (eds.), *Proceedings of the International Archaeological Conference "Cyprus and the Sea,"* 247–253. Nicosia: University of Cyprus.

Ben-Tor, D. 2018. Evidence for Middle Bronze Age Chronology and Synchronisms in the Levant: A Response to Höflmayer *et al.* 2016. *Bulletin of the American Schools of Oriental Research* 379: 43-54.

Bernardini, W. 1996. Transitions in social organization: A predictive model from southwestern archaeology. *Journal of Anthropological Archaeology* 15: 372–402.

Bintliff, J. 1982. Settlement patterns, land tenure, and social structure: A diachronic model. In C. Renfrew and S. Shennan (eds.), *Ranking, Resource, and Exchange: Aspects of the Archaeology of Early European Society,* 106–111. Cambridge: Cambridge University Press.

Birch, J. 2013. Between villages and cities: Settlement aggregation in cross-cultural perspective. In J. Birch (ed.), *From Prehistoric Villages to Cities: Settlement Aggregation and Community Transformation,* 1–22. New York: Routledge.

Bishaw, Z. 2004. Wheat and Barley Seed Systems in Ethiopia and Syria. Unpublished PhD thesis, Wageningen University. Available from: http://edepot.wur.nl/121548—accessed January 2017.

Bissa, E.M.A. 2009. *Governmental Intervention in Foreign Trade in Archaic and Classical Greece.* Leiden, the Netherlands: Brill.

Blanton, R.E., with L.F. Fargher. 2016. *How Humans Cooperate: Confronting the Challenges of Collective Action.* Boulder: University Press of Colorado.

Blanton, R.E., G.M. Feinman, S.A. Kowalewski, and P.N. Peregrine. 1996. A dual-processual theory for the evolution of Mesoamerican civilization. *Current Anthropology* 37: 1–14.

Bolger, D. 2003. *Gender in Ancient Cyprus. Narratives of Social Change on a Mediterranean Island.* Walnut Creek, CA: Altamira Press.

Bolger, D. 2010. The dynamics of gender in early agricultural societies of the Near East. *Signs* 35: 503–531.

Brayshaw, D.J., C.M.C. Rambeau, and S.J. Smith. 2011. Changes in Mediterranean climate during the Holocene: Insights from global and regional climate modelling. *The Holocene* 21: 15–31.

Broodbank, C. 1989. The longboat and society in the Cyclades in the Keros-Syros culture. *American Journal of Archaeology* 93: 319–337.

Brown, M. 2013. Waterways and the political geography of south-east Cyprus in the second millennium BC. *Annual of the British School at Athens* 108: 121–136.

Bruggeman, A., C. Zoumides, and C. Camera. 2015. The effect of climate change on crop production in Cyprus: The Cyprus green-blue water model and scenario modelling. *AGWATER Scientific Report* 8 Deliverable 23. Nicosia: Energy, Environment, and Water Research Group, The Cyprus Institute. Available: http://www.cyi.ac.cy/images/AGWATER_Scientific_Reports/AGWATER_ScientificReport8_WP8_Bruggeman_def.pdf, accessed December 2016.

Carneiro, R.L. 1970. A theory of the origin of the state. *Science* 169: 733–738.

Catling, H.W. 1962. Patterns of settlement in Bronze Age Cyprus. *Opuscula Atheniensia* 4: 129–169.

Ceccarelli, S., S. Grando, and M. Baum. 2007. Participatory plant breeding in water-limited environments. *Experimental Agriculture* 43: 411–435.

Chapman, R.W. 1981. The emergence of formal disposal areas and the "problem" of megalithic tombs in prehistoric Europe. In R.W. Chapman, I.A. Kinnes, and K. Randsborg (eds.), *The Archaeology of Death,* 71–82. Cambridge: Cambridge University Press.

Cherry, J.F. 1983. Evolution, revolution, and the origins of complex society in Minoan Crete. In O. Krzyszkowska and L. Nixon (eds.), *Minoan Society: Proceedings of the Cambridge Colloquium 1981,* 33–45. Bristol: Bristol Classical Press.

Cherry, J.F. 2010. Sorting out Crete's Prepalatial off-island interactions. In W.A. Parkinson and M.L. Galaty (eds.), *Archaic State Interaction: The Eastern Mediterranean in the Bronze Age,* 107–140. Santa Fe: School for Advanced Research Press.

Christakis, K.S. 1999. Pithoi and food storage in Neopalatial Crete: a domestic perspective. *World Archaeology* 31: 1–20.

Christodoulou, D. 1959. *The Evolution of the Rural Land Use Pattern in Cyprus.* London: Geographical Publications Limited.

Cook, B.I., K.J. Anchukaitis, R. Touchan, D.M. Meko, and E.R. Cook. 2016. Spatiotemporal drought variability in the Mediterranean over the last 900 years. *Journal of Geophysical Research: Atmospheres* 121: 2060–2074. doi:10.1002/2015JD023929.

Crewe, L. 2010. Rethinking Kalopsidha: From specialisation to state marginalisation. In D. Bolger and L.C. Maguire (eds.), *The Development of Pre-State Communities in the Ancient Near East*, 63–71. Oxford: Oxbow Books.

Crewe, L. 2015. Expanding and shrinking networks of interaction: Cyprus c. 2200 BC. In H. Meller, H.W. Arx, R. Jung, and R. Risch (eds.), *2200 BCE—Ein Klimasturz als Ursache für den Zerfall der Alten Welt?/2200 BCE—A Climatic Breakdown as a Cause for the Collapse of the Old World? 7th Archaeological Conference of Central Germany October 23–26, 2014 in Halle (Saale)*, 131–148. Halle: Landesmuseum für Vorgeschichte.

de Jong, T. 2013. Astronomical fine-tuning of the chronology of the Hammurabi Age. *Jaarbericht van het Vooraziatisch-Egyptisch Genootschap "Ex Oriente Lux"* 44: 147–167.

Dietler, M., and B. Hayden. (eds.) 2001. *Feasts: Archaeological and Ethnographic Perspectives on Food, Politics, and Power*. Washington, DC: Smithsonian Institution Press.

Ember, C.R. 1983. The relative decline in women's contribution to agriculture with intensification. *American Anthropologist* 85: 285–304.

Fisher, K.D. 2009. Elite Place-making and Social Interaction in the Late Cypriot Bronze Age. *Journal of Mediterranean Archaeology* 22: 183–209.

Food and Agriculture Organization (FAO). 1987. *Improving productivity in dryland areas*. Committee on Agriculture (Ninth Session). COAG/87/7. Rome: FAO.

Food and Agriculture Organization (FAO). 2004. *Carbon Sequestration in Dryland Soils*. World Soils Resources Reports 102. Rome: FAO. http://www.fao.org/docrep/007/y5738e/y5738e00.htm#Contents

Forbes, H. 1989. Of grandfathers and grand theories: The hierarchized ordering of responses to hazard in a Greek rural community. In P. Halstead and J. O'Shea (eds.), *Bad Year Economics: Cultural Responses to Risk and Uncertainty*, 87–97. Cambridge: Cambridge University Press.

Foxhall, L., and H. Forbes. 1982. Sitometreia: The role of grain as a staple food in classical antiquity. *Chiron* 12: 41–90.

Frankel, D. 1974. *Middle Cypriot White Painted Pottery: An Analytical Study of the Decoration*. Studies in Mediterranean Archaeology 42. Göteborg, Sweden: Paul Åströms Förlag.

Frankel, D., and J.M. Webb. 1996. *Marki Alonia: An Early and Middle Bronze Age Town in Cyprus. Excavations 1990–1994*. Studies in Mediterranean Archaeology 123.1. Jonsered, Sweden: Paul Åströms Förlag.

Frankel, D., and J.M. Webb. 2006. *Marki Alonia: An Early and Middle Bronze Age Settlement in Cyprus. Excavations 1995–2000*. Studies in Mediterranean Archaeology 123.2. Sävedalen, Sweden: Paul Åströms Förlag.

Frankel, D., and J.M. Webb. 2007. *The Bronze Age Cemeteries at Deneia in Cyprus*. Studies in Mediterranean Archaeology 135. Sävedalen, Sweden: Paul Åströms Förlag.

Gamble, C. 1986. Hunter-gatherers and the origin of states. In J.A. Hall (ed.), *States in History*, 22–47. Oxford: Basil Blackwell.

Garnsey, P. 1988. *Famine and Food Supply in the Greco-Roman World: Responses to Risk and Crisis*. Cambridge: Cambridge University Press.

Gelfand, M.J., *et al.* 2011. Differences between tight and loose cultures: A 33-nation study. *Science* 332: 1100–1104.

Georgiou, G. 2006. Η Τοπογραφία της Ανθρώπινης Εγκατάστασης στην Κύπρο κατά την Πρώιμη και Μέση Χαλκοκρατία. Unpublished PhD dissertation, University of Cyprus.

Georgiou, G. 2013. 1955–2013: The necropolis of Nicosia *Agia Paraskevi* almost 60 years after Stewart's excavations. In A.B. Knapp, J.M. Webb, and A. McCarthy (eds.), *J.R.B. Stewart—An Archaeological Legacy*, 81–102. Studies in Mediterranean Archaeology 139. Uppsala, Sweden: Åströms Förlag.

Giddens, A. 1979. *Central Problems in Social Theory: Action, Structure, and Contradiction in Social Analysis*. London: Macmillan.

Gilman, A. 1981. The development of social stratification in Bronze Age Europe. *Current Anthropology* 22: 1–23.

Given, M., and A.B. Knapp. (eds.) 2003. *The Sydney Cyprus Survey Project: Social Approaches to Regional Archaeological Survey*. Monumenta Archaeologica 21. Los Angeles: The Cotsen Institute of Archaeology.

Greenfield, H.J. 2010. The Secondary Products Revolution: The past, the present, and the future. *World Archaeology* 42: 29–54.

Griggs, C., C. Pearson, S.W. Manning, and B. Lorentzen. 2014. A 250-year annual precipitation reconstruction and drought assessment for Cyprus from *Pinus brutia* Ten. tree-rings. *International Journal of Climatology* 34: 2702–2714.

Hadjichristodoulou, A. 1982. The effects of annual precipitation and its distribution on grain yield of dryland cereals. *Journal of Agricultural Science* 99: 261–270.

Halstead, P. 2014. *Two Oxen Ahead: Pre-Mechanized Farming in the Mediterranean.* Chichester: Wiley Blackwell.

Halstead, P., and J. O'Shea. (eds.) 1989. *Bad Year Economics: Cultural Responses to Risk and Uncertainty.* Cambridge: Cambridge University Press.

Harris, S.E. 2007. Colonial forestry and environmental history: British policies in Cyprus, 1878–1960. Unpublished PhD dissertation, University of Texas at Austin.

Harris, S.E. 2012. Cyprus as a degraded landscape or resilient environment in the wake of colonial intrusion. *Proceedings of the National Academy of Sciences of the United States of America* 109: 3670–3675.

Hayden, B. 1995. Pathways to power: Principles for creating socioeconomic inequalities. In T.D. Price and G.M. Feinman (eds.), *Foundations of Social Inequality*, 15–86. New York: Plenum Press.

Hayden, B. 2001. Fabulous feasts: A prolegomenon to the importance of feasting. In M. Dietler and B. Hayden (eds.), *Feasts: Archaeological and Ethnographic Perspectives on Food, Politics, and Power*, 23–64. Washington, DC: Smithsonian Institution Press.

Hijmans, R.J., S.E. Cameron, J.L. Parra, P.G. Jones, and A. Jarvis. 2005. Very high resolution interpolated climate surfaces for global land areas. *International Journal of Climatology* 25: 1965–1978.

Hill, G. 1940. *A History of Cyprus. Volume 1: To the Conquest by Richard Lion Heart.* Cambridge: Cambridge University Press.

Hodder, I. 1990. *The Domestication of Europe.* Oxford: Basil Blackwell.

Hodder, I. 2011. Wheels of time: Some aspects of entanglement theory and the Secondary Products Revolution. *Journal of World Prehistory* 24: 175–187.

Höflmayer, F. 2018. An early date for Khyan and its implications for eastern Mediterranean chronologies. In I. Forstner-Müller and N. Moeller (eds.), *The Hyksos Ruler Khyan and the Early Second Intermediate Period in Egypt: Problems and Priorities of Current Research*, 143–171. Ergänzungshefte zu den Jahresheften des Österreichischen Archäologischen Institutes 17. Vienna: Austrian Archaeological Institute.

Höflmayer, F., J. Kamlah, H. Sader, M.W. Dee, W. Kutschera, E.M. Wild, and S. Riehl. 2016a. New evidence for Middle Bronze Age chronology and synchronisms in the Levant: Radiocarbon dates from Tell el-Burak, Tell el-Dab'a, and Tel Ifshar compared. *Bulletin of the American Schools of Oriental Research* 375: 53–76.

Höflmayer, F., A. Yasur-Landau, E.H. Cline, M.W. Dee, B. Lorentzen, and S. Riehl. 2016b. New radiocarbon dates from Tel Kabri support a high Middle Bronze Age chronology. *Radiocarbon* 58: 599–613.

Horden, P., and N. Purcell. 2000. *The Corrupting Sea: A Study of Mediterranean History.* Oxford: Blackwell.

Iacovou, M. 2013. Historically elusive and internally fragile island polities: The intricacies of Cyprus's political geography in the Iron Age. *Bulletin of the American Schools of Oriental Research* 370: 15–47.

Jennings, R.C. 1988. The locust problem in Cyprus. *Bulletin of the School of Oriental and African Studies, University of London* 51: 279–313.

Johnson, G.A. 1978. Information sources and the development of decision-making organisations. In C.L. Redman, M. Berman, F. Curtin, W. Langhorne, N. Versaggi, and J. Wanser (eds.), *Social Archaeology: Beyond Subsistence and Dating*, 87–112. London: Academic Press.

Johnson, G.A. 1982. Organisational structure and scalar stress. In C. Renfrew, M.J. Rowlands, and B.A. Segraves (eds.), *Theory and Explanation in Archaeology: The Southampton Conference*, 389–421. New York: Academic Press.

Kaniewski, D., E. Van Campo, J. Guiot, S. Le Burel, T. Otto, and C. Baeteman. 2013. Environmental roots of the Late Bronze Age crisis. *PLoS ONE* 8.8: e71004. doi:10.1371/journal.pone.0071004

Keswani, P.S. 2004. *Mortuary Ritual and Society in Bronze Age Cyprus.* Monographs in Mediterranean Archaeology 9. London: Equinox.

Keswani, P.S. 2005. Death, prestige, and copper in Bronze Age Cyprus. *American Journal of Archaeology* 109: 341–401.

Keswani, P.S. 2015. Olive production, storage, and political economy at Late Bronze Age Kalavasos, Cyprus. In A. Jacobs and P. Cosyns (eds.), *POCA 2008. Cypriot Material Culture Studies from Picrolite Carving to Proskynitaria Analysis*, 1–24. Brussels: Brussels University Press.

Kissinger, H. 2014. *World Order: Reflections on the Character of Nations and the Course of History*. New York: Penguin.

Knapp, A.B. 1986. Production, exchange, and socio-political complexity on Bronze Age Cyprus. *Oxford Journal of Archaeology* 5: 35–60.

Knapp, A.B. 1990. Production, location, and integration in Bronze Age Cyprus. *Current Anthropology* 31: 147–176.

Knapp, A.B. 2013a. Revolution within evolution: The emergence of a "secondary state" on protohistoric Bronze Age Cyprus. *Levant* 45: 19–44.

Knapp, A.B. 2013b. *The Archaeology of Cyprus: From Earliest Prehistory through the Bronze Age*. Cambridge: Cambridge University Press.

Knox, D. 2012. Making sense of figurines in Bronze Age Cyprus: A comprehensive analysis of ceramic figurative material from ECI–LCIIIA (c.2300BC–c.1100BC). Unpublished PhD thesis, University of Manchester.

Knox, D. 2013. Figurines and figurative vessels at Early Cypriot Bellapais *Vounous*. In A.B. Knapp, J.M. Webb, and A. McCarthy (eds.), *J.R.B. Stewart—An Archaeological Legacy*, 47–57. Studies in Mediterranean Archaeology 139. Uppsala, Sweden: Åströms Förlag.

Kowalewski, S.A. 2013. The work of making community. In J. Birch (ed.), *From Prehistoric Villages to Cities: Settlement Aggregation and Community Transformation*, 201–218. New York: Routledge.

Kypris, D.C. 1996. Cyclic climatic changes in Cyprus as evidenced from historic documents and one century's rainfall records. In A.N. Angelakis and A.S. Issar (eds.), *Diachronic Climate Impacts on Water Resources*, 111–128. NATO ASI 36. Berlin: Springer.

López, M.V., and J.L. Arrúe. 1997. Growth, yield, and water use efficiency of winter barley in response to conservation tillage in a semi-arid region of Spain. *Soil and Tillage Research* 44: 35–54.

Mann, M. 1986. *The Sources of Social Power Volume I: A History of Power from the Beginning to A.D. 1760*. Cambridge: Cambridge University Press.

Manning, S.W. 1993. Prestige, distinction, and competition: The anatomy of socioeconomic complexity in fourth to second millennium B.C.E. Cyprus. *Bulletin of the American Schools of Oriental Research* 292: 35–58.

Manning, S.W. 2013. Cyprus at 2200 BC: Rethinking the chronology of the Cypriot Early Bronze Age. In A.B. Knapp, J.M. Webb, and A. McCarthy (eds.), *J.R.B. Stewart—An Archaeological Legacy*, 1–21. Studies in Mediterranean Archaeology 139. Uppsala, Sweden: Åströms Förlag.

Manning, S.W. 2014. Timings and gaps in the early history of Cyprus and its copper trade: What these might tell us. In J.M. Webb (ed.), *Structure, Measurement, and Meaning. Studies on Prehistoric Cyprus in Honour of David Frankel*, 23–42. Studies in Mediterranean Archaeology 143. Uppsala, Sweden: Åströms Förlag.

Manning, S.W. 2018. Some perspectives on the frequency of significant, historically forcing, drought and subsistence crises in Anatolia and region. In E. Holt (ed.), *Water and Power in Past Societies*, 279-295. IEMA Proceedings, volume 7. Albany, NY: State University of New York Press.

Manning, S.W., F. Höflmayer, N. Moeller, M.W. Dee, C. Bronk Ramsey, D. Fleitmann, T. Higham, W. Kutschera, and E.M. Wild. 2014. Dating the Thera (Santorini) eruption: Coherent archaeological and scientific evidence supporting a high chronology. *Antiquity* 88: 1164–1179.

Manning, S.W., C.B. Griggs, B. Lorentzen, G. Barjamovic, C.B. Ramsey, B. Kromer, and E.M. Wild. 2016. Integrated tree-ring-radiocarbon high-resolution timeframe to resolve earlier second millennium BCE Mesopotamian chronology. *PLoS ONE* 11(7):e0157144. doi:10.1371/journal.pone.0157144.

Marciniak, A. 2011. The Secondary Products Revolution: Empirical evidence and its current zooarchaeological critique. *Journal of World Prehistory* 24: 117–130.

Meller, H., H.W. Arx, R. Jung, and R. Risch. (eds.) 2015. *2200 BCE—Ein Klimasturz als Ursache für den Zerfall der Alten Welt?/2200 BCE—A Climatic Breakdown as a Cause for the Collapse of the Old World? 7th Archaeological Conference of Central Germany October 23–26, 2014 in Halle (Saale)*. Halle: Landesmuseum für Vorgeschichte.

Michaelides, D. 1996. The economy of Cyprus during the Hellenistic and Roman periods. In V. Karageorghis and D. Michaelides (eds.), *The Development of the Cypriot Economy from the Prehistoric Period to the Present Day*, 139–152. Nicosia: University of Cyprus and Bank of Cyprus.

Mona, N. 1986. Structure and responsiveness of barley production in Syria. Unpublished PhD dissertation, Texas A&M University.

Morris, D. 1985. *The Art of Ancient Cyprus*. Oxford: Phaidon.

Padgham, K. 2014. *The Scale and Nature of the Late Bronze Age Economies of Egypt and Cyprus*. BAR International Series 2594. Oxford: Archaeopress.

Papadopoullos, T. 1965. *Social and Historical Data on Population (1570–1881)*. Nicosia: Cyprus Research Centre.

Peltenburg, E. 1993. Settlement discontinuity and resistance to complexity in Cyprus, ca. 4500–2500 B.C.E. *Bulletin of the American Schools of Oriental Research* 292: 9–23.

Peltenburg, E. 1996. From isolation to state formation in Cyprus, c.3500–1500 BC. In V. Karageorghis and D. Michaelides (eds.), *The Development of the Cypriot Economy: From the Prehistoric Period to the Present Day*, 17–44. Nicosia: University of Cyprus and Bank of Cyprus.

Pilides, D. 1996. Storage jars as evidence of the economy of Cyprus in the Late Bronze Age. In V. Karageorghis and D. Michaelides (eds.), *The Development of the Cypriot Economy: From the Prehistoric Period to the Present Day*, 107–124. Nicosia: University of Cyprus and Bank of Cyprus.

Pilides, D. 2014. Windows onto the Bronze Age of Nicosia: Another glimpse. In J.M. Webb (ed.), *Structure, Measurement, and Meaning. Studies on Prehistoric Cyprus in Honour of David Frankel*, 151–159. Studies in Mediterranean Archaeology 143. Uppsala, Sweden: Åströms Förlag.

Porter, A. 2012. *Mobile Pastoralism and the Formation of Near Eastern Civilizations: Weaving Together Society*. Cambridge: Cambridge University Press.

Potts, D.T. 1997. *Mesopotamian Civilization: The Material Foundations*. London: The Athlone Press.

Renfrew, A.C. 1974. Beyond a subsistence economy: The evolution of social organisation in prehistoric Europe. In C.B. Moore (ed.), *Reconstructing Complex Societies: An Archaeological Colloquium*, 69–96. Supplement to the Bulletin of the American School of Oriental Research 20. Boston: American Schools of Oriental Research.

Reemtsma, J.P. 2012. *Trust and Violence: An Essay on a Modern Relationship*. Princeton: Princeton University Press.

Roberts, N., D. Brayshaw, C. Kuzucuoğlu, R. Perez, and L. Sadori. 2011. The mid-Holocene climatic transition in the Mediterranean: Causes and consequences. *The Holocene* 21: 3–13.

Robinson, S.A., S. Black, B.W. Sellwood, and P.J. Valdes. 2006. A review of palaeoclimates and palaeoenvironments in the Levant and Eastern Mediterranean from 25,000 to 5,000 years BP: Setting the environmental background for the evolution of human civilization. *Quaternary Science Review* 25: 1517–1541.

Roscoe, P.B. 1993. Practice and political centralisation: A new approach to political evolution. *Current Anthropology* 34: 111–140.

Şahoğlu, V. 2005. The Anatolian Trade Network and the Izmir region during the Early Bronze Age. *Oxford Journal of Archaeology* 24: 339–361.

Sallares, R. 1991. *The Ecology of the Ancient Greek World*. London: Duckworth.

Scott, J.C. 1985. *Weapons of the Weak*. New Haven: Yale University Press.

Sherratt, A. 1981. Plough and pastoralism: Aspects of the secondary products revolution. In I. Hodder, G. Isaac, and N. Hammond (eds.), *Pattern of the Past: Studies in Honour of David Clarke*, 261–306. Cambridge: Cambridge University Press.

Sherratt, A. 1983. The secondary exploitation of animals in the Old World. *World Archaeology* 15: 90–104.

Smith, A.T. 2003. *The Political Landscape: Constellations of Authority in Early Complex Polities*. Berkeley: University of California Press.

South, A. 2014. From pots to people: Estimating population for Late Bronze Age Kalavasos. In J.M. Webb (ed.), *Structure, Measurement, and Meaning. Studies on Prehistoric Cyprus in Honour of David Frankel*, 69–77. Studies in Mediterranean Archaeology 143. Uppsala, Sweden: Åströms Förlag.

Spencer, C.S. 1993. Human agency, biased transmission, and the cultural evolution of chiefly authority. *Journal of Anthropological Archaeology* 12: 41–74.

Steel, L. 2013. The social world of Early-Middle Bronze Age Cyprus: Rethinking the Vounous bowl. *Journal of Mediterranean Archaeology* 26: 51–73.

Stewart, B. 1908. *My Experiences of Cyprus*. 1st rev. ed. London: George Routledge & Sons.

Stige, L.C., K.-S. Chan, Z. Zhang, D. Frank, and N.C. Stenseth. 2007. Thousand-year-long Chinese time series reveals climatic forcing of decadal locust dynamics. *Proceedings of the National Academy of Sciences of the United States of America* 104: 16188–16193.

Styring, A.K., M. Ater, Y. Hmimsa, R. Fraser, H. Miller, R. Neef, J.A. Pearson, and A. Bogaard. 2016. Disentangling the effect of farming practice from aridity on crop stable isotope values: A present-day model from Morocco and its application to early farming sites in the eastern Mediterranean. *The Anthropocene Review* 3: 1–21.

Talalay, L., and T. Cullen. 2002. Sexual ambiguity in plank figurines from Bronze Age Cyprus. In D. Bolger and N. Serwint (ed.), *Engendering Aphrodite: Women and Society in Ancient Cyprus*, 181–195. Boston: American Schools of Oriental Research.

Todd, I.A. 2013. *Vasilikos Valley Project 12: The Field Survey of the Vasilikos Valley Vol III, Human Settlement in the Vasilikos Valley*. Studies in Mediterranean Archaeology 71.12. Uppsala, Sweden: Åströms Förlag.

Touchan, R., A.K. Christou, and D.M. Meko. 2014. Six centuries of May-July precipitation in Cyprus from tree-rings. *Climate Dynamics* 43: 3281–3292.

Tsipopoulou, M., and A. South. 2012. The economics of monumental buildings. In G. Cadogan, M. Iacovou, K. Kopaka, and J. Whitley (eds.), *Parallel Lives: Ancient Island Societies in Crete and Cyprus. Proceedings of the Conference in Nicosia Organized by the British School at Athens, the University of Crete and the University of Cyprus in November-December 2006*, 209–231. London: The British School at Athens.

Webb, J.M. 2012. Kalopsidha: Forty-six years after SIMA volume 2. In J.M. Webb and D. Frankel (eds.), *SIMA Fifty Years On*, 49–58. Studies in Mediterranean Archaeology 137. Uppsala, Sweden: Åströms Förlag.

Webb, J.M. 2018. Shifting centres: site location and resource procurement on the north coast of Cyprus over the *longue durée* of the prehistoric Bronze Age. *Land* 7, 64; doi:10.3390/land7020064.

Webb, J.M., and D. Frankel. 1999. Characterizing the Philia facies: Material culture, chronology, and the origin of the Bronze Age in Cyprus. *American Journal of Archaeology* 103: 3–43.

Webb, J.M., and D. Frankel. 2010. Social strategies, ritual, and cosmology in Early Bronze Age Cyprus: An investigation of burial data from the north coast. *Levant* 42: 185–209.

Webb, J.M., and D. Frankel. 2013a. Cultural regionalism and divergent social trajectories in Early Bronze Age Cyprus. *American Journal of Archaeology* 117: 59–81.

Webb, J.M., and D. Frankel. 2013b. *Ambelikou* Aletri: *Metallurgy and Pottery Production in Middle Bronze Age Cyprus*. Studies in Mediterranean Archaeology 138. Uppsala, Sweden: Åströms Förlag.

Webb, J.M., D. Frankel, K.O. Eriksson, and J.B. Hennessy. 2009. *The Bronze Age Cemeteries at Karmi Palealona and Lapatsa in Cyprus: Excavations by J.R.B. Stewart*. Studies in Mediterranean Archaeology 136. Sävedalen, Sweden: P. Åströms Förlag.

Weiss, H. 2014. Altered trajectories: The intermediate Bronze Age. In M. Steiner and A.E. Killebrew (eds.), *The Oxford Handbook of the Archaeology of the Levant c.8000–332 BCE*, 367–387. Oxford University Press, Oxford.

Wilkinson, T.J. 2004. *On the Margin of the Euphrates. Settlement, and Land Use at Tell es-Sweyhat and in the Upper Lake Assad Area, Syria*. Chicago: Oriental Institute.

Wossink, A. 2009. *Challenging Climate Change: Competition and Cooperation Among Pastoralists and Agriculturalists in Northern Mesopotamia (c.3000–1600 BC)*. Leiden, the Netherlands: Sidestone Press.

Yoffee, N. 2005. *Myths of the Archaic State: Evolution of the Earliest Cities, States, and Civilizations*. Cambridge: Cambridge University Press.

Zomeni, Z., C. Camera, A. Bruggeman, A. Zissimos, I. Christoforou, and J. Noller. 2014. Digital soil map of Cyprus (1:25,000). *AGWATER Scientific Report* 6 Deliverable D15, D16. Nicosia: The Cyprus Institute. Available: http://www.cyi.ac.cy/images/AGWATER_Scientific_Reports/AGWATER_ScientificReport6_WP3_Soils_def.pdf—accessed December 2016.

PART II

Bronze Age Complexities

4

Negotiating a New Landscape

Middle Bronze Age Fortresses as a Component of the Cypriot Political Assemblage

EILIS MONAHAN AND MATTHEW SPIGELMAN

Introduction

Between the agrarian villages of the prehistoric (Early and Middle) Cypriot Bronze Age, ca. 2400–1750 BCE, and the sociopolitical complexity of Late Cypriot (LC) II, ca. 1450–1200 BCE, lies the Middle Cypriot (MC) III–LC I "transitional" period, ca. 1750–1450 BCE (Manning 2013). This period witnessed a number of rapid transformations in Cypriot society, including the appearance of innovative architectural forms, here classified as fortresses, constructed in the Kyrenia Mountains, the Karpas Peninsula, and the Mesaoria Plain. It is also at this juncture that the development of a hierarchically stratified society on Cyprus is argued to have occurred (e.g., Knapp 2013b; Peltenburg 1996; Manning in this volume). We contend, however, that while this period has been the subject of much scholarly interest, the archaeological dataset remains limited (see endnote), and the mechanisms that drove developments on the island at this time have largely been under-theorized in the search for the predictable rise of a state, as Yoffee (2005: 21) says, a process which has "buried the complexities of development under the single-minded aim of establishing an all-encompassing regularity, a teleology without a god."

The construction of fortresses on Cyprus coincides with the abandonment of many long-lived Bronze Age villages throughout the island (Catling 1962: 141; Georgiou 2011: 478–480). The abandonment and subsequent relocation of settlements paired with the construction of new fortified sites, rather than the construction of defensive walls around existing sites, demonstrates that fortification constituted more than just the introduction of a new element to the built environment. Instead, these fortresses, i.e., sites or structures with marked defensive features, such as stout walls, bastions, reinforced entryways, and locations atop precipitous cliffs, are more productively viewed as part of a suite of interconnected changes that brought about a sharp break from previous lifeways.

The importance of these fortified sites has been downplayed in recent archaeological literature. One factor in this underestimation is the uncertainty surrounding their dating, which has led to a minimalist view of their duration. Despite the recorded presence of chronologically earlier and later ceramic wares at some fortresses (e.g., Red Polished wares associated with the EC and earlier MC at Dhali *Kafkallia* [Catling 1962: 149, no. 27, confirmed by the authors during fieldwork in 2013 and 2016] and White Slip II and Base Ring II, associated with LC IB–LC IIC at Ayios Sozomenos *Glykia Vrysi* [Catling 1962: 161, no. 40; 1975: 197] and Korovia *Nitovikla* [Hult 1992: 48, 70]), the fortresses are generally dated to MC III–LC I (1700–1450 BCE) (e.g., Fortin 1981; Baurain 1984: 80–87; Peltenburg 1996: 30). Merrillees (1994) rejected an earlier MC date for the fortresses' inception, revising the *terminus post quem* further downwards into LC IA, a proposal supported by Peltenburg (2008: 152–153), but simultaneously argued that the fortresses were abandoned before the LC IB (Merrillees 1982: 375). These revisions reduce the fortresses' life span to at most one hundred years.

Rather than considering the tremendous variability in size, materials, architectural forms, and relationships with the landscape constituted by these sites, previous research has also largely discussed the fortresses as a singular phenomenon (e.g., Merrillees 1982: 375; Peltenburg 1996, 2008; Knapp 2008: 144–151; contra Keswani 1996: 219). These analyses viewed the sites caught under the umbrella term *fortress* as components within an emerging settlement hierarchy dedicated to the intensification of copper mining, transport, refining, and export. This industry was organized by (exploitative) emergent elites residing at the newly founded coastal settlements of Enkomi and Morphou *Toumba tou Skourou*. The fortresses were then quickly abandoned as island-wide political hegemony made them no longer necessary or useful (Peltenburg 1996: 35; Keswani and Knapp 2003: 219). This perceived brevity of fortress construction and use and the perpetuation of their received roles as passive components of a security system for the copper trade relegated the Cypriot Bronze Age fortresses to the status of epiphenomenal within a quickly forgotten transitional period.

The MC III–LC I fortresses have received little additional scholarly consideration, aside from repeated attempts to recognize architectural parallels with contemporary fortified sites and to identify a historical impetus for their construction in the Levant, Anatolia, or the Aegean (e.g., Sjöqvist 1940: 138–146; Baurain 1984: 86; Peltenburg 2008) or instead to argue for their local inspiration (e.g., Hult 1992: 75; Merrillees 2007: 93). Further downplaying the sites' significance, one recent article (Devillers *et al.* 2004: Figures 3 and 4) recorded two of the largest fortresses on the Ayios Sozomenos plateau as "livestock enclosures," either unaware of, or disregarding, the presence of extensive internal architecture and nearly 2-meter-thick enclosure walls that go far beyond the needs of simple animal containment. In a rare recent attempt to place the fortifications in a social context, Knapp proposed that they serve as a first attempt in the "trend of 'place-making' by emergent elites that would culminate in the monumental ashlar buildings of the LC II–III," built to "control people's movements and interactions by appropriating, enclosing, and monumentalizing space" (2013a: 360). In this paper we return to Yoffee's critique above, to argue that the significance of the fortresses is not in their construction by an invisible "elite" but rather in the active and generative roles that the fortresses played within the creation of a new social and political assemblage.

Materiality and the Political Assemblage

The material turn in the humanities and social sciences (see Mukerji 2015) has unsurprisingly been embraced by archaeology, where it has developed with an explicit focus on the "meaning" of material culture and its role in the social realm (e.g., Shanks and Tilley 1987). The popular discussion of the "social lives of things" (Appadurai 1986) calls attention to the active role that materials play in the social arena but runs the risk of highlighting the "social" and diminishing the material reality of the "things." This approach also glosses over the critical question of politics, here understood as the negotiation of power as embedded in all social interactions. An understanding of the role of materials and the material world in political relations remains relatively underdeveloped (cf. Smith 2015), as insufficient attention has been paid to how specific things or objects, from pots to fortifications, are active participants in the political domain, operating and acting efficaciously.

Critical theorists of materials and materiality have led an assault on commonly held views of objects simply "expressing," "symbolizing," or "reproducing" social relations. Objects are certainly capable of all these things, but they are also provocative and efficacious, in a way that challenges the traditional subject/object divide (Harman 2010; Frow 2010). In his Actor-Network-Theory, Latour (2005) dismantles the dichotomy between the object and the subject. He argues that non-humans are active participants in social life: things can "determine, authorize, allow, afford, encourage, permit, suggest, influence, block, render possible, forbid, etc." (2005: 72). Latour also cogently argues that social asymmetries are not naturally stable. Relationships must be constantly negotiated and reinforced, so face-to-face contact is insufficient to explain the stark and long-lasting inequalities in human relationships and, writ large, our societies. Instead, social relations are stabilized through the continuous reinforcement granted by the persistent nature of the material world.

Objects do not occur in isolation, but this complicates our understanding of how they operate. DeLanda (2006: 10–11), following Hegel, proposes that object assemblages may be

> both analysable into separate parts and at the same time have irreducible properties, properties that emerge from the *interactions* between parts. . . . In fact, the reason why the properties of a whole cannot be reduced to those of its parts is that they are the result not of an aggregation of the components' own properties but of the actual exercise of their capacities.

This perspective serves as a powerful rejoinder to archaeologists: that objects cannot be understood separately, but only through their relations with other components of their assemblage, human and object alike, and the capacities they exercise. It is for this reason that the Bronze Age fortifications of Cyprus must be studied in the context of their relations with the objects, landscape, and human practices with which they interacted.

In order to investigate these assemblages, we turn to DeLanda's (2006) theorization, in which the relationship between components and the assemblages of which they are part may be conceived in two dimensions or axes (Figure 4.1).

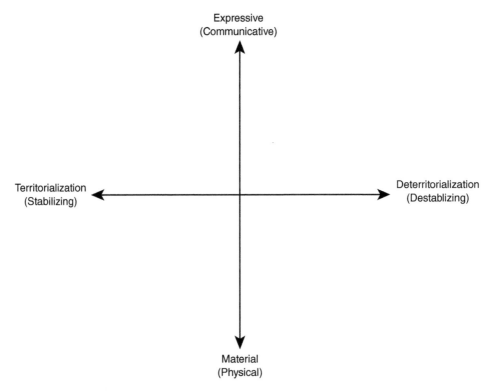

Figure 4.1: Diagram of DeLanda's (2006) theorization of the roles and processes in which components relate to assemblages.

The first axis describes the roles material components play as actors in social interaction, ranging from material to expressive. The second axis defines the processes in which the component plays a role in regard to the definition of the assemblage: processes of territorialization (stabilizing the assemblage by increasing internal homogeneity or sharpening boundaries) and deterritorialization (destabilization by decreasing the homogeneity of the assemblage, or blurring or transgressing boundaries).

Latour's Actor-Network-Theory and DeLanda's assemblage theory together provide a framework within which to study how people, things, and landscapes are actively implicated in the creation of political relations. As a first foray into this methodology, this paper explores the roles played by the landscape in defining the assemblages of the MC III–LC I fortresses and the roles played by these assemblages in the emergence of new systems of social relations and the definition of new social groups. By turning to the material components preserved in the archaeological record, in this example the fortresses and landscapes, we consider the social relations that the assemblage materializes and what affective roles were played by the material components in producing and sustaining relations of inequality and power. This approach creates a framework for investigating the development of political relations using the archaeological record, rather than assuming *a priori* social formations with an invisible elite and the state.

Land and Landscape of Bronze Age Cyprus

We argue that the construction of fortresses in Cyprus during the Bronze Age must be understood as part of the emergence of a new social and political assemblage, of which the landscape is a critical component. Therefore, it is necessary to define what we mean by *landscape*. In doing so we highlight those aspects of the land that we will argue interacted with the fortresses to produce the new social and political landscapes and assemblages of the Middle to Late Bronze Age. Our understanding of landscape is built on that of Gosden and Head (1994: 114), who succinctly state, "Landscapes are both created and creating. Landscapes are shaped by human action through processes such as clearance, erosion and deposition; they are also the shapers of human action encouraging and constraining various forms of land-use and inter-regional connections."

As we look to understand changes in the Cypriot landscape we heed Ingold's (1993: 153) warning of "what the landscape is not. It is not 'land,' it is not 'nature,' and it is not 'space.'" Rather, Ingold (1993: 157–161) argues that a landscape comes into existence through the process of people dwelling within it. As we attempt to understand the place of fortresses within the landscape of Bronze Age Cyprus we necessarily add a political dimension to our understanding of the concept, as we consider how the interaction of fortresses with the landscape serves to shape human relations by providing particular limits on or affordances (i.e., possibilities) for action. It is in this interaction between landscape, built environment, and human activity that inequalities in social relations are created and stabilized.

In working to understand the land of Cyprus as the landscape of the Bronze Age, we identify several key features: the location of agricultural resources (water, fertile soils, pasture), industrial resources (copper bearing minerals, workable clays), routes of land travel (mountain passes, flat plains), and points of access to the sea (bays, sheltered coves). We argue that the landscape of Cyprus is a diverse patchwork and that the reconfiguration of the social and political assemblage requires a reconfiguration of the landscape as well.

The land of Cyprus is dominated by its two mountain ranges: the Kyrenia Mountains to the north and the Troodos Mountains to the south. The remainder of the island is composed of low-lying plains, both in the area between the two mountain ranges and along most of the coastal margins. The Kyrenia Mountains are steep-sided and extend along the north coast of the island, terminating in the Kormakiti Plateau to the west and the Karpas Peninsula to the east. Due to their precipitous slopes, the Kyrenia Mountains can be traversed easily only through a handful of mountain passes. As the Kyrenia Mountains trail off to the northeast, the long and narrow Karpas Peninsula is a mix of hilly areas and fertile valleys, with many sheltered coves along each of its shores.

The Mesaoria Plain is located to the south of the Kyrenia Mountains. It is well watered with fertile soil and easily traversed from east to west. In many places, steep-sided plateaus overlook the margins of the plain. To the west are the Troodos Mountains that compose the southwestern portion of the island. This broad and tall mountain range has rolling foothills and deeply incised valleys. It is extensively forested and encircled by copper-bearing deposits. Small patches of land suitable for growing cereal crops exist within the foothills and river valleys. The Troodos Mountains, however, either are not arable or are better suited to grazing animals and growing orchard fruits.

Within this patchwork, resource acquisition and transport required the negotiation of multiple landscapes and seascapes and could have required interaction with different social groups. We argue that the diversity in the existing natural landscape of Cyprus and the variable human responses during this period to the affordances and limitations created by this landscape (see Manning in this volume) resulted in processes of destabilization and deterritorialization, generating new assemblages and fractured social and political landscapes. At the same time, the introduction of new material practices and expressions of solidarity and connectivity could also have served to counter these destabilizing and deterritorializing processes by strengthening or expanding a social assemblage and its boundaries. It is the role of fortresses in this simultaneous stabilization and destabilization of identity, territory, and connectivity that interests us.

Shifting Bronze Age Assemblages

During the Early Cypriot Bronze Age, a new society emerged on Cyprus with a stable assemblage of people, things, and landscapes. The main components of this assemblage were first introduced to Cyprus, primarily from Anatolia, in the years after 2500 BCE in what is commonly known as the Philia facies or culture. This new social and material assemblage first appeared in the western Mesaoria, likely through processes of trade (e.g., Manning 1993) or migration (Webb and Frankel 1999), and spread through processes of interaction and acculturation (Webb and Frankel 1999: 43) or hybridization (Knapp 2008: 110–130). While initially there is evidence for regular and sustained contact with communities on the Anatolian mainland (Webb et al. 2006), regular contact appears to have ceased by 2300–2250 BCE, when mainland communities went through a period of decreased social complexity and increased mobility while Cypriot communities entered a period of relative insularity (Webb and Frankel 2013a). During this period of insularity and stability, from roughly 2300/2250–2000/1950 BCE, the population on the island grew significantly (Georgiou 2006), and the Early Bronze Age assemblage of people and things spread throughout Cyprus, in conversation with the varying landscapes of the island.

The stable assemblage of Early Bronze Age village society on Cyprus consisted of small communities of several hundred people, a settlement location on a slope near a river or spring providing direct access to both arable farmland and upland pasture, and, for many communities, proximity to nearby copper resources (e.g., Marki *Alonia*: Frankel and Webb 1996; 2006; Sotira *Kaminoudhia*: Swiny et al. 2003). Houses were expanded and conjoined organically, leading to dense habitation areas with many party walls, and cemeteries were located on the surrounding hills. Mortuary and iconographic evidence points to social organization along extended familial lines, and extensive burial rituals provided opportunities for re-negotiating relationships (Keswani 2004; 2005; Webb and Frankel 2013a). There is evidence for regional diversity developing during this period (see Webb and Frankel 2013a) and possibly also the emergence of hereditary elites (Manning 1993; Manning and Swiny 1994; Peltenburg 1994). We argue, however, that these differences are slight when compared with the dramatic changes that followed (cf. Knapp 2013b).

In order to understand later changes, it is important to note what was not included in the assemblage of people, things, and landscape that made up the Early Bronze Age village society of Cyprus. Two absences are particularly notable. First, while weapons were increasingly common accoutrements in burials, there is no evidence for the construction of fortification walls or ditches at any of the Early Bronze Age village sites in Cyprus. Second, few Early Bronze Age village sites were founded in a coastal location (although Kissonerga *Skalia* [Crewe 2014: 137] is a notable exception. The extensive cemeteries at Lapithos also may indicate an as-yet-unlocated coastal settlement; see Diakou in this volume), aquatic resources are largely absent from the excavated settlement assemblages, and foreign objects are practically unknown in settlement and burial contexts. Based on these absences we argue that raiding and large-scale violence were not present (cf. Sneddon 2014) and that maritime trade was negligible during the Early Bronze Age.

The Early Bronze Age assemblage of people, things, and landscapes began to shift and to destabilize social relations during the Middle Cypriot Bronze Age, in the years after 2000/1950 BCE. We argue that the destabilization developed due to changes in assemblage components that originated both internally and externally to the island. Internally, some villages began to focus on specific craft production activities, making use of local affordances granted by their locations in the landscape, and burnt destructions become common, suggesting internecine conflict. Externally, mainland communities underwent a process of re-urbanization and increasing social complexity, resulting in renewed maritime activity and trade throughout the region, including with Cyprus (e.g., Gerstenblith 1983; Marcus *et al.* 2008).

The development of craft specialization in the Middle Bronze Age is most clearly demonstrated in the results of Dikaios's excavations at Ambelikou *Aletri* (Webb and Frankel 2013b). Located on the northern slopes of the Troodos Mountains, close to the large Skouriotissa copper ore body, excavations at Ambelikou *Aletri* showed the development of a community built around multi-crafting, with both copper extraction and ceramic production practiced. Excavations at Pyrgos *Mavrorachi* (Belgiorno 2004), located on the southern slopes of the Troodos Mountains, seem to indicate that many communities on Cyprus adopted a similar multi-crafting strategy during the Middle Bronze Age. The adoption of multi-crafting (Hirth 2009) is a strategy for craft specialization in which a diversity of goods is produced, thereby decreasing the need for extensive distribution or large markets. We argue that the adoption of multi-crafting in villages on the margins of the Troodos Mountains is indicative of the new assemblage of people, things, and landscapes that emerged during the Middle Bronze Age. The formation of this new assemblage from within the existing Early Bronze Age village assemblage is significant, but as we will see it was unstable and required more extensive reorganization.

Burnt destructions in settlements include Marki *Alonia* Area I–IV (MC II: Frankel and Webb 1996: 28–29, Plate 5a; Frankel and Webb 2006: 41), Alambra *Mouttes* (MC I–II: Georgiou 2008: 134; Gjerstad 1926: 23), Ambelikou *Aletri* (MC I: Webb and Frankel 2013b: 62), Kalavasos *Laroumena* (MC II–III: Todd 1993: 87, 91, Figure 3), and Episkopi *Phaneromeni* Area A (LC IA: Carpenter 1981: 62), all of which have previously been explained as the result of isolated accidents or earthquakes (Figure 4.2).

Notably, three of the excavated MC III–LC I fortified sites also had destruction episodes, i.e. *Glykia Vrysi* (Gjerstad 1926: 42), *Nitovikla* (Gjerstad *et al.* 1934: 393), and Enkomi (Dikaios 1969–71: 21, 31–32, 45). The fourth, *Vounari*, had significant deposits of ash and underwent multiple reconstructions, though destruction is not confirmed (Horowitz 2007: 154–158). Only the burning episodes at Ambelikou *Aletri* (Håkansson 1981: 402), Marki *Alonia* (Frankel and Webb 2006: 36, Text Figure 3.4) and Episkopi *Phaneromeni* (Fishman *et al.* 1977: 189) produced radiocarbon determinations, providing a wide date range from ca. 1950–1700 BCE for these destruction episodes on Cyprus (see Paraskeva in this volume). We argue, however, that the prevalence, even ubiquity, of destructions at settlements and fortified sites is strong evidence that violence was an increasing component of Middle Bronze Age society, continuing into the beginning of the Late Bronze Age.

Foreign objects also begin to appear in very small numbers in Cyprus during the Middle Bronze Age (but are limited to funerary sites on the north coast, see Knapp 1994: 281; Webb *et al.* 2009). This shift is contemporaneous with the re-urbanization of the Levant during the MB IIA (Gerstenblith 1983), the re-establishment of maritime exchange between Egypt and the Levantine coast (Marcus *et al.* 2008), and documentary evidence for Cypriot copper abroad (Sasson 1996; Wiseman 1996). These external sources of intrusive material and social components undoubtedly contributed to the destabilization of the Cypriot social assemblage.

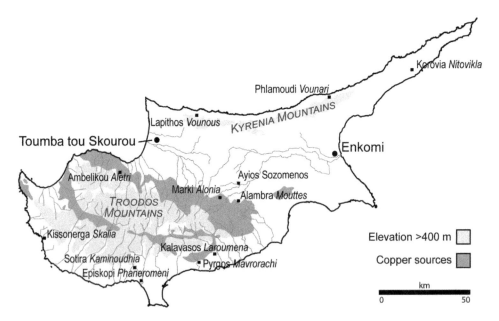

Figure 4.2: Map of MC sites with recorded destructions.

The close of the Middle Bronze Age on Cyprus thus sees the dramatic reor-ganization of the assemblage of people, things, and landscapes (see Manning in this volume). This is particularly clear in the villages located in the foothills of the Troodos Mountains and the northern slopes of the Kyrenia Mountains, all of which were abandoned at this time (Georgiou 2006: 448–454, 465–468, Fig-ures 13.1–13.3; Webb *et al.* 2009: 253–254, Figures 4.44, 4.46). As fortresses were constructed elsewhere, the people of these villages chose to move rather than to encircle themselves with defensive walls. Therefore, we will argue in the next section that the construction of fortifications on Cyprus is more than just the introduction of a new element to the built environment. Rather, it is better viewed as one of a suite of interconnected changes that represents experimentation in the development of a new political and material assemblage in place of the previous assemblage, which had become unstable with the introduction of more intensive craft production, increased foreign trade, and the use of violence on a previously unknown scale.

Diverse Assemblages, Diverse Responses

Fortified sites appeared along the length of the Karpas Peninsula, along the major passes through the Kyrenia Mountains, and on the plateaus of the central and west-ern Mesaoria Plain during the MC III–LC I period, as determined by ceramic assem-blages. Here we emphasize the diversity of landscapes in which these fortresses were built and also the variation in architectural forms produced. The fortified sites on Cyprus are in fact highly variable responses of humans to new material conditions caused by developments both internal and external to the island, and most impor-tantly to the diverse topography and resources of the island itself, rather than a top-down, centralized response to foreign demand for copper. We suggest, however, that the material nature of the fortresses and their interactions with the landscape also shaped human activity, resulting in the creation and reinforcement of emergent hierarchical social relations.

As mentioned previously, scholarly literature on the fortresses has traditionally focused on their presumed involvement in the international copper trade, yet docu-mentary evidence shows only small amounts of Cypriot copper being exported from the island at the time the fortified sites first appear. The argument for the fortified sites being built to guard a single trade route focused on Enkomi in the east (Pelten-burg 1996: 33–34) or a pair of trade routes to the east and the west (Keswani and Knapp 2003: 215) weakens considerably given that many of the fortified sites are located in areas unconnected to the movement of people and goods between these sites and the copper-producing regions on the flanks of the Troodos. Specifically, the locations of clusters of fortified sites on the Karpas Peninsula and on the Kormakiti Plateau and in areas associated with the Kyrenia Pass do not fit such a model, and there are no known fortifications from this period in close proximity to the copper sources themselves (Figure 4.3).

The only copper production site dated to this period that has been excavated, Politiko *Phorades,* has no evidence for fortification or other defensive features

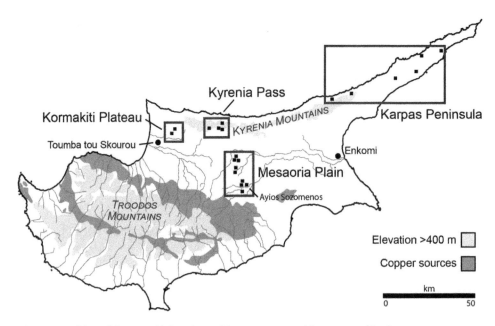

Figure 4.3: Map of Cyprus with locations of fortresses grouped into geographic clusters.

(Knapp and Kassianidou 2008). The fortified sites closest to the Troodos are on the Ayios Sozomenos Plateau in the central Mesaoria, more than 18 km from *Phorades* and more than 10 km from the Sia-Mathiati copper ores and the nearest known ancient mine, Ayia Varvara *Almyras*. *Almyras* is located just 2 km from the MC settlement at Alambra *Mouttes* but dates to the Iron Age, and there is as yet no evidence for Bronze Age mining in this region (Gale *et al.* 1996: 400). If guarding the movement of copper was the primary motivation behind the construction of these fortified structures, leaving the actual sources and smelting sites unprotected requires significant explanation.

Therefore, instead of trying to force the fortified sites into a preconceived model of how Cypriot economic and political organization developed in relation to copper production, we consider the forms and locations of the fortresses within the context of their natural settings, the resources potentially exploited by their inhabitants, and the benefits fortifications might have brought the local populations. For heuristic purposes, a classification of the sites into three broad types based on major architectural characteristics is useful: fortified settlements, outposts, and enclosures (see Figure 4.4 and Table 4.1).

These categories alone suggest very different site functions. Fortification of settlements, even if they are only utilized as short-term refuges, suggests sustained fear of violence. This violence could result over access to territory, or it could be directed at the acquisition of specific resources in the context of raiding for livestock, metals, or other portable wealth. The sites classified as "Fortified Settlements" are

Plamoudhi
Vounari

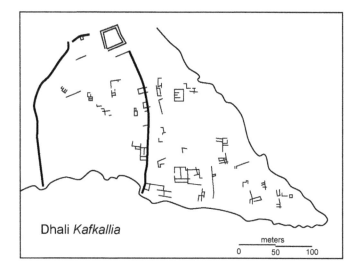

Dhali *Kafkallia*

meters

0   50   100

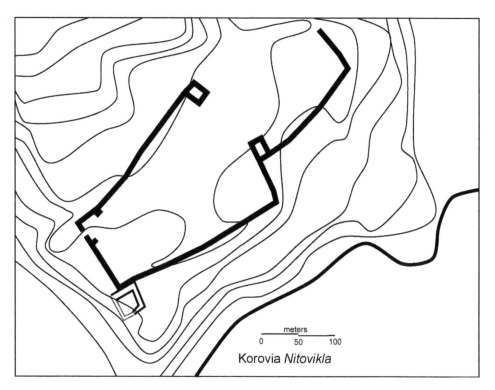

meters

0   50   100

Korovia *Nitovikla*

Figure 4.4: Sketch plans of the fortresses at Phlamoudhi *Vounari* (Outpost; after Horowitz 2008, Figure 48), Korovia *Nitovikla* (Outpost and Enclosure; after Gjerstad *et al.* 1934, Plate IV:2), and Dhali *Kafkallia* (Settlement and Enclosure; after Overbeck and Swiny 1972, Figure 4).

Table 4.1: Summary of Cypriot MC III–LC I fortified sites discussed in text

Region	Site	Dimensions	Features	Type
Yeri Plateau	Yeri *Vrysi ti Panelous*	60 x 90 m	Empty	Enclosure
	Yeri *Phthelia*	4 x 7 m	Single structure, thick walls	Outpost
Ayios Sozomenos Plateau	Dhali *Kafkallia*	150 x 200 m, 250 x 200 x 400 m	Two conjoined enclosures, extensive internal architecture in one	Settlement, Enclosure
	AySz *Nikolidhes*	250 x 250 m	Limited Internal architecture, possible tower and gate	Enclosure
	AySz *Barsak*	250 x 200 m	Double wall and ditch system, empty	Enclosure
	AySz *Glyka Vrysi*	20 x 35 m	Single structure, thick walls	Outpost
Elenja Hills	Elenja *Leondari Vouno*	60 x 40 m	Unknown	Enclosure
	Elenja *Kafezin*	32 x 41 m	Small enclosure, 3 structures	Outpost
	Elenja *Nifkia*	20 x 15 m	Single enclosed space	Outpost
Kormakiti Plateau	Asomatos *Potemata*	100 x 300 m	6x6 m tower, domestic architecture	Settlement
	Karpasha *Styllomenos*	100 x 100 m	Empty	Enclosure
Kyrenia Pass	Dhikomo *Onisia*	80 x 80 m	Empty	Enclosure
	Dhikomo *Pamboulos*	300 x 200 m	Internal architecture	Settlement
	Krini *Merra*	150 x 80 m	Double wall with bastions, empty	Enclosure
	Bellapais *Kapa Kaya*	100 x 100 m	Internal architecture	Settlement
Karpas Penninsula	Phlamoudhi *Vounari*	18 x 18 m	Artificial hill, platform w/ small enclosure	Outpost
	Lythangomi *Troullia*	130 x 60 m	Orthostat slab constructed wall, ditch	Enclosure
	Korovia *Nitovikla*	400 x 200 m, 35 x 40 m	Enclosure, with large structure at corner, gate w/ towers	Outpost, Enclosure

large (>80m × 80m), contain significant remains of stone-built or stone-footed architecture, most likely domestic, and are surrounded by thick (>1m) enclosure walls, often with evidence for bastions, towers, gates, or other defensive elaborations. The significant investment in labor and materials implicated by such architectural remains suggests long-term usage, while sites utilized as temporary refuges would not require such expenditures. Therefore, the sites we have classified as "Empty Enclosures," which consist of large enclosure walls but without internal architecture or significant elaboration of the outer defensive constructions, may be understood as potential protection for livestock but also could have served as potential short-term refuge sites for human populations. Empty enclosures are also understood to have had potential economic affordances, in addition to their defensive capabilities, by facilitating the management of larger herds or providing shelter for mobile trade missions or caravans (Baurain 1984: 87). "Outposts," on the other hand, are individual structures with thick walls that are too small to have contained large numbers of people or amounts of resources, but their isolation and high walls might offer opportunities for secure surveillance, i.e. a concern with possessing knowledge about or exerting control over the actions or movement of others from a defensible location.

Additionally, it must be remembered that the use of such a classificatory typology smooths over variation within categories as well as obscures structures that may transcend such categories by possessing attributes of more than one, or that changed in use as people took advantage of the material affordances provided by the structures. For example, empty enclosures are capable of containing and protecting both humans and animals, but regardless of the original intent, they could have been used opportunistically as refuge or livestock enclosures, dependent on the current conditions and concerns of the local population. Similarly, surveillance should not be understood as a function limited to outposts. The thick, high walls of enclosures and fortified settlements combined with locations in the landscape that provide extensive viewsheds would generate the capabilities of surveillance just as effectively, even if initially the walls were built and the locations selected in order to protect against unwanted physical access.

These factors support our argument that we should not interpret the fortifications of MC III–LC I Cyprus as a uniform phenomenon and that understanding these sites, as with all archaeological research, requires contextual analysis. By recognizing that particular capabilities and limitations are generated by and emerge from the interactions of the components of assemblages, we replace discussion of intent with discussion of affordances. We can then ask how these affordances might have shaped human action. A brief review of the major fortification clusters, based primarily on the records in Fortin's 1981 dissertation, will demonstrate the variation in landscapes and architecture that characterize these sites as well as some of the resulting diverse affordances produced by these sites and will then be followed by a detailed case study of the fortifications on the Karpas Peninsula (Figure 4.3 and Table 4.1).

Kormakiti Plateau Sites

Two fortified sites have been identified atop the Kormakiti Plateau, separated from one another by a little over half a kilometer. Karpasha *Styllomenos* is an empty enclosure while Asomatos *Potemata* is a large fortified settlement with a tower. Both sites look out to the south and west over a fertile plain, which is suitable for agriculture and pasture for animal herds. These sites are also adjacent to the timber and wild animal resources of the forested slopes of the Kyrenia Mountains. Contemporaneous unfortified settlements are visible from the fortified sites, as are, at a significant distance of over 10 km, the navigable Aloupos and Ovgos rivers and the sheltered harbor of Morphou Bay. At such a distance, the sites on the plateau are unlikely to have been able to exert control over trade on the rivers or at the coast, but their proximity to nearby unfortified settlements would allow them to serve as potential refuges. Their topographical situation produces a viewshed that enables the monitoring of movement on the plain below, a capability enhanced by the tower at Asomatos *Potemata*. The structures might also have served as economic infrastructure, as their location and form also creates affordances for the exploitation of forest resources and the protection and management of herds.

Kyrenia Pass Sites

The four fortified sites in the area of the Kyrenia Pass are particularly difficult to access, situated high above the plains and the pass, perched on the edges of steep cliffs. Fortin (1981: 130) observed that these elevations are not conducive to habitation (although Iron Age refuge settlements on Crete might argue otherwise; see Wallace 2003: 257). Åström (1972: 764) suggested that this particular system of fortifications was intended to guard the transport of copper to ports in the north, although no major center from this period is known on the central coast (Catling 1962), a necessary component of such a mercantile assemblage. This cluster of fortified sites, however, does generate the capability of utilizing the pass as a communication route across the Kyrenia Mountains, as the placement of the four fortified sites forms a network or chain of intervisibility that extends from expansive views of the Mesaoria Plain in the south from Krini *Merra*, along the full length of the pass, to a wide swath of the northern coastline. All four sites in this chain are large enclosures, although Dhikomo *Pamboulos* and Bellapais *Kapa Kaya* also contain internal architecture and therefore we classify them as fortified settlements. Krini *Merra*, located 5 km west of the southern entrance of the pass, has a particularly elaborate fortification system including a heavy stone-built double wall and a series of bastions. The apparent emphasis on sightlines and defensive capabilities in these sites, evidenced both through construction techniques and topographical inaccessibility, suggest an overriding concern with defense and long-distance surveillance, potentially concerned with protecting and facilitating trade between the Mesaoria and the north coast. Their inaccessibility, however, makes their utility as long-term settlements associated with agriculture questionable. If the internal architecture proves to be domestic, the association between this assemblage and violent conflict would be strengthened.

Mesaoria Sites: Elenja Hills, and the Yeri and Ayios Sozomenos Plateaus

Each of these three locales in the central Mesaoria has a cluster of fortified sites, often seated on the tops of steep-sided plateaus so as to command views of the plain below. The Elenja Hills (modern Aglantzia) and Yeri Plateau fortifications are significantly smaller than many other recorded fortified sites, thus affording different economic functions or roles in social organization. The sites within each cluster are also of different types and forms, located in close proximity. This arrangement enables a greater diversity of roles and economic functions to be distributed among the sites, while being shared by the assemblage as a whole.

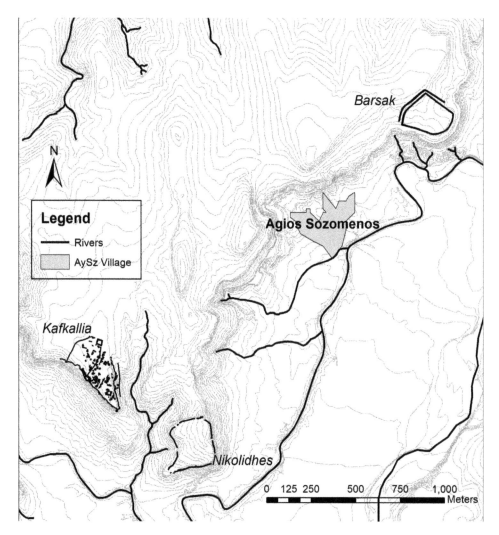

Figure 4.5: Topographic map of the Ayios Sozomenos plateau with fortresses marked.

The fortified sites of the Ayios Sozomenos Plateau are the focus of ongoing research by the authors, in collaboration with Despina Pilides of the Cyprus Department of Antiquities. Here a collection of three sites—Dhali *Kafkallia* (fortified settlement), Ayios Sozomenos *Barsak* (fortified enclosure), and Ayios Sozomenos *Nikolidhes* (fortified enclosure with evidence for limited internal architecture around the perimeter)—is perched atop steep 40–50 m high cliffs on the southern side of a large plateau. A fourth structure, the fortified outpost at *Glykia Vrysi*, was at the base of the cliffs adjacent to a freshwater source and a small settlement. The precipitous cliffs are incorporated into the fortification systems, which also vary significantly between sites. *Nikolidhes* and *Kafkallia* have evidence for towers, while *Kafkallia* consists of two conjoined enclosures, one of which contains extensive domestic architecture (Overbeck and Swiny 1972), and *Barsak* may have had an impressive double wall-and-ditch system. The sites overlook well-watered fertile farmland, with water and pasturage suitable for cattle, and access to uplands suitable for more extensive grazing of sheep and goats. They also overlook a collection of Middle Bronze Age villages, which coalesced into a major Late Bronze Age urban center (Catling 1982: 231; Devillers *et al.* 2004). The central site at *Nikolidhes* is in visual communication with *Barsak* to the north and *Kafkallia* to the west. The individual enclosures have limited viewsheds, but the combined capacities of the components of the assemblage produce a shared viewshed that extends nearly 360 degrees, encompassing much of the Mesaoria. These sites and their relationship with the landscape generate a range of affordances, including housing, monitoring, or managing the movement of people, raw materials, and processed goods across a broad expanse of the island.

Case Study: Karpas Peninsula

While a large number of fortified sites have been identified through extensive survey (Catling 1962; Fortin 1981), only a small number have been intensively mapped or excavated. Two excavated sites, Phlamoudhi *Vounari* and Korovia *Nitovikla*, are located on the Karpas Peninsula, providing an opportunity to study how fortifications developed over time within a distinct region of Cyprus and to investigate whether they formed a common assemblage of people, things, and landscapes within that region. Other fortified sites on the Karpas Peninsula are Dhavlos *Pyrgos*, Lythrangomi *Troullia*, Ayios Thyrsos *Vikla*, and Rizokarpaso *Sylla*. All of these sites, save for Lythrangomi *Troullia*, are situated similarly within the landscape, on low rises overlooking the coast, though these sites are not located in such close proximity as to appear clustered in the manner known in other regions.

Korovia *Nitovikla* is located two-thirds of the way up the Karpas Peninsula, along the southeastern coast, atop a low cliff overlooking a small bay suitable for use as an anchorage or harbor. The northern Levantine coast is just 140 km away, with the large site of Ras Shamra (ancient Ugarit) and the many smaller sites of the Jebleh Plain located due east of *Nitovikla*. The fortification at *Nitovikla* was investigated by the Swedish Cyprus Expedition (Gjerstad *et al.* 1934: 371–407), and the excavated material has subsequently been restudied by Hult (1992), although we adopt the relative chronology for the phasing proposed by Merrillees (1994; also utilized by Crewe 2007).

The Swedish excavations identified a Pre-Period I (late MC III) fill, which underlay a Period I (LC IA) floor, followed by the construction of a fortified building in Period II (LC IA) and its reconstruction in Period III (LC IB). The Period I floor and the fill below it were only exposed in a small area of the site; however, no walls were associated with the Pre-Period I fill, and it was described by the excavators as a "humble settlement" (Gjerstad *et al.* 1934: 394). The Period II fortress, in contrast, was an elaborate construction, with a 20m × 24m interior courtyard and exterior dimensions of 36m × 40m. Entrance to the building was provided by a fortified gateway, its walls formed by ashlar blocks and flanked by towers (Figure 4.6).

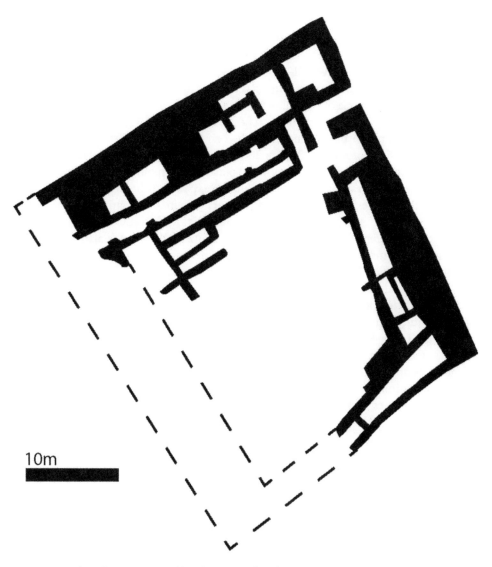

10m

Figure 4.6: Plan of Korovia *Nitovikla* (after Gjerstad *et al.* 1934, 374, Figure 145).

The Period II fortress was destroyed by fire and rebuilt as the Period III fortress along the same lines. Within the courtyard of this final structure there was a stone-built feature with an associated ash deposit. The site was abandoned in the LC IIA period.

Phlamoudhi *Vounari* is located at the base of the Karpas Peninsula, along the northwestern coast, at the mouth of a pass through the Kyrenia Mountains. The site sits atop an anthropogenic hill overlooking the sea (Noller 2008) toward the Anatolian coast, 90 km due north, and the Smooth Cilician Plain, containing Tarsus and other Bronze Age sites, is a further 90 km to the north. A Columbia University expedition excavated *Vounari* (Symeonoglou 1975; Al-Radi 1983), and Horowitz (2007; 2008), whose architectural phasing we adopt, subsequently restudied the excavated material.

Apparently anthropogenic, the clay mound of *Vounari*, Phase 1 at the site, is some 8 m high and likely dates to the same period as the first architectural construction. Horowitz (2007: 342–344) calculates that it would have taken 30 builders 1½ to 3 years, working part-time, to construct the mound. Phase 2 (MC III–LC IA) consisted of a small square structure with 1–2 m thick walls, roughly 5 m to a side, with a sinuous wall extending to the north creating a courtyard area as well as a built stone feature located on the west slope of the hill, which contained an ash deposit (Horowitz 2008: 73–74, Figure 46). This construction was replaced, in Phase 3 (LC IB; Figure 4.7), by a 16 m × 16 m platform, surrounded by a corridor and an exterior wall, with total exterior dimensions of roughly 24 m × 28 m (Horowitz 2008: 74–77, Figures 47–49).

The nature of any architecture atop the platform is unknown. This Phase 3 structure underwent several renovations and minor expansions before being abandoned in the LC IIA (Phase 5). The original excavators dispute the identification of the site as a fortress, but the 1–2 m thick walls of the initial MC III–LC I construction suggest a possible defensible tower structure (Horowitz 2008: 74). We also highlight the monumental nature of the platform in the later phases.

By investigating *Nitovikla* and *Vounari* as part of a new assemblage of people, things, and landscapes that emerged during the LC I period, we avoid the teleology of previous attempts to identify the fortified settlements typologically as pieces of a secular and/or religious administrative apparatus: i.e. military outposts (e.g., Gjerstad *et al.* 1934; Peltenburg 1996), sanctuaries (e.g., Symeonoglou 1975; Al-Radi 1983), or distribution centers (Horowitz 2008). Instead we argue that the assemblage of people, things, and landscapes emerged first and that the construction of fortifications followed in an attempt to negotiate and stabilize this new assemblage, through processes of territorialization. Here we use the evidence of architectural development at both *Nitovikla* and *Vounari* to substantiate this claim.

Both sites are located in direct relation to the sea, presenting a new landscape that was absent from the assemblage of the EC–MC villages. *Nitovikla* looked to the east, *Vounari* to the north. We argue, following Baurain (1984), that the mainland connections that developed at this time were neither wholly peaceful nor strictly violent and that they would have drawn upon both local products and longer distance connections with the Troodos metal deposits. Evidence for direct economic or political ties with a dominant center, however, like that proposed at Enkomi to the south, is lacking.

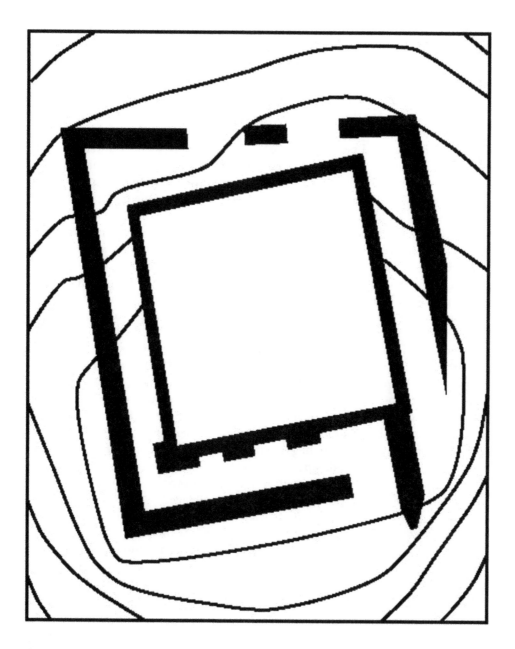

10m

Figure 4.7: Plan of Phlamoudhi *Vounari* (after Horowitz 2008, Figure 48).

At both *Nitovikla* and *Vounari* the initial site choice and construction placed a premium on gaining both vantage over the sea and access to interior regions. In the case of *Nitovikla,* this choice meant locating the site on a natural hill, in the base of a river valley that drained the large and fertile plain upon which the contemporary settlements of *Paleoskoutella* and *Galinoporni* were located (Catling 1962: 140). In the case of *Vounari* it meant artificial construction of a hill, situated on one of the key passes through the Kyrenia Mountains, providing access from the coast to the eastern Mesaoria and the Troodos Mountains. In the case of *Nitovikla, Galinoporni,* and possibly *Paleoskoutella,* the movement of foreign goods is demonstrated by the presence of Canaanite jars (Crewe 2012). It is notable, then, that although both *Nitovikla* and *Vounari* were located at the potentially dangerous interface of land and sea, neither site was initially fortified. The lack of fortifications can be fully appreciated at *Vounari,* where large amounts of labor were expended to construct the hill, yet only a relatively modest structure was initially placed atop it. We thus see that the assemblage of people, things, and landscapes (and seascapes) in the Karpas Peninsula at the beginning of the MC III–LC I contained new means of labor organization and technology to produce surplus goods for export, new routes of movement across both land and sea, and new locations of settlement and types of structures, but fortifications were not yet part of the assemblage.

The second phase of use at both *Nitovikla* and *Vounari* saw the construction of fortified enclosures. In both cases we view this architectural development as an attempt to stabilize an uneven relationship associated with overseas trade. That there was a violent aspect to this instability seems evident from the massive architecture employed and the destruction by fire at *Nitovikla* of the Period II fortress. The walls therefore were a display of group cooperation and membership that had the material effect of protecting and hiding inhabitants and their activities while facilitating the surveillance of the landscape and people outside the walls. In this way, these fortifications, through their material properties and processes of territorialization, attempted to stabilize the social and political assemblage.

We see that these constructions actively negotiated the instability of the assemblage in their continued maintenance and renewal, with walls repaired and reinforced and buttresses constructed over several phases. Therefore, while we cannot categorize the nature of authority during the early years of the Late Cypriot Period, we argue that it was a time in which a new assemblage of people, things, and landscapes emerged, violence or its threat was regularly employed, and fortifications were constructed as a means of mitigating and/or moderating this violence but also served as a unifying force and a potential tool of control.

Stabilization and Deterritorialization: Fortress Abandonment

Such is the lack of study of the LC I period fortifications that we know more about the reasons for their abandonment then we do about the reasons for their construction. All of the known fortifications were abandoned early in the LC II period, sometime after 1500 BCE. This second phase of the Late Bronze Age saw a new stable assemblage of people, things, and landscapes develop across the island as a new political order took hold. This new assemblage was by all accounts peaceful, as there is no evidence for violent destruction of settlements and little or no osteological evidence for warfare; furthermore, fortifications do not reappear on the island until the LC IIC (ca. 1350 BCE: see Fortin 1983: 218).

The changes in the LC II period can be appreciated from several converging lines of evidence, all of which point to a newly legitimated political authority that obviated the need for violent interactions. Throughout the island, new coastal towns were founded and older ones rebuilt. Ashlar buildings became common, often with large-scale storage facilities. Manning (1998) has shown that the construction of the ashlar building at Maroni *Vournes* was designed to block access to a number of chamber tombs, thereby removing them from the assemblage and cutting off lineage-based power structures in favor of a newly centralized political authority. Catling (1962: 144–145), Keswani (1993), and Knapp (1997: 53–63; see also Keswani and Knapp 2003) have modeled the development in LC II of functional site specialization, which is particularly well attested for agricultural surplus (e.g., Aredhiou *Vouppes*: Steel and Thomas 2008; Analiondas *Palioklishia*: Webb and Frankel 1994) and copper production (e.g., Apliki *Karamallos*: Kling and Muhly 2007; Politiko *Phorades*: Knapp and Kassianidou 2008).

Cyprus in the Late Bronze Age therefore sees the development of an interconnected economy, in which property rights and physical security were assured without the use of fortifications. For the purpose of this paper it is unimportant if this was due to the presence of a singular ruler who presided over the island as a whole or to regional powers that interacted with one another peaceably. What matters is that the new LC II assemblages generated social and political conditions that no longer required stabilization and therefore removed the efficacy of fortified enclosures. Their material and communicative affect in territorializing processes in the landscape was no longer needed, and they fell out of use within the assemblage of people, things, and landscapes that produced and reproduced the new social order.

Conclusion

Variation in building technique, form, and location and the resulting variability in potential actions and affects of these fortifications, emphasized by their rapid construction in a short period, argues strongly against their being the product of an organized and hierarchical political system, a proposition for which there is little other evidence. Instead, these sites frequently occur in tight, discrete clusters and in a variety of topographical locations, taking different forms, interacting with each other and the landscape to allow, encourage, or prevent a variety of economic and social activities. In other words, rather than being an island-wide network of fortresses, an assemblage unified by material form, relationship to the landscape, and role in Cypriot Bronze Age society, these fortresses were innovative material components produced as localized responses to the affordances and risks posed by the other material and social components of their particular environment. That the fortifications served to "make places" and control people's movement is certain; that this was the motivation of elites who directed their construction, less so. On the contrary, place-making and the establishment of authority were more likely to have been the byproducts of the far more mundane concerns of daily life, i.e. the security provided through knowledge of surrounding conditions, strong walls against aggression, and a competitive advantage in accessing the best resources. These motivations also would have provided the impetus to mobilize the necessary workforce to build these structures on such an unprecedented and monumental scale in response to a changing and unstable new assemblage of materials and people. We also recognize that fortifications are capable of monumentalizing, controlling movement, curtailing access, and expressing possession and membership, among other actions. Nevertheless, these affordances and limitations to human agency emerge from the interaction between the fortifications and other human and non-human components of the social assemblage and need not be understood as dependent upon initial human intent.

The diverse forms that human responses took to the destabilization of their social assemblages and the varied Cypriot landscape in this period may have led to further destabilization. Social groups competed, split apart, and reformed in new configurations to cooperate in the production of new defensive and economic technologies, processes for which fortifications were both response and stimulus. But this fracturing and militarization of the landscape was temporary. Fortified sites were material components of the social assemblage, built as responses to the challenges of the new social and material assemblages of the time but also capable of new, sometimes unintended, actions and affects that reached far beyond the immediate economic and defensive concerns that likely inspired their initial construction. Individual fortified sites became clusters of fortified sites, each utilizing and producing different affordances within their local assemblages. But most significantly for the development of political complexity on Cyprus, the larger assemblage of the MC III–LC I produced new properties that had not existed on the island previously. From the fortified sites that initially served defensive or economic purposes, protecting and observing the movement and interaction of people and materials, would emerge capabilities for the production of knowledge and the use of force over those people, materials, and the landscape. Walls that were built to protect or outposts built to observe and communicate could also serve to control and constrain. They created and materialized divisions between those with access and knowledge versus those without.

These very affordances allowed an elite group to develop who could manipulate them to produce the first political regime on Cyprus, even if the production of such a system was not the intent of the original construction. The affordances of individual fortresses would have been insufficient to establish such control, but as fortifications spread across the landscape, so too did the affordances of their interactions. It is through the production of this new material assemblage that political authority developed and was reified and reproduced in the built environment of Cyprus. The very properties of the built environment that had initially contributed to the process of destabilization and fracturing of the political landscape would be re-purposed to define a new political assemblage in the hegemony of the LC period.

Acknowledgments

Because this paper contains the seeds of several ideas that the first author has subsequently developed extensively and that feature in her forthcoming dissertation and other publications, the authors have intentionally not updated some aspects of this submission. That said, the authors are most grateful to our two anonymous reviewers for their comments, which we have attempted to address satisfactorily within these confines. Additional thanks are due for the excellent editorial work by Catherine Kearns and the support of Sturt Manning. Any errors are entirely our own.

Endnote

Many of the cemeteries from this period were looted or "excavated" in the nineteenth century with minimal publication. The larger problem, however, is the state of our knowledge concerning human habitation. Excluding evidence from the fortified sites discussed in this paper, settlement evidence for the MC III is limited to Episkopi *Phaneromeni*, Politiko *Troullia*, and Erimi *Laonin tou Porakou*, all awaiting final publication, as well as at Kissonerga *Skalia* and minimal exposures at Kalopsidha (Gjerstad 1926), while, "only Enkomi offers a detailed archaeological record for the earliest phase of the ProBA [i.e. the LC I]" (Knapp 2013b: 33).

References

Al-Radi, S. 1983. *Phlamoudhi* Vounari: *A Sanctuary Site in Cyprus*. Studies in Mediterranean Archaeology 65. Göteborg, Sweden: Paul Åströms Förlag.

Appadurai, A. 1986. *The Social Life of Things: Commodities in Cultural Perspective*. Cambridge: Cambridge University Press.

Åström, P. 1972. *The Swedish Cyprus Expedition*. Vol. 4, part 1B, *The Middle Cypriote Bronze Age*. Lund, Sweden: Swedish Cyprus Expedition.

Baurain, C. 1984. *Chypre et la Méditerranée orientale au Bronze Récent: Synthèse historique*. Paris: École française d'Athènes

Belgiorno, M.-R. 2004. *Pyrgos-Mavroraki: Advanced Technology in Bronze Age Cyprus*. Nicosia: Theopress Ltd.

Bombardieri, L. 2012. Erimi-*Laonin tou Porakou*: 2009 Preliminary Report. *Report of the Department of Antiquities, Cyprus*: 139–168.

Carpenter, J.R. 1981. Excavations at Phaneromeni, 1975–1978. In J.C. Biers and D. Soren (eds.), *Studies in Cypriote Archaeology*, 59–78. Los Angeles: UCLA Institute of Archaeology.

Catling, H.W. 1962. Patterns of settlement in Bronze Age Cyprus. *Opuscula Atheniensia* 4: 129–169.

Catling, H.W. 1982. The ancient topography of the Yalias Valley. *Report of the Department of Antiquities, Cyprus*: 227–236.

Crewe, L. 2007. *Early Enkomi: Regionalism, Trade, and Society at the Beginning of the Late Bronze Age on Cyprus*. Oxford: Archaeopress.

Crewe, L. 2012. Beyond copper: Commodities and values in Middle Bronze Age Cypro-Levantine exchanges. *Oxford Journal of Archaeology* 31.3: 225–243.

Crewe, L. 2013. Regional connections during the Middle-Late Cypriot transition: New evidence from Kissonerga-*Skalia*. *Pasiphae* 7: 47–56.

Crewe, L. 2014. A reappearing Early Bronze Age in western Cyprus. In J.M. Webb (ed.), *Structure, Measurement, and Meaning: Studies on Prehistoric Cyprus in Honour of David Frankel*, 137–149. Studies in Mediterranean Archaeology 143. Uppsala, Sweden: Åströms Förlag.

DeLanda, M. 2006. *A New Philosophy of Society: Assemblage Theory and Social Complexity*. New York: Continuum.

Devillers, B., P. Gaber, and N. Lecuyer. 2004. Notes on the Agios *Sozomenos* Bronze Age settlement (Lefkosia district): Recent palaeoenvironmental and archaeological finds. *Report of the Department of Antiquities, Cyprus*: 85–92.

Dikaios, P. 1969–71. *Enkomi: Excavations 1948–58. Volumes I–IIIB*. Mainz, Germany: Verlag Phillip von Zabern.

Falconer, S., E. Monahan, and P. Fall. 2014. A stone plank figurine from Politiko-*Troullia*, Cyprus: Potential implications for inferring Bronze Age communal behavior. *Bulletin of the American Schools of Oriental Research* 371: 3–16.

Fishman, B., H. Forbes, and B. Lawn. 1977. University of Pennsylvania radiocarbon date XIX. *Radiocarbon* 19.2: 188–228.

Fortin, M. 1981. Military architecture in Cyprus during the second millennium BC. Unpublished PhD dissertation, University of London.

Fortin, M. 1983. Recherches sur l'architecture militaire de l'Age du Bronze a Chypre. *Échos du Monde Classique* 27.2: 206–219.

Frankel, D., and J.M. Webb. 1996. *Marki* Alonia: *An Early and Middle Bronze Age Town in Cyprus. Excavations 1990–1994*. Studies in Mediterranean Archaeology 123.1. Jonsered, Sweden: Paul Åströms Förlag.

Frankel, D., and J.M. Webb. 2006. *Marki* Alonia: *An Early and Middle Bronze Age Settlement in Cyprus. Excavations 1995–2000*. Studies in Mediterranean Archaeology 123.2. Sävedalen, Sweden: Paul Åströms Förlag.

Frow, J. 2010. Matter and materialism: A brief prehistory of the present. In T. Bennett and P. Joyce (eds.), *Material Powers: Cultural Studies, History, and the Material Turn*, 25–37. London: Routledge.

Gale, N., Z. Stos-Gale, and W. Fasnacht. 1996. Appendix 2: Copper and copper working at Alambra. In J.E. Coleman, J.A. Barlow, M.K. Mogelonsky and K.W. Schaar, *Alambra. A Middle Bronze Age Settlement in Cyprus. Archaeological Investigations by Cornell University 1974–1985*, 359–426. Studies in Mediterranean Archaeology 118. Jonsered, Sweden: Paul Åströms Förlag.

Georgiou, G. 2006. Η Τοπογραφία της Ανθρώπινης Εγκατάστασης στην Κύπρο κατά την Πρώιμη και Μέση Χαλκοκρατία. Unpublished PhD dissertation, University of Cyprus.

Georgiou, G. 2008. The settlement at Alambra-*Mouttes* revisited. *Report of the Department of Antiquities, Cyprus*: 133–143.

Georgiou, G. 2011. The central part of Cyprus during Middle Cypriot III to Late Cypriot IA period. In A. Demetriou (ed.), *Proceedings of the 4th International Cyprological Congress, Vol I.2*, 477–482. Nicosia: Society of Cypriot Studies.

Gerstenblith, P. 1983. *The Levant at the Beginning of the Middle Bronze Age*. American Schools of Oriental Research Dissertation Series 5. Boston: The American Schools of Oriental Research.

Given, M., and A.B. Knapp. (eds.) 2003. *The Sydney Cyprus Survey Project: Social Approaches to Regional Archaeological Survey*. Vol. 21. Los Angeles: Cotsen Institute of Archaeology, University of California.

Gjerstad, E. 1926. *Studies on Prehistoric Cyprus*. Uppsala: University of Uppsala.

Gjerstad, E., J. Lindros, E. Sjöqvist, and A. Westholm. 1934. *The Swedish Cyprus Expedition: Finds and Results of the Excavations in Cyprus, 1927–1931. Vol. I*. Stockholm, Sweden: Swedish Cyprus Expedition.

Gosden, C., and L. Head. 1994. Landscape—a usefully ambiguous concept. *Archaeology in Oceania* 29.3: 113–116.

Håkansson, S. 1981. University of Lund radiocarbon dates XIV. *Radiocarbon* 23: 384–403.

Harman, G. 2010. "Object-oriented philosophy." *Towards Speculative Realism: Essays and Lectures*, 93–104. London: Zero Books.

Hirth, K. 2009. Intermittent crafting and multicrafting at Xochicalco. In K. Hirth (ed.), *Housework: Craft Production and Domestic Economy in Ancient Mesoamerica*, 75–91. Archaeological Papers of the American Anthropology Association 19. Hoboken, NJ: Wiley.

Horowitz, M.T. 2007. Monumentality and social transformation at Late Bronze I Phlamoudhi-*Vounari*, Cyprus. Unpublished PhD dissertation, Columbia University.

Horowitz, M.T. 2008. Phlamoudhi-*Vounari*: A multi-function site in Cyprus. In J. Smith (ed.), *Views from Phlamoudhi, Cyprus*, 68–86. Annual of the American Schools of Oriental Research, Volume 63. Boston: American Schools of Oriental Research.

Hult, G. 1992. *Nitovikla Reconsidered*. Medelhavsmuseet Memoir 8. Stockholm: Medelhavsmuseet.

Hult, G. 1994. Qatna and Nitovikla. *Levant* 26.1: 189–197.

Ingold, T. 1993. The temporality of the landscape. *World Archaeology* 25: 152–174.

Keswani, P.S. 1993. Models of local exchange in Late Bronze Age Cyprus. *Bulletin of the American Schools of Oriental Research* 292: 73–83.

Keswani, P.S. 1996. Hierarchies, heterarchies, and urbanization processes: The view from Bronze Age Cyprus. *Journal of Mediterranean Archaeology* 9.2: 211–250.

Keswani, P.S. 2004. *Mortuary Ritual and Society in Bronze Age Cyprus*. Monographs in Mediterranean Archaeology 9. London: Equinox.

Keswani, P.S. 2005. Death, prestige, and copper in Bronze Age Cyprus. *American Journal of Archaeology* 109: 341–401.

Keswani, P.S., and A.B. Knapp. 2003. Bronze Age boundaries and social exchange in north-west Cyprus. *Oxford Journal of Archaeology* 22.3: 213–223.

Kling, B., and J.D. Muhly. 2007. *Joan du Plat Taylor's Excavations at the Late Bronze Age Mining Settlement at Apliki* Karamallos, *Cyprus*. Studies in Mediterranean Archaeology 134.1. Sävedalen, Sweden: Paul Åströms Förlag.

Knapp, A.B. 1994. Emergence, development, and decline on Bronze Age Cyprus. In C. Mathers and S. Stoddart (eds.), *Development and Decline in the Mediterranean Bronze Age*, 271–304. Sheffield: John Collis.

Knapp, A.B. 1997. *The Archaeology of Late Bronze Age Cypriot Society: The Study of Settlement, Survey, and Landscape*. Glasgow: University of Glasgow.

Knapp, A.B. 2008. *Prehistoric and Protohistoric Cyprus: Identity, Insularity, and Connectivity*. Oxford: Oxford University Press.

Knapp, A.B. 2013a. *The Archaeology of Cyprus: From Earliest Prehistory through the Bronze Age*. Cambridge: Cambridge University Press.

Knapp, A.B. 2013b. Revolution within evolution: The emergence of a "secondary state" on Protohistoric Bronze Age Cyprus. *Levant* 45.1: 19–44.

Knapp, A.B., and V. Kassianidou. 2008. The archaeology of Late Bronze Age copper production: Politiko *Phorades* on Cyprus. In Ü. Yalçin (ed.), *Anatolian Metal IV: Frühe Rohstoffgewinnung in Anatolien und seinen Nachbarländern*, 135–147. Die Anschnitt, Beiheft 21. Veröffentlichungen aus dem Deutschen Bergbau-Museum 157. Bochum, Germany: Deutsches Bergbau-Museum.

Latour, B. 2005. *Reassembling the Social: An Introduction to Actor-Network Theory*. Oxford: Oxford University Press.

Manning, S.W. 1993. Prestige, distinction, and competition: The anatomy of socioeconomic complexity in fourth to second millennium BCE. *Bulletin of the American Schools of Oriental Research* 292: 35–58.

Manning, S.W. 1998. Changing pasts and socio-political cognition in Late Bronze Age Cyprus. *World Archaeology* 30: 39–58.

Manning, S.W. 2013. Appendix: A new radiocarbon chronology for prehistoric and protohistoric Cyprus, ca. 11,000–1050 Cal BC. In A.B. Knapp, *The Archaeology of Cyprus: From Earliest Prehistory through the Bronze Age*, 485–533. Cambridge: Cambridge University Press.

Manning, S.W., and S. Swiny. 1994. Sotira *Kaminoudhia* and the chronology of the Early Bronze Age in Cyprus. *Oxford Journal of Archaeology* 13: 149–172.

Marcus, E., Y. Porath, and S. Paley. 2008. The Early Middle Bronze Age IIa in phases at Tel Ifshar and their external relations. *Egypt and the Levant* 18: 221–244.

Merrillees, R.S. 1982. Early metallurgy in Cyprus 4000–500 B.C. In J.D. Muhly, R. Maddin, and V. Karageorghis (eds.), *Early Metallurgy in Cyprus. 4000–500 BC*, 373–376. Nicosia: The Pierides Foundation.

Merrillees, R.S. 1994. Review of G. Hult, *Nitovikla Reconsidered*. *Opuscula Atheniensia* 20: 256–258.

Merrillees, R.S. 2007. The ethnic implications of Tell el-Yahudiyeh ware for the history of the Middle to Late Bronze Age in Cyprus. *Cahiers du Centre d'Etudes Chypriotes* 37.1: 87–96.

Mukerji, C. 2015. The material turn. In R.A. Scott and S.M. Kosslyn (eds.), *Emerging Trends in the Social and Behavioral Sciences*. Wiley Online Library. DOI: 10.1002/9781118900772. Accessed: Dec. 31, 2015.

Noller, J. 2008. Physical foundations of Phlamoudhi. In J. Smith (ed.), *Views from Phlamoudhi, Cyprus*, 25–29. Annual of the American Schools of Oriental Research 63. Boston: American Schools of Oriental Research.

Overbeck, J.C., and S. Swiny. 1972. *Two Cypriot Bronze Age Sites at Kafkallia (Dhali)*. Studies in Mediterranean Archaeology 33. Göteborg, Sweden: P. Åström.

Peltenburg, E. 1994. Constructing authority: The *Vounous* enclosure model. *Opuscula Atheniensia* 20.10: 157–162.

Peltenburg, E. 1996. From isolation to state formation in Cyprus, c. 3500–1500 B.C. In V. Karageorghis and D. Michaelides (eds.), *The Development of the Cypriot Economy from the Prehistoric Period to the Present Day*, 17–44. Nicosia: University of Cyprus and Bank of Cyprus.

Peltenburg, E. 2008. Nitovikla and Tell el-Burak: Cypriot mid-second millennium B.C. forts in a Levantine context. *Report of the Department of Antiquities, Cyprus*: 145–157.

Sasson, J. 1996. Akkadian documents from Mari and Babylonia (Old Babylonian Period). In A.B. Knapp (ed.), *Near Eastern and Aegean Texts from the Third to the First Millennia BC*, 17–19. Altamont, NY: Greece and Cyprus Research Center, Inc.

Shanks, M., and C. Tilley. 1987. *Re-Constructing Archaeology: Theory and Practice*. Cambridge: Cambridge University Press.

Sjöqvist, E. 1940. *Problems of the Late Cypriot Bronze Age*. Stockholm, Sweden: Swedish Cyprus Expedition.

Smith, A.T. 2015. *The Political Machine: Assembling Sovereignty in the Bronze Age Caucasus*. Princeton: Princeton University Press.

Sneddon, A. 2014. Making love not war? An archaeology of violence and some lessons for the study of prehistoric Bronze Age Cyprus. In J.M. Webb (ed.), *Structure, Measurement, and Meaning: Studies on Prehistoric Cyprus in Honour of David Frankel*, 57–67. Studies in Mediterranean Archaeology 143. Uppsala, Sweden: Åströms Förlag.

Steel, L., and S. Thomas. 2008. Excavations at Aredhiou *Vouppes* (*Lithouros*): An interim report on excavations 2005–2006. *Report of the Department of Antiquities, Cyprus*: 227–249.

Symeonoglou, S. 1975. Excavations at Phlamoudhi and the form of the sanctuary in Bronze Age Cyprus. In N. Robertson (ed.), *The Archaeology of Cyprus: Recent Developments*, 61–75. Park Ridge, NJ: Noyes Press.

Swiny, S., G.R. Rapp, and E. Herscher. (eds.) 2003. *Sotira* Kaminoudhia: *An Early Bronze Age Site in Cyprus*. American Schools of Oriental Research Archaeological Reports 8. Boston: American Schools of Oriental Research.

Todd, I. 1993. Kalavasos-*Laroumena*: Test excavation of a Middle Bronze Age settlement. *Report of the Department of Antiquities, Cyprus*: 81–96.

Wallace, S. 2003. The perpetuated past: Re-use or continuity in material culture and the structuring of identity in early Iron Age Crete. *Annual of the British School at Athens* 98: 251–277.

Webb, J.M., and Frankel, D. 1994. Making an impression: Storage and surplus finance in Late Bronze Age Cyprus. *Journal of Mediterranean Archaeology* 7: 5–26.

Webb, J.M., and D. Frankel. 1999. Characterizing the Philia facies: Material culture, chronology, and the origin of the Bronze Age in Cyprus. *American Journal of Archaeology* 103.1: 3–43.

Webb, J.M., and D. Frankel. 2013a. Cultural regionalism and divergent social trajectories in Early Bronze Age Cyprus. *American Journal of Archaeology* 117: 59–81.

Webb, J.M., and D. Frankel. 2013b. *Ambelikou* Aletri: *Metallurgical and Pottery Production in Middle Bronze Age Cyprus*. Studies in Mediterranean Archaeology, Vol. 138. Uppsala, Sweden: Åströms Förlag.

Webb, J.M., D. Frankel, Z.A. Stos, and N. Gale. 2006. Early Bronze Age metal trade in the eastern Mediterranean: New compositional and lead isotope evidence from Cyprus. *Oxford Journal of Archaeology* 25.3: 261–288.

Webb, J.M., D. Frankel, K. Eriksson, and J.B. Hennessy. 2009. *The Bronze Age Cemeteries at Karmi Palealona and Lapatsa in Cyprus. Excavations by J.R.B. Stewart*. Studies in Mediterranean Archaeology 136. Sävedalen, Sweden: Åströms Förlag.

Wiseman, D. 1996. Akkadian documents from Alalakh (Old and Middle Babylonian periods). In A.B. Knapp (ed.), *Near Eastern and Aegean Texts from the Third to the First Millennia BC*, 20. Altamont, NY: Greece and Cyprus Research Center, Inc.

Yoffee, N. 2005. *Myths of the Archaic State: Evolution of the Earliest Cities, States, and Civilizations*. New York: Cambridge University Press.

5

Gray Economics in Late Bronze Age Cyprus

GEORGIA MARINA ANDREOU

Introduction

Researchers working on the eastern Mediterranean Bronze Age, which is characterized by unparalleled mobility, networking, and interaction, have often relied on or been inspired by socioeconomic concepts in order to frame theoretically the politico-economic characteristics of this period. From this perspective, scholars have investigated Cyprus through textual and material evidence of its copper exploitation and have developed models of settlement distribution with the aim to reconstruct the politico-economic organization of the island (e.g., Keswani 1993; 1996; Peltenburg 1996, 2012; Knapp 2013: 349–359). Paramount in these discussions is the unprecedented connectivity observed in the eastern Mediterranean during the later second millennium BCE (e.g., Sauvage 2012; Steel 2013; Knapp and Demesticha 2017), with considerable debate over textual evidence for international diplomacy, such as seen in the Amarna letters (Mynářová 2007) as well as shipwrecks bearing interregional cargo (e.g., Uluburun; see also Pulak 1998; 2008) and the widespread, shared iconographic vocabulary associated with elite groups (Feldman 2006).

Nevertheless, the vestiges of this connectivity are often obscure, especially those related to the structures and processes that facilitated various participants in international trade; in the case of Late Bronze Age (LBA) Cyprus, they are particularly perplexing. Beyond copper, which probably spurred the involvement of the island in broader markets, the processes, agents, and periodization of this involvement are largely enigmatic. I have discussed this topic more extensively in earlier research, in which I proposed that different regions of the island engaged with the eastern Mediterranean economy through a variety of socioeconomic and political mechanisms at different times, as illustrated in the case studies of the Bronze Age Kouris, Vasilikos, and Maroni valleys (Andreou 2014). What arose from this comparative research was a concern for distinguishing modes of what I call economic formality and informality and for understanding how different scales of interaction (local, regional, interregional) articulated and/or co-constructed one another during the Late Cypriot (LC) period. Building on these previous arguments, this paper aims to identify material evidence suggestive of variations in economic formality and informality, as discussed below. This research, then, requires a theoretical framework and a methodological approach that consider the abilities of individuals to operate across different scales as well as the possibility of heterarchical socioeconomic collaboration within exchange networks.

To do so, this paper critically engages with new theoretical and methodological directions. To be more precise, I explore the concept of gray economics, which has been employed in the fields of anthropology and economics as well as policy-making since the 1970s but to date has not appeared in discussions of protohistoric economic complexity and is a novel theoretical direction for studies of the LC. To integrate this framework with archaeological evidence, this work finds alignment with Sherratt and Sherratt's (1991) influential model of the Bronze Age Mediterranean, which envisioned different spatial perspectives of the economy and several types of exchange, expanding from the individual to the state. Their later work (Sherratt and Sherratt 1993), in which they discuss commercial autonomy and entrepreneurial agents operating without the structure of a palace-based centralized economy during the LBA, has also proven insightful. In addition, Monroe's (2009) study on different trade scales in the eastern Mediterranean as well as proposals for a decentralized political configuration during the LC period (Manning and de Mita 1997; Peltenburg and Iacovou 2012; Peltenburg 2012) equally frame and support the conclusions of this research.

Methodologically, this paper builds on a comparative study of published material from both survey and excavation projects in the Vasilikos, Maroni, and Kouris river valleys in Cyprus. In order to identify material evidence for a spectrum of economic relations and networks, I integrate four interrelated types of analysis. First, I compare settlement patterns that appear through spatial analysis in the surveyed material. Based on this comparative analysis, I argue that a lack of homogeneity in these patterns likely indicates regionally specific and possibly significant socioeconomic traditions that seem to have continued from the pre-LC to the LC, despite evidence for change in the settlement patterns. Second, I highlight areas of economic activity located outside of the extensively investigated monumental, administrative structures of the LBA built environments of the three valleys to provide an avenue to discuss the interface between types of formal and informal economic activities. Third, I analyze the abundance and ubiquity of non-local artifacts from intact burial contexts. Using mortuary evidence, I suggest that differences in the quantities of these artifacts as well as in their depositional patterns may signify distinctions in the formality of exchange networks. Finally, I consider interpretations of textual evidence from the Late Bronze Age Mediterranean to ascertain evidence for potential informal economics.

This methodology ultimately tests the hypothesis that variable and seemingly random relationships between settlements and their surrounding environmental contexts, between economic activities and structured built environments, and in the frequencies of imports in mortuary deposits reveal the presence of smaller-scale, probably informal, and more socially embedded economic relations.

The paper begins by introducing the theoretical background and limitations of the concept of gray economics and its relationship to the wider subject of the ancient economy. The next sections examine and conceptualize evidence for economic variability along the four registers outlined above: landscapes, spaces of economic activity, tomb contexts, and textual production. In analyzing the evidence from three river valleys, I argue for the utility of concepts like gray economics for opening up and nuancing our rigid categorizations of Bronze Age economies and settlement hierarchies.

Theoretical Background

Economic anthropology has at times influenced archaeological interpretation of the Bronze Age in Cyprus and in the eastern Mediterranean more broadly. Discussions on reciprocity (Malinowski 1922; Sahlins 1972), redistribution, dualistic spheres of exchange (Bohannan 1959), formalist versus substantivist economics (Polanyi 1944), gifts and commodities (Appadurai 1986), and culturalist approaches have become entwined, especially over the last few decades, with the ways in which ancient historians and archaeologists attempt to understand past communities and the ancient economy (e.g., Scheidel and Von Reden 2002; Manning and Morris 2005; Hirth and Pillsbury 2013). In particular, during the twentieth century, the formalist versus substantivist debate—in which the former advocates for rational and independent economic action against the latter's arguments for economic practices embedded within social and political structures—has figured conspicuously and has been summarized and discussed repeatedly by various scholars of the ancient Near East (e.g., Sherratt and Sherratt 1991; Parkins 1998; Schloen 2001; Morris and Manning 2005; Liverani 2005: 52–53; McGeough 2007; Padgham 2014).

The details of the substantivist versus formalist debate are beyond the scope of this paper, yet because this study uses the modern term of gray economics to discuss the Cypriot Bronze Age, it is necessary to outline the application's relevance to conceptions of embedded as opposed to formal economies. The general distinction between socially embedded and socially disembedded economies derives from the work of Mauss (1925) and Weber (1947) and was principally introduced to studies of the ancient economy through Polanyi's 1944 book *The Great Transformation*. The debate itself considers two conflicting central concepts: on the one hand, formalists such as Hicks (1969) argued that ancient economies operated according to a modern economic rationale, while substantivists such as Polanyi (1944; 1957) and later Finley (1973) claimed that economic decisions were made using socially oriented motives related to and embedded within ancient social structures. For those in the former camp, ancient evidence of market forces, demand, profit, and entrepreneurship can appear in textual and archaeological records when economic actors seem to have made pragmatic and rational decisions independent of social relations. For substantivists, however, these indices of more formalized and modern economic practice are beholden to capitalist understandings of the economy and are thus anachronistic when applied to pre-capitalist and pre-industrialized periods.

Arguments from both camps have their pitfalls. For instance, Polanyi relied on data from the Old Assyrian and Old Babylonian period to argue for a substantive perspective that viewed economic activities in Assur as solely administered by the temple/palace complex and undertaken by trade-agents. This view has since been challenged as incompatible with both textual and material evidence supporting private entrepreneurship in Old Assyrian trade networks, a record that is considered among the best substantiated in ancient history (Liverani 2005: 53). More recently, Monroe (2009: 7) has employed and advocated for a more measured approach that balances the theoretical poles of formalism and substantivism with the aim to address the complex issue of the international Bronze Age economy of the eastern Mediterranean. Monroe examined textual evidence for the relationships between traders and rulers from the polities of Ugarit, Egypt, and Hattuša along with familial and ethnic relationships in the same textual collections. From this approach, he argues convincingly for the contextual and situational nature of these relationships and identifies multiple scales and degrees of formality characterizing economic interactions. Importantly, Monroe discerns both profit-oriented economic activities undertaken by traders and merchants, as well as socially embedded economic behaviors, such as elite gift exchange. Given this complexity, it appears that it is more useful to consider alternative interpretations for the ancient economy that include elements from both embedded practices and the modern market found within the concept of gray economics.

Informality and Gray Economics

As I mentioned above, I engage with the concept of gray economics with the aim to identify material evidence for informal economic interactions and to propose the incorporation of these interactions in broader-scale interpretations of the Cypriot Late Bronze Age. In the spirit of this volume's framework on new methods and analytic schemes, let us define and explore gray economics. Here, the term *economics* combines the rationale, attitudes, activities and particular sociopolitical backgrounds that influenced modes and practices of production, provisioning, distribution, exchange, and consumption of products. *Gray* or *informal* connotes unofficial modes of economic attitudes and activities, lacking dependency on or subjugation to centralized control and monitoring by political and economic administrations or bodies.

For the purposes of this paper, I use the terms *gray economics* or *informal economics* to describe and to begin to categorize archaeologically visible activities that resulted from interactions bearing little material evidence for outside or top-down regulation or control. Such activities may be associated, for example, with household provisioning, and typically emerge in specific contexts of material reciprocation and independent, household-driven economic strategies. Such informality does not appear to be part of the centralized economy or regulated, controlled, or authorized by a formal administration. As such, and following studies discussed in the introduction (particularly Sherratt and Sherratt 1993; Monroe 2009), I do not consider informal economy and state-controlled economy as mutually exclusive but rather as complementary and co-constitutive.

There exist, of course, methodological and terminological limitations to informality and gray economics as concepts when applied to archaeological evidence and frameworks. Although informality is conceived as a widespread phenomenon within the overarching rubric of gray economics, economists often argue that the characteristics and consequences of informality are largely underexplored (Schneider and Enste 2000; Elgin and Oyvat 2013: 36–47; La Porta and Shleifer 2014: 109–110). This concern is exacerbated by a lack of consensus regarding the determinants of economic informality. Furthermore, this confusion is related to difficulties of observing, defining, and measuring informal activities, as they often leave no written or visible records (Sindzingre 2006: 59).

Hart (2006: 21), the British anthropologist who first used the term *gray economics,* proposed a set of inherent characteristics for economic "formality" (in order to distinguish it from "informality") that include order, regularity, and predictability in the production and distribution of goods. These characteristics result from control and standardization by some form of administrative body. In more modern contexts, the International Labour Organisation (ILO) (1972) suggested that the traits for informal economic activities include: ease of entry, family ownership/enterprises, reliance on indigenous resources, small operational scale, unregulated markets, labor-intensive production, and labor skill acquired outside of the formal, state-operated (in modern terms) economy.

Problematically, this definition has been used to assume that informal economic activities are or involve illegal products or services (black market), although in reality they range from nonprofit household-related chores to small enterprises—practices only recently acknowledged as an important component of political economies (Schneider and Enste 2002: 6). For that reason, many have criticized the idea of a juxtaposed formal versus informal economy as a "misplaced dualism" (Lipton 1984: 196; Macharia 1997: 49; Hart 2006: 22) tied to the western concept of the twentieth-century state that has largely ignored the local histories, traditions, and social structures of developing countries.

Macharia's (1997) sociological studies from east Africa provide useful examples and critiques of this misplaced dualism. Through several case studies, he posited that the informal sector had infiltrated larger-scale economic activities to varying degrees, for example in the trade of labor services and the employment of workers or apprentices, especially in the context of developing countries (Macharia 1997: 49, 54). He additionally posited that evidence for formality (for instance market standards and bureaucracy) should not be used to presume the accessibility and participation of communities, particularly in traditional societies (Macharia 1997: 13). Moreover, he discussed how agents from those communities and their practices become legitimate "in the eyes of the society" that often sustains them, despite their deviation from the formal line of economics (Macharia 1997: 55). Given such complex inclusion of both formality and informality within specific social structures and in dialogue with state-level administrations, it becomes more apparent why activities that border or elide into the formal-informal interface, but which are legitimized and socially embedded, are often conceived as gray economics.

In the modern world, these activities include small, often family-run enterprises that operate within delineated social circles and outside the formal, documented, tax-paying, and state-monitored economy. Such practices become legible or visible in the obtainment of goods beyond formal or official trade routes and markets as well as in the moral aspects, obligations, and sentiments surrounding some small-scale economic transactions (Gintis *et al.* 2005; Carballo 2013). Economist and public policy specialist Colin Williams (2004) concluded that a considerable portion of informal economic practices and activities often consist of family, friends, and neighbors paying favors to each other. As such, one can argue that gray economics are deeply entrenched in everyday life. In fact, Hart (2006: 27) argued that gray economics have generally become more frequent and expansive as a result of faster, easier, and improved communication infrastructure starting in the later twentieth century. Moreover, a 2009 study by the Organisation for Economic Co-operation and Development (OECD) concluded that in many parts of the world, practices of informal economy are the norm rather than the exception, involving some two billion people worldwide and including countries with strict economic control measures, such as China (Schneider and Williams 2013: 83).

Such is the gray economy's perseverance and recent pervasiveness that its attendant positive consequences, which include a strong sense of community support, increased entrepreneurship, supply of goods and services via both formal and informal avenues, and economic mobilization, have attracted political attention (Williams 2006: 44). In social terms, the freedom provided by informal economic activities and possible interactions has recently been viewed as strengthening networks and communities and contributing to social peace, which eventually sustains politico-economic systems (Schneider and Enste 2002: 192). In other words, cohesion is a significant stabilizing element in diverse social configurations, and gray economics have cross-culturally played a key role in the maintenance of such networks.

At this point, it should be stressed that evidence for gray economics in ancient societies, drawn from fragmentary records, cannot necessarily support the identification of relative economic status, attitudes, and relations, as opposed to its theoretical application in modern contexts. Instead, the concept can heuristically highlight the integral roles that informal economics play in broader spatial and temporal contexts than just modernity, and interpretations from a case like the Bronze Age Mediterranean may shed new light on our understanding of both past and present societies. In the prehistoric context, arguably comparable to examples from modern traditional societies, informal economic transactions are undoubtedly less discernible than formal, centralized, standardized, and controlled economic networks, which have long held the attention of canonical approaches to the institutions and mechanisms of ancient economies (Schneider and Williams 2013: 12). Despite limitations in visibility, however, one cannot deny that small-scale, agent-driven entrepreneurial trade is an important element that can make more rigorous the models that reconstruct the economic and sociopolitical composition of Late Cypriot society.

Archaeological Background

Longstanding debates and current research on the organization of the Late Cypriot political economy focus on the ways in which the formal economy operated and on how a class of elites was controlling it. As a result, a substantial corpus of research often omits other groups of people, who were part of a socioeconomically heterogeneous population, who also practiced informal economics, and whose contributions were also probably critical to the economic character of the island.

Since the 1960s, one archetypal settlement model has framed our understanding of this period, and despite its gradual elaboration, it has yet to embrace substantively the multiple levels of economic interaction. Based on his extensive survey of especially Bronze Age sites, Catling (1962) initially proposed what has become an exceptionally influential tripartite model of ancient settlement hierarchy, which comprised rich coastal trading centers, inland rural settlements, and small inland production sites mainly associated with copper mining. As multiple excavations since the mid-twentieth century have revealed a variety of additional Late Bronze Age settlements, Keswani (1993) adjusted Catling's model for this specific period to incorporate newly discovered "secondary coastal centers," which were non-coastal settlements associated with ceremonial or religious activities. Problematically, however, she did not explain their relationship to commodity collection and the details of its redistribution in her application of the concepts of staple and wealth finance. The staple finance model involves the collection and redistribution of subsistence resources as tribute, while the wealth finance model is characterized by remuneration of prestigious wealth objects to administrative personnel. Keswani proposed that staple finance was the predominant system at sites with evidence for large-scale storage of agricultural products, such as Kalavasos *Ayios Dhimitrios*, Maroni *Vournes,* and Alassa *Paliotaverna*, and that wealth finance was characteristic of primary settlements, which contained large amounts of prestige artifacts but lacked large and extensive storage facilities. Keswani's (1996) theoretical framing of this settlement model has influenced recent understandings of Late Bronze Age political networks between elites in coastal and inland centers and has engendered a widely accepted argument for regional organization of the island.

Knapp (2013: 437–438) was one of the first scholars to incorporate the relationship between site topography and hierarchy and the flows of goods and agricultural, metallurgical, and social processes into his analysis of settlement patterns, and his remains the most substantive approach to the economic relationships between different levels of settlement (Figure 5.1).

He expanded Catling's (1962) and Keswani's (1993) models, and although they were founded on the same evidentiary lines of settlement distribution, has argued instead for an island-wide sociopolitical configuration, following contemporary written sources that arguably refer to a singular kingdom of Alashiya and its international economic activities (Knapp 2013: 47–438). Alashiya has proven to be a controversial place in these textual sources, although consensus holds that it represented Cyprus. The most detailed information comes from the fourteenth century BCE onwards in the Amarna letters, through a series of exchanges between Egypt and Alashiya (Malbran-Labat 1999), while a discussion on the documentary evidence of Alashiya may be found in Knapp (2013: 438–451; see below).

Despite the plurality of evidence incorporated in the most recent interpretations and models of the Late Bronze Age settlement economy, including excavated

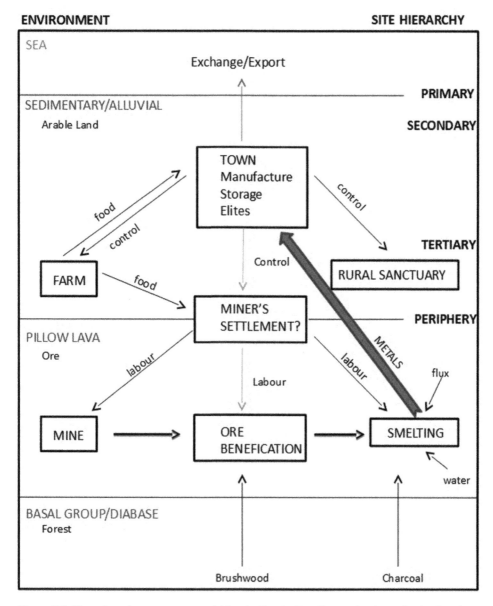

Figure 5.1: Knapp's settlement pattern model for the Cypriot Late Bronze Age (reproduction based on Knapp 2013: 354, Figure 94).

agricultural villages such as Arediou *Vouppes* (Steel 2016), mining villages such as Politiko *Phorades* (Knapp and Kassianidou 2008), and pottery production sites such as Sanidha *Moutti tou Ayiou Serkou* (Todd and Pilides 2004), most scholarship has attended to the category of largest sites, which are interpreted as administering vaguely defined control over sites of lower tiers. The nature of this vertical control between sites of the established tiers, or more horizontally across tiers, is rarely discussed. The reconstruction of economic and sociopolitical ties between various settlement tiers thus remains an open question, with scholars proposing generically that the primary sites formally controlled smaller sites in their periphery. The modes of political organization that were able to manage such control include, for instance, theories of small contact units (Merrillees 1992: 310; Sherratt 1998: 298), heterarchy (Keswani 1996), and states (Knapp 1997; Peltenburg 1996; Webb 1999: 307). The most prominent sites that feature in these investigations are those that bear strong evidence of social and economic differentiation, such as ashlar masonry, seals, script use, and a larger variety of imported artifacts—in other words, materials whose use and distribution suggests elite control (e.g., Webb 2005; Fisher 2009). It is probable, however, that contextual information may provide evidence of the degrees of formality and potential gray economics in their initial or extended uses and histories.

Material Evidence for Informality in the Bronze Age Kouris, Vasilikos, and Maroni Valleys

To explore these contexts, I discuss archaeological evidence from the LC Kouris, Vasilikos, and Maroni valleys of the south-central coast of Cyprus (Figure 5.2). This choice is based on the extensive diachronic investigations of the valleys through previous surveys (Swiny 1981; 2004; Manning and Conwell 1992; Todd 2004) and settlement or cemetery excavations (Benson 1972; Johnson 1980; South and Todd 1985; Todd and Pearlman 1986; MacClellan *et al.* 1988; South and Russell 1989; South 1989; 2000; 2001; Manning *et al.* 1998).

From this rich material record, three excavated and impressive monumental complexes with ashlar buildings dating to the LC period in each of these valleys—Kalavasos *Ayios Dhimitrios* in the Vasilikos Valley (Todd 1989; Fisher *et al.* 2011–2012), Maroni *Vournes* in the Maroni (Cadogan 1989), and Alassa *Paliotaverna* in the Kouris (Hadjisavvas 2017)—have undoubtedly dominated scholarship, often to the analytical subjugation of other aspects of the local economies. These buildings are often viewed as emblematic of urbanization (Fisher 2014b) and signify a sharp contrast to the pre-LC built environment, the available excavations of which have revealed primarily domestic structures. Overall, although the rise of urbanization in Cyprus has received considerable scholarly attention (see summary in Fisher 2014b), the integration of pre-urban, socially embedded economic relations in the new status quo requires a more systematic investigation.

Landscape Archaeology

In this section, I compare the location of LC sites with areas that were intensively occupied during the immediately preceding periods, the Early and the Middle Bronze Age. Scholars have frequently characterized this period as "transitional" (see discussion in Knapp 2013: 348–359), especially in terms of discrete settlement pattern shifts and the establishment of sites closer to the coast at the beginning of the LC period. This shift in the settlement pattern is generally associated with a shift from the pre-LC household-based economy to a LC more formally organized and internationally inte-

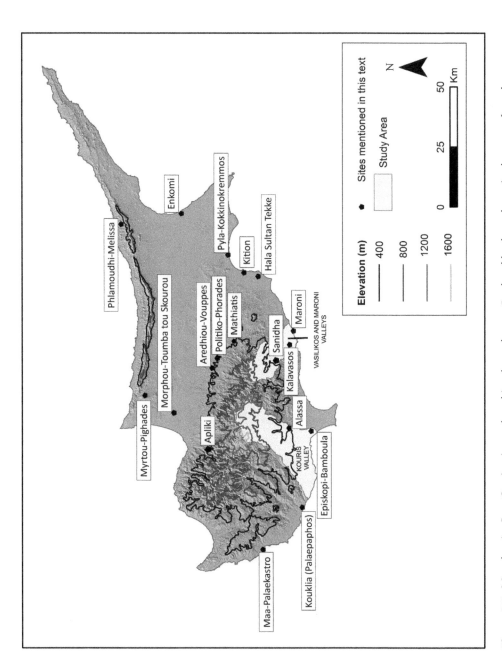

Figure 5.2: Map showing Late Cypriot sites and marking the study area. Produced by the author using basemaps from the Department of Geology, Republic of Cyprus.

grated one. In the context of this paper, I argue that the pre-LC economy appears to be based on informal and more socially embedded practices, whereas the LC economy is subjected to varying levels of control via, for example, the construction of large-scale storage facilities and the use of seals and script. In other words, although for centuries the resources of the island were exploited mainly at a local and regional level via informal, household-based, socially embedded strategies, arguably, much of the available literature on the LC focuses on the textual and material evidence for island-wide formal economics. It is unclear, then, how pre-LC informal economic activities transformed or were ultimately incorporated in the newly founded LC urban landscape.

In the context of archaeological survey, patterns of continuity and discontinuity in habitation may be suggestive of changes of traditional land use patterns and the scale at which certain resources (e.g., copper, timber) and locations (e.g., coast, plateaus) are involved in local economic networks. In this context, juxtaposing significant clusters of EC/MC and LC material on topographical and soil maps in a geographical information systems (GIS) spatial database can highlight regionally distinct links and connections with surrounding and more distant resources (e.g., soil types, sea and coastline, mineral resources).

In this comparative framework, while LC II sites in the Vasilikos and Maroni valleys appear to be established closer to the coast than their EC/MC counterparts, their distance from areas with extensive and dense clusters of EC and MC pottery and known cemeteries is hardly greater than 3 km (Figure 5.3).

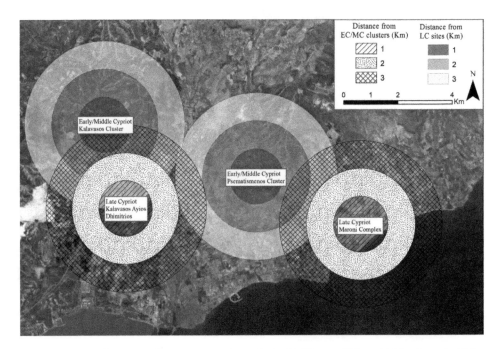

Figure 5.3: Map showing settlement pattern change in the Vasilikos and Maroni Valley from the EC/MC to the LC. Each ring represents a 1 km radius. Produced by the author using Quickbird 2009 satellite imagery from the Geological Survey Department, Republic of Cyprus; and data from Todd 2013; Manning *et al.* 2014.

Moreover, in the Kouris valley, new sites (Alassa *Paliotaverna*, Alassa *Pano Mandilaris* and Episkopi *Bamboula*) are established in much closer proximity to their EC III–LC IA counterparts (Alassa *Palialona*, Episkopi *Phaneromeni*), and throughout the Late Bronze Age they increase in number (Figure 5.4). This indicates a degree of continuity in landscape manipulation strategies and possibly also a continuation in the use of pre-LC economic networks. The small distances discussed above are significant, as Georgiou (2006: 445–446), in his survey of evidence for prehistoric settlement patterns, has estimated that 4 km at the elevation of 100 m can be walked within 30–50 minutes, depending on, among other factors, terrain and direction and means of transportation.

As such, settlement pattern changes or transitions from the EC/MC to the LC in the areas under study do not seem to influence drastically the spatial relation of sites with their surrounding resources, although altering proximity to certain resources and soil types may reflect changes in intensity and scale of their exploitation. The nature of these changes may imply different strategies for managing time and productivity, as well as expansion as opposed to disruption or change of existing economic networks (Andreou 2016: 157–158).

In addition, it seems useful to consider that minor differences in the spatial associations of communities and their surrounding landscape between the EC/MC and the LC in the three valleys is likely related to local traditions stemming from the valleys' continuous habitation and maintenance of potential informal networks that existed prior to the formalization evidenced in the MC III/LC IA urban establishments (e.g., Andreou 2016: 158). In order to identify informal networks, however, it is necessary to understand the characteristics of the formal economic networks.

Contexts for Economic Activity

Having explored local landscape patterns that suggest a possible continuation of pre-LC networks, I turn now to consider the involvements of these communities in exchange networks of both short- and long-distance trade. Given that agents in the Vasilikos, Maroni, or Kouris valley regions likely had multiple opportunities to interact or engage with existing local and regional economic networks (e.g., circulation of certain pottery types), it appears more useful to see how they participated in larger-scale, more formal, island-wide networks. In this context, copper seems to be the most suitable resource to explore, as there is extensive material and textual evidence for its large scale and presumably also centrally controlled (formal) economic exploitation.

Trying to reconstruct various networks of island-wide exchange can be difficult, as evidence for production or distribution of various goods can be limited, although recent investigations of copper production and metallurgy are bringing significant new evidence to light (Figure 5.5).

The Troodos Mountains provide numerous locales suited for copper extraction (Constantinou 1992; Muhly and Kassianidou 2012: 127, Figure 8.5), and archaeological contexts of mining, secondary refinement points, intra-island transportation, and storage of metal, while sometimes difficult to distinguish or date to precise

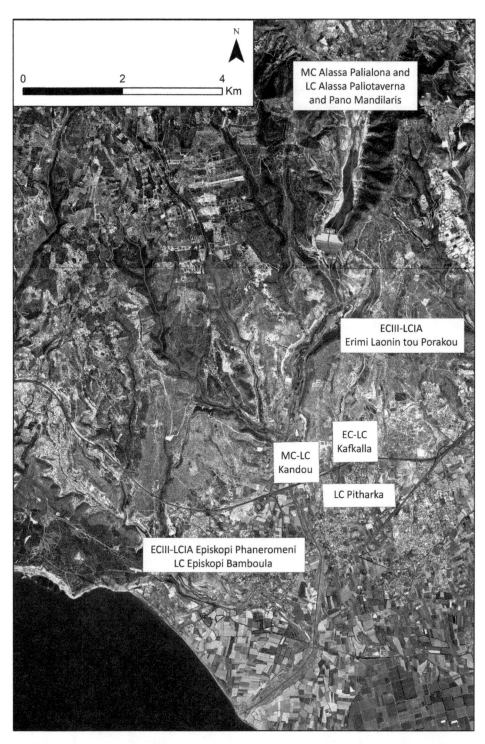

Figure 5.4: Map showing settlement pattern change in the Kouris Valley from the EC/MC to the LC. Produced by the author using Quickbird 2009 satellite imagery from the Geological Survey Department, Republic of Cyprus; and data from Swiny 1981; Bombardieri 2010; Karageorghis and Violaris 2012.

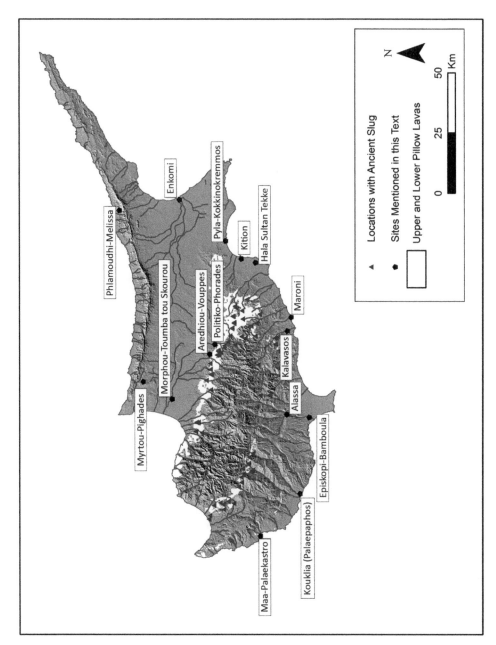

Figure 5.5: Map showing Late Bronze Age sites and their association with Troodos copper resources. Produced by the author using basemaps and data from the Geological Survey Department, Republic of Cyprus.

periods (see also Berranger and Fluzin 2007: 7), have become increasingly more evident through surveys and excavations in the Troodos foothills. The LC copper smelting workshop excavated at Politiko *Phorades* (Knapp and Kassianidou 2008) and the exposure of a deposit of ingot fragments at Mathiatis (Catling 1964: 283; Kassianidou 2009) are just two examples that have markedly elaborated current understandings of copper production and craftsmanship for prehistoric periods.

The *Phorades* workshop was estimated to have produced copper for local consumption with the possibility of some surplus entering extra-community exchange networks (Knapp 2003: 564). As the settlement pattern of the surrounding area was reconstructed from surveyed material, however, it is unclear how this site was integrated into a system developed for the large-scale exportation of copper (e.g., associated storage facilities for copper, measures for controlling production and circulation such as standardized weighting and sealing practices).

Similar conceptions can frame interpretations for Apliki *Karamallos*, another LC production site in the Troodos foothills (Kling and Muhly 2007). The site comprises a smelting workshop in association with domestic spaces and agricultural product storage facilities. Although the site is located inland and close to copper sources, the frequency of imported pottery, such as Mycenaean and Minoan ware (Kling 2007: 149–168), points to consumption patterns that do not conform to the traditional settlement pattern models that usually favor exotica consumption in the primary or secondary sites rather than the supporting villages. This disparity once again appears to require smaller-scale investigation, focusing on less formal and less centrally administered economic interactions, such as the more socially embedded economic activities taking place outside specialized open and structured spaces.

Built Environment

In order to augment the patterns identified in the survey material with stratified archaeological evidence, I return to the Vasilikos, Maroni, and Kouris river valleys to explore architectural evidence for non–centrally administered economic practices. Studies of the significance and instrumentality of LBA architecture in the formation of LC polities and social structures, as explored cogently by Fisher (2007; 2009; 2014a; 2014b; 2014c), provide a rich background for exploring regional differences in built environments that associate with the aforementioned local traditions of spatial associations between surrounding environments and new LC settlements. Here, I focus on the identification of activities that may reveal types of economic agents, with the aim of understanding the degree of their dependence on or independence from LC administrative buildings and monumental complexes.

To begin with, the excavated remains of the major urban sites of Kalavasos *Ayios Dhimitrios*, Maroni *Vournes*, and Alassa *Paliotaverna* in the area under investigation, with their ashlar monumental buildings with large storage capacities (Fisher 2014c; Keswani 2015), also include evidence for domestic units, which have only recently been explored systematically (Fisher 2014a). These probable domestic units often contain storage of goods in *pithoi* (South 1980: 43; Keswani 2009: 114–115; Fisher 2014a), evidence of crafts like metalworking (South 1982: 65; Van Brempt and

Kassianidou 2016) and of material processing (South 1980: 39), access to imported artifacts, script use (in the form of signs; Smith 2002), and non-standardized marking and sealing practices (Smith 2012: 46). Notable are the "semi-official" buildings at Kalavasos *Ayios Dhimitrios*, which are larger than typical domestic units, partially constructed with ashlar masonry, and associated by South (1991: 134) with larger-scale metalworking and agricultural processing.

Considering the variability in the architectural remains, the scales of the various economic activities involved in them, and the role these households played in social interaction and transformation (Fisher 2014a), we can argue that a series of professional identities, ones closely related to the main economic activities of certain individuals and groups, formed an integral part of the LC politico-economic organization. In this vein, one should note that while Episkopi *Bamboula* in the Kouris Valley bears evidence for urbanization and access to imported artifacts, as well as evidence of different socioeconomic identities (Smith 2012: 46), it is not yet associated with excavated monumental structures (Weinberg 1983). This anomaly perhaps points to an even closer incorporation of informal or gray economic activities into a formalized organization, a more traditional trajectory that may further be supported by the relatively long use of family tombs in this area, as discussed in the following section.

Burying Individuals

This section aims to understand the mechanisms of product acquisition at small scales. As the standardization of local and regional pottery can be associated with formalized production and distribution of both pottery and organic materials, I focus here on artifacts whose manufacture was not controlled on the island of Cyprus. The study of the distribution of non-local artifacts aims also to highlight a possible variability in acquisition strategies. It is based on the hypothesis that ubiquitous artifacts were likely acquired via a more centralized and formal economic avenues (market), whereas artifacts that are more scarce in the available burial record may indicate significant patterns of informal acquisition and consumption. The methodology used involves analyzing the available published LBA burial evidence from the three valleys to quantify different artifact types and to examine the degree to which their abundance and ubiquity may be suggestive of informal economic practices. The examples derive from a selection of intact or minimally disturbed tombs, and in the majority of examples, it is not possible to provide a clear association between finds and specific skeletal remains. For that reason, quantitative comparisons in this paper refer to tombs with multiple interments and not to individuals. Finally, quantitative information has been compiled into a spatial database, analyzed using ArcGIS statistical tools and illustrated using Excel.

By comparing assemblages between tombs of particular cemeteries, it is possible to demonstrate that at Kalavasos *Ayios Dhimitrios* and the nearby LC cemetery of Kalavasos *Mangia* in the Vasilikos Valley, from a sample of twenty-two tombs with multiple internments dating between LC IIA and IIC, the majority of tombs contained Mycenaean pottery and other imports. Six unique artifacts include a Hittite figure (tomb 12; see South 2000: 355), glass, faience, and ivory *pyxides*, a set of ivory weights (*Mangia*; see McClellan *et al.* 1988: 205), and faience vessels (Figure 5.6).

The tomb at Kalavasos *Mangia* containing the weights included a set of boat-shaped earrings made of gold (McClellan *et al.* 1988: 203). Although it is unclear if the ubiquitous Mycenaean pottery and the remarkable number of artifacts were acquired through the same large-scale economic networks, one cannot exclude the possibility of intra-site distribution of these goods at varying scales of exchange.

In the Maroni valley, in a sample of forty-seven tombs from Maroni *Tsaroukkas* and Maroni *Vournes* dating between LC IA and IIC, most tombs also contained Mycenaean pottery, while sixteen unique (at Maroni) artifacts were recorded—primarily jewelry (Figure 5.7).

Objects of personal adornment often appear to be unique and personalized, including bull head pendants from T1 (Johnson 1980: 8), silver and gold diadems from T4, T5, T9, and T10 (Johnson 1980: 17–20), a rosette-decorated mouthpiece from T26 (Johnson 1980: 31), gold and silver rings, various shapes of gold beads and silver rings with bezels from T1 and T7 (Johnson 1980: 15, 18–19), and faience scarabs from T4 and T10 (Johnson 1980: 17, 20) and pit 18 from later excavations (Manning *et al.* 1998: 340). Some material assemblages, probably indicating identities relevant in part to economic occupations of either the deceased or those responsible for their burial (likely family), include two terracotta boat models from T1 and T5 (Johnson 1980: 15, 18–19), cylinder seals from pit 18 (Manning *et al.* 1998: 341), bronze weights from T3 (Johnson 1980: 17), and bronze scale pans from T1 and T10 (Johnson 1980: 15, 20). The boat models may be suggestive of links to or expressions of merchant or trader identities. The bronze weights and scales are, on the one hand, suggestive of standardized and likely formal economic interactions, and their low ubiquity across the forty-seven tombs is related to certain individuals or groups (such as families or professional corporations). On the other hand, the wide accessibility of imports like Mycenaean vessels and the abundance of non-ubiquitous artifacts suggest that their circulation was not strictly controlled. This patterning may indicate that a combination of formal and less formal economic relations were influencing or framing the circulation of goods.

Finally, in a sample of thirty-nine multiply interred tombs from Episkopi *Bamboula* dating between LC IA and IIC, Mycenaean pottery was recovered in more than half the corpus (Kiely 2010: 60), and several examples of rare artifacts as well as faience were recorded (e.g., an ostrich egg in T5 and a glass pomegranate in T24; see Benson 1972: 13, 25) (Figure 5.8).

Imported pottery from other locations is less common than the Mycenaean wares and is possibly of Syrian provenance, such as a bichrome jug from T12 (Benson 1972: 16). The burial assemblages that contained the finds discussed above are not distinguished by wealth (large number of finds) or uniqueness (distinct size, shape, or internal arrangement). In other words, it is not possible, based on the available burial record, to pinpoint an individual or a family with more extensive or direct access to imported artifacts and hence participation in larger economic networks.

Finally, although the material evidence discussed indicates a wide accessibility to imports that can suggest a less centralized and controlled distribution of these

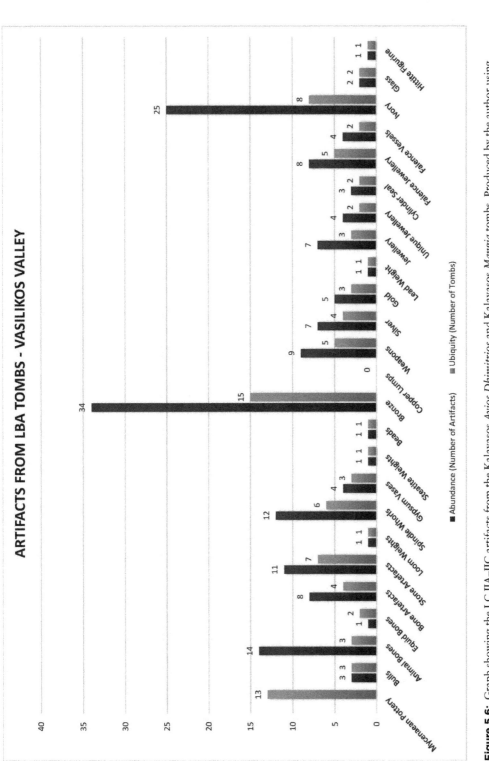

Figure 5.6: Graph showing the LC IIA–IIC artifacts from the Kalavasos Ayios *Dhimitrios* and Kalavasos *Mangia* tombs. Produced by the author using data from South and Todd 1985; Todd and Pearlman 1986; McClellan *et al.* 1988; South and Russell 1989; South 1989; South 2000; South and Steel 2001; South 2002.

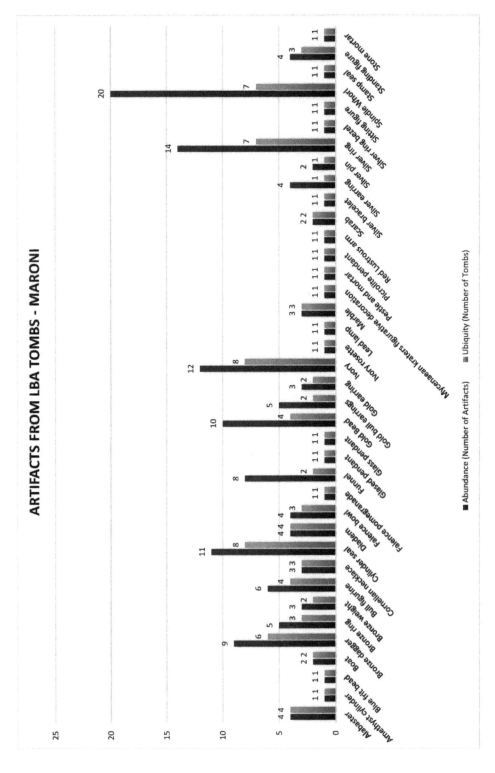

Figure 5.7: Graph showing the LC IIA–IIC artifacts from Maroni *Vournes* and Maroni *Tsaroukkas*. Produced by the author using data from Johnson 1980; Manning *et al.* 1998.

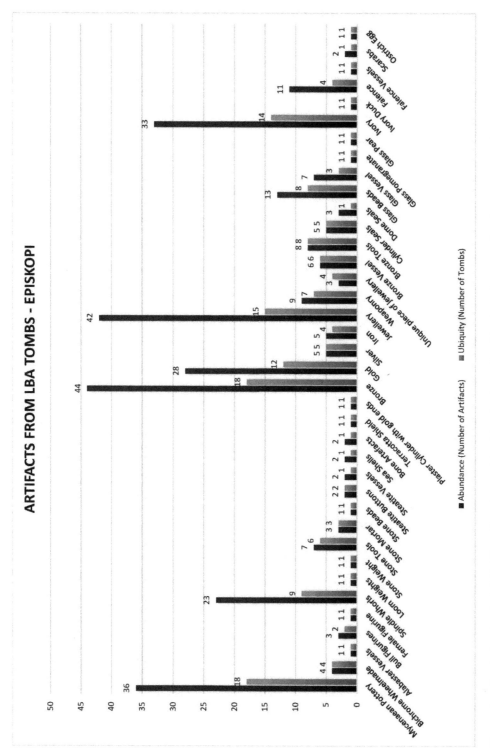

Figure 5.8: Graph showing the LC IA–IIC artifacts from Episkopi *Bamboula*. Produced by the author using data from Benson 1972.

179

artifacts, we cannot ignore the inherent biases of the burial contexts under study. When contrasting the chronological span (often up to one hundred years) and the number of burial interments, it becomes obvious that the available data reflect a small fraction of the mortuary evidence, possibly, as suggested by Manning and Hulin (2005: 17), reflecting those practices limited to elite groups. A greater number of such artifacts and a larger variety of object types probably formed part of the domestic assemblages, and the above example is not representative of any site's total or holistic material culture.

In addition, the details of these objects' direct or indirect import are perplexing. Why and how did almost all investigated burials contain imports? Were different scales of imported vessels or goods associated with different levels of formal politico-economic relations? The aim in this comparison, of course, is not to begin to associate elite versus non-elite artifacts with formal versus informal, public versus private, state versus non-state, or market versus non-market. In contrast, this paper proposes that the variety of materials observed in the scale of imported artifacts is an indication of multiple types of exchange and that their occurrence in tombs can comment on the economic potential and networking of the deceased and/or living who buried them through what were likely important social events reflecting meaningful aspects of identity. To conclude, variability in the abundance and ubiquity of nonlocal artifacts may suggest also a non-standardized exchange system—rather than a tightly controlled or strictly centralized one—in which informal interactions take place, potentially ranging from personal to group levels.

The Textual Evidence

The information derived from spatial and contextual analyses of archaeological material can, on the one hand, point to a possibility of gray economics in the LC period. On the other hand, as noted above, these interpretations raise questions regarding the ways and processes in which imported artifacts were acquired by communities and individuals. To complement those data and to cross-examine the findings, I return to the contemporary textual evidence and its implications for understanding informality. Indeed, available textual evidence has largely fostered debates and competing explanations of the political economy of the LC period, with considerable attention focusing on the identification of "Alashiya" and its potential categorization as a polity (organization, place, network, and entity). While there is little space here to address those concerns, several aspects that emerge from these documents are important for a discussion of formal economics. For these reasons, I focus specifically on textual examples that originate from the fourteenth-century BCE Ugarit and Amarna archives as an entryway to examine representations of informal economic activities.

In these texts, Alashiya is, in general, mentioned as an important diplomatic power, participating in "elite" gift exchange (Peltenburg 2012: 11; Peltenburg and Iacovou 2012: 350), which involved copper exported from Cyprus at seemingly grand scales. In addition, formalized politico-economic relations, for example office holding, are apparent in key words used in the Amarna letters that mention Alashiya, such as the Alashiyan representative in letter EA 35 who addresses the king of Egypt as "brother," intimating a sense of status equality among powerful elites (Knapp 2008: 326). Despite a lack of material evidence substantiating the type of ruler who shaped those written records, one cannot deny that elite groups of Late Bronze Age Cyprus participated in the interregional trade networks and emulated aspects of the Near Eastern ideological sphere, seen in the acquisition of luxury artifacts and symbolic imagery (Webb 2005: 180). The wide distribution of these materials across the island may suggest that multiple sites and multiple agents participated in those formal interaction networks.

Moreover, although Knapp (2008, 2013: 438–447) has elaborated at great length on the correspondence between textual and material evidence, there is no indisputable evidence for island-wide politico-economic integration, such as a distinct administrative building, a distinct (royal) tomb, evidence for veneration of an individual or a group of people (figurative representation), nor is there an established and standardized island-wide sealing practice with irrefutable sphragistic evidence or an archive (Manning and de Mita 1997: 108–109). Indeed, there exists scholarly debate on whether the island had one political power or several competing powers represented in diplomatic exchange, resulting from Alashiya's material and textual diversity. Following Schloen's (2001) study on Ugarit, Peltenburg (2012) has proposed a large (elite) household-based, decentralized Alashiyan political configuration, an approach he considered more consistent with the available material evidence and one that incorporates the agency of diverse elite groups and regional communities. On the other hand, Knapp (2013: 444) takes a maximalist view and argues for a more absolute kind of island-wide authority.

My paper shares Knapp's (2013: 446) skepticism toward interpretations that do not sufficiently incorporate the textual evidence. It also shares his view that the interpretation of the available textual and material evidence relies on the perspective of each researcher. Based on the extensive ethnographic and anthropological data on which the theory of gray economics relies, however, as well as the archaeological data I have presented so far, I am more inclined to follow Peltenburg's (2012) minimalist view that LC local particularities were part of a decentralized political organization that, I believe, may stem from informal socioeconomic interactions. I am less inclined to argue for a more absolute type of island-wide authority, as such an approach does not incorporate and would make even more obscure informal economic interactions, which are already overshadowed by the more widely studied indications for socioeconomic formalization (e.g., the urban components of excavated sites).

Moreover, although more informal and less centrally controlled activities are not included in the available textual evidence of Cyprus, merchants and traders are documented in contemporaneous Near Eastern texts as possessing a multitude of characteristics: sometimes being private entrepreneurs, other times associated with, but not always attached to, a formal politico-economic configuration (Monroe 2009). Monroe investigated written sources that indirectly point to the existence of multiple scales of economic interaction and variable degrees of formality, particularly for the case of the Late Bronze Age kingdom of Ugarit. He also discussed how even the contemporary LBA Egyptian economy, which has been perceived as diachronically monolithic and pharaoh-oriented, permitted entrepreneurial elements (Monroe 2009: 6 with references). He additionally proposed that formal institutions and entrepreneurs were likely linked by various degrees of interdependence (2009: 15). Since the majority of preserved texts from ca. 1350–1175 BCE in the eastern Mediterranean do not demonstrate a depth of information regarding shipping technologies, one might think, as Monroe (2009: 100) has argued, that formal administrators were not concerned with the logistics of moving goods. Could this hypothesis support a more independent character for individuals who owned or could access boats or shipping routes? Although textual and archaeological information regarding merchant activities in LBA Cyprus is limited compared to its Near Eastern counterparts (Manning and Hulin 2005; Knapp 2014: 86–87), the examples mentioned above provide useful paradigms for considering the more informal interactions facilitated by seaborne trade.

For the LC case, which lacks deciphered textual records and instead offers conflicting information deriving from extra-island impressions of Alashiya, things appear more complicated. For instance, letter RS 18.042 of Ugarit mentions a number of jars for a shipment recorded at Ugarit as ". . . 600 jars of oil to Abiramu the Cypriot. . . ." In this text, Abiramu has been interpreted as an agent originally from Alashiya operating in Ugarit and expecting this specific delivery of jars (Monroe 2009: 87–88). Who this person was and how he was related to the Alashiyan economy—a more formal configuration that corresponds with the upper bodies of Near Eastern political structure—remains unclear. We can only speculate on the behavior of Cypriot/Alashiyan merchants reportedly residing in Ugarit (KTU 4.102; UT 119; Monroe 2009: 220; Steel 2013: 30) and their association with what Alashiya may represent. Moreover, seals, pottery, and Cypro-Minoan tablets add further complexity to the peculiar case of Alashiyan migrants (Caubet and Matoïan 1995) and their politico-economic role in Ugarit and Cyprus.

On one hand, in Amarna letter EA39 the king of Alashiya mentions: "these men are my merchants . . . let them go safely and promptly. No one making a claim in your name is to approach my merchants or my ships." This statement, in association with the large amounts of copper reported to be exported from Cyprus, suggests a well-organized, possibly island-wide control of this resource and the agents responsible for its circulation (Knapp 2013: 444). On the other hand, in Amarna letter EA 45 the king of Alashiya mentions: "the people of my land speak to me about the lumber that the king of Egypt receives from me. So, my brother, make the payment to me." This correspondence may indicate that certain individuals or groups of merchants/traders held sufficient influence over the economic dealings of the "land" and "king" of Alashiya; a state of interdependence communicated in the latter's demands for payment by the people. Brown (2013: 11) has noted this ambiguous division between private and state spheres of economic exchange and has associated the textual reference of Alashiyan persons and the overly mercantile attitude of the Alashiyan representative in the available correspondence with the probable existence of formal and informal exchange networks. Prior to that, Liverani (2001: 148–149) discussed the arguably commercial focus of the correspondence between Alashiya and Assyria, and Broodbank (2013: 398–399) has more recently mentioned Alashiya's use of merchants, rather than royal couriers, as messengers.

Overall, I would argue that the juxtaposition of evidence for island-wide control of resources and evidence for regionally and locally independent economic strategies indicates the coexistence of informal or gray economics in such a way that permitted or even encouraged the incorporation of informal economic activities into formalized international economic networks.

Conclusions

The conclusions of this paper are preliminary, as this is an ongoing study at present limited to the south-central coast of the island. Extending research island-wide can provide a more nuanced understanding of different economic scales and degrees of regional informality, as it will involve a wider sample and a larger number of artifacts from secured contexts. Additional useful evidence can derive from recent studies that compiled evidence for seaborne trade that facilitated in varying degrees the transportation of products across the island (Knapp 2014; Knapp and Demesticha 2017).

Given the low archaeological and textual visibility of such gray economics, scholars have naturally attended more closely to monumental remains of state-level production and distribution regimes and interregional exchange networks preserved at the highest levels of socioeconomic class. Despite inevitable theoretical and methodological limitations, this paper has demonstrated the probability that our poor understanding of the details of formal Late Bronze Age economics, particularly regarding the networks linking copper mines and the coast, are largely due to a more decentralized economy than traditionally assumed, including to a large degree socially embedded economic practices.

To conclude, in this paper I have argued that during the LC period, it is plausible that a series of gray economic practices were taking place alongside more materially prominent, formal activities viewed in monumental buildings, large-scale production centers, and storage facilities for agricultural products and the large-scale exploitation of copper. This conclusion is hardly surprising, as such arrangements probably existed and sustained human societies prior to their politico-economic formalization. Gray economics during the LC period arguably coexisted with the formal economy in a non-exclusionary and non-dualistic dynamic. If this type of informal economy benefited elites who organized and profited from state-directed interregional economics, it is likely that they implemented laissez-faire trade or even a policy of close cooperation. Therefore, small-scale units based on informal principles of organization should be viewed as significant, integral parts of the Late Cypriot economy and its general description could be adjusted.

Acknowledgments

This study results from the PhD research I conducted at the University of Edinburgh, under the supervision of Edgar Peltenburg and Gordon Thomas. I would like to thank the Department of Classics at Cornell University and Catherine Kearns, Jeff Leon, and Sturt Manning for organizing this conference. I am very grateful for all inspiring discussions I had with Sturt and A. Bernard Knapp. Finally, I would like to thank Luke Aspland for helping me improve the form and presentation of this paper.

References

Andreou, G.M. 2014. Traversing space: Landscape and identity in Bronze Age Cyprus. Unpublished PhD dissertation, University of Edinburgh.

Andreou, G.M. 2016. Understanding the urban landscape of Late Bronze Age Cyprus: A diachronic perspective from the Vasilikos Valley. *Journal of Mediterranean Archaeology* 29.2: 143–172.

Appadurai, A. 1986. *The Social Life of Things: Commodities in Cultural Perspective.* Cambridge: Cambridge University Press.

Berranger, M., and P. Fluzin. 2007. Organisation de la chaîne opératoire en métallurgie du fer aux IIe-Ier siècle av.J.-C., sur l'oppidum d'Entremont (Aix-en-Provence, Bouches-du-Rhône): La circulation du metal. *ArchéoSciences* 31: 7–22.

Benson, J.L. 1972. *Bamboula at Kourion: The Necropolis and the Finds Excavated by J.F. Daniel.* University of Pennsylvania Museum Monographs. Haney Foundations series 12. Philadelphia: University of Pennsylvania Press.

Bohannan, P. 1959. The impact of money on an African subsistence economy. *Journal of Economic History* 19: 491–503.

Bombardieri, L. 2010. Surveying the Kourion Land: Kouris Valley survey and preliminary excavations at Erimi-*Laonin tou Porakou* (2007–2008). In A.M. Jasink and L. Bombardieri (eds.), *Researches in Cypriote History and Archaeology: Proceedings of the Meeting Held in Florence April 29–30th 2009,* 33–52. Florence: Firenze University Press.

Broodbank, C. 2013. *The Making of the Middle Sea: A History of the Mediterranean from the Beginning to the Emergence of the Classical World.* London: Thames and Hudson.

Brown, M. 2013. Waterways and the political geography of south-east Cyprus in the second millennium BC. *The Annual of the British School of Athens* 108: 121–136.

Cadogan, G. 1989. Maroni and the monuments. In E. Peltenburg (ed.), *Early Society in Cyprus,* 43–51. Edinburgh: Edinburgh University Press.

Carballo, D.M. 2013. Cultural and evolutionary dynamics of cooperation in archaeological perspective. In D.M. Carballo (ed.), *Cooperation and Collective Action: Archaeological Perspectives,* 1–33. Boulder: University Press of Colorado.

Catling, H.W. 1962. Patterns of settlement in Bronze Age Cyprus. *Opuscula Atheniensia* 4: 129–169.

Catling, H.W. 1964. *Cypriot Bronze Work in the Mycenean World.* Oxford: Clarendon Press.

Caubet, A., and V. Matoïan. 1995. Ougarti et l'Égée. In M. Yon, M. Sznycer, and P. Bordneuil (eds.), *Les pays d'Ougarit autour de 1200 av.J.-C.,* 99–112. Paris: Édition Recherche sur les civilisations.

Constantinou, G. 1992. Ancient copper mining in Cyprus. In A. Marangou and K. Psillides (eds.), *Cyprus, Copper, and the Sea,* 43–74. Nicosia: Republic of Cyprus.

D'Altroy, T.N., and T.K. Earle. 1985. Staple finance, wealth finance, and storage in the Inka political economy. *Current Anthropology* 26: 187–206.

Elgin, C., and C. Oyvat. 2013. Lurking in the cities: Urbanization and the informal economy. *Structural Change and Economic Dynamics* 27: 36–47.

Feldman, M.H. 2006. *Diplomacy by Design: Luxury Arts and an "International Style" in the Ancient Near East, 1400–1200 BCE.* London and Chicago: University of Chicago Press.

Finley, M.I. 1973. *The Ancient Economy.* Berkeley and Los Angeles: University of California Press.

Fisher, K.D. 2007. Building Power: Monumental architecture, place, and social interaction in Late Bronze Age Cyprus. Unpublished PhD dissertation, University of Toronto.

Fisher, K.D. 2009. Elite place-making and social interaction in the Late Cypriot Bronze age. *Journal of Mediterranean Archaeology* 22: 183–209.

Fisher, K.D. 2014a. Rethinking the Late Cypriot built environment: Households and communities as places of social transformation. In A.B. Knapp and P. van Dommelen (eds.), *The Cambridge Prehistory of the Bronze and Iron Age Mediterranean,* 399–416. Cambridge: Cambridge University Press.

Fisher, K.D. 2014b. Making the first cities on Cyprus: Urbanism and social change in the Late Bronze Age. In A.T. Creekmore III and K.D. Fisher (eds.), *Making Ancient Cities: Space and Place in Early Urban Societies*, 181–219. Cambridge: Cambridge University Press.

Fisher, K.D. 2014c. The creation and experience of monumentality on Protohistoric Cyprus. In J.F. Osborne (ed.), *Approaching Monumentality in Archaeology*, 355–383. Albany: SUNY Press.

Fisher, K.D., J.F. Leon, S.W. Manning, M. Rogers, and D.A. Sewell. 2017. The Kalavasos and Maroni Built Environments Project: introduction and preliminary report on the 2008 and 2010 seasons. *Report of the Department of Antiquities, Cyprus*: 415–441.

Georgiou, G. 2006. Η τοπογραφία της ανθρώπινης εγκατάστασης στην Κύπρο κατά την Πρώιμη και Μέση Χαλκοκρατία. Unpublished PhD thesis, University of Cyprus.

Gintis, H., S. Bowles, R. Body, and E. Fehr. (eds.) 2005. *Moral Sentiments and Material Interests: The Foundations of Cooperation in Economic Life*. Cambridge: MIT Press.

Hadjisavvas, S. 2017. *Alassa. Excavations at the Late Bronze Age sites of Pano Mantilaris and Paliotaverna 1984-2000*. Lefkosia: Cyprus Department of Antiquities.

Hart, K. 1973. Informal income opportunities and urban employment in Ghana. *Journal of Modern African Studies* 11.1: 61–89.

Hart, K. 2006. Bureaucratic form and the informal economy. In B. Guha-Khasnobis, R. Kanbur, and E. Ostrom (eds.), *Linking the Formal and Informal Economy: Concepts and Policies*, 21–35. Oxford: Oxford University Press.

Hicks, J. 1969. *A Theory of Economic History*. Oxford: Clarendon Press.

Hirth, K., and J. Pillsbury. 2013. *Merchants, Markets, and Exchange in the Pre-Columbian World*. Washington, DC: Dumbarton Oaks Research Library and Collection.

Hodos, T. 2010. Local and global perspectives in the study of social and cultural identities. In S. Hales and T. Hodos (eds.), *Material Culture and Social Identities in the Ancient World*, 3–31. Cambridge: Cambridge University Press.

Johnson, J. 1980. *Maroni de Chypre*. Studies in Mediterranean Archaeology 59. Göteborg, Sweden: Paul Åströms Förlag.

Karageorghis, V., and Y. Violaris (eds.). 2013. *Tombs of the Late Bronze Age in the Limassol Area, Cyprus (17th–13th centuries BC)*. Nicosia: Municipality of Limassol.

Kassianidou, V. 2009. Oxhide ingots in Cyprus. In F. Lo Schiavo, J.D. Muhly, R. Martin, and A. Giumlia-Mair (eds.), *Oxhide Ingots in the Central Mediterranean*, 41–81. Rome: The A.G. Leventis Foundation.

Keswani, P.S. 1993. Models of local exchange in Late Bronze Age Cyprus. *Bulletin of the American Schools of Oriental Research* 292: 73–83.

Keswani, P.S. 1996. Hierarchies, heterarchies, and urbanization processes: The view from Bronze Age Cyprus. *Journal of Mediterranean Archaeology* 9.2: 211–250.

Keswani, P.S. 2009. Exploring regional variation in Late Cypriot II–III pithoi: Perspectives from Alassa and Kalavasos. In I. Hein (ed.), *The Formation of Cyprus in the 2nd Millennium B.C.: Studies in Regionalism during the Middle and Late Bronze Ages*, 107–125. Vienna: Österreichischen Akademie der Wissenschaften.

Keswani, P.S. 2015. Olive production, storage, and political economy at Late Bronze Age Kalavasos, Cyprus. In A. Jacobs and P. Cosyns (eds.), *Cypriot Material Culture Studies from Picrolite Carving to Proskynitaria Analysis. Proceedings of the 8th Annual Postgraduate Cypriot Archaeology Conference Held in Honour of the Memory of Paul Åström at the Vrije Universiteit Brussel (Belgium), 27th–29th November 2008*, 1–24. Brussels: Brussels University Press.

Kiely, T. 2010. Prestige goods and social complexity at Episkopi-*Bamboula*. In A.M. Jasink and L. Bombardieri (eds.), *Researches in Cypriote History and Archaeology: Proceedings of the Meeting Held in Florence April 29–30th 2009*, 53–73. Florence: Firenze University Press.

Kling, B. 2007. Pottery from Apliki *Karamallos*. In B. Kling and J. Muhly (eds.), *Joan du Plat Taylor's Excavations at the Late Bronze Age Mining Settlement at Apliki Karamallos, Cyprus*, 95–227. Studies in Mediterranean Archaeology 134.1. Sävedalen, Sweden: Paul Åströms Förlag.

Kling, B., and J.D. Muhly. (eds.) 2007. *Joan du Plat Taylor's Excavations at the Late Bronze Age Mining Settlement at Apliki Karamallos, Cyprus*. Studies in Mediterranean Archaeology 134.1. Sävedalen, Sweden: Paul Åströms Förlag.

Knapp, A.B. 1993. Thalassocracies in Bronze Age eastern Mediterranean trade: Making and breaking a myth. *World Archaeology* 24: 332–347.

Knapp, A.B. 1997. *The Archaeology of Late Bronze Age Cypriot Society: The Study of Settlement, Survey, and Landscape.* Glasgow: University of Glasgow.

Knapp, A.B. 2003. The archaeology of community on Bronze Age Cyprus: Politiko "Phorades" in context. *American Journal of Archaeology* 107: 559–580.

Knapp, A.B. 2008. *Prehistoric and Protohistoric Cyprus: Identity, Insularity, and Connectivity.* Oxford: Oxford University Press.

Knapp, A.B. 2013. *The Archaeology of Cyprus: From Earliest Prehistory through the Bronze Age.* Cambridge: Cambridge University Press.

Knapp, A.B. 2014. Seafaring and seafarers: The case of Late Bronze Age Cyprus. In J.M. Webb (ed.), *Structure, Measurement, and Meaning: Studies on Prehistoric Cyprus in Honour of David Frankel,* 79–93. Studies in Mediterranean Archaeology 143. Uppsala, Sweden: Åströms Förlag.

Knapp, A.B., and S. Demesticha. 2017. *Mediterranean Connections: Maritime Transport Containers and Seaborne Trade in the Bronze and Early Iron Ages.* New York and London: Routledge.

Knapp, A.B., and V. Kassianidou. 2008. The archaeology of Late Bronze Age copper production: Politiko Phorades on Cyprus. In Ü. Yalçin (ed.), *Anatolian Metal IV: Frühe Rohstoffgewinnung in Anatolien un seinen Nachbarländern,* 135–147. Die Anschnitt, Beiheft 21. Bochum, Germany: Deutsches Bergbau-Museum.

La Porta, R., and A. Shleifer. 2014. Informality and development. *Journal of Economic Perspectives* 28: 109–126.

Lipton, M. 1984. Family, fungibility, and formality: Rural advantages of informal non-farm enterprise versus the urban-formal state. In S. Amin (ed.), *Human Resources, Employment, and Development,* Vol. 5, 189–242. London: MacMillan.

Liverani, M. 2001. *International Relations in the Ancient Near East, 1600–1100 BC.* Basingstoke, U.K.: Palgrave.

Liverani, M. 2005. The Near East: The Bronze Age. In J.G. Manning and I. Morris (eds.), *The Ancient Economy: Evidence and Models,* 47–57. Stanford: Stanford University Press.

Macharia, K. 1997. *Social and Political Dynamics of the Informal Economy in African Cities.* Oxford: University Press of America.

Malbran-Labat, F. 1999. Nouvelles données épigraphiques sur Chypre et Ougarit. *Report of the Department of Antiquities, Cyprus:* 122–124.

Malinowski, B. 1922. *Argonauts of the Western Pacific: An Account of Native Enterprise and Adventure in the Archipelagoes of Melanesian New Guinea.* London: Routledge and Kegan Paul.

Manning, J.G., and I. Morris. (eds.) 2005. *The Ancient Economy: Evidence and Models.* Stanford: Stanford University Press.

Manning, S.W., G.M. Andreou, K.D. Fisher, P. Gerard-Little, C. Kearns, J.F. Leon, D.A. Sewell, and T.M. Urban. 2014. Becoming urban: Investigating the anatomy of the Late Bronze Age complex, Maroni, Cyprus. *Journal of Mediterranean Archaeology* 27.1: 3–32.

Manning, S.W., and D.H. Conwell. 1992. Maroni Valley Archaeological Survey Project: Preliminary report on the 1990–1991 field seasons. *Report of the Department of Antiquities, Cyprus:* 271–283.

Manning, S.W., and F. De Mita. 1997. Cyprus, the Aegean, and Maroni-*Tsaroukkas.* In D. Christou (ed.), *Proceedings of the International Archaeological Conference "Cyprus and the Aegean in Antiquity" from the Prehistoric Period to the 7th Century AD, Nicosia 8–10 December 1995,* 103–141. Nicosia: Department of Antiquities.

Manning, S.W., and L. Hulin. 2005. Maritime commerce and geographies of mobility in the Late Bronze Age of the eastern Mediterranean: Problematizations. In E. Blake and A.B. Knapp (eds.), *The Archaeology of Mediterranean Prehistory,* 270–302. Oxford: Blackwell.

Manning, S.W., S.J. Monks, S. Louise, E. Ribeiro, and J.M. Weinstein. 1998. Late Cypriot tombs at Maroni *Tsaroukkas,* Cyprus. *Annual of the British School in Athens* 93: 297–351.

Manning, S.W., D.A. Sewell, and E. Herscher. 2002. Late Cypriot IA maritime trade in action: Underwater survey at Maroni *Tsaroukkas* and the contemporary east Mediterranean trading system. *Annual of the British School in Athens* 97: 97–162.

Mauss, M. 1990. *The Gift: The Form and Reason for Exchange in Archaic Societies* [1925]. Trans. W.D. Halls. London and New York: Routledge.

McClellan, M.C., P.J. Russell, and I.A. Todd. 1988. Kalavasos-Mangia: Rescue excavations at a Late Bronze Age cemetery. *Report of the Department of Antiquities, Cyprus:* 201–222.

McGeough, K. 2007. *Exchange Relationships at Ugarit.* Leuven, Belgium: Peeters.

Merrillees, R.S. 1992. The government of Cyprus in the Late Bronze Age. In P. Åström (ed.), *Acta Cypria*, Vol. 3, 310–329. Jonsered, Sweden: Paul Åströms Förlag.

Monroe, C.M. 2009. *Scales of Fate: Trade, Tradition, and Transformation in the Eastern Mediterranean, ca. 1350–1175 BCE*. Münster: Ugarit-Verlag.

Morris, I., and J.G. Manning. 2005. Introduction. In J.G. Manning and I. Morris (eds.), *The Ancient Economy: Evidence and Models*, 1–44. Stanford: Stanford University Press.

Muhly, J.D., and V. Kassianidou, Parallels and diversities in the production, trade and use of copper and iron in Crete and Cyprus from the Bronze Age to the Iron Age. In G. Cadogan, M. Iacovou, K. Kopaka and J. Whitley (eds.), *Parallel Lives: Ancient Island Societies in Crete and Cyprus. Proceedings of the Conference in Nicosia Organized by the British School at Athens, the University of Crete and the University of Cyprus in November–December 2006*, 119–140. London: British School at Athens.

Mynářová, J. 2007. *Language of Amarna—Language of Diplomacy: Perspectives on the Amarna Letters*. Prague: Czech Institute of Egyptology.

Padgham, K. 2014. *The Scale and Nature of the Late Bronze Age Economies of Egypt and Cyprus*. Oxford: Archaeopress.

Parkins, H. 1998. Time for change? Shaping the future of the ancient economy. In H. Parkins and C. Smith (eds.), *Trade, Traders, and the Ancient City*, 1–15. New York: Taylor and Francis.

Peltenburg, E.J. 1996. From isolation to state formation in Cyprus, c. 3500–1500 BC. In V. Karageorghis and D. Michaelides (eds.), *The Development of the Cypriot Economy from the Prehistoric Period to the Present Day*, 17–43. Nicosia: University of Cyprus and Bank of Cyprus.

Peltenburg, E.J. 2012. Text meets material in Late Bronze Age Cyprus. In A. Georgiou (ed.), *Cyprus: An Island Culture: Society and Social Relations from the Bronze Age to the Venetian Period*, 1–23. Oxford: Oxbow Books.

Peltenburg, E.J., and M. Iacovou. 2012. Crete and Cyprus: Contrasting political configurations. In G. Cadogan, M. Iacovou, K. Kopaka, and J. Whitley (eds.), *Parallel Lives: Ancient Island Societies in Crete and Cyprus. Proceedings of the Conference in Nicosia Organized by the British School at Athens, the University of Crete and the University of Cyprus in November–December 2006*, 343–363. London: British School at Athens.

Polanyi, K. 1944. *The Great Transformation*. Boston: Beacon Press.

Polanyi, K. 1957. *Trade and Market in the Early Empires: Economies in History and Theory*. Glencoe: Free Press.

Pulak, C. 1998. The Uluburun shipwreck: An overview. *International Journal of Nautical Archaeology and Underwater Investigation* 27: 188–124.

Pulak, C. 2008. The Uluburun shipwreck and Late Bronze Age trade. In J. Aruz, K. Benzel, and J.M. Evans (eds.), *Beyond Babylon: Art, Trade, and Diplomacy in the Second Millennium BC*, 289–310, 313–314. New York, New Haven, and London: Metropolitan Museum of Art, Yale University Press.

Sahlins, M. 1972. *Stone Age Economics*. Chicago: Aldne-Atherton.

Sauvage. C. 2012. *Routes Maritimes et Systéme D'Échanges Internationaux au Bronze Récent en Méditerranée Orientale*. Lyon: Travaux de la Maison de L'Orient et de la Méditerranée.

Schloen, D.J. 2001. *The House of the Father as Fact and Symbol: Patrimonialism in Ugarit and the Ancient Near East*. Winona Lake: Eisenbrauns.

Scheidel, W., and S. Von Reden. (eds.) 2002. *The Ancient Economy*. New York: Routledge.

Schneider, F., and D.H. Enste. 2002. *The Shadow Economy: An International Survey*. Cambridge: Cambridge University Press.

Schneider, F., and C.C. Williams. 2013. *The Shadow Economy*. London: The Institute of Economic Affairs.

Sewell, D.A. 2015. The seafarers of Maroni. In C.F. MacDonald, E. Hatzaki, and S. Andreou (eds.), *The Great Islands: Studies of Crete and Cyprus Presented to Gerald Cadogan*, 186–191. Athens: Kapon Editions.

Sherratt, A., and S. Sherratt. 1991. From luxuries to commodities: The nature of Mediterranean Bronze Age trading systems. In N. Gale (ed.), *Bronze Age Trade in the Mediterranean*, 351–386. Studies in Mediterranean Archaeology 90. Jonsered, Sweden: Paul Åströms Förlag.

Sherratt, S. 1998. "Sea peoples" and the economic structure of the late second millennium in the eastern Mediterranean. In S. Gitin, A. Mazar, and E. Stern (eds.), *Mediterranean Peoples in Transition: Thirteenth to Early Tenth Centuries BCE*, 292–313. Jerusalem: Israel Exploration Society.

Sherratt, S., and A. Sherratt. 1993. The growth of the Mediterranean economy in the early first millennium BC. *World Archaeology* 24: 361–378.

Sindzingre, A. 2006. The relevance of the concepts of formality and informality: A theoretical appraisal. In B. Guha-Khasnobis, R. Kanbur, and E. Ostrom (eds.), *Linking the Formal and Informal Economy: Concepts and Policies*, 58–74. Oxford: Oxford University Press.

Smith, J.S. (ed.) 2002. *Seal and Script Use on Cyprus in the Bronze and Iron Ages.* Boston: Archaeological Institute of America.

Smith, J.S. 2012. Seals, scripts, and politics at Late Bronze Age Kourion. *American Journal of Archaeology* 116: 39–103.

Södebaum, F. 2006. Blocking human potential: How formal policies block the informal economy in the Maputo corridor. In B. Guha-Khasnobis, R. Kanbur, and E. Ostrom (eds.), *Linking the Formal and Informal Economy: Concepts and Policies*, 163–178. Oxford: Oxford University Press.

South, A.K. 1980. Kalavasos-*Ayios Dhimitrios* 1979: A summary report. *Report of the Department of Antiquities, Cyprus*: 22–53.

South, A.K. 1982. Kalavasos-*Ayios Dhimitrios* 1980–1981. *Report of the Department of Antiquities, Cyprus*: 60–68.

South, A.K. 1989. From copper to kingship: Aspects of Bronze Age society viewed from the Vasilikos Valley. In E. Peltenburg (ed.), *Early Society in Cyprus*, 315–324. Edinburgh: Edinburgh University Press.

South, A.K. 1991. Kalavasos-*Ayios Dhimitrios* 1990. *Report of the Department of Antiquities, Cyprus*: 133–145.

South, A.K. 2000. Late Bronze Age burials at Kalavasos-*Ayios Dhimitrios*. In G.K Ioannides and S. Hadgistilles (eds.), *Πρακτικά του Γ΄ Διεθνούς Κυπρολογικού Συνεδρίου (Λευκωσία, 16–20 Απριλίου 1996) Α΄: Αρχαίο Μέρος*, 345–364. Nicosia: Society of Cypriot Studies—The A.G. Leventis Foundation.

South, A.K. 2002. Late Bronze Age settlement patterns in Southern Cyprus: The first kingdoms. *Cahier du Centre d'Études Cypriotes* 32: 59–72

South, A.K., and P. Russell. 1989. Tombs 1–7 and 10. In I.A. Todd (ed.), *Vasilikos Valley Project 3 Kalavasos-Ayios Dhimitrios II. Ceramics, Objects, Tombs, Specialist Studies*, 41–57. Studies in Mediterranean Archaeology 71.3. Göteborg, Sweden: Paul Åströms Förlag.

South, A.K., and L. Steel. 2001. The White Slip sequence at Kalavasos. In V. Karageorghis (ed.), *The White Slip Ware of Late Bronze Age Cyprus, Proceedings of an International Conference Organized by the Anastasios G. Leventis Foundation, Nicosia in Honour of Malcolm Wiener, Nicosia, 29th–30th October 1998*, 65–74. Vienna: Verlag der Österreichischen Akademie der Wissenschaften.

South, A.K., and I.A. Todd. 1985. In quest of Cypriot copper traders: Excavations at *Ayios Dhimitrios*. *Archaeology* 38.5: 40–47.

Steel, L. 2013. *Materiality and Consumption in the Bronze Age Mediterranean.* New York and Abingdon: Routledge.

Steel, L. 2016. Exploring Aredhiou: New light on the rural communities of the Cypriot hinterland during the Late Bronze Age. *American Journal of Archaeology* 120: 511–536.

Swiny, S. 1981. Bronze Age settlement patterns in southwest Cyprus. *Levant* 13: 51–87.

Swiny, S. 2004. The role of intuitive and small scale surveys in landscape archaeology. In M. Iacovou (ed.), *Archaeological Field Survey in Cyprus: Past History, Future Potentials. Proceedings of a Conference Held by the Archaeological Research Unit of the University of Cyprus, 1–2 December 2000*, 55–61. London: British School at Athens.

Todd, I.A. 1989. *Vasilikos Valley Project 3: Kalavasos-Ayios Dhimitrios II, Ceramics, Objects, Tombs, Specialist Studies.* Studies in Mediterranean Archaeology 71.3. Göteborg, Sweden: Paul Åströms Förlag.

Todd, I.A. 2004. *Vasilikos Valley Project 9: The Field Survey of the Vasilikos Valley Vol. I.* Studies in Mediterranean Archaeology 71.9. Sävedalen, Sweden: Paul Åströms Förlag.

Todd, I.A. 2013. *Vasilikos Valley Project 12: The Field Survey of the Vasilikos Valley Vol. III, Human Settlement in the Vasilikos Valley.* Studies in Mediterranean Archaeology 71.12. Uppsala, Sweden: Åströms Förlag.

Todd, I.A., and D. Pearlman. 1986. Appendix: List of Kalavasos Village Tombs. In I.A. Todd (ed.), *Vasilikos Valley Project 1, The Bronze Age Cemetery in Kalavasos Village*, 188–218. Studies in Mediterranean Archaeology 71.1. Göteborg, Sweden: Paul Åströms Förlag.

Todd, I.A., and D. Pilides. 2004. The site of Sanidha-*Moutti tou Ayiou Serkou*. In I.A. Todd (ed.), *Vasilikos Valley Project 9: The Field Survey of the Vasilikos Valley Vol. I*, 161–171. Studies in Mediterranean Archaeology 71.9. Sävedalen, Sweden: Paul Åströms Förlag.

Van Brempt, L., and V. Kassianidou. 2016. Facing the complexity of copper-sulphide ore smelting and assessing the role of copper in south-central Cyprus: A comparative study of the slag assemblage from Late Bronze Age Kalavasos-*Ayios Dhimitrios*. *Journal of Archaeological Science Reports* 7: 539–553.

Van de Mieroop, M. 1997. *The Mesopotamian City*. Oxford: Clarendon Press.

Webb, J.M. 1999. *Ritual Architecture, Iconography, and Practice in Late Bronze Age Cyprus*. Studies in Mediterranean Archaeology 77. Jonsered, Sweden: Paul Åströms Förlag.

Webb, J.M. 2005. Ideology, iconography, and identity: The role of foreign goods and images in the establishment of social hierarchy in Late Bronze Age Cyprus. In J. Clarke (ed.), *Archaeological Perspectives on the Transmission and Transformation of Culture in the Eastern Mediterranean*, 177–182. Oxford: Oxbow Books.

Weber, M. 1947. *The Theory of Social and Economic Organization*. Ed. T. Parsons, *Wirtschaft und Gesellschaft* I. Trans. A.R. Henderson. London: Free Press.

Weinberg, S. 1983. *Bamboula at Kourion: The Architecture*. Philadelphia: University of Pennsylvania.

Williams, C.C. 2004. *Cash-in-Hand Work: The Underground Sector and the Hidden Economy of Favours*. Basingstoke: Palsgrave Macmillan.

Williams, C.C. 2006. *The Hidden Enterprise Culture: Entrepreneurship in the Underground Economy*. Northampton: Edward Elgar.

6

Tracing the Foundation Horizon of Palaepaphos

New Research on the Early History of the Paphos Region

ARTEMIS GEORGIOU

Middle Cypriot III–Late Cypriot I: The Dawn of a New Era

The period that spans the latter part of the Middle and the beginning of the Late Bronze Age (LBA) in Cyprus constitutes a time of major transformation in the socioeconomic environment, settlement patterns, and material culture of the island (Figure 6.1). While the agropastoral scheme that had sustained Cypriot communities for almost a millennium during the long and largely uneventful Early and Middle Bronze Age was retained as the basis of the LBA economy (but see Manning in this volume; see also Webb and Frankel 2013 for the emergence of divergent social trajectories early in the EBA), the inception of the Late Cypriot (LC) period marked the end of simple subsistence villages (Knapp 1997: 29–30). By the mid-second millennium BCE onwards, the Cypriot economy centered on the heavy industry of copper and the extra-insular export of the processed metal (Peltenburg 1996: 29–31; Knapp 2013: 28–29). Pyrotechnological implements used for the processing of the ores and the production of copper, such as tuyères, crucibles, and bellows, provide ample documentation of the progress achieved in the technology of copper smelting during the dawn of the LC period (Kassianidou 2008: 258–265; 2011: 45–46; Knapp 2012). Such implements, as well as copper slag, the residue of smelting, were excavated at special function sites situated inland, such as Politiko *Phorades* (Knapp and Kassianidou 2008: 140–144), as well as at coastal centers, for example at Enkomi (Dikaios 1969–71: 500) and Morphou *Toumba tou Skourou* (Vermeule and Wolsky 1990: 43–45; see also Muhly 1989: 299; Kassianidou 2013a: 133–134). No oxhide ingots of the LC I period are preserved on the island, but the introduction of schematically depicted oxhide ingots on cylinder seals begins in this period (Papasavvas 2009: 90), indicating that this standardized shape emerged at around this time. Lead isotope analyses on copper oxhide ingots found in Late Minoan IB contexts at Zakros, Mochlos, Syme, and Gournia on Crete suggest a Cypriot origin (Stos-Gale 2011: 223–226; Kassianidou 2014) and confirm the intensification of the island's external

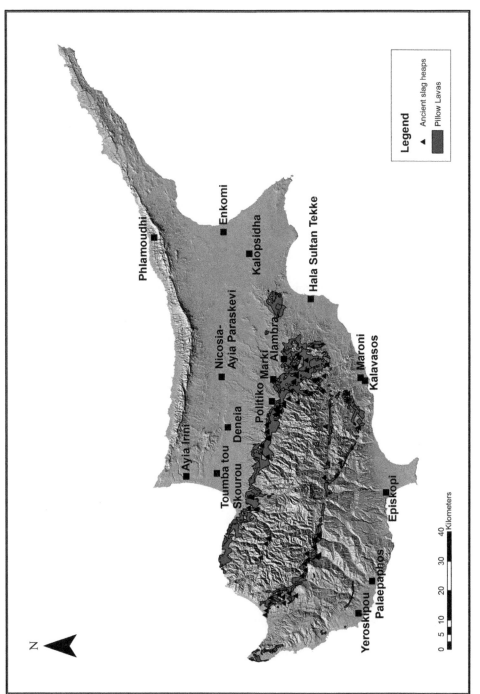

Figure 6.1: Map of Cyprus with sites mentioned in the text, showing the Pillow Lavas and the distribution of ancient slag heaps. Digital data courtesy of the Geological Survey Department, Cyprus; map drafter by the author.

connections. Contemporary textual evidence from outside Cyprus is also enlightening. A number of texts from Mari, Babylonia, and Alalakh dating to the first half of the eighteenth century BCE mention Alashiya, which is commonly equated with Cyprus (Goren *et al.* 2003), as a supplier of copper (Knapp 1996: 17–30). The earliest use of a syllabic script, conventionally referred to as "Cypro-Minoan" (Ferrara 2012: 267–269), indicates the establishment of sociopolitical structures on the island that necessitated a scribal system.

The exponential increase of Cypriot pottery deposited in settlement and mortuary contexts in the Levant and Egypt manifests Cyprus's participation in the eastern Mediterranean trading networks at the close of the Middle Cypriot (MC) period. Cypriot wares were mostly concentrated on the Hyksos-controlled Nile Delta, predominantly at Tell el-Dab'a (Maguire 1995; 2009) and sites along the Levantine coast (see Oren 2001; Bergoffen 2001; 2005; Crewe 2007a: 14–15; Eriksson 2007: 71–74; Yener 2012: 162–163; Knapp 2013: 34–35). In its majority, this corpus consisted of ceramic wares associated with production in the east of the island (Crewe 2010: 63).

The marked upsurge of exotica deposited in LC I tombs (Keswani 2004: 136–139) further demonstrates the island's participation in trading networks (see Andreou in this volume). Imported ceramics include Tell el Yahudiyeh juglets from Egypt, Canaanite jars from the Levant, and Late Minoan and Late Helladic finewares from the Aegean (Pecorella 1973; Kaplan 1980: 77–80; Crewe 2007a: 15–16; 2012: 227–229; A. Georgiou 2016: 192). Cylinder seals, socketed axes, faience, and ivory artifacts, all imported from the Levant and Egypt, were also deposited in mortuary contexts (Courtois 1986: 76–79; Philip 1991: 80–82; Knapp 2013: 34–35).

The transition from the MC III to the LC IA in Cyprus also incorporated substantial transformations within the island's ceramics production (see Crewe 2007a: 32–40). While the traditional White Painted, Red Polished, and Black/Red Slip wares—characteristic of MC pottery production—persisted, the archaic versions of the Base Ring and White Slip wares, known by the terms *Proto–Base Ring* and *Proto–White Slip*, were developed during the LC IA period in the northwestern and central parts of the island (Merrillees 1971: 62; Åström 2001a; Herscher 2001: 13–16; Manning 2001: 80–81). The dawn of the LBA signals the earliest use of the potter's wheel for the manufacture of pottery on the island, which Crewe considers to form part of the Levantine innovations introduced during this time (2007b: 213).

The shift from an agropastoral economy to an industrial and commercial one, combined with increasing contact with the outside world, intensified the level of complexity within Cypriot societies (Manning in this volume). Mortuary data reflect the endeavors of rising elite groups to establish status and authority through the adoption of prestige and symbolic paraphernalia associated with elite practices in the rest of the eastern Mediterranean (Knapp 1993: 97–98; 2013: 28–35; Keswani 1996: 238; 2005: 392–393; Webb 2005: 180–181). These seminal forces of societal transformation were exponentially augmented during the nucleation processes that characterized this period, when populations originating from heterogeneous backgrounds accumulated at newly founded coastal centers (Keswani 1996: 220; 2004: 87–88; G. Georgiou 2006: 457).

The Settlement Pattern of Cyprus at the Opening of the Late Bronze Age

The demise of the agropastoral economic system brought about the abandonment of the majority of the centuries-old villages, which were—as a rule—located inland, close to stretches of arable land and perennial water sources. Marki *Alonia* and Alambra *Mouttes*, two extensive settlements that thrived during the early part of the second millennium BCE, were abandoned before the end of the MC period (Frankel and Webb 2006; Coleman *et al.* 1996; Dikomitou-Eliadou in this volume). Settlements such as Nicosia *Ayia Paraskevi* and Deneia, however, established from as early as the third millennium BCE, continued to be successively inhabited during the LBA owing to their strategic geographical location along the routes that linked the metalliferous zones to the coast (G. Georgiou 2006: 281–285) (Figure 6.1).

The dramatic transformations of the settlement pattern at the dawn of the LBA are epitomized by the foundation of new settlements by or near the coast (G. Georgiou 2006: 457; Crewe 2007a: 41–47; Knapp 1997). The main impetus for the foundation of the coastal settlements is associated with the consolidation of the heavy industry of copper as the focal point of the Cypriot economy, considering that the metal's maritime export necessitated the establishment of coastal emporia (Peltenburg 1996: 30–35; Keswani 2005: 293–294; Iacovou 2012: 58–60).

The newly founded settlement at Enkomi, exposed in roughly contemporaneous expeditions by the French Mission (see Schaeffer 1952; 1971; Courtois 1981; 1984) and the Department of Antiquities of Cyprus led by Dikaios during the 1940s and 1950s (Dikaios 1969–71), has presented the most critical evidence for these processes. The foundation of Enkomi has been considered as a means of facilitating the movement of goods from Kalopsidha, and possibly other areas as well, by population groups seeking to join in the ideological and economic connectivity of the eastern Mediterranean (Crewe 2007a: 152, 158; 2010: 69; cf. Webb 2012: 54–56). Kalopsidha was an early participant in the eastern Mediterranean market economy judging by the plethora of imported Levantine goods and the indication for metalworking activities (Crewe 2010: 69–70). Its significance was undermined following Enkomi's establishment, but the settlement was not altogether abandoned (Webb 2012: 55).

The large structure of Area III at Enkomi, known as the "Fortress," was established during Level IA ([of LC IA2 date according to Crewe 2007a: 73] Dikaios 1969–71: 16–34). Its substantial built and independent character prompted Pickles and Peltenburg to suggest that the "Fortress" constituted the administrative center of early Enkomi (1988: 87). The excavation of tuyères, crucibles, and furnaces from the "Fortress" attests to some degree of metallurgical activities taking place within this structure (Muhly 1989: 299–300; Kassianidou 2012: 104; 2013a: 134).

The construction of a number of roughly contemporary fortified sites at key locations on the north and central parts of the island and the Karpas Peninsula (see Fortin 1989: 247–248; Crewe 2007a: 49–61; G. Georgiou 2006: 472–475) were considered as indications of Enkomi's regional control over the resources (but see Monahan and Spigelman in this volume). Peltenburg suggested that the strategic location of a number of these "forts" indicates that these functioned as a means of securing the movement of copper from the mining regions to Enkomi and exerting regional control (1996: 30–31, 35–36; see also Webb 1999: 305–308). Based on the distribution pattern of the "forts" and the regional variability of the period's ceramic repertoire, Crewe has suggested that the fortified settlements underscore the regionalism of the LC I period rather than promoting the domination of a single center (Crewe 2007a: 66, 158–159). Regardless of their *raison d'être*, the "forts" entail a series of diversified and not necessarily matching phenomena and function as a prime indicator of the transformative forces in the island's social, economic, and political spheres at the inception of the LBA (Monahan and Spigelman in this volume). It is further noteworthy that all the establishments collectively referred to as "forts" ceased to exist by the end of LC IIA period. Unlike the also newly founded coastal settlements, which developed into sophisticated urban centers during the latter part of the Late Bronze Age, the "forts" had no long-lasting impact on the Cypriot landscape.

With the exception of Enkomi, the LC coastal settlements present minimal evidence of their foundation horizons. On the northwestern coast, the settlement of Morphou *Toumba tou Skourou* was established near the Morphou Bay on top of a mound that was severely damaged by modern bulldozing activities (Vermeule and Wolsky 1990: 7). Morphou *Toumba tou Skourou* was occupied from at least the LC IA period, with mortuary evidence attesting to an even earlier MC III phase (Vermeule and Wolsky 1990: 287–307). The site revealed evidence for industrial facilities pertaining to the manufacture of pottery (i.e., the "Basin Building" used for purifying clay) in addition to possible metalworking activities. The mortuary evidence from Morphou *Toumba tou Skourou* attests to the site's connections with other areas of the Mediterranean, especially Minoan Crete (Vermeule and Wolsky 1990: 381; Keswani 2004: 121). A wealthy LC I cemetery excavated at the site of Ayia Irini *Palaeokastro* within the Morphou Bay to the north of *Toumba tou Skourou* (Pecorella 1977; Quilici 1990) contained numerous exotica, including imported finewares from the Aegean (Pecorella 1973).

The site of Phlamoudhi *Melissa* on the north coast appears to have been continually occupied from the MC III to LC IIC periods. In the early phase of occupation there is evidence for a pottery kiln (Smith 2008: 49). At the neighboring hilltop site of Phlamoudhi *Vounari* a small monumental structure was built at around the time of *Melissa*'s foundation but was abandoned before the end of LC IIA (Horowitz 2008: 70).

Hala Sultan Tekke on the southeastern coast of the island was also founded during the MC–LC transition, although the site is much better known by its final phase in the twelfth century BCE, when it functioned as a cosmopolitan harbor town (Åström 1996: 10; Fischer 2016). Material dating to the town's early phases is largely residual and relatively sparse, found mostly in trial trenches and mortuary contexts (e.g., Åström *et al.* 1983: 66, 74, 147, 150, 153; Åström 2001b: 57–61; Fischer and Bürge 2015: 33–34; 2016: 41, 44; Fischer and Bürge 2017: 174–184).

The earliest architectural features at the site of *Vournes*, close to the village of Maroni on the south-central coast, date to the LC IA period but are much disturbed by later activity (Cadogan 1992: 51–53; 1996: 15; Manning 1998). During the LC

IIA–B period a free-standing structure with a sunken basin known as the "Basin Building" was established at Maroni *Vournes*. It was designed to be impermeable to liquids, but its use remains unclear (Cadogan 1984: 6–7). Excavations at the coastal site of Maroni *Tsaroukkas* revealed evidence for occupation early in the LC period (Manning and De Mita 1997: 136; Manning *et al.* 2014).

Finally, the area of Episkopi, at the terminal point of the Kouris valley on the south coast, presents limited evidence for the MC III–LC IA period. A short period of occupation was assigned to the LC IA period at the site of Episkopi *Phaneromeni* (Herscher 2001: 15). At Episkopi *Bamboula*, excavations by Daniel revealed scanty residential contexts, the earliest of which date to the LC IA period and a few contemporary mortuary remains (Benson 1972: 4–5; see also Kiely 2011).

Palaepaphos: The Foundation Horizon

Palaia (Old) Paphos is situated on the southwestern coast of Cyprus, within the modern-day village of Kouklia (Figure 6.2).

The site is renowned for its monumental Sanctuary, originally constructed at the opening of the twelfth century BCE, which continued to function as a place of adoration for a female deity, later known as Aphrodite, down to late antiquity. An abundance of epigraphic testimonies from as early as the seventh century BCE designate the site as the administrative center for the polity of Paphos (Satraki 2012: 218–236). It became known by the name *Palaepaphos* only after the end of the fourth century BCE, when the kingdom's capital shifted to Nea (New) Paphos some 15 km to the northwest (Iacovou 2013: 287–288).

The Evidence from the Palaepaphos Nucleus

The site possesses an impressively long and continuous history, from the time of its earliest establishment to the present day. As a result of its uninterrupted occupation, no stratified data corresponding to the site's foundation horizon has been brought to light so far. The town's foundation horizon is exclusively known by means of residual ceramic fragments and disturbed mortuary remains. Despite the limited and fragmentary nature of Palaepaphos's earliest strata, the evidence for an early occupation spanning the MC III–LC I phase in the area is unequivocal.

Excavations by the earliest archaeological expedition in the area of Kouklia, the Cyprus Exploration Fund, in 1888 (see Hogarth *et al.* 1888) revealed five vessels dating to the MC III phase, now at the Ashmolean Museum, Oxford, which were said to originate from the locality of Kouklia *Evreti*. They entail an almost complete White Painted (WP) V–VI jar, a zoomorphic vessel of WP III ware, a juglet of Black Slip incised ware and two WP III Pendent Line style bottles (Frankel 1983: 86–87, 108). The latter two are of questionable origin, since the accession registry of the Ashmolean Museum lists both Kouklia and Aglatzia *Leondari Vouno* as their find-spots. A body fragment of a WP V jar, now also at the Ashmolean, was collected from Kouklia *Evreti*, following Catling's very brief surface survey in western Cyprus in 1953 (1962: 165; Frankel 1983: 107).

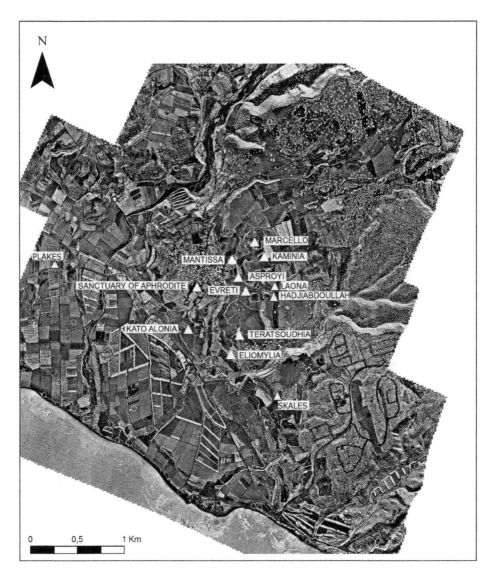

Figure 6.2: Orthophoto map of the Kouklia village with localities. Courtesy of the "Palaepaphos Urban Landscape Project," used by permission of the director.

The investigations by the British Mission under Mitford and Iliffe during the first half of the 1950s revealed a number of tombs at Kouklia, which regrettably remain largely unpublished. In a very brief and preliminary report, Catling assigned a date early in the LC sequence for the finds contained within Tombs VIII and X at *Evreti* and Tombs II and IX at *Asproyi* (1979: 274–275). Catling's more detailed publication of the exceptionally wealthy Tomb VIII of *Evreti* includes burial gifts assigned to the LC I period (Catling 1968: 165–166). The majority of the mortuary equipment from this tomb dates to the LC IIC–IIIA periods, but a few White Slip I and Base Ring I vessels corroborate an earlier phase.

The archaeological remains unearthed by the British Mission were distributed to the Museums of Liverpool, St. Andrew's, the regional Kouklia Museum, and the Cyprus Museum in Nicosia. The St. Andrew's part of the share was transferred to the National Museums of Scotland, following the closure of the institution's gallery. A very limited number of finds from the Palaepaphos mortuary contexts were displayed as part of a temporary exhibition and are thus known by means of the exhibition's catalogue (Goring 1988: 65). This publication includes two White Slip I bowls, two Base Ring I jugs, and a White Lustrous bottle dating to LC IB from Kouklia *Asproyi* Tomb IX, out of the twenty objects that Catling has registered in his preliminary report for this context (Goring 1988: 65–66, 69). The catalogue further incorporates a faience necklace with a carnelian bead in the form of a stylized *udjat* eye, which was possibly imported from Egypt (Goring 1988: 77, No. 93), and a dark blue cast glass pendant in a Hathor-like form, both found deposited in *Asproyi* Tomb II (Goring 1988: 77, No. 94). The glass pendant belongs to a well-known type of the sixteenth and fifteenth centuries BCE that was imported from northern Mesopotamia (Goring 1988: 77).

The material transferred by the Kouklia British Mission to the Liverpool Museum remains largely unknown. An interim list cataloguing the Cypriot antiquities stored at Liverpool includes, among others, three Red Slip sherds dating to the MC III period from Kouklia *Evreti* Tomb X and a so-called White-on-Black sherd from *Evreti* Tomb IIIA (Tsielepi and Bienkowski 1988: 7). Investigations in the wider area of *Evreti* and *Asproyi* by the same mission revealed material dated to the end of the MC period inside pits, including fragments of WP IV–V, Red Polished III–IV, and Black Slip ware vessels (Maier and von Wartburg 1985a: 104–105).

The long-term fieldwork operations in the area of Kouklia by the Swiss-German team under the direction of the late Franz-Georg Maier also brought to light material assigned to the polity's earliest strata. Investigations during 1967–68 in the area of *Evreti* revealed two wells (TE III and TE VIII) filled with a mixture of pottery, stones, animal bones, and small faience, ivory, and bronze objects, which correspond to the living and working contexts of the area (Maier and von Wartburg 1985a: 110–113; 1985b: 147–148). The entire corpus from these very significant contexts was recently published in a comprehensive publication (von Rüden *et al.* 2016). The vast majority of the finds dates to the LC IIC–IIIA span, but the earliest phases are also represented by a few residual remains. Keswani's ceramic analyses of the pithos assemblage from the *Evreti* wells suggest that a significant number of the storage vessels correspond to the so-called Drab Polished ware and are indicative of an early LC date (Keswani 2016: 218–222). A point of reference is a rim fragment of an imported Late Minoan IA cup (Maier and von Wartburg 1985a: 110, Plate XIV:1; A. Georgiou 2016: 191, Figures 1a, 1b), which illustrates the site's maritime connections with other Mediterranean polities early in the LBA. Further excavations in the wider area of *Evreti-Asproyi* by the Swiss-German Mission produced a number of stray finds dating to the MC–LC transition, such as fragments of Red Polished III–IV, Coarse Monochrome, White Painted, and Bichrome Wheelmade ware (Maier and von Wartburg 1985a: 119, Plate XVI:11).

In the area of Kouklia *Marcello* the Swiss-German Mission uncovered unstratified ceramic remains dated to the MC III–LC IA periods. This material consists of small sherds, mostly of Red Polished III–IV, Black Slip (Reserved Line), Proto–Base Ring, and Proto–White Slip wares (Maier and von Wartburg 1986: 60; Maier 2008: 185–186).

There were also numerous White Slip I and Base Ring I fragments dating to the LC IB–IIB periods (Maier 2008: 188–189). Preliminary reports of the Swiss-German Mission's excavations make reference to early imports from the Greek mainland, assigned to the Late Helladic IIB–IIIA1 phase. This corpus includes fragments of stirrup jars, kylikes, and a cup with a stipple filling (Maier 1983: 230–231, Plates 22f, 23a–c).

Fieldwork expeditions at the site of Kouklia *Teratsoudhia* by the Department of Antiquities revealed wealthy tomb groups that span the entire LC sequence. The earliest material is dated to the LC IA period and was found within Tomb 104 (Area F: sherds of Black Slip [Reserved Band] jugs [Karageorghis 1990: 28, 57, Plate V], Chamber K, nos. 14 and 27: Black Slip III ware jugs [Karageorghis 1990: 29–30, Plates XVIII, XLVII]) and Chamber B of Tomb 105, with plentiful of examples of Proto–Base Ring and Black Slip III ware (nos. 42, 43, 45 [Karageorghis 1990: 44, Plates XXXIII, LXVIII]). The following LC IB–IIB phase is very well represented in the material from almost all contexts. Numerous complete and fragmentary jugs, juglets, bowls, and more rarely tankards of Base Ring I ware were deposited in the *Teratsoudhia* tombs. White Slip I ware is also represented by several examples, almost exclusively "milk-bowls" (see commentary in Karageorghis 1990: 54–73). There were also three White Lustrous Wheelmade vessels and the much rarer version of White Lustrous Handmade (from Well No. 67 [Karageorghis 1990: 53, Plates XLI, LXXV]). A large krater found inside a well at *Teratsoudhia* is a rare example of Bichrome Wheelmade pictorial ware, with the depiction of a man and a bull (Karageorghis 1990: 52, Plates XLI, LXXV). The mortuary corpus at *Teratsoudhia* included a number of imported artifacts dating to LC I, including three fragmentary Late Minoan I cups (from Tomb 104, Chamber O and Tomb 105, Pit C [Karageorghis 1990: 37, 71–72, Plate IV]), similar to the examples found at Ayia Irini (Pecorella 1973). Tomb 104 contained a stone vessel fragment imported from Egypt, with the cartouche of a pharaoh, tentatively identified as Ahmose I, the founder of the New Kingdom during the sixteenth century BCE (Clerc 1990).

The fieldwork expeditions of the "Palaepaphos Urban Landscape Project," a long-term program initiated in 2006 by Iacovou (2008a) under the auspices of the University of Cyprus, have exposed critical evidence elucidating Palaepaphos's earliest establishment. Aiming to investigate the polity's urban landscape in a diachronic framework, the Palaepaphos Urban Landscape Project has been undertaking fieldwork at targeted areas of the village at Kouklia (see Iacovou 2008a; 2012: 60; 2013: 282–285 for preliminary reports). The investigation of the extension of the rampart on the hill of Kouklia *Marcello* produced residual sherds spanning the MC III–LC I period. These included WP, Black/Red Slip, Red Polished III–IV ware, and Proto–White Slip fragments. *Marcello* has also revealed two Red-on-Black sherds, which were evidently imported from the eastern part of the island. There were also numerous White Slip I and Base Ring I sherds (Sherratt in press). The program's investigations on the plateau of *Hadjiabdullah* also produced evidence for the town's early occupation. The wares represented include Bichrome Wheelmade, Black Slip Incised, Proto–White Slip and numerous examples of White Slip I and Base Ring I ware. The material from *Hadjiabdullah* suggests that this locality was probably established during LC IA–IB period, slightly later than *Marcello*. The ongoing excavations at the man-made tumulus of Kouklia *Laona*, constructed with overlapping strata of red soil brought in from surrounding areas, as well as marl (Iacovou 2017), also shed light on Palaepaphos's early phases. The ceramic contents of this feature consist of a mixture of sherds dating from as early as the MC III period. The early material found at *Laona* includes Black/Red Slip and Red Polished III–IV sherds, a fragment of a Black Slip Handmade (Reserved Band) jug (Figure 6.3), three Proto–White Slip fragments (e.g., Figure 6.4), and plentiful White Slip I and Base Ring I examples.

Figure 6.3: Body fragment of a Black Slip (Reserved Band Ware) jug. From Palaepaphos *Laona*. Courtesy of the "Palaepaphos Urban Landscape Project," used by permission of the director.

Figure 6.4: Rim fragment of a Proto–White Slip bowl. From Palaepaphos *Laona*. Courtesy of the "Palaepaphos Urban Landscape Project," used by permission of the director.

The date of the material we can attribute to the foundation of the settlement at Palaepaphos suggests that the first populations were established during the MC III–LC IA period. The limited quantities of the evidence corresponding to Palaepaphos's earliest occupation and the lack of contextual data pose substantial constraints to our understanding of the transformative forces that resulted in the site's establishment and its character at the time of its foundation. In order to trace the processes that instigated the foundation of Palaepaphos, it is essential to move beyond the limits of the polity's nucleus and expand into the wider Paphos region.

The Evidence from the Paphos Region

The area of research is defined as the hydrological zone of Paphos, the drainage basin in southwest Cyprus that forms a geographical unity (Christodoulou 1959: 18). This extended landscape is dominated by the foothills and the mountainous range of Troodos on the north/northeast and the wide coastal plains on the south/southwest. It is further defined by smaller watersheds created by four large rivers: the Chapotami, Dhiarizos, Xeros (or Xeropotamos), and Ezousa that spring from the Troodos foothills and flow in an almost parallel northeast/southwest axis toward the coast.

Datasets Used

The evidence presented in this section is based on the results of three interrelated categories of analysis: surface surveys, systematic and rescue excavations, and doctoral and master dissertations. For pedestrian survey, distinct segments of the wider region have been examined through several projects. The Canadian Palaipaphos Survey Project (CPSP) of Brock University conducted extensive, semi-intensive, and systematic survey campaigns from 1979 to 1991 in the area around Kouklia village using zones along the Ezousa, Xeros, and Dhiarizos rivers (Sørensen and Rupp 1993; Diacopoulos 2004; Rupp 2004 with further references). The Lemba Archaeological Project, in addition to the excavations conducted at the sites of Lemba and Kissonerga, has surveyed large parcels in the villages of Lemba, Kissonerga, Peyia, and Stavros tis Psokas in search of prehistoric sites (Baird 1985; Bolger *et al.* 2004). Smaller-scale surface surveys were conducted by the Department of Antiquities at Kouklia, Kissonerga, and the Akamas Peninsula (Hadjisavvas 1977). The area around Polis, situated to the north of the Paphos catchment area, was surveyed by the Polis-Pyrgos Archaeological Project (Maliszewski 2007; 2013). Surface surveys have proven invaluable in identifying sites of archaeological interest within an extended landscape, such as that of the Paphos catchment area. It should, nonetheless, be maintained that the identification of the size, character, and extent of a site based exclusively on pottery scatters should be treated cautiously (Diacopoulos 2004: 72; Given 2004; Bintliff 2013; see discussions by Satraki and Kearns in this volume), in particular considering that a large amount of the evidence collected in the Paphos region remains unpublished.

Archaeological excavations of prehistoric sites within the Paphos catchment area are particularly limited beyond the Kouklia nucleus. These include the long-term excavation programs of the University of Edinburgh at Lemba (Peltenburg *et al.* 1985), Kissonerga (Peltenburg *et al.* 1998), and Souskiou (Peltenburg 2006); the ongoing excavation project of the University of Manchester at Kissonerga *Skalia* (Crewe *et al.* 2008; 2013); and the Prasteio Mesorotsos Archaeological Project (PMAP) (McCarthy *et al.* 2010). In addition, the Department of Antiquities has been conducting rescue excavations within the wider Paphos area (i.e. Raptou and Villain 2018).

Finally, the present research makes use of specialized master and doctoral theses dealing with the extended Paphos region. The site registry and commentary compiled by G. Georgiou (2006) offers an invaluable insight into the settlement patterns of the entire island from the Late Chalcolithic to the opening of the LBA. Agapiou's (2010) master's thesis, which analyzes the use of space within the Paphos catchment area using Geographical Information Systems (GIS), is of additional value, as is Christodoulidou's (2014) master's thesis that focuses on the available pottery evidence. Finally, the doctoral dissertation of Zomeni (2012) examines the geological character of the Paphos region, with significant information on the natural resources and changes to the ancient coastline.

Examining the Settlement Pattern in the Wider Paphos Region

Maier and Karageorghis (1984: 46) have noted the practical absence of an Early Bronze Age horizon at Palaepaphos and the overall paucity of EC evidence within the wider Paphos area. The same picture is also conveyed by survey expeditions (Sørensen and Rupp 1993: 4; Diacopoulos 2004: 76). It is as yet unclear whether this truly corresponds to limited occupation during the EC period, or whether the presumed "vacuum" is projected by the demonstrably regional character of ceramic production of the Paphos area, which is difficult to synchronize with that of the rest of the island (see discussion in Herscher 1980; G. Georgiou 2006: 460; Crewe 2014: 137).

Kissonerga *Mosphilia* is so far the only site in the Paphos catchment area that presents a continuous occupation from the Late Neolithic period to the Philia phase (Peltenburg *et al.* 1998: 240–259). Recent investigations at Kissonerga *Skalia*, a possible segment of the *Mosphilia* settlement, suggest continuous occupation at the site from the Philia phase to the MC III/LC IA period, although the early phases at *Skalia* are mostly evidenced by residual pottery (Crewe 2013: 49; 2014: 146). Excavations by the Department of Antiquities at the area of Kissonerga *Ammoudhia* revealed an extensive cemetery site that spans the entire EC–MC period (Graham 2012; 2013: 136–137).

An EC III horizon has also been recognized at sites near the village of Prasteio, within the Dhiarizos valley, some 15 km inland. Rescue excavations at the cemetery site of Prasteio *Agkathera* revealed limited material that possibly spans the EC III–LC IA period (Christodoulou 1971: 80), similar to the date proposed for the site of Prasteio *Lakridhes* by the CPSP (Sørensen and Rupp 1993: 4). Preliminary reports by PMAP suggest that the site's life span coincides with the entire EC–MC period and that *Mesorotsos* was abandoned early in the LC I period (McCarthy *et al.* 2010: 65).

Based on the results of surface survey projects, a small rise in the number of sites within the Paphos catchment area can be traced during the MC I–II periods. The sites of Ayia Marinoudha *Akoni*, Kedhares *Pouspoutis/Soumatzera,* and Kissonerga *Choiromandres* were established early during the MC period (G. Georgiou 2006: 382, 386, 389). A number of other sites such as Ayios Dhimitrianos *Vouni*, Koloni *Anatoliko*, Kritou Marottou *Piknopitia/Arkoklima*, Mamonia *Kalamos*, and Trachypedoula *Kapsales* have also been dated to the MC period (G. Georgiou 2006: 382–383, 389, 393–394). These sites are known only via limited surface data, and as such their chronological designation is tentative (Sørensen and Rupp 1993: 6).

The region of Paphos witnessed an unprecedented upsurge in the number of identified sites during the subsequent MC III and LC IA periods (Figure 6.5).

This picture is mostly illustrated by surface surveys but is further corroborated by small-scale excavations. The majority of the MC III–LC IA sites were situated along the watersheds of the Ezousa and Dhiarizos rivers and to some extent within the Yeroskipou watershed to the west (Agapiou 2010: 104). Occupation along the Xeros watershed appears to have been particularly sparse; it is unclear whether this represents an actual scarcity of settlements, or whether this impression is due to the fact that the Xeros watershed was not surveyed as intensively as the Ezousa and Dhiarizos.

During the MC III–LC IA phase, the focus of occupation along the Ezousa watershed was the inland area of the Paphos forest on the one hand and the coastal area where the river flows on the other. A cluster of sites can be observed near the village of Kritou Marottou (Figure 6.5), ca. 25 km inland at a height of around 600 m above sea level (Sørensen and Rupp 1993: 6; G. Georgiou 2006: 392–393). The terminal

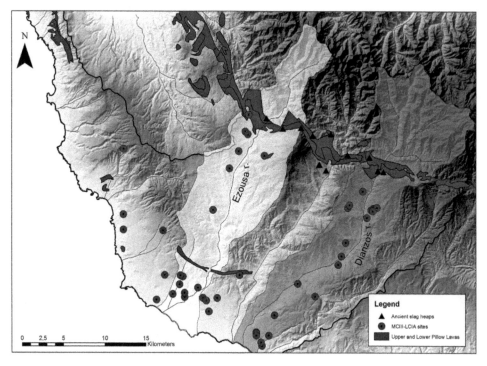

Figure 6.5: Map of the Paphos hydrological zone, showing the distribution of MC III–LC IA sites, the Upper and Lower Pillow Lavas, and the distribution of ancient slag heaps in the Paphos forest. Digital data courtesy of the Geological Survey Department, Cyprus.

point of the Ezousa River was marked by a cluster of sites, namely Ayia Marinoudha *Kotsiatis/Akoni*, Ayia Varvara *Teratsin*, Timi *Sentouzin tou Rafti*, and Anarita *Retzepis* (Figure 6.6) (G. Georgiou 2006: 424–428).

Rescue excavations at the latter two sites revealed tomb groups with significant finds spanning the MC III–LC IA sequence. At Timi, rescue excavations by the St. Andrews and Liverpool Museums Expedition in 1951 exposed two chamber tombs (Catling 1979: 274). The mortuary gifts accompanying these burials remain unpublished, except for two ceramic spindle-whorls (Goring 1988: 74, Figures 83–84) and a Black Slip incised jug (Iliffe 1952: 32). Close to the village of Anarita, the Department of Antiquities conducted rescue excavations in 1995 within a tomb situated between the localities *Retzepis* and *Kousoulatos*. Its burial gifts also remain unpublished, except for a brief report, which illustrates a Black Slip III jug with punctured decoration on the neck and body, evidently imitating Tell el-Yahudiyeh ware jugs (Figure 6.7) (cf. Negbi 1978 for comparable examples from *Toumba tou Skourou*), a Red Slip IV jug (Figure 6.8), and a bronze dagger (Christou 1996: 1061–1062, Figures 24–26).

The route of the Dhiarizos River is marked by denser occupation during this period, particularly at the area from which the river springs in the mountainous northern limits of the Paphos zone. Surface surveys at sites close to the villages of Arminou, Kedhares, and Trachypedoula revealed significant amounts of material that dates to the MC III–LC IA period (Sørensen and Rupp 1993: 6–7; G. Georgiou

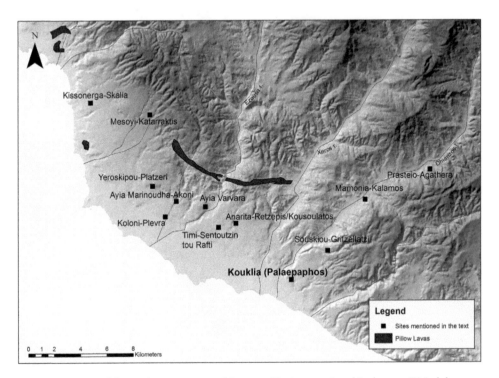

Figure 6.6: Map of the southwestern coast of Cyprus with sites mentioned in the text. Digital data courtesy of the Geological Survey Department, Cyprus.

Figure 6.7: Jug of Black Slip III ware with punctured decoration. From Anarita *Retzepis/Kousoulatos*. PM. 3271.11. Used by permission of the Department of Antiquities, Cyprus.

2006: 384, 386–387, 398). At the site of Kedhares *Skales* (Figure 6.5), the Department of Antiquities conducted rescue excavations inside a tomb, the results of which still remain unpublished. A brief report illustrates two bronze daggers, a bronze chisel, and a Proto–White Slip jug with a long cylindrical neck and a spherical body. This form is particularly rare. The vessel is decorated with vertical panels filled with

Figure 6.8: Jug of Red Slip IV ware. From Anarita *Retzepis/Kousoulatos*. PM. 3271.4. Used by permission of the Department of Antiquities, Cyprus.

elaborate zigzag bands alternating with a row of cross-hatched lozenges (Figure 6.9) (Christou 1996: 1062–1063, Figures 27–30; Åström 2001a: 49).

A distinct cluster of sites dated to the MC III–LC I period can be observed to the west of the Ezousa River (Figure 6.6). Kissonerga *Skalia* and possibly also *Ammoudhia* continue to be occupied during this period (Crewe 2013: 49). At Mesoyi *Katarraktis* a tomb dated to the MC III–LC IA period contained the remains of two individuals and their burial gifts, which included Drab Polished and Red Polished IV vessels (Herscher and Fox 1993).

Figure 6.9: Jug of Proto–White Slip ware. From Kedhares *Skales*. PM. 3290.2. Used by permission of the Department of Antiquities, Cyprus.

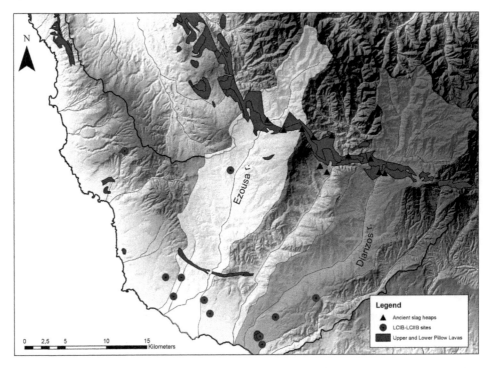

Figure 6.10: Map of the Paphos hydrological zone showing the distribution of LC IB–LC IIB sites, the Upper and Lower Pillow Lavas, and the distribution of ancient slag heaps in the Paphos forest. Digital data courtesy of the Geological Survey Department, Cyprus.

The subsequent LC IB period in the wider Paphos catchment area presents a dramatic change in settlement patterns, with a remarkable decrease in the number of the sites (Figure 6.10) (Diacopoulos 2004: 77; Agapiou 2010, 105). The most evident alteration is the practical desertion of occupation at the Troodos foothills (Figure 6.5) (Sørensen and Rupp 1993: 6–7, Figure 3).

The focus of occupation was transferred to the coast, as is evidenced by the plethora of sites identified near the terminal points of the Ezousa (e.g., Ayia Varvara *Hadjiyiannokoudhis* and *Pladhia Petra*, Ayia Marinoudha *Argakin* and *Akonin*, Anarita *Eliouthkia*, Koloni *Plevra* [Figure 6.6]) and the Dhiarizos River, near the villages of Kouklia and Souskiou (e.g., *Gritzellatzi*) (see analyses in Sørensen and Rupp 1993: 6–7, Figure 3). In this period, occupation within the area of Kouklia becomes much more substantial. The settlement was henceforth on track to develop into the prime center of the Paphos region.

Elucidating the Foundation Horizon of Palaepaphos

The transformation of the settlement pattern in the Paphos region during the MC III–LC IA period, illustrated by the sharp rise in the number of sites, is unequivocally conveyed not only by means of ceramic surface scatters but also by limited excavations. The proliferation in the number of identified sites at the close of the MC period in the Paphos catchment area may reflect a population increase, which in turn would indicate a potential movement of people from other centers. The candidates for this postulated population shift are the neighboring areas of Episkopi to the southeast and Morphou *Toumba tou Skourou* to the northwest. The links in the material culture are particularly strong between the Paphian sites and the settlements at Episkopi and *Toumba tou Skourou*. This is evident mostly in terms of the popularity of Black Slip III (Punctured Style) ware imitating Tell el-Yahudiyeh wares, stylistic associations in the production of storage vessels (Crewe 2013: 52), and the popularity in the Proto–White Slip and Proto–Base Ring wares.

During the MC III–LC IA period, the Paphos and the Polis catchment areas were both dotted by a plethora of sites, especially close to the cupriferous zones of the Troodos foothills (G. Georgiou 2006, Periphery 11; Maliszewski 1997; 2007). We can speculate on a possible population movement departing from Morphou *Toumba tou Skourou* toward the Polis Bay and subsequently toward the Troodos foothills within the Paphos hydrological zone. The shift of the Cypriot economy and society toward the procurement of copper and the prospects of attaining wealth and status through the new economic order are not unrelated to possible population shifts in search of exploitable copper sources (G. Georgiou 2006: 429). This speculation remains to be corroborated by further investigation in the northwestern part of the island in relation to the Paphos hydrological zone.

The routes of the Ezousa and the Dhiarizos rivers were also marked by dense occupation during the MC III–LC IA period. A substantial number of sites were clustered at the terminal point of Ezousa, extending toward the mouth of Xeros. Among these stand out the MC III–LC IA tombs excavated at Timi *Sentouztin tou Rafti* and Anarita *Retzepis* that were equipped by wealthy ceramic and metallic finds, illustrating the prosperity attained by these communities at the opening of the LBA. The tombs at Timi and Anarita further illustrate the emergence of stratified societies and the rise of a new class of social elites, who gained power in relation to the control of production and trade. Mortuary display was evidently one arena of social competition (Keswani 2005: 392–393).

The MC III–LC IA period also marks the earliest establishment in the area of Kouklia. From the available data pertaining to the foundation horizon of Palaepaphos it is possible to infer elements that characterize urban societies, such as some level of social stratification and intra- and extra-insular contacts (Keswani 2004: 140–142); however, the evidence corresponding to the site's earliest occupation is insufficient to suggest a fully developed urban-oriented community. Rather, at the time of its establishment, the community at Kouklia is best described as a "gateway" center. Gateway communities develop and flourish at passage points, near natural corridors of communication, located at the edge of their hinterland (Hirth 1978: 36–37). The prerequisites for the establishment of such communities are the inland areas of productivity, in this case metallurgical, and the external demand for such products. According to Hirth (1978: 37), "[i]ndividual communities throughout the hinterland are linked to the gateway community via a linear or dendritic market network." The initial settlement at Palaepaphos thus acted as the regional gateway center of the Dhiarizos valley, linking a chain of settlements that extended from the metalliferous zones of the Troodos foothills to the coast and by extension to long-distance trade (Iacovou 2012: 61–62; see Andreou in this volume).

In the LC IB period, the settlement pattern in the wider Paphos catchment zone was substantially altered. The majority of the sites that appear to have been established at the close of the MC period in the mountainous range of Paphos present no evidence for continuity after the end of LC IA. At the same time, and throughout the LC IB–IIA, the activity at the coastal areas, and especially at Kouklia, becomes much more prominent. There is an apparent nucleation, both in terms of population and economic focus, toward Palaepaphos, whose coastal location granted strategic and commercial importance. During the LC IB–IIA periods, the settlement of Kouklia must have comprised an agglomeration of diversified communities previously dispersed over an extended area that accumulated at the coast (Iacovou 2012: 57–58). The continuing nucleation at Kouklia shifted the focus of interest from the hinterland to the coast and concurrently instigated the processes that enabled the coastal center to control and manage the movement of goods within the extended Dhiarizos watershed. The LC IB–IIA periods mark the emergence of the political and economic mechanisms that replaced early exchange networks dealing with the flow of goods within the Dhiarizos valley. In that respect, the prerequisite for direct occupation near the cupriferous zones and along the routes was minimized to only a limited number of secondary centers.

The LC IB–IIA periods also saw an upsurge in the contacts of Palaepaphos with other areas of Cyprus and other regions of the Eastern Mediterranean, such as Minoan Crete, Egypt, and the northern Levant. Trade and the import of exotica were important factors in the processes that stimulated and maintained power differentials in the community, at a time when status and wealth were negotiated within a relatively new establishment (Knapp 1993: 97–98; 2013: 39–40; Keswani 1996: 220; 2004: 136–139). The deposition of imported artifacts and other prestige goods in the LC I tombs at Palaepaphos illuminate these processes, whereby rising elites chose to exhibit their wealth and consolidate power.

The area of Yeroskipou at the terminal point of the Ezousa River remained inhabited throughout the LBA, but there is no evidence for the concurrent development of a major urban center in the area, similar to Palaepaphos. Excavations at *Platzeri* close to Yeroskipou suggest that the area was used as a cemetery from as early as the LC IB to the end of the LC IIC period (Nicolaou 1983; Maier and Karageorghis 1984: 102–104). Yeroskipou appears to have been continuously occupied during the LBA, but its significance appears to have been minimized following the rise of Palaepaphos as the prime center in the region.

The reasons why Palaepaphos was selected for the establishment of a nucleated community at the opening of the LC period remain unclear. Situated near the flow of the Dhiarizos River, Palaepaphos was established on top of a series of high-rising plateaus, which afforded a commanding and uninterrupted view toward the sea and the land. More importantly, Palaepaphos must have been equipped with a natural anchorage, which facilitated the docking of ships and enabled extra-insular contacts and long-distance trade. Nowadays, this anchorage is invisible. The memory of a lagoon that had silted up in antiquity, however, is portrayed in the work of Archimandrite Kyprianos dating to the eighteenth century CE. The area of *Loures*, a narrow strip of land situated to the east of the sacred plateau, has been put forward by Iacovou as a possible candidate (Iacovou 2012: 60–62; 2014: 39). Zomeni (2012: 257–264, Figure 4.28) has alternatively argued for four possible locations for the establishment of a port during the LBA. All four are located within the flat plain immediately below the Alonia plateau, which accommodated the megalithic Sanctuary of the *Kypris* from 1200 BCE onwards.

The foundation of Palaepaphos and its development into an urban center are relevant to the island-wide transformations happening at the beginning of the LBA, in relation to the establishment of a new economic order converging on the procurement of copper and the extra-insular exportation of final metal products and other commodities (Keswani 1996: 219–220; G. Georgiou 2006: 457; Iacovou 2012: 61). The ancient exploitation of the Upper and Lower Pillow Lavas and other cupriferous formations found on the northern limits of the Paphos catchment area is confirmed by the distribution of slag heaps dispersed throughout the Paphos forest (Iacovou 2014: 44–45). These are located near the villages of Peravasa, Pano Panaghia, Vrecchia, Ayios Nicolaos, Mamountali, and Asproyia and range in size from small patches to massive mounds (Fox *et al.* 1987; Stos-Gale *et al.* 1998: 239, Nos. 63–76; Zomeni 2012: 198–204; Kassianidou 2013b: 58–59). A number of the slag heaps situated within the Paphos Forest were quarried for road foundation material (Zomeni 2012: 205–209, Table 4.1), and the overall topography of the Paphos forest was substantially transformed in the course of the modern era (see Iacovou 2014: 44–45). Absolute dates by means of radiocarbon (^{14}C) analysis were provided for a very limited number of samples from Peravasa and Sideropunji (close to Peravasa), which indicated a chronology within the Roman era, specifically the fourth century CE (Stos-Gale *et al.* 1998: 246; Zomeni 2012: 207–208; Iacovou 2014: 44). Despite the lack of a corroborative chronology, the exploitation of the ore bodies in the Paphos Forest from as early as the mid-second millennium BCE is not unlikely. It is in fact conspicuous how, during the emergence of a new economic system based on copper exploitation during the MC III–LC IA period, the focus of human occupation was centered on the mountainous regions of the Paphos Forest, in close proximity to the cupriferous Pillow Lavas. The excavation of a substantial fragment of copper slag from the Late Bronze Age strata of the Palaepaphos sanctuary (Megaw 1951: 258) and the Late Bronze Age contexts of Kouklia *Evreti* (Maier and von Wartburg 1985a: 120) elucidate the connection between the flourishing of this LBA polity and the exploitation of the area's mineral resources.

Conclusions

Despite the limited visibility of the earliest occupation levels at Palaepaphos, the study of the overall settlement pattern within the general catchment area renders the foundation horizon of this polity a prominent case study for the investigation of societal, economic, and political transformations in Cyprus at the dawn of the LBA. The evidence presented here is neither exclusive nor conclusive, since it is largely based on data deriving from surface pottery scatters or evidence that remains largely unpublished. Further investigation at Kouklia and the wider Paphos area will shed light on the processes that instigated the establishment of the site that was destined to become the prime center of southwestern Cyprus until the fourth century BCE, when the capital center shifted to Nea Paphos.

Palaepaphos developed gradually from a coastal port of export into an internationally connected, socially complex LC urban community (Iacovou 2008a: 2; 2012: 64; Von Rüden et al. 2016; A. Georgiou 2017). This process culminated in the LC IIIA period, the twelfth century BCE, when the polity managed to nucleate resources and man power (Iacovou 2008b: 626–627), expressed by the construction of the monumental Sanctuary at around 1200 BCE (Maier and Karageorghis 1984: 81–102; A. Georgiou 2017: 212–213). Together with the contemporary Temple 1 at Kition, this Sanctuary constitutes the earliest truly monumental structure built on the island.

Acknowledgments

I would like to extend my thanks to Sturt Manning, Katie Kearns, and Jeffrey Leon for the invitation to be part of the "New Directions in Cypriot Archaeology" workshop and for their warm hospitality. I am also grateful to Maria Iacovou for permission to include unpublished material from the Palaepaphos Urban Landscape Project (Figures 6.3, 6.4) and to the Department of Antiquities, Cyprus for the permission to illustrate Figures 6.7, 6.8, and 6.9. The article was prepared while the author was a Marie Curie Fellow (Career Integration Grants) at the Archaeological Research Unit of the University of Cyprus, for the Project "ARIEL" (Archaeological Investigations of the Extra-Urban and Urban Landscape in Eastern Mediterranean centers: a case study at Palaepaphos, Cyprus). The project was funded from the People Programme (Marie Curie Actions) of the European Union's Seventh Framework Programme FP7/2007–2013/under REA grant agreement no. 334271.

References

Åström, P. 1996. Hala Sultan Tekke: A Late Cypriot harbour town. In P. Åström and E. Herscher (eds.), *Late Bronze Age Settlement in Cyprus: Function and Relationship*, 9–14. Studies in Mediterranean Archaeology PB 126. Jonsered, Sweden: Paul Åströms Förlag.

Åström, P. 2001a. The relative and absolute chronology of Proto White Slip ware. In V. Karageorghis (ed.), *The White Slip Ware of Late Bronze Age Cyprus. Proceedings of an International Conference Organized by the A.G. Leventis Foundation, Nicosia, in Honour of Malcolm Wiener*, 49–50. Vienna: Österreichische Akademie der Wissenschaften.

Åström, P. 2001b. *Hala Sultan Tekke 11: Trial Trenches at Dromolaxia-Vyzakia Adjacent to Areas 6 and 8*. Studies in Mediterranean Archaeology 45.11. Jonsered, Sweden: Paul Åströms Förlag.

Åström, P., E. Åström, A. Hatziantoniou, K. Niklasson, and U. Öbrink. 1983. *Hala Sultan Tekke 8, Excavations 1971–79*. Studies in Mediterranean Archaeology 45.8. Göteborg, Sweden: Paul Åströms Förlag.

Agapiou, A. 2010. Τοπογραφία θέσεων της ευρύτερης περιοχής Πάφου κατά την 3η και 2η χιλιετία π.Χ. και μελέτη της πορείας αστικοποίησης με την υποστήριξη Συστημάτων Γεωγραφικών Πληροφοριών. Unpublished M.A. thesis, University of Cyprus, Nicosia.

Baird, D. 1985. Survey in Peyia Village territory, Paphos, 1983. *Report of the Department of Antiquities, Cyprus*: 340–349.

Benson, J.L. 1972. *Bamboula at Kourion: The Necropolis and the Finds*. Philadelphia: University of Pennsylvania Press.

Bergoffen, C.J. 2001. The Base Ring pottery from Tell el-'Ajjul. In P. Åström (ed.), *The Chronology of Base-ring Ware and Bichrome Wheel-made Ware*, 31–50. Stockholm: Kungl. Vitterhets Historie och Antikvitets Akademien.

Bergoffen, C.J. 2005. *The Cypriot Bronze Age Pottery from Sir Leonard Wolley's Excavations at Alalakh (Tell Atchana)*. Vienna: Österreichische Akademie der Wissenschaften.

Bintliff, J. 2013. Intra-site artefact surveys. In C. Corsi, B. Slapšak, and F. Vermeulen (eds.), *Good Practice in Archaeological Diagnostics*, 193–207. Cham, Switzerland: Springer International Publishing.

Bolger, D.L., C. McCartney, and E. Peltenburg. 2004. Regional interaction in the prehistoric west: Lemba Archaeological Project Western Cyprus Survey. In Iacovou, M. (ed.), *Archaeological Field Survey in Cyprus: Past History, Future Potentials. Proceedings of a Conference Held by the Archaeological Research Unit of the University of Cyprus, 1–2 December 2000*, 105–123. London: The British School at Athens.

Cadogan, G. 1984. Maroni and the Late Bronze Age of Cyprus. In V. Karageorghis and J.D. Muhly (eds.), *Cyprus at the Close of the Late Bronze Age*, 1–10. Nicosia: The A.G. Leventis Foundation.

Cadogan, G. 1992. Maroni VI. *Report of the Department of Antiquities, Cyprus*: 51–58.

Cadogan, G. 1996. Maroni: Change in Late Bronze Age Cyprus. In P. Åström and E. Herscher (eds.), *Late Bronze Age Settlement in Cyprus: Function and Relationship*, 15–22. Studies in Mediterranean Archaeology PB 126. Jonsered, Sweden: Paul Åströms Förlag.

Catling, H.W. 1962. Patterns of settlement in Bronze Age Cyprus. *Opuscula Atheniensia* 4: 129–169.

Catling, H.W. 1968. Kouklia: *Evreti* Tomb 8. *Bulletin Correspondance Hellénique* 92.1: 162–169.

Catling, H.W. 1979. The St. Andrews–Liverpool Museums Kouklia tomb excavation 1950–1954. *Report of the Department of Antiquities, Cyprus*: 270–275.

Christodoulidou, E. 2014. Ο ιδρυτικός ορίζοντας της Παλαιπάφου με βάση την κεραμεική. Unpublished Masters thesis, University of Cyprus.

Christodoulou, A. 1970. Δραστηριότητες του κλάδου αρχαιολογικής επισκοπήσεως κατά το 1970. *Report of the Department of Antiquities, Cyprus*: 80–85.

Christodoulou, D. 1959. *The Evolution of the Rural Land Use Pattern in Cyprus*. Regional Monograph 2: Cyprus. London: The World Land Use Survey.

Christou, D. 1996. Chronique des fouilles et découvertes archéologiques à Chypre en 1995. *Bulletin Correspondance Hellénique* 120.2: 1051–1100.

Clerc, G. 1990. Un fragment de vase au nom d'Ahmosis (?) à Palaepaphos-*Teratsoudhia*. In V. Karageorghis (ed.), *Tombs at Palaepaphos, 1. Teratsoudhia, 2. Eliomylia*, 95–103. Nicosia: A.G. Leventis Foundation.

Coleman, J.E., J.A. Barlow, M.K. Mogelonsky, and K.W. Schaar. 1996. *Alambra: A Middle Bronze Age Site in Cyprus*. Studies in Mediterranean Archaeology 118. Jonsered, Sweden: Paul Åströms Förlag.

Courtois, J.-C. 1981. *Alasia II: Les tombes d'Enkomi, Le mobilier funéraire*. Paris: Mission archéologique d'Alasia.

Courtois, J.-C. 1984. *Alasia III: Les objets des niveaux stratifiés d'Enkomi (Fouilles C.F.-A. Schaeffer 1947–1970)*. Paris: Editions recherches sur les Civilisations, Mémoire 32.

Courtois, J.-C. 1986. A propos des apports orientaux dans la civilisation du Bronze Récent à Chypre. In V. Karageorghis (ed.), *Acts of the International Archaeological Symposium "Cyprus between the Orient and the Occident,"* 69–90. Nicosia: Department of Antiquities, Cyprus.

Crewe, L. 2007a. *Early Enkomi: Regionalism, Trade, and Society at the Beginning of the Late Bronze Age on Cyprus*. British Archaeological Reports, International Series 1706. Oxford: Archaeopress.

Crewe, L. 2007b. Sophistication in simplicity: The first production of wheelmade pottery on Late Bronze Age Cyprus. *Journal of Mediterranean Archaeology* 20.2: 209–238.

Crewe, L. 2010. Rethinking Kalopsidha: From specialization to state marginalization. In D. Bolger and L.C. Maguire (eds.), *The Development of Pre-State Communities in the Ancient Near East. Studies in Honour of Edgar Peltenburg*, 63–71. Oxford and Oakville: Oxbow Books.

Crewe, L. 2012. Beyond copper: Commodities and values in Middle Bronze Cypro-Levantine exchanges. *Oxford Journal of Archaeology* 31: 225–243.

Crewe, L. 2013. Regional connections during the Middle-Late Cypriot transition: New evidence from Kissonerga-*Skalia. Pasiphae* 7: 47–55.

Crewe, L. 2014. A reappearing Early Bronze Age in western Cyprus. In J.M. Webb (ed.), *Structure, Measurement, and Meaning: Studies on Prehistoric Cyprus in Honour of David Frankel*, 137–149. Studies in Mediterranean Archaeology 143. Uppsala, Sweden: Åströms Förlag.

Crewe, L., P. Croft, L. Graham, and A. McCarthy. 2008. First preliminary report of excavations at Kissonerga-*Skalia. Report of the Department of Antiquities, Cyprus*: 105–120.

Diacopoulos, L. 2004. Investigating social complexity through regional survey: "Second generation" analysis of Bronze Age data from the Canadian Palaipaphos Survey Project, Southwestern Cyprus. *Journal of Mediterranean Archaeology* 17.1: 59–85.

Dikaios, P. 1969–71. *Enkomi, Excavations 1948–1958*. Mainz am Rhein, Germany: Philipp von Zebern.

Eriksson, K.O. 2007. *The Creative Independence of Late Bronze Age Cyprus: An Account of the Archaeological Importance of White Slip Ware*. Vienna: Österreichische Akademie der Wissenschaften.

Ferrara, S. 2012. *Cypro Minoan Inscriptions 1: Analysis*. Oxford: Oxford University Press.

Fischer, P.M. 2016. The Late Bronze Age harbour city of Hala Sultan Tekke: Results from the New Swedish Cyprus Expedition 2010–2015. In G. Bourogiannis and C. Mühlenbock (eds.), *Ancient Cyprus Today: Museum Collections and New Research*, 69–78. Studies in Mediterranean Archaeology PB 184. Uppsala, Sweden: Åströms Förlag.

Fischer, P.M., and T. Bürge. 2015. The new Swedish Cyprus Expedition 2014 excavations at Hala Sultan Tekke: Preliminary results. *Opuscula* 8: 27–79.

Fischer, P.M., and T. Bürge. 2016. The new Swedish Cyprus Expedition 2015 excavations at Hala Sultan Tekke: Preliminary results. *Opuscula* 9: 33–58.

Fischer, P.M., and T. Bürge. 2017. Tombs and offering pits at the Late Bronze Age metropolis of Hala Sultan Tekke, Cyprus. *Bulletin of the American Schools of Oriental Research* 377 :161–218.

Fortin, M. 1989. La soi-disant forteresse d'Enkomi (Chypre) à la fin du Bronze Moyen et ay début du Bronze Récent. In R. Laffineur (ed.), *Transition, Le monde Egéen du Bronze Moyen au Bronze Récent*, 239–249. Aegaeum 3. Liège: Université de Liège.

Fox, W., S. Zacharias, and U. Franklin. 1987. Investigations of ancient metallurgical sites in the Paphos District, Cyprus. In D.W. Rupp (ed.), *Western Cyprus: Connections,* 169–184. Studies in Mediterranean Archaeology 77. Göteborg, Sweden: Paul Åströms Förlag.

Frankel, D. 1983. *Corpus of Cypriote Antiquities: 7. Early and Middle Bronze Age Material in the Ashmolean Museum, Oxford*. Studies in Mediterranean Archaeology 20:7, Göteborg, Sweden: Paul Åströms Förlag.

Frankel, D., and J.M. Webb. 2006. *Marki-Alonia: An Early and Middle Bronze Age Settlement in Cyprus. Excavations 1995–2000*. Studies in Mediterranean Archaeology 123.1. Sävedalen, Sweden: Paul Åströms Förlag.

Georgiou, A. 2016. The imported Late Helladic and Late Minoan pottery. In C. Von Rüden, A. Georgiou, A. Jacobs, and P. Halstead (eds.), *Feasting, Craft, and Depositional Practice in Late Bronze Age Palaepaphos: The Well Fillings of Evreti*, 191–196. Rahden, Germany: Verlag Marie Leidorf.

Georgiou, A. 2017. Flourishing amidst a "crisis": The regional history of the Paphos polity at the transition from the 13th to the 12th centuries BCE. In P.M. Fischer and T. Bürge (eds.), *Sea Peoples Up-to-Date: New Research on Transformations in the Eastern Mediterranean in the 13th–11th Centuries BCE*, 207–227. Vienna: Österreichische Akademie der Wissenschaften.

Georgiou, G. 2006. Η τοπογραφία της ανθρώπινης εγκατάστασης στην Κύπρο κατά την Πρώιμη και Μέση Χαλκοκρατία. Unpublished PhD thesis, University of Cyprus.

Given, M. 2004. Mapping and manuring: Can we compare sherd density figure? In S.E. Alcock and J.F. Cherry (eds.), *Side-by-side Survey: Comparative Regional Studies in Mediterranean World*, 13–21. Oxford: Oxbow Books.

Goren, Y., F. Bunimovitz, I. Finkelstein, and N. Na'aman. 2003. The location of Alashiya: New evidence from petrographic investigation of Alashiyan tablets from El-Amarna and Ugarit. *American Journal of Archaeology* 107: 233–255.

Goring, E. 1988. *A Mischievous Pastime: Digging in Cyprus in the nineteenth century. A Catalogue of the Exhibition "Aphrodite's Island: Art and Archaeology of Ancient Cyprus" Held in the Royal Museum of Scotland*. Edinburgh: National Museums of Scotland, Bank of Cyprus Cultural Foundation.

Graham, L. 2012. The necropolis at Kissonerga-*Ammoudhia*: New ceramic evidence from the Early-Middle Bronze Age in Western Cyprus. In A. Georgiou (ed.), *Cyprus: An Island Culture. Society and Social Relations from the Chalcolithic to the Venetian Period*, 38–47. Oxford: Oxbow Books.

Graham, L. 2013. The trouble with typologies: Stewart's pottery classifications and regional styles. In A.B. Knapp, J.M. Webb, and A. McCarthy (eds), *J.R.B. Stewart, An Archaeological Legacy*, 133–140. Studies in Mediterranean Archaeology 139. Uppsala, Sweden: Åströms Förlag.

Hadjisavvas, S. 1977. The archaeological survey of Paphos: A preliminary report. *Report of the Department of Antiquities, Cyprus*: 222–231.

Herscher, E. 1980. Southern Cyprus and the disappearing Early Bronze Age. *Report of the Department of Antiquities, Cyprus*: 17–21.

Herscher, E. 2001. Early Base Ring Ware from *Phaneromeni* and Maroni. In P. Åström (ed.), *The Chronology of Base-ring Ware and Bichrome Wheel-made Ware*, 11–21. Stockholm: Kungl. Vitterhets Historie och Antikvitets Akademien.

Herscher, E., and S.C. Fox. 1993. A Middle Bronze Age tomb from western Cyprus. *Report of the Department of Antiquities, Cyprus*: 69–86.

Hirth, K.G. 1978. Inter-regional trade and the formation of prehistoric gateway communities. *American Antiquity* 43: 35–45.

Hogarth, D.G., M.R. James, R.E. Smith, and E.A. Gardner. 1888. Excavations in Cyprus, 1887–8. Paphos, Leontary, Amargetti. *Journal of Hellenic Studies* 9: 147–271.

Horowitz, M.T. 2008. Phlamoudhi-*Vounari*: A multi-function site. In J.S. Smith (ed.), *Views from Phlamoudhi, Cyprus*, 69–85. Boston: American Schools of Oriental Research.

Iacovou, M. 2007. Site size estimates and the diversity factor in Late Cypriot settlement histories. *Bulletin of American Schools of Oriental Research* 348: 1–23.

Iacovou, M. 2008a. "The Palaepaphos Urban Landscape Project": Theoretical background and preliminary report 2006–2007. *Report of the Department of Antiquities, Cyprus*: 1–17.

Iacovou, M. 2008b. Cultural and political configurations in Iron Age Cyprus: The sequel to a protohistoric episode. *American Journal of Archaeology* 112.4: 625–657.

Iacovou, M. 2012. From regional gateway to Cypriot kingdom: Copper deposits and copper routes in the chora of Paphos. In V. Kassianidou and G. Papasavvas (eds.), *Eastern Mediterranean Metallurgy and Metalwork in the Second Millennium BC: A Conference in Honour of James D. Muhly, Nicosia, 10th–11th October 2009*, 56–67. Oxford: Oxbow Books.

Iacovou, M. 2013. Paphos before Palaepaphos: New approaches to the history of the Paphian Kingdom. In D. Michaelides (ed.), *Epigraphy, Numismatics, Prosopography, and History of Ancient Cyprus: Studies in Honour of Ino Nicolaou*, 275–292. Studies in Mediterranean Archaeology PB 179. Uppsala, Sweden: Åströms Förlag.

Iacovou, M. 2014. Political economies and landscape transformations: The case of ancient Paphos. In J.M. Webb (ed.), *Structure, Measurement, and Meaning. Studies on Prehistoric Cyprus in Honour of David Frankel*, 35–48. Studies in Mediterranean Archaeology 143. Uppsala, Sweden: Åströms Förlag.

Iacovou, M. 2017. Ο τύμβος της Λαόνας στην Παλαίπαφο. Από την αναγνώριση στη μέθοδο διερεύνησης. In V. Vlachou and A. Gadolou (eds.), *Τέρψις. Studies in Mediterranean Archaeology in Honour of Nota Kourou*, 317–329. Brussels: CReA-Patrimoine.

Iliffe, J.H. 1952. Excavations at Aphrodite's sanctuary at Paphos (1951). *Liverpool Bulletin* 2: 29–66.

Kaplan, M.F. 1980. *The Origin and Distribution of Tell el Yahudiyeh Ware*. Studies in Mediterranean Archaeology 62. Göteborg, Sweden: Paul Åströms Förlag.

Karageorghis, V. 1990. *Tombs at Palaepaphos, 1. Teratsoudhia, 2. Eliomylia*, Nicosia: A.G. Leventis Foundation.

Kassianidou, V. 2008. The formative years of the Cypriot copper industry. In I. Tzachili (ed.), *Aegean Metallurgy in the Bronze Age*, 249–267. Athens: Ta Pragmata Publications.

Kassianidou, V. 2011. Blowing the wind of change: The introduction of bellows in Late Bronze Age Cyprus. In P.P. Betancourt and S.C. Ferrence (eds.), *Metallurgy: Understanding How, Learning Why. Studies in Honor of James D. Muhly*, 41–47. Philadelphia: INSTAP Academic Press.

Kassianidou, V. 2012. Metallurgy and metalwork in Enkomi: The early phases. In V. Kassianidou and G. Papasavvas (eds.), *Eastern Mediterranean Metallurgy and Metalwork in the Second Millennium BC*, 94–106. Oxford: Oxbow Books.

Kassianidou, V. 2013a. The production and trade of Cypriot copper in the Late Bronze Age. An analysis of the evidence. *Pasiphae* VII: 133–145.

Kassianidou, V. 2013b. The exploitation of the landscape: Metal resources and the copper trade during the Age of the Cypriot city-kingdoms. *Bulletin of the American Schools of Oriental Research* 370: 49–82.

Kassianidou, V. 2014. Oxhide ingots made of Cypriote copper found in Crete. In V. Karageorghis and A. Kanta (eds.), *Kypriaka in Crete: From the Bronze Age to the End of the Archaic Period*, 307–311. Nicosia: INSTAP and Leventis Foundation.

Keswani, P.S. 2004. *Mortuary Ritual and Society in Bronze Age Cyprus*. London: Equinox.

Keswani, P.S. 1996. Hierarchies, heterarchies, and urbanization processes: The view from Bronze Age Cyprus. *Journal of Mediterranean Archaeology* 9.2: 211–249.

Keswani, P.S. 2005. Death, prestige, and copper in Bronze Age Cyprus. *American Journal of Archaeology* 109: 341–401.

Keswani, P.S. 2016. Fragmentary pithoi. In C. Von Rüden, A. Georgiou, A. Jacobs, and P. Halstead (eds.), *Feasting, Craft, and Depositional Practice in Late Bronze Age Palaepaphos: The Well Fillings of Evreti*, 217–234. Rahden, Germany: Verlag Marie Leidorf.

Kiely, T. 2011. Episkopi-*Bamboula*: The rise and fall of a Late Cypriot urban settlement. In A. Demetriou (ed.), *Proceedings of the 4th International Cyprological Congress*, 549–559. Nicosia: Leventis Foundation.

Knapp, A.B. 1993. Social complexity: Incipience, emergence, and development on Prehistoric Cyprus. *Bulletin of the American Schools of Oriental Research* 292: 85–106.

Knapp, A.B. 1996. *Sources for the History of Cyprus. Volume 2: Near Eastern Texts from the Third to the First Millennia BC*. Albany: State University of New York.

Knapp, A.B. 1997. *The Archaeology of Late Bronze Age Cypriot Society: The Study of Settlement, Survey and Landscape*. Glasgow: University of Glasgow.

Knapp, A.B. 2012. Metallurgical production and trade on Bronze Age Cyprus: Views and variations. In V. Kassianidou and G. Papasavvas (eds.), *Eastern Mediterranean Metallurgy and Metalwork in the Second Millennium BC*, 14–25. Oxford: Oxbow Books.

Knapp, A.B. 2013. Revolution within evolution: The emergence of a "secondary state" on Protohistoric Bronze Age Cyprus. *Levant* 45.1: 19–43.

Knapp, A.B., and V. Kassianidou. 2008. The archaeology of Late Bronze Age copper production: Politiko-*Phorades* on Cyprus. In Ü. Yalçin (ed.), *Anatolian Metal IV*, 135–147. Der Anschnitt Beiheft 21. Bochum, Germany: Deutsches Bergbau-Museum.

Maguire, L.C. 1995. Tell el Dab'a: The Cypriot connection. In W.V. Davies and L. Schofield (eds.), *Egypt, the Aegean, and the Levant. Interconnections in the Second Millennium BC*, 54–65. London: British Museum.

Maguire, L.C. 2009. *The Cypriot Pottery and its Circulation in the Levant*. Tell el Dab'a 21. Vienna: Österreichische Akademie der Wissenschaften.

Maier, F.G. 2008. *Nordost-Tor und persische Belagerungsrampe in alt-Paphos*. Alt-Paphos 6. Mainz am Rhein, Germany: Konstanz Universitätsverlag.

Maier, F.G., and V. Karageorghis. 1984. *Paphos: History and Archaeology*. Nicosia: A.G. Leventis Foundation.

Maier, F.G. 1983. New evidence for the early history of Palaepaphos. *British School at Athens* 78: 229–233.

Maier, F.G., and M.-L. von Wartburg. 1985a. Excavations at Kouklia (Palaepaphos): Thirteenth preliminary report: Seasons 1983 and 1984. *Report of the Department of Antiquities, Cyprus*: 100–125.

Maier, F.G., and M.-L. von Wartburg. 1985b. Reconstructing history from the earth: c. 2800 B.C.–1600 A.D.: Excavating at Palaepaphos, 1966–1984. In V. Karageorghis (ed.), *Archaeology in Cyprus 1960–1985*, 142–172. Nicosia: A.G. Leventis Foundation.

Maier, F.G., and M.-L. von Wartburg. 1986. Excavations at Kouklia (Palaepaphos): Fourteenth preliminary report: Season 1985. *Report of the Department of Antiquities, Cyprus*: 55–61.

Maliszewski, D. 1997. Notes on the Bronze Age settlement patterns of Western Cyprus, c. 2500–c. 1050 BC. *Report of the Department of Antiquities, Cyprus*: 65–84.

Maliszewski, D. 2007. Neolithic, Chalcolithic, and Bronze Age sites in northwestern Cyprus: First assessment. *Report of the Department of Antiquities, Cyprus*: 87–103.

Maliszewski, D. 2013. *Chalcolithic and Bronze Age Pottery from the Field Survey in Northwestern Cyprus 1992–1999*. BAR International Series 2547. Oxford: Archaeopress.

Manning, S.W. 1998. Changing pasts and socio-political cognition in Late Bronze Age Cyprus. *World Archaeology* 30: 39–58.

Manning, S.W. 2001. The chronology and foreign connections of the Late Cypriot I period: Times they are a-changin. In P. Åström (ed.), *The Chronology of Base-ring Ware and Bichrome Wheel-made Ware*, 69–94. Stockholm: Kungl. Vitterhets Historie och Antikvitets Akademien.

Manning, S.W. 2013. Appendix: A new radiocarbon chronology for prehistoric and protohistoric Cyprus, ca. 11000–1050 Cal BC. In A.B. Knapp, *The Archaeology of Cyprus: From Earliest Prehistory through the Bronze Age*, 485–533. Cambridge: Cambridge University Press.

Manning, S.W., and F. De Mita. 1997. Cyprus, the Aegean, and Maroni-*Tsaroukkas*. In D. Christou (ed.), *Proceedings of the International Archaeological Conference: Cyprus and the Aegean in Antiquity, from the Prehistoric Period to the 7th Century A.D.*, 103–141. Nicosia: Department of Antiquities.

Manning, S.W., G.M. Andreou, K.D. Fisher, P. Gerard-Little, C. Kearns, J.F. Leon, D.A. Sewell, and T.M. Urban. 2014. Becoming urban: Investigating the anatomy of the Maroni Late Bronze Age complex, Cyprus. *Journal of Mediterranean Archaeology* 27.1: 3–32.

McCarthy, A., B. Blakeman, D. Collard, P. Croft, L. Graham, C. McCartney, and L. Stork. 2010. The Prasteio-*Mesorotsos* archaeological expedition: Second preliminary report of the 2009 excavations. *Report of the Department of Antiquities, Cyprus*: 53–76.

Megaw, A.H.S. 1951. Archaeology in Cyprus 1949–1950. *Journal of Hellenic Studies* 71: 258–260.

Merrillees, R.S. 1971. The early history of Late Cypriote I. *Levant* 3: 56–79.

Muhly, J.D. 1989. The organisation of the copper industry in Late Bronze Age Cyprus. In E.J. Peltenburg (ed.), *Early Society in Cyprus*, 298–314. Edinburgh: Edinburgh University Press.

Nicolaou, K. 1983. A Late Cypriote necropolis at Yeroskipou. *Report of the Department of Antiquities, Cyprus*: 142–152.

Oren, E.D. 2001. Early White Slip Pottery in Canaan: Spatial and chronological perspectives. In V. Karageorghis (ed.), *The White Slip ware of Late Bronze Age Cyprus: Proceedings of an International Conference Organized by the A.G. Leventis Foundation, Nicosia, in Honour of Malcolm Wiener*, 127–144. Vienna: Österreichische Akademie der Wissenschaften.

Papasavvas, G. 2009. The iconography of the oxhide ingots. In F. Lo Schiavo, J.D. Muhly, R. Maddin, and A. Giumlia-Mair (eds.), *Oxhide Ingots in the Central Mediterranean*, 83–132. Rome: A.G. Leventis Foundation.

Pecorella, P.E. 1973. Mycenaean pottery from Ayia Irini. In V. Karageorghis (ed.), *The Mycenaeans in the Eastern Mediterranean*, 19–24. Nicosia: Department of Antiquities, Cyprus.

Pecorella, P.E. 1977. *Le Tombe dell'età del Bronzo Tardo della necropoli a mare di Ayia Irini "Paleokastro."* Rome: Instituto per gli Studi Micenei ed Egeo-Anatolici.

Peltenburg, E. 1996. From isolation to state formation in Cyprus, c. 3500–1500 BC. In V. Karageorghis and D. Michaelides (eds.), *The Development of the Cypriot Economy, from the Prehistoric Period to the Present Day*, 17–44. Nicosia: University of Cyprus and Bank of Cyprus.

Peltenburg, E. 2006. *The Chalcolithic Cemetery of Souskiou-Vathyrkakas, Cyprus: Investigations of Four Missions from 1950–1997*. Nicosia: Department of Antiquities.

Peltenburg, E. (ed.) 1985. *Lemba Archaeological Project (Cyprus) I. Excavations at Lemba-Lakkous, 1976–1983*. Studies in Mediterranean Archaeology 70.1. Göteborg, Sweden: Åströms Verlag.

Peltenburg, E. (ed.) 1998. *Lemba Archaeological Project (Cyprus) II.1A. Excavations at Kissonerga-Mosphilia, 1979–1992*. Studies in Mediterranean Archaeology 70.2. Jonsered, Sweden: Åströms Verlag.

Philip, G. 1991. Cypriot bronzework in the Levantine world: Conservatism, innovation, and social change. *Journal of Mediterranean Archaeology* 4.1: 59–101.

Pickles, S., and E. Peltenburg. 1998. Metallurgy, society, and the Bronze/Iron transition in the east Mediterranean and the Near East. *Report of the Department of Antiquities, Cyprus*: 67–100.

Quilici, L. 1990. *La Tomba dell'età del Bronzo Tardo dall'abitato di Paleokastro presso Ayia Irini*. Rome: Instituto per gli Studi Micenei ed Egeo-Anatolici.

Raptou, E. and S. Villain. 2018. Nouvelles tombes du bronze récent dans la region de Paphos. *Report of the Department of Antiquities, Cyprus*: 277–326.

Rupp, D.W. 2004. Evolving strategies for investigating an extensive *terra incognita* in the Paphos District by the Canadian Palaipaphos Survey Project and the Western Cyprus Project. In Iacovou, M. (ed.), *Archaeological Field Survey in Cyprus. Past History, Future Potentials, Proceedings of a Conference Held by the Archaeological Research Unit of the University of Cyprus, 1–2 December 2000*, 63–76. London: The British School at Athens.

Satraki, A. 2012. Κύπριοι βασιλείς. Από τον Κόσμασο μέχρι τον Νικοκρέοντα. Archaeognosia 9. Athens: University of Athens.

Schaeffer, C.F.-A. 1952. *Enkomi-Alasia I. Nouvelles Missions en Chypre 1946–1950*. Paris: Klincksieck.

Schaeffer, C.F.-A. 1971. *Alasia I (première série). Mission Archélogique d'Alasia*. Paris: Klincksieck.

Sherratt, E.S. n.d. The Palaepaphos Urban Landscape Project 2006–2008: The Bronze Age pottery from Marcello. *Report of the Department of Antiquities, Cyprus*.

Smith, J.S. 2008. Settlement to sanctuary at Phlamoudhi-*Melissa*. In J.S. Smith (ed.), *Views from Phlamoudhi, Cyprus*, 45–68. Boston: American Schools of Oriental Research.

Sørensen, L.W., and D.W. Rupp. (eds.) 1993. *The Land of the Paphian Aphrodite, Volume 2. The Canadian Palaipaphos Survey Project. Artifact and Ecofactual studies*. Studies in Mediterranean Archaeology 104.2. Göteborg, Sweden: Paul Åströms Förlag.

Stos-Gale, Z.A., S.G. Maliotis, and N. Gale. 1998. A preliminary survey of the Cypriot slag heaps and their contribution to the reconstruction of copper production on Cyprus. In T. Rehren, A. Hauptmann, and J.D. Muhly (eds.), *Metallurgica Antiqua in Honour of Hans-Gert Bachmann and Robert Maddin*, 235–262. Der Anschnitt, Beiheft 8. Bochum, Germany: Deutsches Bergbau-Museum.

Stos-Gale, Z.A. 2011. "Biscuits with ears": A search for the origin of the earliest oxhide ingots. In P.P. Betancourt and S.C. Ferrence (eds.), *Metallurgy: Understanding How, Learning Why. Studies in Honor of James D. Muhly*, 221–229. Philadelphia: INSTAP Academic Press.

Tsielepi, S.C., and P. Bienkowski. 1988. *Cypriot Pottery in the Liverpool Museum. An Interim list*. Liverpool: National Museums and Galleries on Merseyside Occasional Papers.

Vermeule, E., and F.Z. Wolsky. 1990. *Toumba tou Skourou, A Bronze Age Potters' Quarter on Morphou Bay in Cyprus*. Boston: Harvard University Press.

Von Rüden, C., A. Georgiou, A. Jacobs, and P. Halstead. (eds.) 2016. *Feasting, Craft, and Depositional Practice in Late Bronze Age Palaepaphos: The Well Fillings of Evreti*. Rahden: Leidorf.

Webb, J.M. 1999. *Ritual Architecture, Iconography, and Practice in the Late Cypriot Bronze Age*. Studies in Mediterranean Archaeology 75. Jonsered, Sweden: Paul Åströms Förlag.

Webb, J.M. 2005. Ideology, iconography, and identity: The role of foreign goods and images in the establishment of social hierarchy in Late Bronze Age Cyprus. In J. Clarke (ed.), *Archaeological Perspectives in the Transmission and Transformation of Culture in the Eastern Mediterranean*, 176–182. Oxford: Oxbow Books.

Webb, J.M. 2012. Kalopsidha: Forty-six years after SIMA Volume 2. In J.M. Webb and D. Frankel (eds.), *SIMA Fifty Years On*, 49–58. Studies in Mediterranean Archaeology 137. Uppsala, Sweden: Åströms Förlag.

Webb, J.M. and D. Frankel. 2013. Cultural regionalism and divergent social trajectories in Early Bronze Age Cyprus. *American Journal of Archaeology* 117.1: 59–81.

Yener, K.A. 2012. Late Bronze Age Alalakh and Cyprus: A relationship of metals? In V. Kassianidou and G. Papasavvas (eds.), *Eastern Mediterranean Metallurgy and Metalwork in the Second Millennium BC*, 163–168. Oxford: Oxbow Books.

Zomeni, Z. 2012. Quaternary marine terraces on Cyprus: Constraints on uplift and pedogenesis, and the geoarchaeology of Palaipafos. Unpublished PhD dissertation, Oregon State University.

PART III

Diachronic Landscapes

7

Alambra

From "A Middle Bronze Age Settlement in Cyprus" to a Royal District

ANNA SATRAKI

Introduction: Regionalism as a Diachronic Phenomenon in Cypriot History

From the beginning of the Late Bronze Age (ca. 1700 BCE), early forms of complex political organization appeared on Cyprus, arguably as a result of increasing demand for Cypriot copper from surrounding Mediterranean states. Newly founded coastal settlements emerged that gradually (and certainly by the thirteenth century BCE) developed from gateway emporia to urban centers (Satraki 2012: 103–110 with references; see also Manning *et al.* 2014). The last half-century of archaeological research has indeed come to this consensus on Cypriot state formation. Yet this proposed notion of copper driving state formation is valid as long as it is considered to describe the idiosyncratic response of the island as a whole toward social transformation, as opposed to other areas of the ancient world to which Cyprus can be held as comparable, for instance Crete, where different paths to complexity were followed and different (temporal and spatial) scales were involved (Peltenburg and Iacovou 2012).

Once we begin to explore the individual histories of the island's micro-regions, however, major discrepancies from this overarching axiom begin to appear. For example, a recent study by Webb and Frankel (2013) demonstrated that already from the Early Cypriot (EC) I–II period, a rise of hierarchical social relations within sites on the northern coast was evidenced through pottery production and funerary practices, suggesting an earlier trajectory toward complexity. These sites seem to have sustained long-distance trading activities and to have exerted control over inland resources. Moreover, although the prevalent copper trade model has rarely been contested, never do two administrative sites provide identical evidence as to how an economy primarily invested in copper (a process that would imply control over the mineral, its inland transportation, and its overseas trade) functioned within each Late Cypriot polity (see Andreou in this volume). Finally, it is true that coastal emporia, from Enkomi to (clockwise) Kition, Hala Sultan Tekke, Maroni *Vournes*, Kalavasos *Ayios Dhimitrios*, and Kouklia *Palaepaphos*, which lie a maximum distance of 5 km from the sea were the leading settlements within their respective territories (for a recent synthesis and bibliography, see Knapp 2013). Similarly, there is consensus that control over trading (export and import) activities was pivotal in social transformation and the formation of power structures. Yet the excavation of a site further inland, namely Alassa *Paliotaverna* (Hadjisavvas 1996), challenged this model and provided insights to alternative modes of geopolitical relationships within the Late Bronze Age (Figure 7.1).

Evidently, the Cypriot physical landscape, characterized by mountains, hilly zones, river valleys, and plains, is structured into regionally distinct territories. These geographic regions provided the economic background on which political territories were shaped. This reality shaped a phenomenon, commonly referred to as "regionalism," that defined the Bronze and Iron Ages (for a review of the use of the term in relation to the Bronze Age, see G. Georgiou 2006: 37–44; in relation to the Iron Age, see Satraki 2012: 378–383; see also Knapp 1997: 46–47).

The most profound argument for Cypriot regionalism is the interpretation that pre-Ptolemaic Cyprus was never a unitary state but rather was fragmented into autonomous polities (for a different view on the Late Bronze Age, see Knapp 2008). In the course of the Late Bronze and Iron Age periods, the number of separate Cypriot polities fluctuated in time, thus resulting in constant negotiation of their political territories. For example, during the Late Bronze Age, on the south-central coast, there were two major centers, Kalavasos *Ayios Dhimitrios* and Maroni *Vournes*. Large architectural complexes recovered there (South 1996; Cadogan 1996; Manning *et al.* 2014), which were massively constructed with ashlar masonry and comprised tomb assemblages (suggesting that the tomb owners had access to luxuries and imported goods), indicate that the two important towns dominated large areas—presumably the Vasilikos and Maroni river watersheds, respectively—where contemporary settlements have been located by surface survey (South 2002: 64–65; Andreou in this volume). South (2002: 68) has described perceptively how the organization of these areas transformed during the transition to the Iron Age in the early first millennium BCE: "in the case of Kalavasos and Maroni, these two prosperous Late Bronze Age polities . . . were completely abandoned by about 1200 BC . . . Indeed, in this region the political pattern changed out of all recognition, with Amathus taking over as the centre of a kingdom, and the Maroni and Vasilikos valleys found themselves in the borderlands at the outer edge of the hypothesized extent of the kingdom."

In the context of the Cypriot Iron Age, epigraphic and archaeological evidence suggests that territories changed political affiliation through coercion (e.g., Idalion was besieged and conquered by Kition at some point in the fifth century BCE) or as a result of an economic transaction (a *chorion*, most probably Tamassos, was sold by its king Pasikypros to Pummayaton, king of Kition, for fifty *talanta*; see Athenaeus 4.167 c–d) or by means that we still need to understand (Fourrier 2002: 138–139).

Alambra is situated in the heart of the central part of the island, although "Central Cyprus" is not a formal geographic division. Rather, it is a geographically diverse region that has been the topic of at least two other studies (G. Georgiou

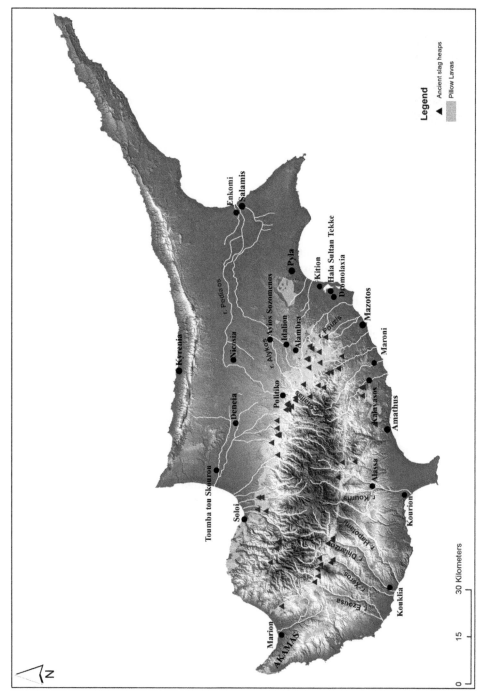

Figure 7.1: Map of Cyprus indicating sites mentioned in the text. Digital geological data from the Cyprus Geological Survey Department.

2011; Pilides 2017). In the context presented here, the Alambra region is considered to comprise part of the south-central Mesaoria Plain and the eastern hilly zone of the Troodos complex (and thus the easternmost metalliferous pillow lavas of the Troodos ophiolites), namely the lands through which the Alykos and Gialias rivers pass to the north and the Tremithos river to the south (for the geographical and geological characteristics of the area, see Karouzis 2000: 70–71, 97–103).

The aim of the present paper is to identify the processes that led to the incorporation of the prehistoric landscape at Alambra—and consequently the wider central part of the island—within the political and economic regions of the Late Bronze Age, and subsequently its emergence as a royal territory within the Iron Age polity of Idalion. More broadly, it attempts to illuminate and to interpret the establishment, the territorial and political development, and finally the abolition of the Idalion polis.

The Making of a Bronze Age Landscape

The survey conducted by the Cornell team in the 1970s and 1980s revealed a small cluster of Early and Middle Bronze Age sites (mostly cemeteries) in the area of modern Alambra. The Middle Cypriot (MC) settlement at Alambra *Mouttes* was excavated and soon after published in a monograph by the same team (Coleman *et al.* 1996; see Dikomitou-Eliadou in this volume).[1] The Alambra cluster of Middle Bronze Age sites belongs to a densely occupied region, with major groups located around Nicosia, Politiko, Marki, and Ayios Sozomenos (G. Georgiou 2006: 83). These settlements and necropoleis are located either close to springs or on the flow of the two major rivers, the Pediaios and Gialias. Similarly, the sites near Alambra are located close to a spring of Tremithos that flows downstream to the south and meets another cluster of Early-Middle Bronze Age sites at the vicinity of Dromolaxia (Markou 2013) (Figure 7.2).

None of these protohistoric Bronze Age sites at Alambra—certainly not the settlement at *Mouttes*—continued into the Late Bronze Age. "Not even a single Late Bronze Age sherd was found in any of our investigations at Alambra," Coleman reports (1996: 5). He goes on to describe what appears to be a peaceful abandonment of the settlement already by MC I or II. In the context of the island's central region, and also of island-wide trends, the abandonment of the sites at Alambra is not an isolated phenomenon. As Webb and Frankel (2013) describe, significant changes in settlement pattern took place during the Middle Cypriote period: in MC II some villages were abandoned, while a more or less contemporary increase at other sites suggests a process of nucleation into larger villages and towns (Iacovou *et al.* 2008: 286).

So, where were the people of Alambra headed when they left their homes during the Middle Bronze Age? Did they move to Deneia, as suggested by Frankel in this volume? Or did they move toward another center, such as Nicosia *Ayia Paraskevi*?

---

1. The site of Alambra *Mouttes* is currently the focus of a new project; see Sneddon 2015.

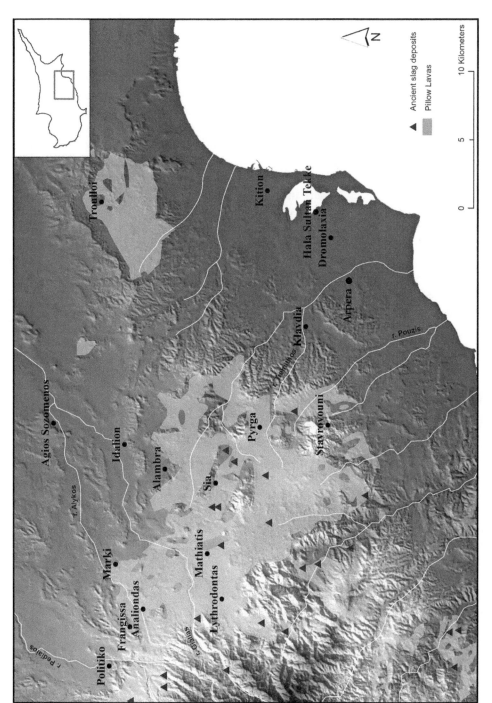

Figure 7.2: Map of Cyprus indicating sites Bronze and Iron Age sites of central and southeastern Cyprus. Digital geological data from the Cyprus Geological Survey Department.

Whatever their destination, the important point is that MC III regional centers soon began to decline when new settlements were established on the coast at the start of the Late Bronze Age (ca. 1700 BCE) in response to increasing interregional demand for Cypriot copper.[2] Markou (2013: 111) has recently recorded an expansion of sites into the igneous pillow lavas of the eastern Troodos Mountains during the Late Bronze Age at the localities of Mathiatis, Sia, and (further south) Pyrga, occurring around the same time as the coastal MC III development, in the context of the island-wide phenomenon of the development of extractive metallurgy.

This late MC settlement pattern provided the platform for a new order of relationships that transformed the economic and political landscape during the initial phase of the Late Cypriot period. The construction of a number of fortified sites toward the end of the Middle Bronze Age, however, suggests that this new order underwent a period of increasing instability (Monahan and Spigelman in this volume). Interestingly, among twenty such buildings, two are located on the northern coast, five in the southern foothills of the northern range, four in the Karpass peninsula, one in the Mesaoria Plain, and nine (almost half of the total number) in central Cyprus (Crewe 2007: 49–61).

So: what was this major reorganization of the landscape in central Cyprus aiming at? Or, stated another way, what was the guiding and managing force behind this restructuring? Was it part of a polity-formation process structured around a local dominating center, or was it caught in a tug-of-war between emerging powers based outside this region? Before we attempt to untangle this complex issue, let us first take a comparative glance at the rest of the island.

The Formation of Territories

The complexity of the issue of the political organization in central Cyprus during the early part of the Late Bronze Age is characteristic of comparable questions that challenge our knowledge of territorial organization across the island. The major evidentiary basis that persists through time is that of the geographical characteristics of each region. For example, watersheds and mountains often generate the borders of different, constructed geographical regions. Most importantly, in the ancient Greek language the word *oros* means both "mountain" and "landmark," a testimony to the importance of mountains as landmarks, as defining features of the landscape (Della Dora and Terkenli 2012: 141).

For the western and southern part of the island, the Cypriot landscape breaks into micro-regions, typically around river valleys and major watersheds. These micro-regions, which emerge as categories based on select geomorphological components of the landscape, more or less corresponded to the hinterland, the *chora*, of the emerging political centers based around the coasts. For example, the Dhiarizos River

---

2. For the clusters of sites around Deneia and Ayia Paraskevi, with bibliography see Georgiou 2006: 154–55 and 145, respectively. On their abandonment upon the inception of the LC period, see Georgiou 2006: 302–305 and 281–82.

constitutes the backbone of the Palaepaphos region (see A. Georgiou in this volume). Along with the watersheds of Chapotami, Xeros, and Ezousa, these rivers produce a self-contained catchment area (Agapiou 2010), with the theorized constituents of a Cypriot polity, namely a port, agricultural land, and mining areas (Iacovou 2007: 18). We may justifiably deduce that this zone created the hinterland of Palaepaphos (Iacovou 2014; Satraki 2012: 338, 341–343, 352–353, 358).

Similarly, the Kouris River constitutes the backbone of another self-contained region, one in which the Late Bronze Age center at Alassa and the Iron Age center at Kourion dominated their contemporary settlements (Satraki 2012: 151, 343–344, 351). On the Chrysochous River drainage framed by the northern foothills of the Troodos massif, the site of Marion appeared as the sole dominating power during the Iron Age (Satraki 2012: 338). The northwestern foot of the Troodos Mountains and the western Mesoria plain, penetrated by a number of rivers that flow downstream toward Morphou Bay, formed the hinterland of a Late Bronze Age administrative center (to which Morphou *Toumba tou Skourou* must have been attached) and Iron Age Soloi (Satraki 2012: 144–146, 340). Likewise to the south, the Late Bronze Age administrative centers at Kalavasos *Ayios Dhimitrios* and Maroni *Vournes* seem to have controlled the Vasilikos and Maroni river valleys, respectively (South 2002). This relatively "straight-forward" territorial organization of river valleys with political cohesion, however, does not apply to the central and eastern part of the island.

Power Centers in Central Cyprus

So let us return to the Alambra area and consider: was this geographically diverse central region part of one single polity during the Late Bronze Age, or was it fragmented into multiple entities? The identification of any administrative centers that may have appeared inside this area is crucial. Since the surveys conducted by Catling during the 1950s and 1960s, Cypriot archaeologists have theorized that an early regional center appeared at Ayios Sozomenos, which was succeeded by a settlement at Idalion *Ambelleri* before the end of the Bronze Age (Catling 1982: 231). Let us then briefly examine the archaeological evidence pertaining to the two sites.

Ayios Sozomenos: Primary Center or a Cluster of Secondary Sites?

The plateau of Ayios Sozomenos is located on the flow of the Alykos River, a tributary of the Gialias River. Surface survey projects from the 1950s located high concentrations of Middle and Late Bronze Age sites on the upper and lower areas of the plateau and also in the lowland zones of the valley (Overbeck and Swiny 1972; Devillers *et al.* 2004; Brown 2013: 122). Three sites located on the plateau and one just below, to the south, have been interpreted as MC III–LC IA forts (Monahan and Spigelman in this volume). From one of the lowland sites, known as *Ampelia*, Catling collected surface sherds that include Canaanite jars, Levantine ceramics, Late Helladic IIIA-B vases, and fragments of faience, ivory, and bronze objects (Catling 1982: 231).

A recent project of the Department of Antiquities directed by Despina Pilides (The Ayios Sozomenos Survey and Excavation Project—ASESP) aims at resurveying the area with targeted excavation at important sites (Pilides 2017). Two of the forts located on the plateau have been investigated with impressive results. At *Barsak* a double circuit wall with a deep ditch on the exterior was revealed. In the course of the LCII period *Barsak* was abandoned and a new fort was built at *Nikolides*, which was strengthened during its lifespan by the addition of an ashlar tower. The ASESP also located a large settlement site at the foot of *Barsak* (at a site called *Tzirpoulos*, at a distance of approximately 350m across from *Ampelia*), with evidence for a variety of workshop activities in one of the buildings excavated there. Despite their prominent location at the confluence of the Alykos and Yialias rivers, on the communication route to the east, supervising a fertile valley with agricultural produce, it seems that the Ayios Sozomenos cluster of sites was abandoned before the end of the LCII (Pilides 2017).

Earlier survey projects suggested a function oriented toward agricultural activities for the sites at Ayios Sozomenos. The excavations of the ASESP attest to the accumulation of wealth and provide evidence for supra-regional political organization. According to Catling (1982: 231), "this [*Ampelia*] was the major Middle and Late Bronze Age settlement in the valley, a position it subsequently yielded to Idalion." He also wrote that "it may be held that in the Late Bronze Age the area was in fairly close contact with the rich port towns in the region of Larnaka, and may even have been an entrepôt for trade between those towns and more remote settlements to the north and north-west" (Catling 1982: 232).

It certainly seems possible that the Ayios Sozomenos cluster of Late Bronze Age sites was functioning in close contact with (or under the authority of) a major coastal urban center, but it is not wholly convincing that that major site was located on the coast of Larnaka. It seems equally plausible that Ayios Sozomenos's location on the flow of the Gialias River was of critical importance to Enkomi, since it would have secured the procurement of agricultural goods to that eastern port town (Satraki 2012: 147–148). Peltenburg (1996) cogently suggested that the MC III–LC I fortified sites across the central areas of the island were part of Enkomi's system of secondary sites, which linked its primary coastal settlement with its mining and agricultural hinterland. Indeed, the site cluster at Ayios Sozomenos claims three such forts in the area of the plateau, while two more are located a short distance to the south.

I would even go further to suggest that this route from Enkomi into the Troodos began at Analiondas, where the spring of the Alykos River is located. At the site of Analiondas *Palioklishia*, archaeologists located an agricultural production and storage center of the thirteenth century BCE through surface evidence. It seemed to have operated as a support village within a regionally based system of exchange (Webb and Frankel 1994).

Therefore, it seems that the cluster of sites at Ayios Sozomenos managed to consolidate supra-regional control (of the wider area) at the very beginning of the Late Bronze Age but failed to maintain its territorial organization, as its system collapsed just before the LCIIC, the phase that witnessed the climax of urban development in Bronze Age Cyprus (Negbi 1986). Unless the new and very important excavation project directed by Pilides changes this state of affairs, what we can make of the cluster of sites at Ayios Sozomenos is a group of dynamic inland centers engaged in the processing of agricultural commodities and possibly connected with Enkomi.

Idalion: A "Polis" of the Late Bronze Age?

The twelfth century BCE witnesses for the first time the documentation of as many as eight Cypriot place names on an Egyptian royal text, dated to the reign of Ramesses III on the Great Temple at Medinet Habu (see Edgerton and Wilson 1936; Snodgrass 1994: 169). It has been argued that the list dates back to the thirteenth century BCE. The sites mentioned on this royal monument have been interpreted as Salamis, Kition, Marion, Soloi, Idalion, Akamas, Kourion, and Kyrenia. Although some of the names on the list are dubiously identified with actual place names in Cyprus, it remains strongly plausible that at least some of these identifications are valid and represent political entities on the island. Thus, if we accept the suggestion that the name of Idalion was mentioned on this Ramesside inscription, then it becomes evident that Idalion was entering a phase of supra-regional consolidation by the LC IIC period.

In terms of the archaeological record, mortuary evidence and pottery scatters confirm occupation at the site of Idalion at least by the thirteenth century BCE (Schulte-Campbell 1989; Hadjicosti 1999: 36). A complex of rooms with workshop and storage installations (in close proximity to the palace of the Cypro-Archaic and Cypro-Classical period) was uncovered and has been dated to the twelfth to eighth centuries BCE (Hadjicosti 1999: 37–38). It is anticipated that the publication of the rescue excavations conducted by the Department of Antiquities over the past few decades will add substantial data for the LC II period settlement at Idalion.

As it stands, the published LC IIIA occupation strata are well documented. The hill of Idalion *Ambelleri* (the Iron Age acropolis that accommodated first the palace of the Greek-speaking "*basileus* of Idalion" and then the administrative center of the Phoenician "*mlk* of Kition and Idalion") was fortified in order to protect several structures and a "cult-house" complex (Gjerstad *et al.* 1935: 624). This sanctuary site, as identified by Gjerstad and verified by Webb (1999: 84–91), is one among only sixteen securely identified sacred spaces of the Late Bronze Age in Cyprus. This earliest *temenos* atop the Idalion acropolis produced evidence pertaining to ritual food consumption and drinking activities, while other finds include eight terracotta bull figurines and one made of ivory; gold jewelry and gold leaves; maceheads; seals and cylinder seals; copper and iron slag; a fragment of an ingot; and an iron knife. The evidence is unequivocal for the operation of an institutionalized, formal cult on the summit of the hill that soon after became the region's administrative acropolis. The highly symbolic significance of the *temenos*'s paraphernalia points toward an organized society that was in charge of administering the copper procured in the catchment area and the management of the territory that contained the metalliferous zones.

Interestingly, the emergence of Idalion as a potentially powerful player in the context of the LC IIC/LC IIIA coincides with a recession of settlement in the Gialias valley. The Ayios Sozomenos cluster and also Analiondas *Palioklishia* are abandoned around or soon after 1200 BCE (Webb and Frankel 1994: 20). Could this state of affairs substantiate the hypotheses that the Gialias network of secondary centers was linked to Enkomi and that the rise of Idalion triggered instability within the established yet fragile system of Enkomi's contacts? We need to keep in mind that the rearrangement of the area's geopolitical organization may have been initiated by the same people who sustained Enkomi's inland economics for a couple of centuries. It was perhaps the populations of the Gialias rural settlements who triggered the phenomenon of *synoikismos* (the "gathering together," the concentration of the population in a single polis) and initiated the establishment of a primary center within their area.

Contrary to the Ayios Sozomenos cluster, the newly founded settlement at Idalion managed to consolidate—well before the end of the Late Bronze Age—a state-formation process within the limits of the central part of the island. Archaeological documentation is still pending, but it is highly possible that this process was based on the need to control and to manage the local extraction of copper of the Mathiatis-Sia-Pyrga ores and consequently its trade in Cypriot and foreign markets. Located at a strategic point so as to control as much as possible of the rich agricultural land of the eastern Mesaoria Plain (generously irrigated by the Alykos and Gialias river in the winter months) and surrounded to the south by the rich copper deposits of the eastern Troodos's pillow lavas and with easy access to Larnaka bay, the polis of Idalion claimed a vital economic and political territory. The choice of place for the new establishment was a successful one, as Idalion proved to be a resilient seat of local administration. This endurance is amply reflected in the late narrative of King Chalkenor who, according to Stephanus of Byzantium (*Ethnica* "'Ιδάλιον, πόλις Κύπρου"), wandered for days before the sun itself (as was the oracle's dictate) pointed out the right place to found his new polis.[3] Chalkenor (translated as "the man of copper") must have preserved, through the realm of myth, the historical conditions that determined the foundation of the Idalion polis.

Southeastern Partnerships: Idalion and the Coastal Centers of the Larnaka Bay

At this point we have to consider one central issue that defines the diachronic history of Idalion during the Iron Age and most probably the Bronze Age as well. It concerns the constant need of Idalion to orientate toward the coast, where the copper resources that were procured within its territory would be exported from a harbor. One strong hypothesis suggests that Idalion established a seaport on the coast between Kiti and Mazotos, at the mouths of the rivers Tremithos and Pouzis, whose watersheds both cross the cupriferous pillow lavas and the fertile coastal plain (Leonard 2000: 135–137). Given that no port that would date to the Late Bronze and Iron Ages has been located there, however, and more importantly that

---

3. For a classical synthesis of the foundation myths of the Iron Age poleis of Cyprus, see Gjerstad 1944; for a recent approach on the Nostoi and their historical implications, see Iacovou 2008a.

the area is considered inhospitable to the functions of a port or harbor, we are obliged to dismiss this (Markou 2013: 111).

For this reason, the Iron Age history of Idalion was defined by the changing relations of control and primacy with the urban center of Kition. Even before the fifth century BCE when Idalion was conquered and subsequently annexed by Kition (Satraki 2012: 289–290 with references), textual sources imply that Idalion was heavily dependent on the port city of Kition in order to ensure a gateway to coastal trade networks (Iacovou 2013: 148). Unlike during the Iron Age, however, in the Late Bronze Age period there were not one but two major port towns on the southeast coast of Cyprus: Kition and Hala Sultan Tekke. Are we to assume that Idalion had already developed a link with Kition, defying the existence of Hala Sultan Tekke? I think not, because Kition must have been in direct control of the copper resources at Troulloi, a minor outcrop of the Troodos complex, to the north of Larnaka (on copper mining in the area of Troulloi, see Kassianidou 2012: 233). Rather, Hala Sultan Tekke needed to have control over mineral resources that lay at some distance from the port, namely the pillow lavas of the easternmost part of the Troodos (around Sia, Mathiatis, Lythrodontas, Pyrga, and Stavrovouni) (see Satraki 2012: 149–150). Idalion and Hala Sultan Tekke may have developed as allied political and economic centers in an effort to manage the geological assets of their territory. The communication between the two centers must have been focused around the Tremithos drainage system (Markou 2013: 105).

This "partnership" did not last for long. Before the end of the Late Bronze Age, the coastal urban center at Hala Sultan Tekke was peacefully abandoned due to the silting of its harbor, the *raison d'être* of the coastal urban center (Åström 1986: 8; Devillers *et al.* 2015). The same seems to have been the case with the mining sites at Mathiatis, Lythrodontas, and Sia (Hadjicosti 1991) as well as the inland sites at Dromolaxia *Trypes*, Arpera *Mosphilios,* and Klavdia *Tremithos*. Before the consolidation of its geopolitical region, therefore, Idalion was being challenged by the island-wide transformations that were generated in the context of the close of the Late Bronze Age (Iacovou 2008a; A. Georgiou 2011). At the onset of the Early Iron Age, the excavated eleventh-century BCE strata at Idalion and Kition (see Satraki 2012: 180–182 with bibliography) remain the sole archaeologically visible evidence of settlement in the southeastern part of the island.

The Idalion Tablet: The Consolidation of the Landscape

The Early Iron Age is the chronological horizon that encapsulates the formation of the Cypriot city-states (Satraki 2012: 175–210). The culmination of these processes belongs to a new cycle of Cypriot political organization, one that can rightfully be described as the era of the kingdoms (Satraki 2012: 211–374). The Neo-Assyrian royal texts that officially claim a number of Cypriot leaders as kings constitute the *termini ante quos* for the crystallization of the royal institution and the ascendance of the hereditary *basileis* (Iacovou 2002: 81–83; Satraki 2013: 125–126). The royal prism of Esarhaddon from 673 BCE officially affirms the primacy of Idalion in the central part of Cyprus. Among the listed Cypriot cities and their rulers, Akestor of Idalion appears first in the catalogue (Luckenbill 1968: 265–266; Satraki 2012: 215).

Figure 7.3: Replica of the "Bronze Tablet of Idalion" exhibited at the Local Museum of Ancient Idalion. Courtesy of the Department of Antiquities, Cyprus.

The Cypro-Archaic period (ca. 750–500 BCE) is a time of consolidation with regard to the territorial extent of each of these kingdoms and their political institutions. Already from the end of the seventh century BCE, royal iconography manifests in statuary in the context of Idalion's urban and peri-urban sanctuaries (Satraki 2008). Before the end of the sixth century BCE, coins bearing royal symbols and names of the ruling dynasty appear (Satraki 2012: 286). Moreover, recent work has documented a "full" Archaic landscape in the upper Tremithos drainage, comprising a more extensive settlement system than what has been recorded for earlier periods (Markou 2013: 112), which indicates territorial consolidation and a fully developed economic and political organizational scheme with respect to the Idalion *chora*.

One of the last official documents that belong to the era of the autonomous kingdom of Idalion is the famous bronze tablet that was found on the administrative acropolis (Masson 1983: No. 217) (Figure 7.3).

This lengthy inscription records invaluable information on the Idalion polity, such as the existence of state officials and their names (*basileus Stasikypros* and a dignitary named Filokypros Onasagoras) and of public and royal land. It also provides historical data regarding the last years or perhaps months of the kingdom of Idalion itself. It is on this precious document that we find for the first time the name of Alambria, denoting an οιρωνι, translated by Masson as "district" (1983: 244). Interestingly, this term is probably connected to the Mycenaean Greek word *orojo* that is found on Linear B tablets to describe administrative regions (Fourrier 2002: 142). Indeed, Coleman's survey at Alambra located sites that date to the Cypro-Archaic period (Coleman *et al.* 1996: 519–520), archaeological evidence that supports the claim that the Alambra area may have been abandoned before the end of the Middle Bronze Age, but it was later settled again and developed into a secondary site within the Idalion *chora*.

This tablet also records that during the reign of this king Stasikypros, Idalion witnessed a stressful siege on behalf of *"the Medes and the Kitians."* Evidently the partnership that presumably linked the inland polis with the coastal one must have undergone a severe break. This siege was successfully resisted, as the document seems to suggest, but soon after, probably through coercion, the two fifth-century BCE powers of central and southeastern Cyprus—Idalion and Kition—joined together.

Joining Powers: The Kingdom of Kition and Idalion

Sometime during the fifth century BCE, the kings of Kition eventually absorbed and incorporated the kingdom of Idalion. This event is revealed in two royal inscriptions written in the Phoenician alphabet (Figures 7.4 and 7.5). In these inscriptions (one

Figure 7.4: Marble architectural feature with Phoenician inscription. Local Museum of Ancient Idalion (No. CCM 6500). Courtesy of the Department of Antiquities, Cyprus.

Figure 7.5: Marble stele with Phoenician inscription. Local Museum of Ancient Idalion (no. PH1). Courtesy of the Department of Antiquities, Cyprus.

of unknown provenance and the other allegedly found at Idalion but with no exact provenance), King Baalmilk II is designated as king of "Kition and Idalion." While his father, King Ozibaal, is also designated as king of "Kition and Idalion," his grand-father, Baalmilk I, is simply called the king of Kition (Yon 2004: Nos. 45 and 46). The annexation of Idalion is, therefore, an achievement attributed to Ozibaal.

In spite of its absorption by the kingdom of Kition, however, Idalion was never deprived of its prominent economic role in copper extraction and production (Sznycer 2004). This retention is made evident by the fact that the archaic administrative center of the Greek kingdom continued to be used by Phoenician rulers. Most importantly, the recent excavations of the administrative complex have revealed an archive in the Phoenician alphabet comprised of more than seven hundred inscriptions that record economic activities down to the end of the fourth century BCE (Hadjicosti 1997).

Sometime during the fourth century BCE, "Kition and Idalion" also managed to take possession of the inland site of Tamassos. What is not often acknowledged in modern scholarship is that only one king of Kition, Pummayaton, ever bore the title "King of Kition, Idalion, and Tamassos." The epigraphic evidence states that he did not bear this triple title to the end of his kingship. In fact, Pummayaton is named "king of Kition, Idalion, and Tamassos" in a single non-royal inscription on a marble altar of unknown provenance, securely dated to 341 BCE (the twenty-first year of his reign) (Yon 2004: No. 1002). A number of inscriptions from Kition that date from the thirty-fourth year of his reign, however, describe Pummayaton as king of only "Kition and Idalion" (Yon 2004: No. 1029). This nomenclature allows us to reach the conclusion that Tamassos was lost to the kingdom of Kition before the abolition of all the Cypriot kingdoms by Ptolemy Soter.

From Analiondas to Pyla: The Territory of the Kingdom of "Kition and Idalion"

The conquest of Tamassos (close to the site of modern Politiko) was evidently a short affair. As was the case during the Late Bronze Age, the network of sites along the Pediaios River was out of the reach of the Idalion polity and the later "Kition and Idalion" combined kingdom. On the contrary, the Gialias waterway, from its spring close to Analiondas to at least as far as the Ayios Sozomenos plateau, was by the Classical period fully incorporated within the kingdom of "Kition and Idalion." This territorial shift, I think, is established by a series of extra-urban sanctuaries, located on the northern bank of the river Gialias (within the rural land of modern Dali), which seem to demarcate the northern frontier area of the kingdom (Figure 7.6).

Influenced by de Polignac's (1984) model, the proliferation of extra-urban sanc-tuaries during the Archaic period is believed to have demonstrated intentions of ter-ritorial domination and sovereignty on behalf of the Cypriot ruling classes (Fourrier 2002; 2007; Papantoniou 2012). Arguably, the presence of a number of sanctuaries on the banks of the Gialias could have provided the authorities of "Kition and Idalion" with the means to organize and to control the northern extremity of their periphery.

Two digraphic and bilingual inscriptions (in Phoenician and Greek; see Yon 2004: Nos. 70 and 71) found at Analiondas, at a sanctuary site known as *Frangissa*, may point to the western frontier zone of "Kition and Idalion" (Figure 7.7).

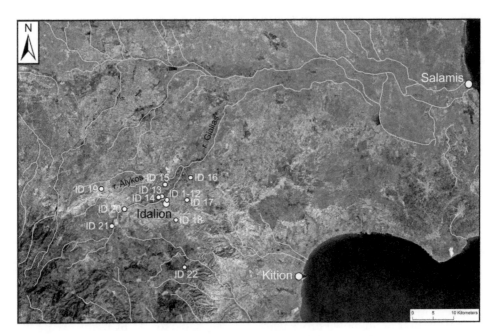

Figure 7.6: Map indicating sites identified by Ulbrich (2008: Plate 34) as urban and peri-urban sanctuaries of Idalion (Nos. ID 1–ID 22). Digital geological data from the Cyprus Geological Survey Department.

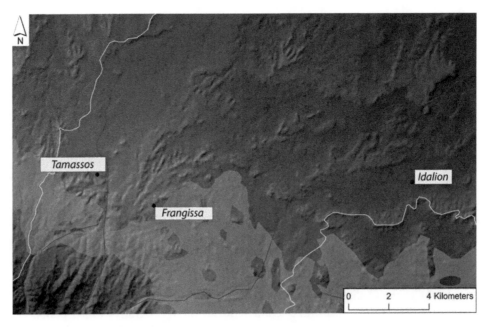

Figure 7.7: Map indicating the site of Frangissa between Tamassos and Idalion. Digital geological data from the Cyprus Geological Survey Department.

These two inscriptions record the act of dedication of two statuettes in the seventeenth and thirtieth years of Milkyaton, king of "Kition and Idalion," testifying to the potential inclusion of this area within the kingdom (Satraki 2012: 329).

Just a few decades before the abolition of the Cypriot city-kingdoms by Ptolemy Soter (finalized by the year 310 BCE), the central part of Cyprus merged with the coastal region of Kition, extending perhaps from the Pentaskhinos River to the area of Pyla. Every single royal inscription that mentions kings Baalmilk I, Ozibaal, Baalmilk II, Milkyaton, and Pummayaton, however, invariably reproduces that same royal title: king of "Kition and Idalion," bearing testimony to the fact that the royal dynasty of Kition had wisely acknowledged the deeply rooted necessity of the existence of Idalion as a regional center. It is no coincidence that five royal inscriptions were dedicated to the sanctuary of Apollo at Idalion (Yon 2004: Nos. 45, 68, 69, 180, 181), while only one was found at Kition (Yon 2004: No. 1144). The regional center at Idalion remained to the end of the fourth century BCE a robust focal point of territorial organization within central Cyprus.

Epilogue

As stated at the beginning of the paper, the aim was to identify the processes that led to the emergence and the geopolitical development of the Iron Age polity of Idalion. Considering that only a small part of the excavated archaeological record from Idalion itself has been published, this can be considered a preliminary interpretation of the issues pertaining to the formation of this inland city-kingdom. It is hoped, however, that the paper has opened up a new reading of the available (that is, published) archaeological record and has also added a new dimension to the study of the material culture of the ancient city, through the spectrum of historicity.

Acknowledgments

I am most grateful for the opportunity I was given in the context of this conference to focus on the territory of Alambra and Idalion, using it as a case study for approaching a region and its idiosyncrasies in order to investigate the geopolitical organization of Cyprus during the Late Bronze Age and Iron Age periods. The choice of case study was guided by my strong wish to pay homage to the Cornell archaeological mission, which, several decades ago, lovingly and respectfully explored Alambra—both ancient and new. This paper is dedicated to Professor John E. Coleman and his Cornell team of students, who revealed, documented, and preserved the high antiquity of my topos that continues to bare its ancient name today.

I wish to express my deepest gratitude to Sturt Manning and his team of students and also to the organizers of this conference, Katie Kearns and Jeff Leon, for their kind invitation to participate in this inspiring gathering. I would also like to thank Vassilis Trigkas, who prepared the maps for this paper, and Artemis Georgiou for reading early drafts of the text and for providing constructive criticism.

References

Agapiou, A. 2010. Τοπογραφία θέσεων της ευρύτερης περιοχής Πάφου, κατά την 3η και 2η χιλιετία π.Χ., και μελέτη της πορείας της αστικοποίησης, με την υποστήριξη Συστημάτων Γεωγραφικών Πληροφοριών. Unpublished MA dissertation, University of Cyprus.

Åström, P. 1986. Hala Sultan Tekke: An international harbour town of the Late Cypriot Bronze Age. *Opuscula Atheniensia* 16.1: 7017.

Brown, M. 2013. Waterways and the political geography of south-east Cyprus in the second millennium BC. *Annual of the British School at Athens* 108: 121–136.

Cadogan, G. 1996. Maroni: Change in Late Bronze Age Cyprus. In P. Åström and E. Herscher (eds.), *Late Bronze Age Settlement in Cyprus: Function and Relationships*, 15–22. Studies in Mediterranean Archaeology 126. Jonsered, Sweden: Paul Åströms Förlag.

Catling, H.W. 1982. The ancient topography of the Yialias Valley. *Report of the Department of Antiquities, Cyprus*: 227–236.

Coleman, J.E, J.A. Barlow, M.K. Mogelonsky, and K.S. Schaar. 1996. *Alambra: A Middle Bronze Age Settlement in Cyprus*. Studies in Mediterranean Archaeology 118. Jonsered, Sweden: Paul Åströms Förlag.

Crewe, L. 2007. *Early Enkomi: Regionalism, Trade, and Society at the Beginning of the Late Bronze Age on Cyprus*. British Archaeological Report Series 1706. Oxford: Archaeopress.

Della Dora, V., and T.S. Terkenli. 2012. Cultural geographies. In I. Vogiatzakis (ed.), *Mediterranean Mountain Environments*, 137–158. West Sussex: Wiley-Blackwell.

Devillers, B., M. Brown, and C. Morhange. 2015. Paleo-environmental evolution of the Larnaca Salt Lakes (Cyprus) and the relationship to second millennium BC settlement. *Journal of Archaeological Science, Report* 1: 73–80.

Devillers, B., P. Gaber, and N. Lecuyer. 2004. Notes on the Ayios Sozomenos Bronze Age settlement (Lefkosia District): Recent palaeoenvironmental and archaeological finds. *Report of the Department of Antiquities, Cyprus*: 85–92.

de Polignac, F. 1984. *La naissance de la cité grecque*. Paris: Éditions La Découverte.

Edgerton, W.F., and J.A. Wilson. 1936. *Historical Records of Ramesses III: The Texts in Medinet Habu*. Studies in Ancient Oriental Civilization 12. Chicago: University of Chicago Press.

Fourrier, S. 2002. Les territoires des royaumes chypriotes archaïques: Une esquisse de géographie historique. *Cahier du Centre d'Études Chypriotes* 32: 135–146.

Frankel, D. 2009. What do we mean by "regionalism"? In I. Hein (ed.), *The Formation of Cyprus in the 2nd Millennium B.C. Studies in Regionalism during the Middle and Late Bronze Age*, 16–25. Vienna: Verlag der Österreichischen Akademie der Wissenschaften.

Georgiou, A. 2011. The settlement histories of Cyprus at the opening of the twelfth century BC. *Cahier du Centre d'Études Chypriotes* 41: 109–131.

Georgiou, G. 2006. Η τοπογραφία της ανθρώπινης εγκατάστασης στην Κύπρο κατά την Πρώιμη και Μέση Εποχή του Χαλκού. Unpublished PhD dissertation, University of Cyprus.

Georgiou, G. 2008. The settlement at Alambra-*Mouttes* revisited. *Report of the Department of Antiquities, Cyprus*: 133–143.

Georgiou, G. 2011. The central part of Cyprus during Middle Cypriot III to late Cypriot IA period. In A. Demetriou (ed.), *Πρακτικά του Τέταρτου Διεθνούς Κυπρολογικού Συνεδρίου*, vol. Α΄2, 477–483. Nicosia: The A.G. Leventis Foundation.

Gjerstad, E., J. Lindros, E. Sjöqvist, and A. Westholm. 1935. *The Swedish Cyprus Expedition. Finds and Results of the Excavations in Cyprus 1927–1931, Vol. II, Text and Plates*. Stockholm: The Swedish Cyprus Expedition.

Gjerstad, E. 1944. The colonization of Cyprus in Greek legend. *Opuscula Archaeologia* 3: 107–123.

Hadjicosti, M. 1991. The Late Bronze Age Tomb 2 from Mathiatis (New perspectives for the Mathiatis region). *Report of the Department of Antiquities, Cyprus*: 75–91.

Hadjicosti, M. 1997. The kingdom of Idalion in the light of new evidence. *Bulletin of the American Schools of Oriental Research* 308: 49–61.

Hadjicosti, M. 1999. Idalion before the Phoenicians: The archaeological evidence and its topographical distribution. In M. Iacovou and D. Michaelides (eds.), *Cyprus: The Historicity of the Geometric Horizon*, 35–54. Nicosia: Archaeological Research Unit, University of Cyprus.

Hadjisavvas, S. 1996. Alassa: A regional centre of Alasia? In P. Åström and E. Herscher (eds.), *Late Bronze Age Settlement in Cyprus: Function and Relationship*, 23–38. Studies in Mediterranean Archaeology PB 126. Jonsered, Sweden: Paul Åströms Förlag.

Iacovou, M. 2007. Site size estimates and the diversity factor in Late Cypriot settlement histories. *Bulletin of the American Schools of Oriental Research* 348: 1–23.

Iacovou, M. 2008a. Cyprus: From migration to hellenisation. In G.R. Tsetskhladze (ed.), *Greek Colonization. An Account of Greek Colonies and Other Settlements Overseas, Vol. II*, 219–288. Leiden and Boston: Brill.

Iacovou, M. 2008b. Cultural and political configurations in Iron Age Cyprus: The sequel to a proto-historic episode. *American Journal of Archaeology* 112: 625–657.

Iacovou, M. 2013. The political geography of Iron Age Cyprus: The Cypriot syllabary as a royal signature. In P.M. Steele (ed.), *Syllabic Writing on Cyprus and its Context*, 133–152. Cambridge: Cambridge University Press.

Iacovou, M. 2014. Political economies and landscape transformations: The case of ancient Paphos. In J.M. Webb (eds.), *Structure, Measurement, and Meaning: Studies on Prehistoric Cyprus in Honour of David Frankel*, 161–174. Studies in Mediterranean Archaeology 143. Uppsala, Sweden: Åströms Förlag.

Iacovou, M., J.M. Webb, E.J. Peltenburg, and D. Frankel. 2008. Chypre: Des premières communautés néolithiques à l'émergence de l'urbanisme. *Études Balkaniques, Cahiers Pierre Belon* 15: 277–293.

Karouzis, G. 2000. Σύγχρονη γεωγραφία της Κύπρου. Τόμος 5. Γεωγραφικές περιφέρειες της Κύπρου. Nicosia: Selas.

Kassianidou, V. 2012. The origin and use of metals in Iron Age Cyprus. In M. Iacovou (ed.), *Cyprus and the Aegean in the Early Iron Age: The Legacy of Nicolas Coldstream*, 229–259. Nicosia: Bank of Cyprus Cultural Foundation.

Knapp, A.B. 1997. *The Archaeology of Late Bronze Age Cypriot Society: The Study of Settlement, Survey, and Landscape*. Occasional Paper Series No. 4. Glasgow: University of Glasgow.

Knapp, A.B. 2008. *Prehistoric and Protohistoric Cyprus: Identity, Insularity, and Connectivity*. Oxford: Oxford University Press.

Leonard, A. 2000. The Larnaka Hinterland Project: A preliminary report on the 1997 and 1998 seasons. *Report of the Department of Antiquities, Cyprus*: 117–146.

Manning, S.W., G.M. Andreou, K.D. Fischer, P. Gerard-Little, C. Kearns, J.F. Leon, D.A. Sewell, and T.M. Urban. 2014. Becoming urban: Investigating the anatomy of the Late Bronze Age complex, Maroni, Cyprus. *Journal of Mediterranean Archaeology* 27.1: 3–32.

Markou, F. 2013. Θέσεις και χρήσεις της υδρολογικής λεκάνης των ποταμών Τρέμιθου και Πούζη από την Πρώιμη Κυπριακή Χαλκοκρατία ως τη Ρωμαϊκή περίοδο. Επιφανειακή και αρχειακή έρευνα. Unpublished MA thesis, University of Cyprus.

Masson, O. 1983. *Les inscriptions chypriotes syllabiques: Recueil critique et commenté*. Études chypriotes I, 2nd ed. Paris: De Boccard.

Negbi, O. 1986. The climax of urban development in Bronze Age Cyprus. *Report of the Department of Antiquities, Cyprus*: 97-121.

Overbeck, J.C., and S. Swiny. 1972. *Two Cypriot Bronze Age Sites at Kafkallia (Dhali)*. Studies in Mediterranean Archaeology 33. Göteborg, Sweden: Paul Åströms Förlag.

Papantoniou, G. 2012. *Religion and Social Transformations in Cyprus: From the Cypriot Basileis to the Hellenistic Strategos*. Leiden: Brill.

Peltenburg, E.J. 1996. From isolation to state formation in Cyprus, c. 3500–1500 B.C. In V. Karageorghis and D. Michaelides (eds.), *The Development of the Cypriot Economy from the Prehistoric Period to the Present Day*, 17–44. Nicosia: University of Cyprus and Bank of Cyprus.

Peltenburg, E.J., and M. Iacovou. 2012. Crete and Cyprus: Contrasting political configurations. In G. Cadogan and M. Iacovou (eds.), *Parallel Lives: Ancient Island Societies in Crete and Cyprus. Proceedings of the Conference in Nicosia Organized by the British School at Athens, the University of Crete, and the University of Cyprus in November–December 2006*, 345–363. London: British School at Athens.

Pilides, D. 2017. Η κεντρική Κύπρος στην Ύστερη Εποχή του Χαλκού: οι ανασκαφές στον Άγιο Σωζόμενο. In Ν. Παπαδημητρίου and Μ. Τόλη (eds), *Αρχαία Κύπρος. Πρόσφατες εξελίξεις στην αρχαιολογία της ανατολικής Μεσογείου*, 93-134. Athens: Museum of Cycladic Art.

Satraki, A. 2008. Manifestations of royalty in Cypriot sculpture. In G. Papantoniou (ed.), *Postgraduate Cypriot Archaeology 2005: Proceedings of the Fifth Annual Meeting of young researchers on*

Cypriot Archaeology, Trinity College Dublin, 2005, 27–35. British Archaeological Report International Series 1803. Oxford: Archaeopress.

Satraki, A. 2012. *Κύπριοι Βασιλείς από τον Κόσμασο μέχρι το Νικοκρέοντα: η πολιτειακή οργάνωση της αρχαίας Κύπρου από την Ύστερη Εποχή του Χαλκού μέχρι το τέλος της Κυπροκλασικής περιόδου με βάση τα αρχαιολογικά δεδομένα.* Arheognosia 9. Athens: University of Athens.

Satraki, A. 2013. The iconography of basileis in Archaic and Classical Cyprus: Manifestations of royal power in the visual record. *Bulletin of the American Schools of Oriental Research* 370: 123–144.

Schulte-Campbell, C.C. 1989. A Late Cypriot IIC tomb: Idalion tomb 1.76. In L.E. Stager and A.M. Walker (eds.), *American Expedition to Idalion, Cyprus, 1973–1980*, 119–166. Oriental Institute Communications 24. Chicago: The Oriental Institute of the University of Chicago.

Sneddon, A. 2015. Revisiting Alambra *Mouttes*: Defining the spatial configuration and social relations of a prehistoric Bronze Age settlement in Cyprus. *Journal of Mediterranean Archaeology* 28.2: 141–170.

Snodgrass, A.M. 1994. Gains, losses, and survivals: What we can infer for the eleventh century B.C. In V. Karageorghis (ed.), *Proceedings of the International Symposium Cyprus in the 11th Century B.C.*, 167–173. Nicosia: The A.G. Leventis Foundation.

South, A. 1996. Kalavasos-*Ayios Dhimitrios* and the organization of Late Bronze Age Cyprus. In P. Åström and E. Herscher (eds.), *Late Bronze Age Settlement in Cyprus: Function and Relationships*, 39–49. Studies in Mediterranean Archaeology 126. Jonsered, Sweden: Paul Åströms Förlag.

South, A. 2002. Late Bronze Age settlement patterns in southern Cyprus: The first kingdoms. *Cahier du Centre d'Études Chypriotes* 32: 59–72.

Sznycer, M. 2004. Idalion: Capital économique des rois phéniciens de Kition et d'Idalion. *Cahier du Centre d'Études Chypriotes* 34: 85–100.

Ulbrich, A. 2008. *Kypris: Heiligtümer und Kulte weiblicher Gottheiten auf Zypern in der kyproarchaischen und kyproklassichen Epoche (Königszeit).* Alter Orient und Altes Testament 44, Munich: Ugarit-Verlag.

Webb, J.M. 1999. *Ritual Architecture, Iconography, and Practice in Late Bronze Age Cyprus.* Studies in Mediterranean Archaeology 75. Jonsered, Sweden: Paul Åströms Förlag.

Webb, J.M., and D. Frankel. 1994. Making an impression: Storage and surplus finance in Late Bronze Age Cyprus. *Journal of Mediterranean Archaeology* 7.1: 5–26.

Webb, J.M., and D. Frankel. 2013. Cultural regionalism and divergent social trajectories in Early Bronze Age Cyprus. *American Journal of Archaeology* 117.1: 59–81.

Yon, M. 2004. *Kition dans les textes: Testimonia littéraires et épigraphiques et corpus des inscriptions. Kition-Bamboula 5.* Paris: Editions Recherche sur les civilisations.

8

The Archaeology of the North Coast of Cyprus

The Evidence from Lapithos

STELLA DIAKOU

Introduction

The Early Iron Age in Cyprus is known almost exclusively through cemeteries and tombs. Lapithos, on the north coast of the island (Figure 8.1), is no exception to this general rule; archaeological fieldwork during the end of the nineteenth and the first half of the twentieth centuries revealed extensive cemeteries and groups of tombs dating to the Early and Middle Bronze Age (ca. 2250–1750/1700 BCE) and the Cypro-Geometric (CG) period (ca. 1050–750 BCE).

Only one settlement has been identified and excavated in Lapithos: the Swedish Cyprus Expedition (SCE) uncovered a Neolithic settlement at the end of the 1920s at the locality *Plakes* (also called *Alonia ton Plakon*; Gjerstad *et al.* 1934: 13–33). Catling's surface survey in the 1950s (Catling 1962; 1971; 1973; 1975) identified a number of possible settlement sites, as well as a significant number of burial sites, ranging in date from the Neolithic to the Hellenistic periods. Nonetheless, because the collected material—in particular anything post–Bronze Age—was not published or otherwise analyzed (cf. Georgiou 2006), these identifications remain tentative. This almost complete absence of excavated settlements is only one of the problems embedded in the archaeology of the north coast in general and of Lapithos in particular.

The Turkish invasion of 1974 and the resulting occupation of approximately the northern half of Cyprus put an end to all legal archaeological projects in that region. Under UNESCO conventions, no legal archaeological work can be carried out in the occupied area (UNESCO 1957: 44; Davis 2014: 41).[1] This "politically

---

1. "VI.32. In the event of armed conflict, any Member State occupying the territory of another State should refrain from carrying out archaeological excavations in the occupied territory. In the event of chance finds being made, particularly during military works, the occupying Power should take all possible measures to protect these finds, which should be handed over, on the termination of hostilities, to the competent authorities of the territory previously occupied, together with all documentation relating thereto" (UNESCO 1957: 44).

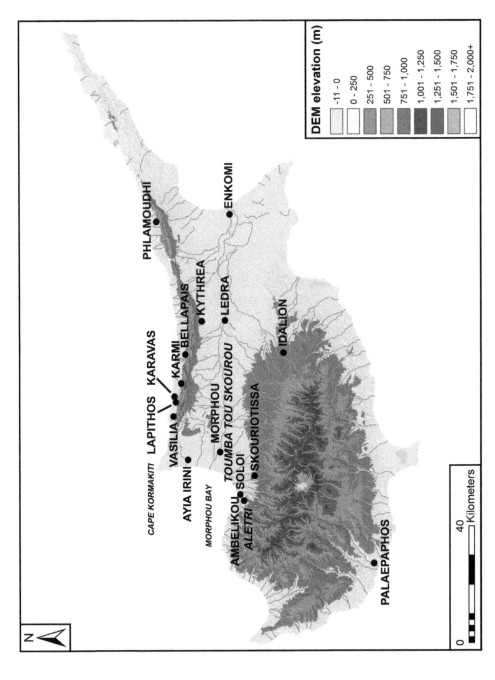

Figure 8.1: Major sites and localities mentioned in text. Created by C. Kearns; basemap provided by the Geological Survey Department of Cyprus.

imposed situation" (Knapp 2013: 31) has created an imbalance and a disparity not only in active fieldwork but also in synthetic and interpretive studies of the ancient society of Cyprus. Even though the north coast was once considered "one of the richest areas on the island since the earliest human occupation" (Herscher 1978: 1), its archaeology, particularly post-1974, has remained underexplored or unknown (if we consider illegal and/or unpublished excavations). The last ten years have seen a renewed interest in the archaeology of the north coast due to the efforts of archaeologists to "revisit" old excavations and to look at material under new light (see for example Smith 2008a; 2008b; Webb 2016; 2017; Webb and Frankel 2010; 2013a; 2013b; Webb et al. 2009).

An additional concern hampers our understanding of the archaeology of Lapithos and in particular that of the later, post-prehistoric periods: there is a puzzling absence of maps showing the exact locations of excavated cemeteries. The archaeological expeditions at Lapithos took place in the early part of the twentieth century, yet they failed to illustrate and to discuss the relationships between the excavated cemeteries themselves, both spatially and temporally. In addition to the unpublished state of the majority of the excavated material, the finds, dispersed in museums worldwide, have not been associated with their locational context and have never been discussed as complete burial assemblages (cf. Diakou 2013).

In an effort to remedy this archaeological disparity, this paper explores the archaeology of the north coast of Cyprus during the Bronze and Early Iron Ages. Using Lapithos as a case study, this analysis reconstructs the socio-political and economic landscape of the region. This is achieved with use of new sets of spatial data and the creation of comprehensive maps showing the excavated cemeteries of Lapithos. The study area corresponds to the municipality of Lapithos as it was defined until 1974. The name *Lapithos* denotes an Iron Age "kingdom" or polity (cf. Iacovou 2013b: 16n2) known through coins from the end of the sixth century BCE (Satraki 2012: 307–309) and mentioned in literary texts describing the events of the abolition of the Cypriot kingdoms by Ptolemy I Soter at the end of the fourth century BCE (Diod. Sic. 19.79.4). The Iron Age polity of Lapithos, however, remains archaeologically and historically elusive (Iacovou 2013b: 16, 27, 30, 31). With the help of maps, photographs, and other archival documents, it is possible to reconstruct the ancient topography of a region now lost and inaccessible, both because of the passage of time and the political conditions.

Taking a landscape approach, this paper uses new sets of spatial data and attempts to provide a diachronic account of the history of the site of Lapithos. For the purposes of this analysis, I define *landscape* not only "as the backdrop against which archaeological remains are plotted" but also as the space that takes on a multitude of meanings and importance "by virtue of its being perceived, experienced, and contextualized by people" (Knapp and Ashmore 1999: 1). Within this context, a landscape approach is considered particularly useful in that it allows us to explore people's dynamic relationships "with the physical, social, and cultural dimensions of their environments across space and over time" (Anschuetz et al. 2001: 159; see also Van Dyke and Alcock 2003).

The goals of this discussion are threefold: to present the available sources for the study of the archaeology of Lapithos despite its current inaccessibility, to reconstruct the topography of Lapithos with an emphasis on the CG period, and finally, to explore diachronic changes in the landscape and their implications. It is argued that the development of such methodologies and the creation of new data can contribute much-needed resolution to the study of the archaeology of the north coast.

The Landscape of Lapithos

Lapithos sits on the northwest slopes of the Pentadaktylos, the Kyrenia mountain range that defines the north coast of Cyprus (Figure 8.1). The Pentadaktylos varies in altitude from 700 to 1024 m above sea level and extends from Panagra in the west to Eftakomi in the east. The northern slopes of the mountain range are steep and are characterized by ravines and gorges created by rivers flowing toward the sea. Between the mountain range and the sea to the north there is a narrow and fertile alluvial plain that reaches a maximum width of 5 km. Three passages through the range provide access to the rest of the island: at Panagra, ca. 9 km west of Lapithos, at Agirdha, ca. 12 km east of Lapithos, and at Akanthou, farther to the east (Figure 8.2).

The village of Lapithos is situated on the foothills below Kyparissovouno, the highest peak of the Pentadaktylos, and extends all the way to the coast (Figure 8.3). Lapithos is bordered by Vasilia to the west and by Karavas to the east (Figure 8.4). The villages of Larnakas Lapithou, Agridaki, and Sysklipos border Lapithos to the south and are located on the southern slopes of the Pentadaktylos. One of the two most important springs of the Pentadaktylos is in Lapithos; the second one is at Kythrea, on the southern slopes of the mountain range.

The Hilarion Limestone, which is located below the two villages, acts as the largest reservoir of water in the island. Both Lapithos and Kythrea owe their water abundance and fertility of soils to this formation (Myres 1940/45: 73; Christodou-

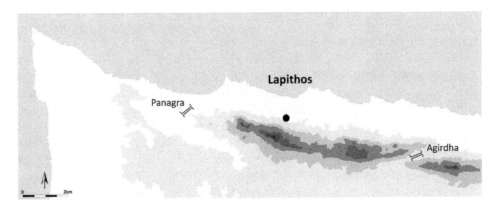

Figure 8.2: Map of northwest Cyprus showing location of Lapithos.

Figure 8.3: View of Lapithos on the north slopes of the Pentadaktylos Mountain. Photograph by the author.

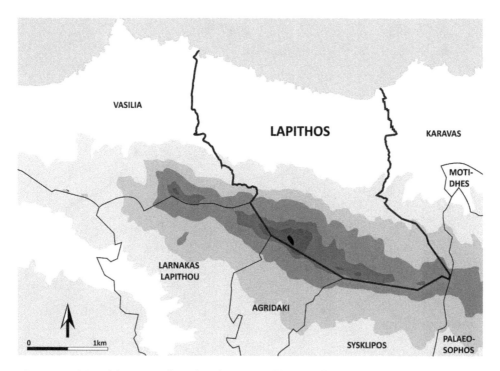

Figure 8.4: Map of the region of Lapithos showing neighboring villages.

lou 1959: 40, 118). Until 1974, when the demography and layout of the village were significantly altered, Lapithos consisted of six parishes, each developed around a church: *Ayia Anastasia* and *Ayia Paraskevi* in the upper village, *Timios Prodromos* and *Ayios Loukas* in the center, *Ayios Theodoros* to the west, and *Ayios Minas* (*Sphinarin*) to the east (Figure 8.5). Each parish not only had its own mayor, community council, and church board but also a distinct cemetery.

A seventh parish, the Turkish one, was located between the parishes of *Ayios Theororos* and *Ayios Loukas* and had its own mosque, school, and cemetery. The layout and growth of the village of Lapithos mirrors its particular landscape. The upper village is made up of rocky limestone plateaus and is characterized by dramatic changes in altitude and visibility. The most prominent plateau is the one in the center of Lapithos with the church of Ayia Anastasia, reaching a height of ca. 140 m above sea level.

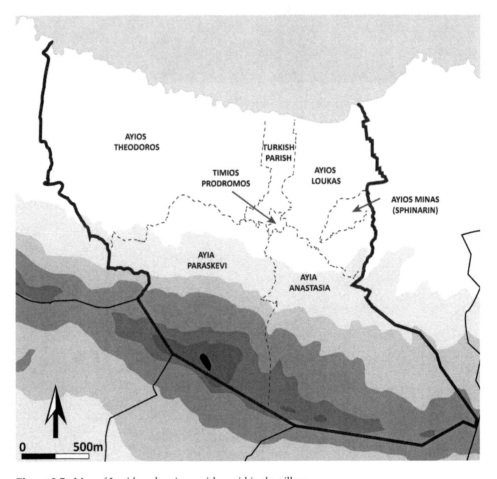

Figure 8.5: Map of Lapithos showing parishes within the village.

Archaeological Fieldwork at Lapithos

Lapithos attracted the interest of archaeologists before the end of the nineteenth century (Ohnefalsch-Richter 1893; Myres and Ohnefalsch-Richter 1899; Dalton 1900; 1906; Tatton-Brown 2001: 174; Merrillees 2009). The first organized excavations were carried out in 1913 by Myres and Markides on behalf of the Cyprus Museum Committee. Myres and Markides excavated Classical remains at *Lampousa* (Myres 1940/45: 74–78) as well as seventy-five tombs of the Early and Middle Bronze Age at *Vrysin tou Barba* (Myres 1940/45: 78–85, Plates 24–29) (Figure 8.6).

These excavations were only preliminarily published. Shortly afterwards, Markides excavated three tombs at the plateau of *Ayia Anastasia*, which contained both Late Cypriot (LC) and Early Iron Age layers (Markides 1916; Gjerstad 1926: 8). These excavations also lack proper recording, although the tombs were later reinvestigated by the Swedish Cyprus Expedition (SCE; Gjerstad *et al.* 1934: 162–163), and two of them were published by Pieridou (1966; 1972).

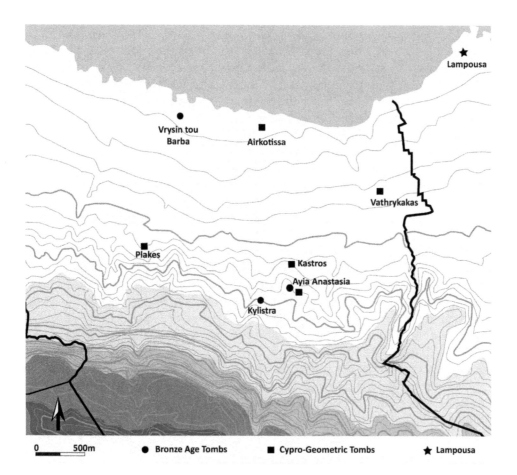

Figure 8.6: Map of Lapithos with excavated sites mentioned in the text.

The SCE worked at Lapithos in 1927–1928 and excavated tombs of the Bronze and Early Iron Ages. In particular, the Swedish team excavated twenty-three tombs of the Early and Middle Bronze Age at *Vrysin tou Barba* (Gjerstad *et al.* 1934: 33–162), two tombs of the Middle and Late Bronze Age at *Kylistra* (Gjerstad *et al.* 1934: 164–172), twenty-eight CG tombs at *Kastros* (Gjerstad *et al.* 1934: 172–264), and three CG tombs at *Plakes* (Gjerstad *et al.* 1934: 265–276). The excavations and finds were published shortly thereafter. In fact, Gjerstad extensively used the finds from Lapithos to create the typology of CG pottery (Gjerstad 1948; Adelman 1976: 48).

The year 1931 marked the beginning of the third and last systematic expedition at Lapithos. The Pennsylvania Cyprus Expedition (PCE) was directed by Hill, a former director of the American School of Classical Studies at Athens, and funded by the University of Pennsylvania Museum of Archaeology and Anthropology (Herscher 2007; Diakou 2016: 24). The expedition arrived in Lapithos in September 1931, only three years after the SCE, and within four months it had excavated sixty-five tombs of the Bronze and Iron Ages. In particular, the PCE excavated Early and Middle Bronze Age tombs at *Vrysin tou Barba* (Grace 1940; Herscher 1978), the same locality at which the SCE had previously excavated an extensive Bronze Age cemetery. In addition, they excavated two contemporary CG cemeteries, the so-called *Lower Geometric* cemetery, on the coast, at the locality *Airkotissa* (Donohoe 1992) and one in the center of the village, the so-called *Upper Geometric* or *Kato Kastros* cemetery (Diakou 2013). Despite the large number of tombs excavated at three separate cemeteries, the results of the PCE at Lapithos remained for the most part unpublished and unknown to the archaeological community.

The only exception is Pieridou's publication of Tomb 474 from the *Upper Geometric* cemetery, the so-called *Prostemenos* tomb (1965). Tomb 474 was the richest CG tomb excavated by the American team and, in accordance with the Antiquities Law of 1905 (Tsolakis 1997: 22–24), the only tomb awarded to the Cyprus Museum. In her publication, Pieridou (1965: 75n2) erroneously assigned the tomb to a site called *Prostemenos*: "According to Miss Grace's diary the site where this tomb was discovered is called 'prostemenos.'" Both the names *Upper Geometric* and *Prostemenos* appear on the title page of the field notebook, prompting the incorrect identification of the location of the tomb. The name *Prostemenos* (εμπρός + τέμενος), however, refers to a location southeast of the village of Lapithos, where the PCE excavated the scant remains of a sanctuary of the Classical period (Grace 1931/32: 157–184). Despite Pieridou's thorough ceramic analysis, Tomb 474 was taken out of its context and was not studied as part of the *Upper Geometric* cemetery. The publication by Pieridou, however important, did not succeed in acknowledging the existence of two additional extensive Geometric cemeteries but treated Tomb 474 as an isolated burial assemblage (Donohoe 1992: 11n14).

Sources for the Study of the Archaeology of Lapithos

Despite these excavations as well as additional rescue work by the Department of Antiquities of Cyprus (Table 8.1), the tomb assemblages from Lapithos have not been associated with their locational context and as such cannot be discussed in a meaningful way.

Nonetheless, there are a number of sources available for the study of the archaeology of Lapithos, and their employment allows for the creation of new spatial data, the construction of maps, and the identification of the excavated cemeteries in order to explore the sociopolitical and economic environment of this region.

Table 8.1: Archaeological fieldwork at Lapithos with relevant publications

Location	Excavators	Year of excavation	Type of site	Chronology	Publication
Ayia Anastasia	M. Markides	1914; 1915; 1917	Necropolis: 3 tombs T. 501–503	Late Bronze Age and Cypro-Geometric	Markides 1916
	SCE	1927–1928		Late Bronze Age and Cypro-Geometric	Gjerstad *et al.* 1934: 162–164 Pieridou 1966 (T. 502) Pieridou 1972 (T. 503)
Kastros	SCE	1927–1928	Necropolis: 28 tombs T. 401–429	Cypro-Geometric	Gjerstad *et al.* 1934: 172–264
Kylistra	SCE	1927–1928	Necropolis: 2 tombs T. 701–702	Middle and Late Bronze Age	Gjerstad *et al.* 1934: 164–172
Lampousa	J. L. Myres and M. Markides	1913	Acropolis?		Myres 1940/45: 72–78
Lower Geometric	PCE	1931	Necropolis: 20 tombs T. 451–470	Cypro-Geometric	Unpublished See Donohoe 1992
Plakes/ Alonia ton Plakon	SCE	1927–1928	Settlement	Neolithic/ Chalcolithic?	Gjerstad *et al.* 1934: 13–33
	SCE	1927–1928	Necropolis: 3 tombs T. 601–603	Cypro-Geometric	Gjerstad *et al.* 1934: 265–276
Prostemenos	PCE	1931–1932	Sanctuary	Archaic/ Classical?	Unpublished See Grace 1931/32, 157–184
Upper Geometric	PCE	1931	Necropolis: 16 tombs T. 471–486	Cypro-Geometric	Unpublished See Diakou 2013 Pieridou 1965 (T. 474)
Vathyrkakas	Department of Antiquities	1950s	Necropolis: 4 tombs	Cypro-Geometric	Pieridou 1964
Vrysin tou Barba	J. L. Myres and M. Markides	1913; 1917	Necropolis: 75 tombs	Early and Middle Bronze Age	Myres 1940/45: 78–85
	SCE	1927–1928	Necropolis: 23 tombs	Early and Middle Bronze Age	Gjerstad *et al.* 1934: 33–162

(*Continued*)

Table 8.1:—*cont.*

Location	Excavators	Year of excavation	Type of site	Chronology	Publication
	PCE	1931	Necropolis: 38 tombs T. 801–838	Early and Middle Bronze Age	Unpublished See Herscher 1978 Grace 1940 (T. 806A)
Unknown	M. Ohnefalsch-Richter	—	Tomb	Early Graceo-Phoenician tomb with "late Mykenaean vases"	Ohnefalsch-Richter 1893: plate XCVIII: 1, 6, 9 Myres and Ohnefalsch-Richter 1899: 7–8
Unknown	Department of Antiquities	1973	Tombs	Cypro-Geometric	Unpublished See Nicolaou 1975/76: 45

The first source, the excavation records of the American expedition to Lapithos, is located in the archives of the University of Pennsylvania Museum of Archaeology and Anthropology (Ruwell 1984). In addition to excavation journals, there are detailed tomb plans, tomb photographs taken during the excavation, cemetery plans, and the excavation permits that Hill received. The second source is the excavation records of the SCE at the Museum of Mediterranean Antiquities (Medelhavsmuseet) in Stockholm. The Swedish team published two relevant maps: a contour map with the position of the excavated cemeteries (Gjerstad *et al.* 1934: Plan III.1) and a cemetery plan (Gjerstad *et al.* 1934: Plan V.2). The members of the SCE also took photographs, including both general views of the village and close-ups of the cemetery and the tombs. The third source consists of maps and photographs from the Department of Lands and Surveys of Cyprus, including (1) cadastral maps of 1918, (2) aerial photographs of the region of 1957 and 1963, (3) satellite images of 2003, and (4) a road map of Lapithos of 2004 created in collaboration with the Lapithos municipality. All these sources were integrated into ArcGIS software in order to create a basemap and to georeference in real space the cemeteries, surveyed sites, and specific plots of land. The decision to use ArcGIS stemmed first and foremost from the nature of the area under study. As an occupied region, where legal archaeological work is prohibited, it was considered imperative to use software that would permit the location of sites in real space regardless of issues of accessibility.[2]

---

2. While access in the occupied part of Cyprus is allowed since 2003, any archaeological work is prohibited under UNESCO conventions. For this reason, the author did not take new geospatial references on the identified cemeteries and used only archival sources for their identification.

The Bronze Age Evidence from Lapithos

The identification of the Bronze Age cemeteries of Lapithos is quite straightforward. The largest excavated cemetery is located on the coast of Lapithos at the locality *Vrysin tou Barba* (Figure 8.6), less than 2 km north of *Ayia Anastasia*. Nonetheless, out of the 136 excavated tombs (Keswani 2004: 188, Table 3.1), only half have been studied and only one-fifth of them have been properly published. The SCE also excavated two tombs of the Middle and Late Bronze Age at the locality of *Kylistra*, ca. 300 m southwest of *Ayia Anastasia*. The tombs are located by the side of the road leading from *Ayia Paraskevi* to *Kefalovryso* and were partially destroyed during its construction.

The Early and Middle Bronze Age is well represented at Lapithos with wealthy tombs at *Vrysin tou Barba* that cover the span from Early Cypriot (EC) II to the end of the Middle Cypriot (MC) period. In its earliest phase (EC II–IIIA) only 40 percent of the chambers contained metal artifacts, most commonly knives, hook-tang weapons, and pins (Keswani 2004: Table 4.11a; Webb and Frankel 2010: 204). At the transitional phase, EC IIIB/MC I, 74 percent of the chambers contained metal artifacts (Keswani 2004: Table 4.11b; Webb and Frankel 2010: 205), which increased to 96 percent during MC I–III (Keswani 2004: Table 4.11c), indicating an intensification of the metal consumption at a community-wide level (Keswani 2004: 67–69). During the final phase of use (MC I–III), imported objects, such as gold, silver, and faience ornaments also increase and are distributed more broadly throughout the cemetery. The distribution and types of metal artifacts suggest that the mortuary ritual was used as an arena for displaying, negotiating, affirming, and enhancing status and prestige (Keswani 2004: 71). The material culture associated with the tombs at *Vrysin tou Barba* (e.g., pottery, ceremonial vessels, metal artifacts, and imported objects) speaks for a wealthy society with (1) access to copper sources or to the networks of circulation of either raw materials and/or finished objects and (2) participation in the external trade networks (Webb *et al.* 2009: 251–252; Webb and Frankel 2013a: 76; 2013b: 220).

Following a dynamic Early and Middle Bronze Age, during which Lapithos became preeminent over other centers on the north coast (see below), the Late Bronze Age on the north coast is characterized by a significant decrease in the number of identifiable sites. The burial record at Lapithos diminishes dramatically, and the extensive cemetery at *Vrysin tou Barba* receives its last burials at the end of the Middle Bronze Age. A few Late Bronze Age burials were excavated at *Kylistra* and at *Ayia Anastasia* in the center of the village. This pattern of contraction is also evident in the survey evidence, not only in Lapithos but also on the north coast in general (Georgiou 2006: 415, Figure 11.5, 425–426, Table 11.2, 448–449; Webb *et al.* 2009: 254, Figure 4.46). The reduction of sites is observed already at the transition from the Middle to the Late Bronze Age and may be attributed either to decreased archaeological visibility or, more likely, to a decrease in population numbers and sites or even to a movement to another center.

Identifying the Cypro-Geometric Cemeteries

At the transition from the Late Bronze Age to the Geometric period, the mortuary record in Cyprus undergoes a dramatic change. During the eleventh century BCE cemeteries are established on new locations on the island (Iacovou 1994: 158; 1999: 148).

This significant topographical transformation provides the context in which we should evaluate the CG cemeteries of Lapithos. Contrary to the Bronze Age cemeteries, the majority of which are shown on the maps of the SCE, the locations of the CG cemeteries of Lapithos had not been securely identified. Nonetheless, this period constitutes the only chronological horizon with concrete evidence after the Early and Middle Bronze Age and before the Cypro-Archaic (CA) period, when the excavation record again becomes mute.

The location of the *Kastros* cemetery is discussed first because its positioning on the basemap was instrumental in the identification of the *Upper Geometric* cemetery. The toponym *Kastros* corresponds to the plateau on which the boys' school is built in the center of the village. Overlaying the map produced by the SCE on the basemap shows that the *Kastros* cemetery is located on top of the plateau, to the east of the school (Figure 8.7).

A street running east to west borders the cemetery to the south, whereas to the north is the edge of the *Kastros* plateau. Further to the south the *Kastros* plateau continues and reaches the base of the plateau of *Ayia Anastasia*, which looms 25 m above the present level of *Kastros* (Gjerstad *et al.* 1934: 173). The tombs are located almost directly north of the hotel built on the plateau of *Ayia Anastasia*.

The so-called *Upper Geometric* or *Kato Kastros* cemetery, excavated by the PCE, is also located in the center of the village. Neither of these names is mentioned in the gazetteer of toponyms for Cyprus (Christodoulou and Konstantinidis 1987), nor

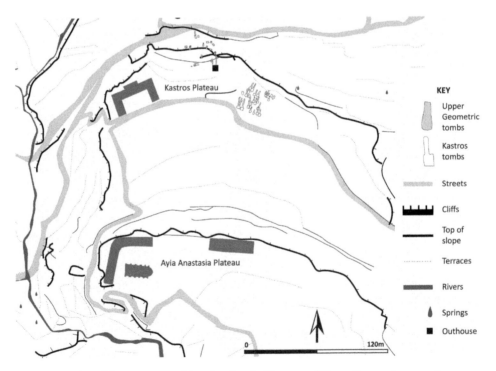

Figure 8.7: Plan of the center of Lapithos showing the *Kastros* and *Upper Geometric* cemeteries.

were they recognized as toponyms during interviews with the displaced inhabitants of Lapithos. Moreover, in the archival records of the American expedition there is, surprisingly, no direct reference to the Swedish excavations, which had taken place only three years earlier. It seems likely that these names were assigned by the excavators: in the case of *Kato Kastros*, the excavators wished to highlight that the tombs are located at the lower part of the *Kastros* plateau and, in the case of *Upper Geometric*, to distinguish it from the Geometric tombs excavated on the coast of Lapithos at a much lower elevation (see below). According to the excavation permits, Hill was allowed to excavate in the plots east of the boys' school. The first trenches were opened in plot 40 (Grace 1931/32: 9). Additional spatial references that helped in anchoring the tomb plan on the basemap were identified in the excavation journals. In particular, these notes made repeated references to the "outhouse"—the school's restrooms—when speaking about the orientation of the tombs (Grace 1931/32: 9, 12, 14). In addition, on the bottom right corner of the cemetery plan there is a rectangular building, the point of reference from which tombs were measured (Figure 8.8).

On the plan this structure is designated as "closets," another word for toilets, which was identified as the same "outhouse" of the school mentioned in the field notebooks. No such building was located in the cadastral maps. However, a promising building was discernible on the aerial photograph of 1963, which allowed the anchoring of the tomb plan northeast of the boys' school (Figure 8.7). The "outhouse" of the current school stands at the exact same location today. The evidence for the placement of the tombs at this location is strengthened by the fact that the tombs follow the cliffs and slopes of the plateau. Finally, the majority of the *Upper Geometric* tombs are indeed at a lower elevation (approximately 10m) than the *Kastros* tombs.

The next question to ponder is the spatial relationship of the two cemeteries. The only "primary source" regarding the relationship of the two cemeteries comes from Grace's unpublished report: "the latter group [*Upper Geometric*] formed part of a very extensive Iron Age cemetery, tombs of which have been discovered at various points from 1 km W of the village to 2 km E of it" (Grace 1937). It is likely that Grace refers to the *Kastros* tombs and possibly to the tombs excavated at *Ayia Anastasia*. Grace seems to consider the two cemeteries connected. It is not clear, however, whether her observation is based on the specific geographic location of the cemeteries or on the fact that the two cemeteries are largely contemporaneous. On the other hand, Donohoe (1992: 403–404), in her study of the *Lower Geometric* cemetery, takes a different approach, emphasizing the existence of "at least three and probably four distinct cemeteries" that were in use during the Early Iron Age, each associated with a separate community. It seems likely that Donohoe's conclusion is based on the available brief descriptions of the excavated cemeteries.

Plotting the two cemeteries on the map of Lapithos shows that they could in fact be part of the same extensive cemetery (Figure 8.7). The *Upper Geometric* tombs are located less than 30 m northwest of the *Kastros* tombs. Both cemeteries are located on the *Kastros* plateau, with the *Upper Geometric* tombs extending over its slopes. A group of tombs from the *Upper Geometric* cemetery is located on top

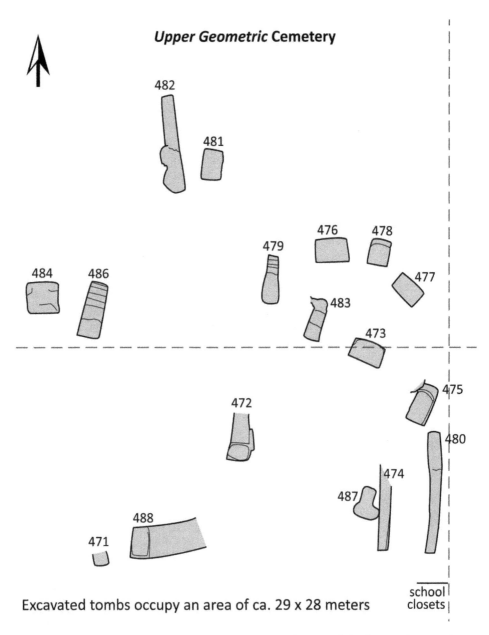

Figure 8.8: Plan of the *Upper Geometric* cemetery. Based on the original plan by Dorothy Hannah Cox, courtesy of the University of Pennsylvania Museum of Archaeology and Anthropology.

of the *Kastros* plateau, at the same elevation as the *Kastros* tombs, which are now covered by the enlargement of the school building. The rest of the tombs are located directly to the north and below the first cliff bordering the plateau. Access to the *Kastros* plateau was from the west, possibly through the same path that leads to the plateau today. A river also runs to the west of the plateau, in the gorge created by the foothills of the Pentadaktylos. Following the river from that site, one reaches the sea. It is unclear how comprehensive the investigation in the area between the two cemeteries was. It should be emphasized here that the school building, which goes back to the early twentieth century, and in particular the outhouse and the courtyard, are occupying the area to this date, meaning that no excavation could take place there. Nonetheless, taking into account references about other tombs in the field notebooks (Grace 1931/32: 9), it is most likely that there are additional tombs in the area between the two cemeteries.

These topographical observations indicate that the *Upper Geometric* and *Kastros* cemeteries, the two most extensive and richest CG cemeteries in Lapithos, are part of the same cemetery and, as such, they should be studied together. Adding up to a total of forty-eight chamber tombs with multiple burials spanning the entire CG period, their analysis provides a window into the Early Iron Age society of Lapithos, the different communities that comprise it, differential access to wealth, and status variations. The distribution of the tombs and the changes in elevation reveal different clusters within the cemetery that may reflect chronological patterns as well as social aspects. The dispersal of the tombs and their relative dating (Diakou 2013: 69–70) show that the earliest tombs are at the top of the plateau. After CG II the cemetery expanded from the top of the plateau to the slopes. In addition, the spatial ordering of the tombs is not random. The analysis of the tombs and finds (Diakou 2013) suggests that the primary and most prominent part of the cemetery is the one on top of the plateau, with the richest and earliest tombs.

The other excavated CG burial sites (Figure 8.6) consist of spatially distinct groups of tombs, and thus their identification is more straightforward. Three tombs with Late Bronze Age and Early Iron Age layers were excavated on the plateau of *Ayia Anastasia*. Tomb 502 preserves the only known instance of a tomb opened in LC IIC/IIIA and reused in CG IA (Pieridou 1966; Georgiadou 2012: 87). Tomb 503 preserves the very unusual phenomenon of a LC IIIB tomb reused from CG IA onward (Pieridou 1972; Iacovou 1994: 152). Despite the lack of a plan, the plateau of *Ayia Anastasia* is marked by the presence of the church with the same name and is visible from nearly all vantage points within the village. During the reinvestigation of the plateau by the SCE, the tombs were located at the southern part of the plateau, among the houses, and close to the road leading up to it (Gjerstad *et al.* 1934: 164–165). The *Lower Geometric* cemetery is located close to the sea, about 1 km east of the prehistoric tombs excavated at *Vrysin tou Barba* and ca. 1.6 km north of *Ayia Anastasia* at the locality *Airkotissa*. This cemetery consists of much poorer tomb assemblages and seems to represent a distinct community of CG Lapithos. Three tombs were excavated by the Swedish team at the locality *Plakes* in the western part of the village, ca. 1.4 km west of *Ayia Anastasia*. The tombs disturb the remains of a Neolithic settlement, also excavated by the SCE. In the 1950s the Department of Antiquities excavated four Early Iron Age tombs at the locality Karavas *Vathyrkakas* (Megaw 1954: 173). The tombs, which were later published by Pieridou (1964), located between the villages of Karavas and Lapithos to the east of the Vathyrkakas River, form yet another distinct cemetery.

Geometric society on Cyprus is characterized by striking similarities in the mortuary record across the island (Iacovou 1999: 148; 2005: 131; Janes

2013: 325): the use of extramural cemeteries with chamber tombs, the preference for inhumation, the presence of secondary burials in large vessels, and the types of grave goods are all features observed in contemporary cemeteries, both at Lapithos and elsewhere on the island. The homogeneous character of the CG culture is also visible in pottery production and specifically in the development of the White Painted ware, as shapes and decorative motifs are repeated and found throughout the island (Iacovou 1994: 159; 1999: 148–149), albeit in regional production centers (Georgiadou 2013).

Within this context, the analysis of the tombs and finds from the Lapithos cemeteries, and in particular of the *Upper Geometric* cemetery (Diakou 2013), highlights a society with differential access to wealth and/or resources. Despite the complex and imperfect nature of the dataset and the fact that wealth variations in a mortuary context are not a direct reflection of the society of the living, such variations in mortuary ritual may well be attributed to wealth and status distinctions and may therefore reflect social asymmetries. In fact, two sets of artifacts were distinguished among the *Kastros* tombs as belonging to individuals holding or assigned a special status. Set A consisted of gold headdresses, jewelry, and pins made of precious materials, and Set B consisted of iron *obeloi* (spits used for roasting meat) (Karageorghis 1974; Åström *et al.* 1986; Strøm 1992; Iacovou 2013a: 138–140; 2013b: 17), tools, and bronze artifacts. The same sets of artifacts were found at the richest tombs at Palaepaphos *Skales* (Karageorghis 1983), highlighting the existence of a shared system of prestige symbolism and ideology. The analysis of artifacts indicates social differentiation that is expressed in the deposition of prestige items in tombs. At the same time, there is a wide range in the distribution of wealth in the tombs, varying from tombs that may represent the "aristocracy" of the society, such as some of the Kastros tombs (Coldstream 1989; Steel 1993: 205), and tombs that may have belonged to "humble fishermen," such as those found in the *Lower Geometric* cemetery (Donohoe 1992: 403–406).

The Topography of CG Lapithos

Once we move beyond the mortuary landscape, the exploration of the topography of CG Lapithos remains incomplete without a discussion of possible habitation sites. First, it should be emphasized that with the exception of the *Lower Geometric* cemetery, which is contemporary to the other CG cemeteries of Lapithos (Donohoe 1992: 90–92), the excavated cemeteries are located in the southern part of the village, on the lower foothills of the Pentadaktylos. The cemeteries occupy the highest part of the village, overlooking the coastal plain, without encroaching on flat agricultural land. The landscape of Lapithos with its abundant water sources would allow for the development of multiple communities, something evident in the layout and recent history of the village. In the absence of any excavated contemporary settlements, we may postulate that each cemetery corresponded to a different community, as is suggested by the location of the *Lower Geometric* cemetery, at a significant distance from the other cemeteries. Alternatively, the cemeteries in the southern part of the village are close enough to one another that they may correspond to a single large community. The physical separation of the cemeteries in this case may be attributed to a variety of issues such as social position or landholding.

The character of the prominent plateau of *Ayia Anastasia* in the central part of the village remains undefined and problematic (Figure 8.7). The size of the plateau is estimated to be around 2.5 ha. It is naturally defended, and its north and northwest sides are characterized by vertical rock formations, whereas its south and east sides, a continuation of the Pentadaktylos foothills, are smoother. A river runs to the west of the plateau, providing access from the southwest. The Cyprus Survey identified the plateau as a Bronze Age and Early Iron Age cemetery (Catling 1962). The question is whether it is possible to propose the existence of a settlement on the plateau or whether we should hypothesize the presence of another extensive cemetery. There are a number of issues with both propositions. On the one hand, taking into account the clear separation of habitation and burial sites that emerged during the Early Iron Age period, the presence of CG tombs on the plateau of *Ayia Anastasia* make any hypothesis of CG settlement at the same location unlikely. If we reconstruct the plateau of *Ayia Anastasia* as another CG cemetery, then this fits well with the other CG cemeteries of Lapithos along the southern border of the village. In this case, the contemporary settlement of Lapithos should be sought elsewhere. On the other hand, CG burial grounds are established as a rule on new locations (Iacovou 1999: 148). This transformation is attested across all CG sites on the island and is considered a primary feature of the CG period (Janes 2008: 326). This shift in practice would potentially make the identification of *Ayia Anastasia* as both a Bronze Age and an Early Iron Age cemetery problematic. One may suggest that the excavated CG tombs on the plateau are not part of a cemetery but are isolated and peculiar instances. Is it possible that the existence of these tombs points to the special nature of the plateau? Might we reconstruct a Late Bronze Age settlement on *Ayia Anastasia* with intramural burials, one whose tombs were reused, in order to establish and emphasize continuity between the Late Bronze Age and the CG periods?

Another candidate for the location of a CG settlement, and possibly the site of the later Iron Age polity, is *Lampousa* (Figure 8.6). The location of *Lampousa* on the coast and its diachronic importance evidenced by remains and finds dating from the Bronze Age to the Byzantine period (Nicolaou 1976) make it a suitable candidate. Myres (1940/45: 73) identified the location of the Iron Age kingdom of Lapithos with *Lampousa* and suggested that the excavated cemeteries in the village of Lapithos are to be associated with it. Nonetheless, the investigation of the so-called acropolis in 1913 (Myres 1940/45) and of the Troulli hill to the east of the acropolis in 1915 (Markides 1916) produced very little in the way of stratified remains because of earlier extensive quarrying and looting of the site (Merrillees 2009: 390, Figure 1). In his account Myres mentions fragments of Bronze and Iron Age pottery and concludes that *Lampousa* was a small coastal town in the Late Bronze Age and the Classical times (Myres 1940/45: 78). The continuous occupation of the site would account for the obliteration of the earlier evidence. The identification of *Lampousa* as the Early Iron Age polity of Lapithos brings the focus of habitation areas back to the coast with the Early Iron Age cemeteries to the south at a higher elevation on the Pentadaktylos foothills.

Lapithos in Context

New research on the archaeology of the north coast in the Early and Middle Bronze Ages and, more specifically, the publication of sites long ago excavated, demonstrates the rise and demise of centers close to the passes that controlled access to and connected the north coast with inland sites and especially with the central part of the island and the cupriferous foothills of the Troodos Mountains (Webb *et al.* 2009; Webb and Frankel 2010; 2013a; 2013b). This ebb and flow is observed already from the Philia Early Cypriot period (ca. 2450/200–2300/2250 BCE) with the settlement of Vasilia at the northwest end of the Pentadaktylos maintaining control of the Panagra pass (Webb *et al.* 2009: 248, Figure 4.43). Analysis of objects from the tombs at Vasilia (Webb *et al.* 2006) shows that this community was a part of networks that accumulated and circulated copper and tin around Anatolia, Cyprus, and the Cyclades in the third millennium BCE. For the efficient functioning of these external networks and for Vasilia to maintain a role as a "gateway community," that is a community located on trade routes at a key point for regulating the movement of goods (Hirth 1978), we may postulate internal networks of sites that connected the north coast to the copper ores on the foothills of the Troodos Mountains (Webb *et al.* 2009: 247–248).

Following the collapse of the Philia Culture and the abandonment of the settlement at Vasilia, the north coast underwent a reconfiguration of the settlement pattern and witnessed the rise of Bellapais *Vounous* on the north side of the Pentadaktylos, close to the Agirdha pass (Webb *et al.* 2009: 249, Figure 4.43). At the same time, Lapithos and Karmi, to the northwest of Agirdha, were also established. The mortuary evidence from *Vounous* shows that during EC I–II (ca. 2300/2250–2150/2100 BCE), *Vounous* replaced Vasilia, and access to and from the north coast moved to the Agirdha pass (Webb *et al.* 2009: 249; Webb and Frankel 2013a: 72–73).

The expansion of Lapithos and Karmi during EC III (ca. 2150/2100–2000/1950 BCE), as part of a general increase in population and settlement density in the northwest part of the island (Georgiou 2006: 414, Figure 11.4), and the subsequent rise of Lapithos as the preeminent center on the north coast signify another major shift in settlement focus (Webb *et al.* 2009: 251, Figure 4.44). In addition to the excavated tombs at *Vrysin tou Barba*, which display a significant increase of metal consumption (Keswani 2004: Table 11b), survey evidence shows a general increase in burial and habitation sites within Lapithos (Georgiou 2006: 112–114). Lapithos during EC III/MC I has been described as either a "centralized state" controlling copper routes running through the Agirdha pass (Stewart 1962: 299) or as a center for the manufacture of metal objects with copper from the Skouriotissa mines (Catling 1962: 139; cf. Ben-Yosef *et al.* 2011; Muhly and Kassianidou 2012: 126–128; Kassianidou 2013). Despite the uncertain nature of such assumptions, the renewed external demand of Cypriot copper at this time is evident in the foundation of mining villages at Ambelikou (Webb and Frankel 2013b), Katydata (Boutin *et al.* 2003), and elsewhere, possibly under the control of Lapithos. In fact, the analysis of the material from the Middle Cypriot I site of Ambelikou *Aletri* suggests that the export of copper, and possibly the exploitation of the ores themselves, was controlled by the north coast and likely by Lapithos (Webb and Frankel 2013b: 205).

MC Lapithos is characterized by an increase of identified sites and a widespread consumption of metal artifacts. The abundance of metal objects from the Lapithos tombs and the fact that almost all known imports of this period to Cyprus were found on the north coast "leaves little doubt that both foreign relations and the metal trade were once again in the hands of north coast entrepreneurs" (Webb and Frankel 2013a: 76). For Lapithos to maintain this dominant role in the movement and export of copper, we need to postulate close connections with different site networks extending along the south slopes of the Pentadaktylos and reaching the foothills of the Troodos Mountains (Webb and Frankel 2013b: 220). For the case of Ambelikou, Webb and Frankel suggested that the region was accessible by boat around Cape Kormakiti or overland via Morphou Bay, if indeed it was inhabited at this time, as well as through the Panagra pass (Webb and Frankel 2013b: 205, 221, 223).

The transitional MC III/LC IA period witnessed yet another major restructuring of settlement patterns on the north coast and the south slopes of the Pentadaktylos. Sites at Lapithos and Karavas were abandoned (Georgiou 2006: 415, Figure 11.5; Webb *et al.* 2009: 254, Figure 4.46). The establishment of new sites in the eastern part of the Pentadaktylos (e.g., Akanthou, Dhavlos, and Phlamoudhi; see Georgiou 2006: 448–449) and the occupation of the area around Morphou Bay (e.g., Ayia Irini *Palaeokastro*, Morphou *Toumba tou Skourou*, and Pendayia; see Webb *et al.* 2009: 253) indicate a reorientation of communication routes. Despite previous interpretations that postulated the continuous importance of Lapithos in the Late Bronze Age and assigned the lack of sites to issues of archaeological visibility (Catling 1962: 142), this drastic transformation of settlement patterns can likely be attributed to a combination of factors (see Manning in this volume). The establishment of coastal centers, especially *Toumba tou Skourou* and Enkomi with better harbors, extensive cultivable land, and more direct access to copper sources possibly drew populations from sites that were not able to sustain larger communities. As Peltenburg (1996: 31) has observed, "no other Cypriot center was as successful as Enkomi in securing a steady supply of copper, and the desertion of important cemeteries like Lapithos *Vrysin tou Barba* and *Vounous* whose earlier prosperity was so closely linked with copper exploitation, mirrors the rise of Enkomi." The establishment of the coastal centers and their growth, in turn, may have been triggered by a reorientation of copper trade routes toward Egypt and the Levant (Webb *et al.* 2009: 253). The construction of the so-called forts at this time (Fortin 1981; 1983) and specifically the group of six forts on the south and north slopes of the Pentadaktylos, close to the passes of Panagra and Agirdha, may explain the establishment of *Toumba tou Skourou* and Enkomi and the control of transportation routes (Peltenburg 1996: 30–31; Georgiou 2006: 472–475, Figure 13.4; Crewe 2007: 65–66; cf. Monahan and Spigelman in this volume). Finally, the occupation of the Morphou Bay area, which may have become possible after a drying out of the land from a lowering of the sea level, "provided a more efficient outlet for copper from the Skouriotissa region" (Webb *et al.* 2009: 253–254, with reference to Frankel 1974: 10).

The end of the Late Bronze Age is associated with the collapse of the international trading system that was responsible for the efficient circulation of raw materials and products in the Aegean, the Mediterranean, and beyond. For reasons that are still unclear, the archaeological record of Lapithos picks up again in the eleventh century BCE and continues throughout the Geometric period (Satraki 2012: 305–307). While the lack of identified settlements is puzzling, this absence should most probably be attributed to issues of archaeological visibility and gaps in fieldwork and research. Even though the CG record is more consistent than that of the Late Bronze Age, the distribution pattern of excavated sites continues to be nucleated with a focus of occupation along the foothills of the Pentadaktylos. The CG cemeteries of Lapithos occupy the natural plateaus of the region, forming a semicircle around the southernmost edge of the village, overlooking the sea, and seemingly leaving the coastal plain devoid of any occupation.

The political form and significance of Lapithos from the Early Iron Age onwards, as well as its relationship with neighboring polities, remain enigmatic. The excavated CG cemeteries of Lapithos exhibit the same general characteristics observed elsewhere on the island. The analysis of the finds from the cemeteries shows variation in the deposition of wealth. Nonetheless, unlike the preceding periods, there is nothing in the CG cemeteries of Lapithos that would suggest regular or intense contacts with the outside world. While the Iron Age witnesses the establishment and development of a number of important polities on the island (Iacovou 2013b; see Satraki and Kearns in this volume), which flourish until their abolition by Ptolemy I Soter in the fourth century BCE (Papantoniou 2012: 7–15; 2013), the status of Lapithos in this period is elusive.

The paucity of archaeological data from Lapithos beyond the CG cemeteries and the current inaccessibility to the area hamper our efforts to elucidate the processes that resulted in the "kingdom" of Lapithos. The name features in the Greek historian Diodorus Siculus' account (Diod. Sic. 19.79.4) from the first century BCE in his discussion of the abolition of the Cypriot polities, and it is also known from coins found in the Lapithos area dating from the mid-sixth century BCE onward (Satraki 2012: 307–309). While it may be unnecessary to try to pinpoint when Lapithos became established as a kingdom (Iacovou 2013b: 17), the presence or absence of Lapithos in the limited textual sources highlights the complexity and the dynamic nature of the political landscape of Cyprus during the Iron Age. For example, three centuries before Diodorus, in 673 BCE, the Neo-Assyrian king Esarhaddon inscribed on his prism the names of ten Cypriot rulers and their respective city-states (Luckenbill 1968; Lipinski 1991). While Lapithos is not mentioned on the prism, we learn about Chytroi—the village of modern Kythrea on the southern slopes of the Pentadaktylos Mountain. With the exception of four CG tombs (Nicolaou 1965), however, there are no archaeological correlates for the existence of Kythrea as a long-lived Iron Age polity. In fact, in Diodorus' account, at the time of the abolition of the kingdoms, there is no mention of any inland polity, suggesting that between the seventh and the fourth centuries BCE, a number of complex processes took place that altered the political landscape of the island (Iacovou 2013b: 27–28). The relationship of Lapithos with the neighboring polities of Kythrea, of Soloi in the Morphou Bay on the west, and of Ledra and Idalion, all of which are mentioned on the prism of Esarhaddon, remains puzzling.

Conclusions

Geometric Lapithos "sits" in isolation as long as the evidence of the Late Bronze Age and the CA period is missing. The preceding discussion illustrates the importance of a landscape approach to sites and regions whose archaeologies are complex and lack consistent data. The particular landscape of the north coast, its physical and resulting cultural isolation, and its dependence on copper sources are all factors that must have affected the life and development of its settlements. When the conditions were favorable, the north coast, whether through Vasilia, Vounous, or Lapithos, was a key player in the circulation of raw material and metal objects, both internally and externally (see Manning and Kearns in this volume). A change in the external demand for copper and the reorientation of site communication networks away from Lapithos and toward other coastal centers, such as the one observed in the Late Bronze Age, led to the isolation of the north coast. Such an understanding places the exploitation of copper sources in the center of the economic development and prosperity of these settlements. Indeed, copper continued to be the major export commodity of Cyprus during the Iron Age (Iacovou 2013b: 21–22), as it has been recently confirmed by Kassianidou's (2013) archaeometallurgical analyses.

The maps presented here, while restricted within the boundaries of modern Lapithos, demonstrate the potential both of this methodology and of this material. A thorough analysis of site patterns and communication networks on the north coast, however, as a well-defined region on the basis of geography and landscape from the CG period onward, will become necessary in order to move forward with these research questions. For example, only with more research can we hope to elucidate the relationship of the polity of Lapithos with the polity of Kythrea or with Kyrenia, which in the final episode in the history of the Iron Age polities (Papantoniou 2013: 178–179n21) was governed by the same ruler as Lapithos (Diod. Sic. 19.79.4)

This study has positioned the north coast of Cyprus back on the map and has drawn attention to the complicated archaeology of the region. Even though the north coast is currently inaccessible to fieldwork, our understanding of the archaeology of this region should not be perceived as stagnant. New research and approaches such as the ones presented in this paper add to our knowledge of the archaeology of the north coast and serve as a step toward achieving a comprehensive assessment of the archaeology of Cyprus in its entirety, despite current political divisions.

Acknowledgments

This chapter derives from my doctoral dissertation, carried out at Bryn Mawr College. A first version of this chapter was produced in the framework of a project entitled "Cultural and Political Landscapes: The View from the North Coast of Cyprus," funded by the Irish Research Council, Government of Ireland, and hosted at the Department of Classics of the University of Dublin, Trinity College (2014–2015). The chapter was reworked during a postdoctoral fellowship at the Department of

History and Archaeology of the University of Cyprus (2015–2017). The following editions on Lapithos tombs were published too late to incorporate into this paper and are therefore not referenced: S. Diakou, The Upper Geometric at Lapithos. University of Pennsylvania Museum excavations 1931–1932. *Studies in Mediterranean Archaeology* 146 (2018), Uppsala, Sweden: Paul Åströms Förlag; J.M. Webb, Lapithos Vrysi tou Barba, Cyprus, Early and Middle Bronze Age tombs excavated by Menelaos Markides, *Studies in Mediterranean Archaeology* 148 (2018), Nicosia: Paul Åströms Förlag. I would like to thank the organizers (C. Kearns, J. Leon, and S. Manning) for the invitation to participate in the conference. I also thank the University of Pennsylvania Museum of Archaeology and Anthropology and the Museum of Mediterranean Antiquities (Medelhavsmuseet) in Stockholm for allowing me to study their collections, both material and archival. I am grateful to J. Tabolli for helping greatly in the production of the maps. Finally, I want to thank J. Best, G. Papantoniou, and A. Georgiou for reading and commenting on earlier drafts of this article. I remain responsible however for any information and arguments put forward.

References

Ancient Authors:

Athenaeus, *Deipnosophistai*
Diodorus Siculus, *Library of History*

Adelman, C.M. 1976. *Cypro-Geometric Pottery: Refinements in Classification*. Studies in Mediterranean Archaeology 47. Göteborg, Sweden: Paul Åströms Förlag.
Anschuetz, K.F., R.H. Wilshusen, and C.L. Scheick. 2001. An archaeology of landscape: Perspectives and directions. *Journal of Archaeological Research* 9.2: 157–211.
Åström, P., R. Maddin, J.D. Muhly, and T. Stech. 1986. Iron artifacts from Swedish excavations in Cyprus. *Opuscula Atheniensia* 16.3: 27–41.
Ben-Yosef, E., R. Shaar, L. Tauxe, T.E. Levy, and V. Kassianidou. 2011. The Cyprus Archaeomagnetic Project (CAMP): Targeting the slag deposits of Cyprus and the Eastern Mediterranean. *Antiquity* 85: 330
Boutin, A., A.B. Knapp, I. Banks, M. Given and M. Horrowitz. 2003. Settlement and cemetery in and around Katydata village: From prehistory to the Roman era. *Report of the Department of Antiquities, Cyprus*: 335–349.
Catling, H.W. 1962. Patterns of settlement in Bronze Age Cyprus. *Opuscula Atheniensia* 4: 129–169.
Catling, H.W. 1971. Cyprus in the Early Bronze Age. In I.E.S. Edwards, C.J. Gadd, and N.G.L. Hammond (eds.), *Cambridge Ancient History* I.2, 808–803. Cambridge: Cambridge University Press.
Catling, H.W. 1973. Cyprus in the Middle Bronze Age. In I.E.S. Edwards, C.J. Gadd, and N.G.L. Hammond (eds.), *Cambridge Ancient History* II.1, 165–175. Cambridge: Cambridge University Press.
Catling, H.W. 1975. Cyprus in the Late Bronze Age. In I.E.S. Edwards, C.J. Gadd, N.G.L. Hammond, and E. Sollberger (eds.), *Cambridge Ancient History* II, 188–216. Cambridge: Cambridge University Press.
Christodoulou, D. 1959. *The Evolution of the Rural Land Use Pattern in Cyprus*. The World Land Use Survey. Regional Monograph No. 2. London: Geographical Publications Ltd.
Christodoulou, M.N., and K. Konstantinidis. 1987. *A Complete Gazetteer of Cyprus*. Nicosia: Cyprus Permanent Committee for the Standardization of Geographical Names.
Coldstream, J.N. 1989. Status symbols in Cyprus in the eleventh century BC. In E.J. Peltenburg (ed.), *Early Society in Cyprus*, 325–335. Edinburgh: Edinburgh University Press.
Crewe, L. 2007. *Early Enkomi: Regionalism, Trade, and Society at the Beginning of the Late Bronze Age on Cyprus*. British Archaeological Reports, International Series 1706. Oxford: Archaeopress.

Dalton, O.M. 1900. A Byzantine silver treasure from the district of Kerynia, Cyprus, now preserved in the British Museum. *Archaeologia* 67: 159–174.

Dalton, O.M. 1906. A second silver treasure from Cyprus. *Archaeologia* 60: 1–24.

Davis, T. 2014. History of research. In M.L. Steiner and A.E. Killebrew (eds.), *The Oxford Handbook of the Archaeology of the Levant c. 8000–332 BCE*, 35–43. Oxford: Oxford University Press.

Diakou, S. 2013. Lapithos: The Upper Geometric Cemetery. Unpublished PhD dissertation, Bryn Mawr College.

Diakou, S. 2016. Histories of pots and people: Rediscovering the archaeology of Cypro-Geometric Lapithos. In G. Bourogiannis and C. Mühlenbock (eds.), *Ancient Cyprus Today: Museum Collections and New Research*, 21–30. Studies in Mediterranean Archaeology PB 184. Uppsala, Sweden: Åströms Förlag.

Donohoe, J.M. 1992. The Lapithos-Lower Geometric cemetery: An Early Iron Age cemetery in Cyprus. Report of the 1931–32 Excavations of the Cyprus Expedition of the University of Pennsylvania Museum. Unpublished PhD dissertation, University of Pennsylvania, Philadelphia, Pennsylvania.

Fortin, M. 1981. Military architecture in Cyprus during the second millennium B.C. Unpublished PhD dissertation, University of London.

Fortin, M. 1983. Recherches sur l'architecture militaire de l'Âge du bronze à Chypre. *Échos du monde classique* 27: 206–219.

Frankel, D. 1974. *Middle Cypriot White Painted Pottery. An Analytical Study of the Decoration.* Studies in Mediterranean Archaeology 42. Göteborg, Sweden: Paul Åströms Förlag.

Georgiadou, A.P. 2012. The early Cypro-Geometric pottery: Examining the evidence from Lapithos Tomb 502. In A. Georgiou (ed.), *Cyprus, An Island Culture: Society and Social Relations From the Bronze Age to the Venetian Period*, 84–103. Oxford: Oxbow Books.

Georgiadou, A.P. 2013. La céramique géométrique de Chypre (XIe-VIIIe s. av. J.-C.): Étude des ateliers régionaux. Thèse des universités Aix-Marseille/Athènes.

Georgiou, G. 2006. Η Τοπογραφία της Ανθρώπινης Εγκατάστασης στην Κύπρο κατά την Πρώιμη και Μέση Χαλκοκρατία. Unpublished PhD dissertation, University of Cyprus, Nicosia, Cyprus.

Gjerstad, E.J. 1926. *Studies on Prehistoric Cyprus.* Uppsala, Sweden: A.-b. Lundequistska bokhandeln.

Gjerstad, E.J. 1948. *The Swedish Cyprus Expedition IV.2. The Cypro-Geometric, Cypro-Archaic and Cypro-Classical Periods.* Stockholm: Swedish Cyprus Expedition.

Gjerstad, E.J., J. Lindros, E. Sjöqvist, and A. Westholm. 1934. *The Swedish Cyprus Expedition I. Finds and Results of the Excavations in Cyprus, 1927–1931.* Stockholm: Swedish Cyprus Expedition.

Grace, V.R. 1931/32. Upper Geometric-Prostemenos. Unpublished field notebook, University of Pennsylvania Museum of Archaeology and Anthropology, Philadelphia.

Grace, V.R. 1937. Lapithos, 1931: Geometric Tombs. Unpublished report, University of Pennsylvania Museum of Archaeology and Anthropology, Philadelphia.

Grace, V.R. 1940. A Cypriote tomb and Minoan evidence for its date. *American Journal of Archaeology* 44.1: 10–52.

Herscher, E. 1978. The Bronze Age cemetery at Lapithos, Vrysi Tou Barba, Cyprus: Results of the University of Pennsylvania, museum excavation, 1931. Unpublished PhD dissertation, University of Pennsylvania, Philadelphia, Pennsylvania.

Herscher, E. 2007. Lapithos 1931: An unofficial ASCSA excavation in Cyprus. *Ákoue: Newsletter of the American School of Classical Studies at Athens* 57.8: 21.

Hirth, K.G. 1978. Interregional trade and the formation of prehistoric gateway communities. *American Antiquity* 43.1: 35–45.

Iacovou, M. 1994. The topography of eleventh century B.C. Cyprus. In V. Karageorghis (ed.), *Proceedings of the International Symposium: Cyprus in the 11th Century BC*, 149–165. Nicosia: Leventis Foundation.

Iacovou, M. 1999. Excerpta Cypria Geometrica. Materials for a history of Geometric Cyprus. In M. Iacovou and D. Michaelides (eds.), *Cyprus: The Historicity of the Geometric Horizon*, 141–166. Nicosia: Archaeological Research Unit, University of Cyprus.

Iacovou, M. 2005. Cyprus at the dawn of the first millennium BCE: Cultural homogenization versus the tyranny of ethnic identifications. In J. Clarke (ed.), *Archaeological Perspectives on the Transmission and Transformation of Culture in the Eastern Mediterranean*, 125–134. Levant Supplementary Series 2. Oxford: Oxbow Books.

Iacovou, M. 2013a. The Cypriot syllabary as a royal signature: The political context of the syllabic script in the Iron Age. In P. Steele (ed.), *Syllabic Writing on Cyprus and its Context*, 133–152. Cambridge Classical Studies. Cambridge and New York: Cambridge University Press.

Iacovou, M. 2013b. Historically elusive and internally fragile island polities: The intricacies of Cyprus's political geography in the Iron Age. *Bulletin of the American Schools of Oriental Research* 370: 15–47.

Janes, S. 2008. The Cypro-Geometric horizon, a view from below: Identity and social change in the mortuary record. Unpublished PhD dissertation, University of Glasgow, Glasgow.

Janes, S. 2013. Death and burial in the age of the Cypriot city-kingdoms: Social complexity based on the mortuary evidence. *Bulleting of the American Schools of Oriental Research* 370: 145–168.

Karageorghis, V. 1974. Pikes or obeloi from Cyprus and Crete. In D. Levi, P. Carratelli, and G. Rizza (eds.), *Antichità cretesi: Studi in onore di Doro Levi* II, 168–172. Catania, Italy: Università di Catania, Istituto di archeologia.

Karageorghis, V. 1983. *Palaepaphos-Skales: An Iron Age cemetery in Cyprus*. Konstanz, Germany: Universitätsverlag.

Kassianidou, V. 2013. Mining landscapes of prehistoric Cyprus. *Metalla* 20, 36–45

Keswani, P.S. 2004. *Mortuary Ritual and Society in Bronze Age Cyprus*. London: Equinox Pub.

Knapp, A.B. 2013. *The Archaeology of Cyprus: From Earliest Prehistory through the Bronze Age*. Cambridge: Cambridge University Press.

Knapp, A.B., and W. Ashmore. 1999. Archaeological landscapes: Constructed, conceptualized, ideational. In W. Ashmore and A.B. Knapp (eds.), *Archaeologies of Landscape*, 1–30. Malden, MA: Blackwell.

Lipinski, E. 1991. The Cypriot vassals of Esarhaddon. In M. Cogan and I. Eph'al (eds.), *Ah, Assyria . . . Studies in Assyrian History and Ancient Near Eastern Historiography Presented to Hayim Tadmor*, 58–64. Jerusalem: Magnes Press.

Luckenbill, D.D. 1968. *Ancient Records of Assyria and Babylonia*. New York: Greenwood Press.

Markides, M. 1916. *Annual Report of the Curator of Antiquities 1915*. Nicosia: The Government Printing Office.

Megaw, A.H.S. 1954. Archaeology in Cyprus, 1953. *Journal of Hellenic Studies* 74: 172–176.

Merrillees, R.S. 2009. The modern history of the first Lambousa treasure of Byzantine silverware from Cyprus. *The Antiquaries Journal* 89: 389–403.

Muhly, J.D., and V. Kassianidou. 2012. Parallels and diversities in the production, trade, and use of copper and iron in Crete and Cyprus from the Bronze Age to the Iron Age. In G. Cadogan, M. Iacovou, K. Kopaka, and J. Whitley (eds.), *Parallel Lives: Ancient Island Societies in Crete and Cyprus. Proceedings of the Conference in Nicosia Organized by the British School at Athens, the University of Crete, and the University of Cyprus in November–December 2006*, 119–140. British School at Athens Studies 20. London: British School at Athens.

Myres, J.L. 1940/45. Excavations in Cyprus, 1913. *Annual of the British School at Athens* 41: 53–104.

Myres, J.L., and M. Ohnefalsch-Richter. 1899. *A Catalogue of the Cyprus Museum with a Chronicle of Excavations Undertaken since the British Occupation and Introductory Notes on Cypriote Archaeology*. Oxford: Clarendon Press.

Nicolaou, K. 1965. Γεωμετρικοί τάφοι Κυθρέας. *Report of the Department of Antiquities, Cyprus*: 30–73.

Nicolaou, K. 1975/76. Archaeology in Cyprus, 1969–76. *Archaeological Reports* 22: 34–69.

Nicolaou, K. 1976. Ancient fish-tanks at Lapithos, Cyprus. *The International Journal of Nautical Archaeology and Underwater Exploration* 5.2: 133–141.

Ohnefalsch-Richter, M. 1893. *Kypros, the Bible, and Homer: Oriental Civilization, Art, and Religion in Ancient Times*. London: Asher & Co.

Papantoniou, G. 2012. *Religion and Social Transformation in Cyprus: From the Cypriot Basileis to the Hellenistic Strategos*. Mnemosyne Supplement 347; History and Archaeology of Classical Antiquity 347. Leiden: Brill.

Papantoniou, G. 2013. Cypriot autonomous polities at the crossroads of empire: The imprint of a transformed islandscape in the Classical and Hellenistic periods. *Bulletin of the American Schools of Oriental Research* 370: 169–205.

Peltenburg, E. 1996. From isolation to state formation in Cyprus, c. 3500–1500 B.C. In V. Karageorghis and D. Michaelides (eds.), *The Development of the Cypriot Economy from the Prehistoric Period to the Present Day*, 17–44. Nicosia: University of Cyprus and Bank of Cyprus.

Pieridou, A. 1964. A Cypro-Geometric cemetery at "Vathyrkakas," Karavas. *Report of the Department of Antiquities, Cyprus*: 114–129.

Pieridou, A. 1965. An early Cypro-Geometric tomb at Lapethos. *Report of the Department of Antiquities, Cyprus:* 74–111.

Pieridou, A. 1966. A tomb-group from Lapithos "Agia Anastasia." *Report of the Department of Antiquities, Cyprus:* 1–12.

Pieridou, A. 1972. Τάφος υπ' αρ. 503 εκ Λαπήθου, "Αγία Αναστασία." *Report of the Department of Antiquities, Cyprus:* 237–250.

Ruwell, M.E. 1984. *A Guide to the University Museum Archives of the University of Pennsylvania.* Philadelphia: The Museum.

Satraki, A. 2012. *Κύπριοι Βασιλείς από τον Κοσμασό Μέχρι τον Νικοκρέοντα.* Αρχαιογνωσία 9. Athens: University of Athens.

Smith, J.S. 2008a. Bringing old excavations to life. *Near Eastern Archaeology* 71.1/2: 30–40.

Smith, J.S. 2008b. From expedition to exhibition. In J.S. Smith (ed.), *Views from Phlamoudhi, Cyprus,* 1–13. Annual of the American Schools of Oriental Research 63. Boston: American Schools of Oriental Research.

Steel, L. 1993. Burial customs in Cyprus at the transition from the Bronze Age to the Iron Age. Unpublished PhD dissertation, University College London.

Stewart, J.R. 1962. The Early Cypriote Bronze Age. In P. Dikaios and J.R. Stewart (eds.), *The Swedish Cyprus Expedition* IV.1A. *The Stone and the Early Bronze Age in Cyprus,* 203–401. Lund, Sweden: The Swedish Cyprus Expedition.

Strøm, I. 1992. Obeloi of pre- or proto-monetary value in the Greek sanctuaries. In T. Linders and B. Arloth (eds.), *Economics of Cult in the Ancient Greek World. Proceedings of the Uppsala Symposium 1990,* 41–51. *Boreas* 21. Uppsala, Sweden: S. Academiae Ubsaliensis.

Tatton-Brown, V. 2001. Excavations in ancient Cyprus: Original manuscripts and correspondence in the British Museum. In V. Tatton-Brown (ed.), *Cyprus in the 19th Century AD. Fact, Fancy, and Fiction,* 168–183. Oxford: Oxbow Books.

Tsolakis, K.A. 1997. Valuation and Administration of Lands Containing Antiquities in Cyprus. Unpublished thesis, University of New Brunswick, Fredericton, Canada.

UNESCO. 1957. *Records of the General Conference: Ninth Session New Delhi 1956: Resolutions.* Paris: UNESCO.

Van Dyke, R.M., and S.E. Alcock. 2003. Archaeologies of memory: An introduction. In R.M. Van Dyke and S.E. Alcock (eds.), *Archaeologies of Memory,* 1–13. Malden, MA: Blackwell.

Webb, J.M. 2016. Lapithos revisited: A fresh look at a key Middle Bronze Age site in Cyprus. In G. Bourogiannis and C. Mühlenbock (eds.), *Ancient Cyprus Today: Museum Collections and New Research,* 57–67. Studies in Mediterranean Archaeology PB 184. Uppsala, Sweden: Åströms Förlag.

Webb, J.M. 2017. Lapithos Tomb 322: Voice, context and the archaeological record. In E. Minchin and H. Jackson (eds.), *Text and the Material World: Essays in Honour of Graeme Clarke,* 1–12. Studies in Mediterranean Archaeology PB 185. Uppsala, Sweden: Åströms Förlag.

Webb, J.M., and D. Frankel. 2010. Social strategies, ritual, and cosmology in Early Bronze Age Cyprus: An investigation of burial data from the north coast. *Levant* 42: 185–209.

Webb, J.M., and D. Frankel. 2013a. Cultural regionalism and divergent social trajectories in Early Bronze Age Cyprus. *American Journal of Archaeology* 117: 59–81.

Webb, J.M., and D. Frankel. 2013b. *Ambelikou Aletri: Metallurgy and Pottery Production in Middle Bronze Age Cyprus.* Studies in Mediterranean Archaeology 138. Uppsala, Sweden: Åströms Förlag.

Webb, J.M., D. Frankel, Z.A. Stos, and N. Gale. 2006. Early Bronze Age metal trade in the eastern Mediterranean: New compositional and lead isotope evidence from Cyprus. *Oxford Journal of Archaeology* 25: 261–288.

Webb, J.M., D. Frankel, K.O. Eriksson, and J.B. Hennessy. 2009. *The Bronze Age Cemeteries at Karmi Palealona and Lapatsa in Cyprus: Excavations by J.R.B. Stewart.* Studies in Mediterranean Archaeology 136. Sävedalen, Sweden: Åströms Förlag.

9

Discerning "Favorable" Environments

Science, Survey Archaeology, and the Cypriot Iron Age

CATHERINE KEARNS

Introduction

In 1879, the colonial surveyor Lord H. H. Kitchener observed that "Cyprus is an island of sudden changes. Both climate and landscape are subject to rapid variations" (quoted in Shirley 2001: 57). As put forward in recent work by Webb and Frankel (2013) and others (e.g., Iacovou 2014b; Manning in this volume), the island's richly diverse topography and ecology are among the critical components that anchor archaeological interpretations of local settlement dynamics, economies of land and sea, and geopolitical interactions, both within Cypriot society and with the surrounding east Mediterranean. When considering the import of Kitchener's observations, two concerns emerge for examining the island's more ancient environments. The first constitutes a traditional focus on environmental constraints and the asymmetrical vocabulary that we have used to describe Cypriot human-environment relationships as constricting past populations with the forces of "immutable" geography (e.g., Iacovou 2013: 19; Satraki in this volume; see also Braudel 1980: 31). Some recent work has rightly challenged the island's historical epithet *makarios*, meaning "blessed," in reference to its productivity, by drawing attention to the shifty marginality and erratic nature of Cypriot environments (Christodoulou 1959: 41–42; Iacovou 2013: 19; Manning in this volume). Yet a recurring theme in Cypriot archaeology foregrounds how ancient populations and their activities were ostensibly shaped by topography, climate, and the location of valuable resources, most notably copper (e.g., Iacovou 2012).

A second concern stems from our lack of information on abrupt or "sudden" changes in past landscape and climates on Cyprus, as opposed to increasingly detailed records in other places of the Mediterranean ecumene, such as Anatolia (e.g., Haldon *et al.* 2014; see also Kearns 2013). In many ways, longstanding archaeological interest in Cyprus's topography and surface features has obscured historical changes in rainfall, vegetation cover, river courses, and maritime routes in and around which past societies organized their practices (Held n.d.; Stanley Price 1979; Butzer and Harris 2007; Devillers *et al.* 2015). Given new directions in several branches of archaeology toward examining environmental histories and human-nature entanglements (e.g., Kintigh *et al.* 2014: 15–19), it seems timely to question how these sudden or persistent climates on Cyprus feature in archaeological epistemologies.

In this paper, I present new data from diachronic paleoclimate records related to precipitation and water availability as an entryway for thinking substantively about social and environmental changes during the Iron Age. The shifts recorded in these scientific data raise opportunities for exploring how, and why, scholars aim to associate and to synchronize historical and climatic episodes, such as the rise of polities or the collapse of interconnected economic systems. As a complement to existing narratives, I assert that landscapes—defined here as the interactions between people and their real and imagined surroundings, which are socially constructed and dynamic (following scholars such as Alcock 1993; Wilkinson 2003; Smith 2003)—are further generated by the practices of both humans and materials, like water, soils, and trees, which make up the surrounding environment: the rich world of biota as well as inanimate matter that shape and are shaped by their own forces, physical climatic changes and long-term anthropogenic modifications (see e.g., Crumley 1994; Morrison 2014; Bauer and Kosiba 2016).

In discerning landscape change, I focus on its nonlinear complexity and its often dramatic intersections with human practice and social order, and question the moral underbelly inherent to vocabulary such as "favorable" as opposed to "deleterious" climates that characterize recent literature on past human-environment relationships (see e.g., Diamond 2005; cf. Kouki 2013; Hulme 2016). My aim is not to identify nor to privilege either climatic or anthropogenic agents but to advocate an integrated approach that combines scientific and archaeological data—balancing the *archaeo-* with the *-metry* (Pollard and Bray 2014)—to avoid overgeneralizations of cultural and social florescence, on the one hand, or the restrictive nature of climate and environment on passive human subjects, on the other (Middleton 2012). Without denying that environmental or ecological systems do indeed exert considerable influence in human decision-making (on environmental determinism, see e.g., Hulme 2011: 246), this approach underscores the ways in which human groups and environmental constituents such as water courses, fields and soils, and ores of copper recursively produced new forms of society during the Iron Age. Moreover, studying past environmental changes requires critical inquiry into ideological and cultural ideas and experiences of climate through "weathered" experiences (Hulme 2016).

This paper begins with a brief review of the existing paleoenvironmental record for Cyprus in order to sketch out recent directions in human-environment studies. A second section then turns to our archaeological constructions of past climate and social change, using one case study from the ninth to eighth centuries BCE as a platform from which to interrogate "favorable" climatic conditions and sociopolitical development in the transition to the first millennium BCE. As a method for interpreting past precipitation change in this period, the third section discusses recent carbon stable isotope analysis of archaeological charcoal from selected sites on the island. To complement the scientific data, I discuss both legacy and recent archaeological survey evidence from one region in south-central Cyprus, the Vasilikos and Maroni valleys, which reveals complicated settlement and place-making practices and the investment in landscapes that characterized emerging communities on the edge of a rising coastal power, Amathus (see Petit 2001). These analyses provide space to consider the intervention of environmental materials and their mediations in human social change as well as the give and take between new social inequalities and "sudden" climates that fostered what we call the Cypriot Iron Age.

Paleoenvironments of Cyprus

There is a long history of mapping the ancient surfaces and topography of Cyprus, even before the major trigonometric survey of Kitchener in 1878–1883 (Kearns 2013: 122–123). From antiquarian observations about the geographical positions of sites during the eighteenth and nineteenth centuries to the archaeological distribution maps of Gjerstad (1926) and Catling (1962) in the twentieth century, this topographic tradition has greatly enhanced our understanding of site position and regional variation, a central concern of prehistoric archaeology (e.g., Bolger 1989; Webb and Frankel 2013). Indeed, the early focus on topography brought sophisticated survey methods to the island before they reached many other regions of the Mediterranean (see Iacovou 2004). According to these studies, ancient interactions between humans and their surroundings were often governed by marked characteristics of the local geology, such as the presence of cupriferous igneous rocks or the imposing peaks of the Kyrenia mountain range along the northern coast. Given this attention to the active role of conspicuous topography in the bounding and shaping of ancient societies, we have remained largely in the dark about the composition and changes of the island's ancient environments (Noller 2010); the ways in which human communities engineered, negotiated, or challenged their shifting surroundings; and how those surroundings mediated human practices.

For instance, archaeobotanical investigations are still not widely implemented on the island, despite the very early interest in preserving seeds and wood charcoal during the pioneering excavations of du Plat Taylor (1952) and Stewart (Stewart and Stewart 1950) in the early twentieth century. Due to the scarcity of paleoenvironmental records, we know little about past vegetation cover, the composition of forests that may have extended further into the lowlands, or paleosols, and archaeologists have needed to rely on other regional Mediterranean archives (Noller 2010; see also Wasse 2007; Kearns 2013: 126–127). There is an apparent presumption that the environments of Cyprus have remained relatively the same throughout its long human occupation—hot dry summers and cold wet winters, with some significant coastline change (e.g., Gifford 1985; Morhange 2000)—which has also contributed to the absence of rigorous paleoclimatic research (Held n.d.). Recent work is, however, restoring this imbalance (e.g., Kaniewski *et al.* 2013; Griggs *et al.* 2014; Devillers *et al.* 2015; Knapp and Manning 2016).

An additional problem in constructing an ancient environmental record is the arbitrary cutoff between prehistory and history that still pervades Cypriot archaeology (Iacovou 2008: 625). Those scholars working in the prehistoric periods, generally up until the Late Bronze Age in the second half of the second millennium BCE, tend to study human-environment relationships more than those working in the historical periods. The intense focus on mortuary, sanctuary, and urban contexts in studies of the late second and first millennia BCE often render landscapes as backgrounds to political and social history, rather than as dynamic contexts with their own agency (cf. Iacovou 2014a: 796–797). Indeed, as others have noted, the rural practices, utilitarian objects, economic strategies, and domestic spaces of the Iron Age need intensive research in order to fill in the gaps created by years of study skewed to monumental buildings and tomb offerings (see Rupp 1997; Given and Smith 2003; Toumazou *et al.* 2011). Perhaps most critical to this divergence of history from prehistory and protohistory, however, is the general absence of absolutely dated remains for the Iron Age (although on Iron Age slag-related dating, see Kassianidou 2013: Appendix I; 2014), as opposed to the revolutionary radiometric analysis currently underway for illuminating the island's prehistoric periods (see e.g., Paraskeva in this volume).

Dynamic Human-Environment Relationships: What Is a "Favorable" Climate?

Past climatic and landscape changes on Cyprus thus require more attention, since they had varied effects on the shape and consistency of local ecosystems as well as diverse resonances and material relationships within societies (Manning in this volume). In line with a growing movement to study environments and climate across the humanities and the social sciences, this paper argues that Cypriot landscapes were (and are) constantly in flux, forming and re-forming the island in concert with developing human activity (see e.g., Given and Knapp 2003; Given *et al.* 2013; see also Horden and Purcell 2000). This approach seeks to investigate the complex ways in which human groups experienced shifts such as decreasing or increasing water availability, interannual harvest variability, and eustatic sea level rise. Using an informed selection of interdisciplinary methods, we can question how these fluctuations became entangled with human technological developments, such as the construction of new roads and harbors, or manipulations of existing irrigation or pastoral strategies (Frankel *et al.* 2013; Morrison 2014). The recent study of terraces at Politiko *Troullia* in the northeast foothills of the Troodos massif provides one example of how, between the second and first millennium BCE, people altered their wall construction and maintenance practices to accommodate different environmental and socioeconomic needs (Fall *et al.* 2012). This work suggests that potential changes in rainfall and erosion, which might have required better soil management strategies on the part of those working the land, interacted with the altered organization of landscape control within this region.

Following the work of archaeologists interested in the social and political dimensions of human-environment interfaces (e.g., Rosen 2007; Fisher *et al.* 2009; Frankel *et al.* 2013; Morrison 2014; Crumley *et al.* 2015; Bauer and Kosiba 2016), we note that humans are not grouped into monolithic entities that act or react to external shifts in uniform ways. Nor are rigidly defined environments passive in the reproduction of social structures or institutions. The capacity of authorities to manage and to take control of environmental concerns such as water shortage, for example, may build on and reinforce existing social boundaries, while the materiality of copper ores, involving a nexus of soils, waters, igneous lithologies, and forest vegetation, may mediate asymmetrical economic relationships involving the production, distribution, or consumption of copper objects (see Appadurai 2015). Moreover, changes in vegetation patterns or precipitations levels do not exist as a separate external *explanans* driving societal transformation but instead must be analyzed in tandem with the ordering of daily practice within a society (Smith 2003: 278–279; Hulme 2016; Kearns 2017). The case study on Iron Age settled landscapes that follows in this chapter offers one example of what might be called this environmental *habitus* and reveals the spectrality of human agency and regional environmental fluctuations that mediate and co-create change.

Across the humanities and social sciences, we are seeing increasing interest—associated, in many ways, with global anxieties—in environmentally constrained collapse and the diversity of human involvement in or responsibilities for ecological degradation (e.g., Butzer 2012; Middleton 2012). As others have noted (Harris 2013: 5), the debilitating crises in human society that often follow or coincide with regional or global climatic changes seem relatively easier to study in the historical and textual record than episodes of "prosperous" human-environment entanglements and indeed have often stood in as markers for periodization schemes in archaeological chronologies. Such axioms, often correlating macro-scalar phenomena such as depopulation with poorly resolved proxy information on global warming or cooling episodes and natural disasters, have found considerable purchase in explanations for major social and political transitions, like the collapse of the Akkadian empire during an abrupt aridification event around 2200 BCE (e.g., Weiss and Bradley 2001). For the end of the Bronze Age in the late second millennium BCE, scholars have argued from recent pollen analysis that a prolonged drought episode caused the breakdown of the network of complex polities engaged in interregional trade and gift exchange, forcing communities to move continuously in search of basic resources during the overly arid Early Iron Age (Kaniewski *et al.* 2013; cf. Knapp and Manning 2016: 102–112). In the early modern period, the deterioration of Cyprus's forests witnessed by travelers during the Ottoman Empire has provided a more recent example of caustic foreign imperial policy and weakened stability linked to environmental spoiling (Butzer and Harris 2007).

In these reconstructions, which focus predominantly on discerning causality or environmental impacts on human life and which often skew unevenly either toward scientific or toward archaeological or textual evidence (see Pollard and Bray 2014), societies either fail to adapt or lose their resilience in the face of physical forces beyond their control (e.g., Diamond 2005). Many rely on what Coombes and Barber (2005: 304–305) call "black box" determinism, which employs only approximate, imprecise, or overly macro-scale data and creates reductive relationships between climate and society (see Hulme 2011), projected back onto fragmentary archaeological or textual archives. If the climate gets worse, in many scenarios, conditions are created in which agropastoral economies suffer due to unsustainable reliance on diminishing harvests, dependent state powers fall apart, and chaos reigns. Yet taking this dualism to its opposite polarity, particularly in the Mediterranean constructs of wet/warm optima and of dry/cold minima, if the climate gets "better," do new communities or states form and prosper? Do populations necessarily start growing? Does farming become less risky, with reduced interannual variability of harvests, better soil quality, and more chances to control erosion, all combining to allow new or altered political economies reliant on agricultural commodities to develop? How does "favorable" climate affect different social groups and political modalities? This equation has certainly received less attention, although recent work has provided provocative examples (e.g., Manning 2013a; Pederson *et al.* 2014) that nevertheless create a moral economy of environmental conditions, marked by value-laden terms such as *prosperous, destructive,* or *favorable.* These terms do little to explain *how* climates stimulate development or inequalities or *how* communities or social groups imagined, experienced, or conceived of shifting ecologies. If paleoclimatic research is increasingly becoming a rich exercise of self-reflexive engagement with reconstructing physical climates, it behooves archaeologists and environmental historians interested in past records to analyze and examine the imaginations and experiences of climate discursively made and mediated through culture (Hulme 2016).

In the same way that the reductive links between "bad" climate and collapse can mask the intricacies of complex human-environment relationships, "favorable" conditions require careful analysis to explore their equally varied interactions within human populations (Kouki 2013: 211). In other words, we might ask, favorable to or for whom or which groups? Given the accumulating anthropological work on variegated perceptions and politics of knowledge of climate and environment (e.g., Hulme 2015; Barnes and Dove 2015), in what ways do we understand a regional setting or climatic phase as "favorable" and project that onto non-linear complex landscapes? In light of the recent study of a period of unprecedented warm and moist climate coinciding with the rise of the Mongol Empire of Genghis Khan during the thirteenth century CE (Pederson *et al.* 2014), for example, we can question how one emerging authority took control of rain-induced steppe productivity and concentrated labor and agricultural resources, while scores of other people were subjugated or displaced by new imperialist land use mechanisms and labor practices. How do more reliable growing seasons intersect with contingent practices that act to constrain or generate the mechanisms that produce social order? How is any human ordering of climatic conditions, whether prolonged drought or an onset of cooler temperatures, linked to political authority and social practice? This perspective calls for examining not just whether societies expanded and developed new technologies during periods of seemingly "better" climate but also how new conditions interacted with the apparatus of land management, political economies, and the emergence of cultural and social values of landscape and environments within and between societies. From the standpoint of these dynamic human-environment relationships, I argue for studying "landscapes in the making," to reorient a phrase from Hoskins (1955), and place emphasis on the recurring and accumulating processes, experiences, and perceptions that shape human interactions with their real and imagined surroundings.

The revolutionary social, political, and economic changes occurring around the Mediterranean during the early first millennium BCE, at the onset of a new Iron Age world, provide a case study for exploring this perspective (for the complex periodization, see Kotsonas 2016). Recent work in paleoenvironmental studies is elucidating a "sudden" climatic change around the mid-ninth century BCE marked by a shift from cooler and more arid conditions to wetter, warmer ones by the seventh century BCE (van Geel et al. 2004; Manning 2010: 43–44). This apparent turn to climates "favorable" to Cypriot topography and terrain—with more rainfall and likely more reliable growing seasons and fewer extended droughts—happens a few centuries after the end of the Late Bronze Age (e.g., Manning 2013b). It therefore offers an example with which to study the interrelationships between shifting environments and the regeneration of sociopolitical complexity, forms of mercantile trade, and new cultural practices occurring around the eastern Mediterranean (Sherratt and Sherratt 1993; Morris 2009; Broodbank 2013: 445–505). Rather than assume that this climatic change immediately led to growth in population, innovation, and prosperity from the Near East to the Aegean Sea and on to the Atlantic, the following analysis breaks down the scientific and archaeological evidence from two proximal watersheds on Cyprus to investigate these altered human-environment relationships.

Climatic and Environmental Change

While recent paleoclimatic research has sought to illuminate the dry episode in the Mediterranean that coincides with the end of the Bronze Age and its unique political economies (e.g., Rohling et al. 2009; Langgut et al. 2013; Drake 2012; Kaniewski et al. 2013; Knapp and Manning 2016: 102–112), less attention has gone to the probable wetter episode that follows, around the ninth and eighth centuries BCE. The lack of precise, high-resolution data for this period, especially for places like Cyprus, exacerbates this problem. Nevertheless, studies are increasingly showing that a potentially global shift from drier to wetter physical climates occurred, with different regional effects across the Mediterranean (Roberts et al. 2012; see Bar-Matthews et al. 1998; Manning 2010; 2013a: 112–114; Mayewski et al. 2004; cf. Drake 2012).

These indirect records of a wetter climate come from contexts such as peat bogs in northern Europe as well as the southern hemisphere (van Geel et al. 2000; van Geel et al. 2004; Chambers et al. 2007; Swindles et al. 2007), sediment profiles in Turkey and northern Africa (Hassan 1997), pollen cores from lakes in the Mediterranean (Roberts et al. 2011; Langgut et al. 2013; Kaniewski et al. 2013), and proxies for sea surface temperatures and salinity in the Atlantic Ocean and the Mediterranean (Emeis et al. 2000). Indirect records for water availability in northeastern Iberia drawn from charcoal show a cool and dry period, on the other hand, likely reflecting differences in eastern and western Mediterranean climates during this Iron Age episode (Ferrio et al. 2006; see Roberts et al. 2012). Scholars have suggested that this type of synchronous cooling was triggered by a reduction in solar activity, also known as a "solar minimum," which increased the amount of cosmic rays in the atmosphere leading to cloud and precipitation formation (e.g., van Geel et al.

2000; Bond *et al.* 2001; Manning 2013: 114). The radiocarbon curve documents this dramatic drop in solar activity, marking a decrease in sunspots and therefore a generally less warm period starting around 800 BCE and followed by warming (Manning 2010: 43).

Carbon Stable Isotope Analysis

We still lack precise information for this climatic change on Cyprus (cf. Kaniewski *et al.* 2013). In order to create a local record for potential climatic shifts, I performed stable isotope analysis on archaeological charcoal recovered from several sites on the island (for the premise of this technique, see McCarroll and Loader 2004). A growing number of international studies have explored the correlations between carbon stable isotope composition ($\delta^{13}C$) in plants and climatic variation, particularly factors related to water availability, humidity, and moisture conditions (e.g., Ferrio *et al.* 2006; Riehl *et al.* 2008; Wallace *et al.* 2013). The changes in a plant's isotopic values are complicated by various forms of water input and loss, temperature, light intensity, and even soil nutrients. For semi-arid areas such as Cyprus, rainfall is the most prominent force of environmental change and is almost always unreliable and often inadequate in lowland areas that are susceptible to high evaporation rates. During periods of water shortage, a plant's carbon isotope ratios will exhibit this discrimination in water availability as an increase in the heavier isotope ^{13}C (compared to the lighter ^{12}C). Since charcoal is a ubiquitous feature of archaeological deposits, it is a relatively available source with which to study broad trends in water availability during the late Holocene, although problems in the representation of original wood material in preserved charcoal require additional analysis, as discussed below.

For the archaeological charcoal, I obtained approximately 170 individual samples from Cyprus to measure carbon stable isotopic composition, summarized in Table 9.1. These samples, which come from both excavated sites and geomorphological sampling at sites, represent varied stratified contexts: tombs, building material, kilns, and floor deposits. The sites also cover different bioclimatic parts of the island as well as both urban and non-urban contexts (Figure 9.1).

Several samples originate in immediate coastal environments, such as Zygi *Petrini*, Amathus, and Kition, with an average annual precipitation range between 300–400 mm, while others represent inland foothills landscapes, such as Apliki *Karamallos*, where average annual precipitation can reach 800 mm. The samples extend from the mid-third millennium BCE to the mid-first millennium CE and cluster in three major periods: the Late Bronze Age, the Archaic and Classical periods, and the Roman to Late Roman periods. Thus, the earliest part of the first millennium BCE (e.g., eleventh to ninth centuries) is not well represented, except for a few samples from an early Cypro-Geometric (CG) deposit at the site of Idalion. In addition, four samples were sent for radiocarbon dating, while the remaining samples are dated from stratigraphic records. For this reason, some of the chronological resolution for samples remains poor, covering multiple centuries. Despite the limitations of this initial study and the problems with diluting climatic change to only "wet" or

Table 9.1: Charcoal data derived from archaeological sites on Cyprus, catalogued by site, species, number of samples, chronological period and corresponding date range, and archaeological context

Site name	Species	No. of samples	Chronological period	Date range (approx.)	Context
Alambra Mouttes	*Olea eur.*	2	MC III	1750–1650 BCE	Room debris
Maroni Tsaroukkas	*Olea eur.*	2	LC IIA/LC IIB	1500–1350 BCE	Tomb
Kalavasos *Ayios Dhimitrios*	*Pinus sp.*	76	LC IIB/LC IIC	1400–1300 BCE	Roof debris; Pithos hall
Alassa Paliotaverna	*Olea eur.*	1	LC IIIA	1200–1050 BCE	Room and pit deposits
	Pinus sp.	3	LC IIC	1340–1200 BCE	Room and pit deposits
	Pinus sp.	3	LC IIIA	1200–1050 BCE	Room and pit deposits
Apliki Karamallos	*Pinus sp.*	11	LC IIC/LC IIIA	1350–1250 BCE	Room debris
	Pistacia ter.	1	LC IIC/LC IIIA	1350–1250 BCE	Room debris
Idalion	*Quercus sp.*	1	Cypro-Geometric	1050–800 BCE	Pit deposit
	Quercus sp.	16	Cypro-Classical	500–300 BCE	Pit deposit
	Pistacia ter.	5	Cypro-Classical	500–300 BCE	Pit deposit
Amathus	*Quercus sp.*	4	Cypro-Archaic	800–500 BCE	Pit deposit, floor debris
	Pinus sp.	12	Cypro-Archaic	800–500 BCE	Pit deposit, floor debris
	Olea eur.	1	Cypro-Archaic	800–500 BCE	Pit deposit, floor debris
	Pistacia ter.	2	Hellenistic	300–30 BCE	Destruction layer
	Quercus sp.	6	Hellenistic	300–30 BCE	Destruction layer
	Olea eur.	5	Hellenistic	300–30 BCE	Destruction layer
	Pinus sp.	11	Roman	30 BCE–200 CE	Room debris
	Quercus sp.	5	Roman	30 BCE–200 CE	Room debris
Kition *Pervolia*	*Olea eur.*	7	Classical	500–400 BCE	Tomb
Zygi *Petrini*	*Pinus sp.*	68	Late Roman	200–400 CE	Kiln feature

"dry" (Rosen and Rosen 2001), the data provide a reasonable diachronic range of relative changes in water availability, and ongoing research for this project is working toward collecting more samples with more precise dating.

The samples fall into a standard range of mostly low-elevation endemic taxa on Cyprus: pine (*Pinus brutia* Ten., *Pinus nigra*), oak (*Quercus sp.* evergreen), olive (*Olea europaea*), and terebinth (*Pistacia terebinthus*). To differentiate between the high-elevation and low-elevation species of pine endemic to Cyprus (*P. nigra* and *P. brutia*, respectively) as a possible source of isotopic variation, select samples were identified with a scanning electron microscope (SEM). The samples were

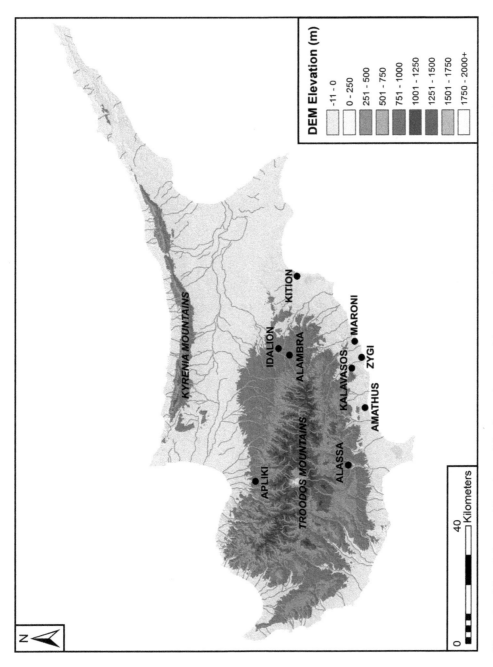

Figure 9.1: Map of sites providing charcoal for this study. Created by C. Kearns; basemap provided by the Geological Survey Department.

then prepared by sectioning along ring boundaries with an average of 5.9 ± 3.2 rings and were run on an elemental analyzer coupled with an isotope ratio mass spectrometer, following common procedure (e.g., Ferrio *et al.* 2006). The results were then calibrated against Antarctic ice core values to account for changes in atmospheric CO_2 in the past, in order to calculate carbon isotope discrimination, $\Delta^{13}C$ (Farquhar *et al.* 1989; Ferrio *et al.* 2006; the $\delta^{13}C$ values used for the Cypriot charcoal ranged from −6.37 to −6.52 ppm). To assess the variability in isotopic composition of charcoal due to the charring process, experimental carbonization tests were performed on modern *P. brutia* from Limassol Forest (see Czimczik *et al.* 2002; Turney *et al.* 2006; Resco *et al.* 2011). Additionally, some basic outlier analysis was used to eliminate likely anomalous values caused by non-climatic trends, such as lower $\delta^{13}C$ values that often occur in the first few decades of a tree's growth (Gagen *et al.* 2008; see also Kearns 2015: 131–166). It is important to state that these data form an impartial paleoclimatic record for Cyprus but highlight the necessity of continuing to build up paleoenvironmental information, especially for later periods.

Results

The preliminary data from the carbon stable isotope analysis suggest certain trends in past water availability on Cyprus and support other proxy records for a shift to wetter conditions by the eighth to seventh centuries BCE. Figure 9.2 shows the average $\Delta^{13}C$ values for periods from all sites, coded according to each of the species analyzed, and their standard deviations.

The material from the earlier second millennium BCE at the inland Middle Cypriot (MC) site of Alambra *Mouttes* reflects an apparent drier period, with a potential turn to wetter conditions in Late Cypriot (LC) IIB, around the beginning of the fourteenth century BCE, at Kalavasos *Ayios Dhimitrios*. In comparison to the drier values of the Late Bronze Age, also represented by charcoal from the site of Alassa *Paliotaverna* in the Kouris Valley and room debris from the inland site of Apliki *Karamallos*, the material from the eighth to fifth centuries BCE from the Cypro-Archaic (CA) period at Amathus on the southern coast has considerably higher $\Delta^{13}C$ values, reflecting an increase in the amount of water available during the growth of the trees sampled. The relatively similar values for the Cypro-Classical, Hellenistic, Roman, and Late Roman periods also correspond well with other records showing a generally stable end of the first millennium BCE and early first millennium CE, including the radiocarbon curve (Manning 2010: 43; 2013a).

While the samples from the LC IIIA inland copper production settlement of Apliki *Karamallos* are likely the higher-elevation *P. nigra* species and therefore may reveal a difference in isotopic discrimination compared to lowland taxa from sites at Kalavasos *Ayios Dhimitrios* and Amathus, the pine, oak, and olive samples from CA levels at Amathus all show high $\Delta^{13}C$ values, affirming the shift from drier to wetter conditions by the eighth to seventh centuries BCE. The overall pattern of a drier period in the twelfth to eighth centuries, moreover, aligns with the recent pollen record drawn from the Larnaka Salt Lake (Kaniewski *et al.* 2013; on the problems

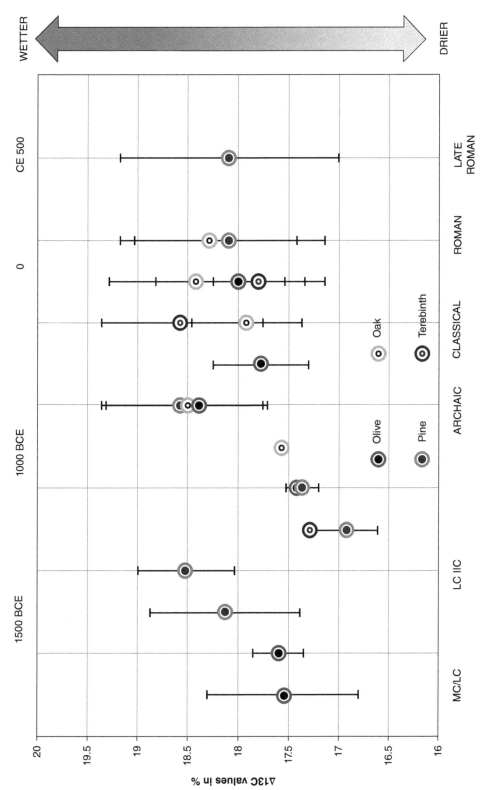

Figure 9.2: Graph of results from carbon stable isotope analysis, coded according to species (*Pinus sp.*, *Quercus sp.*, *Olea eur.*, *Pistacia ter.*) and grouped by period. Average values shown with approximate error 0.05 ppm.

with this study's chronological resolution, see Knapp and Manning 2016), and this aridity is supported by the lower value for the sample of *Quercus sp.* recovered from Idalion dating to the tenth to ninth centuries BCE.

Social and Political Change

Having introduced a scientific framework to begin building a paleoclimatic record for Cyprus and its shifting physical climates and acknowledging that this local record needs more data and other paleoenvironmental studies in order to refine its accuracy, archaeological evidence can help elucidate how these transformations became entangled with new land use, settlement, and industrial practices. To do so, I draw on archaeological survey material collected in the Vasilikos and Maroni valleys of south-central Cyprus (Kearns 2016; 2017), integrated with geophysical survey and geographic information systems (GIS) analysis that models rural landscape dynamics (see Bevan 2002). These river valleys, which radiate out from the Troodos Mountains to the coast, cutting through igneous and sedimentary zones before reaching the coastal plain, have supported agriculture as well as copper mining and production for several millennia (Wagstaff 1978; Gomez 1987; Figure 9.3). Scholars have traditionally looked to this region for its prominent early prehistoric sites, such as Kalavasos *Tenta* and Khirokitia *Vounoi*, and for two LC urban polities, Kalavasos *Ayios Dhimitrios* and Maroni *Vournes*, which sat on an important east-west coastal route (South 2002; Todd 2013: 92–97; Andreou in this volume).

Less examined are its post–Bronze Age occupations, particularly the CG III–CA II period, ca. 900–500 BCE, when numerous settlements appear on the grounds of earlier sites as well as in newly occupied areas throughout the two valleys (see South 2002; Todd 2013: 97–102). Although the borders of the island's first-millennium BCE polities are debated (see e.g., Fourrier 2002; Satraki and Diakou in this volume), scholars conjecture that this region was involved in the economic, cultural, and likely political apparatus of the coastal polity of Amathus, 20 km to the west (Hermary 1992; Aupert 1996: Figure 2; Todd 2013: 99–103).

Two earlier interdisciplinary projects, the Vasilikos Valley Project (VVP; see Todd 2004; 2013; 2016) and the Maroni Valley Archaeological Survey Project (MVASP; see Manning *et al.* 1994), with quite divergent methods and survey areas (VVP = 151 sq. km, MVASP = 14.5 sq. km), conducted extensive and intensive survey in these valleys. They recorded diachronic surface material ranging from earliest prehistory to the modern period and interpreted several fluctuations in occupation. While both projects catalogued diagnostic Iron Age material, the settlement patterns in this region after the end of the Bronze Age remain unclear, in part due to problems in recognizing (and lack of attention to) local, coarse Iron Age wares through surface survey (Given and Smith 2003: 271; Janes and Winther-Jacobsen 2013). Moreover, the incompatibility of the two survey datasets and their incommensurate sampling strategies, ranging from intuitive topographical walking to total collection intensity, make a substantive regional comparison exceedingly difficult (on this issue, see Alcock and Cherry 2004; Kearns 2015: 171–186). "Chasing" the Iron Age via survey results therefore requires spatial and material synthesis (*sensu* Pettegrew 2001).

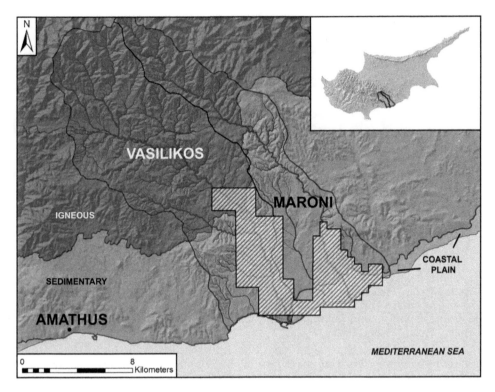

Figure 9.3: Physiographical map of the Vasilikos and Maroni valleys, showing igneous, sedimentary, and coastal zones, with survey areas in gray box. Created by C. Kearns; data provided by the Geological Survey Department of Cyprus.

For this case study, I employed "front to back" re-survey as a way to examine these changes (see Thompson 2004). This method entails the return to a region previously surveyed, often decades earlier, to distinguish modifications in assemblage as well as visibility and surface composition (see Diacopoulos 2004).

Despite methodological constraints in both the Vasilikos and Maroni valleys, the survey evidence, illustrated below as discrete assemblages of material (and not densities), shows significant drops in settlement numbers in the early CG period (twelfth to ninth centuries BCE), with only three sites with CG III material (ca. 900–800/750 BCE) recorded in the first publications of the Vasilikos Valley, as opposed to roughly seventy-five settlements and tombs for the Late Bronze Age period (Todd 2013: 92–96). A more recent intensive study of the VVP material has found several more indications of scattered CG III material, suggesting increased activity around 800 BCE, but in low frequencies that also correspond to areas with material from the late second millennium BCE (Georgiadou 2016: 104). Very little recovered CG material was found in the southern Maroni valley following the abandonment of Maroni *Vournes* and Maroni *Tsaroukkas* (Manning *et al.* 1994: 353–356) (Figure 9.4).

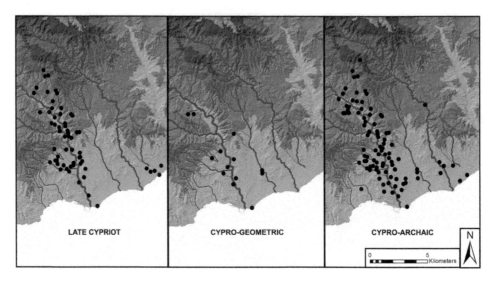

Figure 9.4: Map of settlements in the Vasilikos and Maroni valleys recorded through archaeological survey, separated into Late Bronze Age, Cypro-Geometric (III), and Cypro-Archaic periods. Created by C. Kearns; basemap provided by the Geological Survey Department of Cyprus.

Ongoing research at the site of Tochni *Lakkia* on the coast near the mouth of the Vasilikos river indicates some continued presence and activity at this probable anchorage site during the CG period (on Tochni *Lakkia,* see Andreou *et al.* 2017). This tenuous continuity suggests the clustering, or contraction, of communities in selected settlements after the apparent breakdown of the local center of Kalavasos *Ayios Dhimitrios.* Thus the broad picture that emerges in this region and across the island (e.g., Rupp 1987; Petit 2001) during the eleventh to ninth centuries BCE is one of limited permanent occupation with some preserved maintenance of important coastal trading sites and access to major transregional routes that connected the east and west of the island. Vessel sizes seem to have decreased, or we lack significant evidence for large storage jars known from Late Bronze Age centers (requiring technological investment), implying also a shift in daily practice and strategies for maintaining and distributing goods (Pilides 1996: 110, 119–120; Hadjisavvas 1996: 133; see Halstead and O'Shea 1989: 123–124).

By the late ninth to eighth centuries BCE, however, this apparent contraction of the local population is countered by the expansion of numerous re-settlements as well as original establishments, particularly tomb sites, throughout the two survey areas, indicating a complex shift to more sedentary practices. From the site of Tochni *Lakkia* on the coast, up the valleys into the foothills of the Troodos, clusters of sites appear with CA I ceramic material (750–600 BCE), with several large concentrations surrounded by smaller installations likely involved in agricultural, pastoral, and industrial activities (Georgiadou 2016: 104–106). The distribution of these sites indicates the potential bounding of emergent communities, providing access up the river valleys to goods brought in from the coast or from the important east-west coastal road that endured into the Roman period (Bekker-Nielsen 2004: 194–196). In addition, evidence of olive oil production at survey sites in the Vasilikos Valley may point to the increasing permanence of collective agropastoral practice (Todd 2013: 101).

The prominent spacing of cemeteries on previously unoccupied ground in the lower part of the Vasilikos Valley, shown in Figure 9.5, suggests intentional demarcations of mortuary places linked to new social organization and arguably to the revitalization of the fertile coastal plain (for a similar case in nearby Amathus, see Janes 2013). For the Vasilikos and Maroni watersheds, the coastal plain is where marine terraces conspicuously stick up, marking prominent places that became the grounds for these new Archaic collective burials, intervisible due to the relatively flat sloping terrain. In these clusters of tombs, excavated materials point to the contemporary underscoring of social inequality, potentially linked to access to emerging productive landscapes and interregional markets like Tochni *Lakkia*. An increase in the number of fragments of decorated drinking and dining wares points to feasting-like practices, perhaps as settings for the display of social power (Hamilakis and Sherratt 2012).

We can discern these changes in a handful of salvage operations on CGIII/CAI tombs at Mari (Hadjicosti 1997), Maroni (Karageorghis 1972: 1017–1019; Christodoulou 1972), and Khirokitia (Karageorghis 1984: 922; Flourentzos 1985). These singular examples consist of mostly small-scale burials of a few individuals, with some evidence of re-burial at later phases during the early fifth century BCE (a general trend; see Hamilakis and Sherratt 2012: 200). The presence of bronze jewelry, uncommon ceramic forms, and iron swords, adzes, and knives far outside the urban polity at Amathus may hint at a local elite adopting the mortuary warrior aesthetic appearing elsewhere on the island during the early first millennium BCE in iconography and "epic" funerary objects (Hamilakis and Sherratt 2012: 195; on contemporary mortuary practices, see e.g., Rupp 1987; Blackwell 2010). While presumably these emerging elites linked themselves to the nearby coastal center to the west in order to access the growing interregional trade in luxury goods as well as agropastoral commodities (Greene *et al.* 2013), the place-making practices in the Maroni and Vasilikos valleys do suggest alternate forms of social bounding (Georgiadou 2016: 106). Survey data from the region of Amathus (Petit 1996), for example, in the hills surrounding the site where elites built distinct necropoleis showcasing monumental performativity (Janes 2013) indicate much less continuity with second-millennium inhabitation and landscape practices than the Vasilikos and Maroni region, where Middle Bronze Age and Late Bronze Age settlements provided apparent salience during the transition to the Iron Age.

Spatial analysis of the VVP and MVASP data indicate that these settlements were intensifying local land by managing small watersheds (e.g., 6 ha) and re-occupying terraces higher up the slopes of the valley than in the Late Bronze Age where the soil was potentially more fertile. Data from previous surveys in the region as well as my own recent re-survey of these sites illustrate the wide-ranging use of slopes and terraces along the valley sides and perennial streams that seem to have been unoccupied and unworked in the preceding CG I–II period (see Kearns 2016; 2017). The mapping of terrace walls (notoriously difficult to date) in several of these drainages suggests renewed attention to curating soil and rainwater in this period, based on the presence of CA ceramics nearby (see Wagstaff 1992). These findings correspond

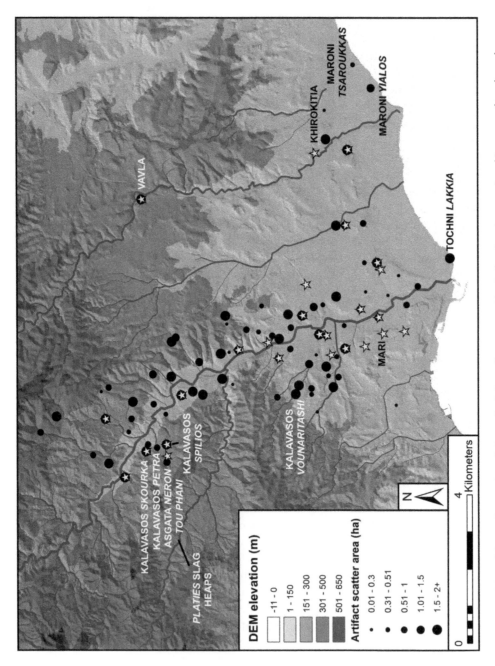

Figure 9.5: Map of Cypro-Geometric and Cypro-Archaic artifact scatters (dots), showing sites mentioned in text, and tombs and cemeteries (stars), indicating new mortuary landscape in southern valleys. Created by C. Kearns; data provided by the Geological Survey Department of Cyprus.

well with evidence recorded to the west in the nearby Amathus hinterland, where the French survey also found a network of rock-cut installations that likely date to the early first millennium BCE, when new communities began reworking the landscape and increasing agricultural production (see Petit 1996: 178–179, 182, Figure 171).

While survey data lack chronological precision, it becomes clear that by roughly the eighth century BCE, this region had developed landscape practices that brought people together to manage their surroundings and to invest in permanent infrastructure, such as soil management and industrial installations, with which they could sustain themselves and potentially produce for wider markets. The strengthening of access routes to the east and the west, as well as to anchorages such as Tochni *Lakkia* along the coast, brought people and goods to new settlements or gathering places such as ritual centers. For example, groups reused the visible monumental Bronze Age ruins at Maroni *Vournes* to construct a conspicuous shrine with potential pilgrimage attraction, whose votive offerings (ca. eighth to third centuries BCE) were oriented toward fertility and herding and were situated near features related to olive oil production (Cadogan 1983: 156–157; Ulbrich 2012; 2013: 36). Additional survey work has revealed probable small shrines and sanctuaries of the Archaic and Classical periods at sites like Vavla *Kapsalaes* (Morden and Todd 1994; Papantoniou *et al.* 2015), Vavla *Metaxa* (Flourentzos 2008: 82), and Maroni *Yialos* (Karageorghis 1978: 881–882; Johnson 1980: 6). Such pockets of evidence hint at a series of differentiated ritual landscapes that may have accommodated diverse social groups and countryside pilgrimage practices across the Vasilikos and Maroni valleys (see Given and Smith 2003: 275–276).

To give one example of such local growth of social boundaries, the settlements that arise in this arguable period of increasing sedentism near the important Kalavasos copper mines in the Vasilikos Valley, roughly 11 km from the coast, point to a potential reclaimed organization of mineral as well as charcoal resources. These eighth to fifth century BCE production activities built up dependent economic practices tied to forests, soil, and mineral sources and seem to have belonged to a settlement zone integrating mining with cultivation and possibly pastoralism. A few radiocarbon dates from prominent slag heaps in this mining area, at Kalavasos *Petra* and Kalavasos *Platies*, indicate the exploitation of these mines by the CA period (Kassianidou 2013: 75; Table 9.2).

Table 9.2: Published radiocarbon dates from charcoal in slag heaps in the Kalavasos area (Kassianidou 2013: 75, Appendix I)

Site Name	Context	Published date (Zwicker 1986)	^{14}C date before present	Calibrated date (68.2%)	Calibrated date (95.4%)	Period
Kalavasos	"biggest" slag heap	430 ± 85 BCE	2376 ± 83 BP	552–382 BCE	770–354 BCE	Cypro-Archaic
Kalavasos *Platies*	Slag heap?	410 ± 70 BCE	2357 ± 68 BP	541–375 BCE	670–352 BCE	Cypro-Archaic
Kalavaos *Platies*	Slag heap?	450 ± 40 BCE	2399 ± 30 BP	510–434 BCE	544–396 BCE	Cypro-Classical

Slag around the first-millennium BCE survey sites of Asgata *Neron tou Phani* and Kalavasos *Spilios* suggests that emerging communities were taking advantage of the igneous pillow lavas in conjunction with an area of relatively stable slopes and access to streams with extant check dam features. Later, toward the middle of the first millennium BCE, this charged geologic zone of mining and copper production had become the location of religious practice, seen in the remains of a small structure with multiple Cypro-Classical (fifth century BCE) ceramic figurines in the slag heap at Kalavasos *Skourka* (Flourentzos 2008: 102; Todd 2013: 135–140). Over the course of centuries of close investment in these copper resources, local communities had come to link the landscape of mining and igneous geology with a repertory of cultural practice involving deposited sacred objects. Perhaps these ritual practices were also aimed at the health of nearby forests of pine that fueled their local and transregional mining economy.

Recent fieldwork at the site of Kalavasos *Vounaritashi*, situated in a small side valley of the Vasilikos River roughly 4 km from the coast, provides an opportunity for more substantive analysis of the relationships between people and changing landscapes (Figure 9.6). Pedestrian and geophysical survey as well as targeted soil tests around a large multi-period site first identified by the VVP (Todd 2004:

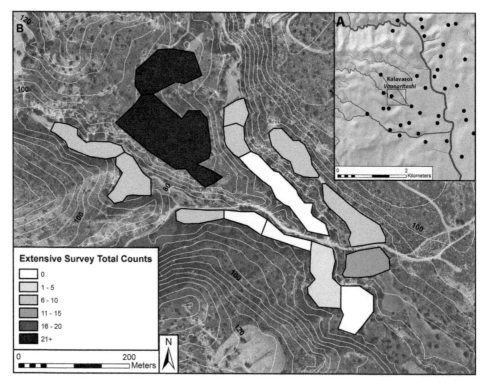

Figure 9.6: Position of Kalavasos *Vounaritashi* in mid-valley amid Archaic settlements (A) and satellite image showing extensive survey results surrounding the site (B). 5 m contours. Created by C. Kearns; data provided from Geological Survey Department and Department of Lands and Surveys of Cyprus.

58–60) and undertaken through the Kalavasos and Maroni Built Environments Project (KAMBE) indicate a prominent assemblage of CA materials amid limestone and gypsum outcrops (Kearns 2016). Extensive survey (10 m transect spacing) has further suggested some type of settlement on the plateau with fewer ceramic fragments in the nearby alluvial drainages, which retain relic cross-channel walls, perhaps even dating to the Bronze Age (Wagstaff 1992). The dense surface scatters, discretely bounded by the rich soils of the limestone and gypsiferous ridge, include significant fragments of large storage vessels (*pithoi*), basket-handled amphorae, grinding (*mortaria*) and cooking vessels, and arrangements of stone blocks, suggesting activities related to storage, production, consumption, and probable habitation (Figure 9.7).

The proximity to deep alluvial soils points to agropastoral tasks and the maintenance of valued land and water management features. Intended future excavations at the site and its associated walls and possible enclosures, as well as the remains of plant and animal economies, will provide a closer look at the area's environmental practices as they became a part of or potentially challenged interregional developments associated with nearby Amathus or other coastal centers.

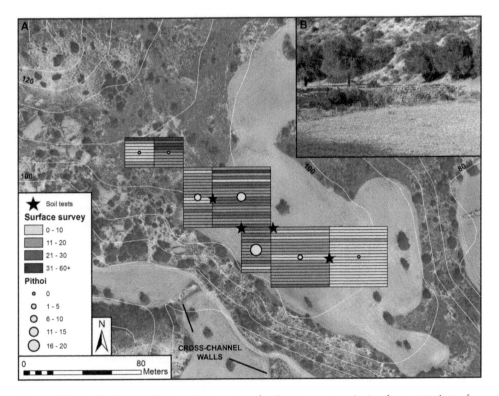

Figure 9.7: Satellite image with intensive survey results (2 m transect spacing) and concentrations of large storage vessels (*pithoi*) (A) and cross-channel wall (B). 5 m contours. Created by C. Kearns; data provided from Geological Survey Department and Department of Lands and Surveys of Cyprus.

Discussion and Conclusion

At the macro-scale, the apparent synchronous correlation between a sudden growth in communities and renewed exploitation of mines in this south-central area of Cyprus around the eighth century BCE and a turn to wetter, "favorable" conditions as shown in new paleoenvironmental records seems apt for a causal relationship between climatic and social change. The climate got "better," potentially marked by more winter rainfall, warmer temperatures, and more reliable and consistent growing seasons. These conditioned the growth and expansion of communities, fostering hierarchical organization and the command of local resources through emerging institutions such as property that helped formulate novel Iron Age political systems. And yet, while the local signature of a healthy growing sequence may point to the regeneration of nearby forests and more water to harvest for cultivation, we need more archaeological and paleoenvironmental research to discern how ancient communities might have manipulated these resources in an emerging set of economic and social practices and how environmental shifts mediated the responses of various groups within Archaic society. As this paper has shown, climatic and social temporalities are difficult to weave together and require a balancing of scientifically and archaeologically informed work. Excavation of non-urban, first-millennium BCE sites and terraces in valleys like these thus becomes critical, especially for Cyprus (see e.g., Rautman 2000; Sørensen and Winther-Jacobsen 2006; Toumazou *et al.* 2011; Given *et al.* 2013), as does more archaeobotanical, zooarchaeological, and geomorphological research on soil quality, crop production, and practices such as shepherding and animal husbandry (see Leon 2016).

Such a preliminary project can conclude not with definite claims about the first-millennium BCE countryside and its processes of development but with suggestions for further points of discussion on social formation and human-environment recursivity. Within the apparatus of Iron Age political authority, how might a shift to more stable growing seasons have aligned with mechanisms of rule, economy, and culture that were just taking shape? Our knowledge of the political institutions of the major urban centers and their potential capacities for controlling agropastoral production remains limited but offers avenues for fruitful research. For the watersheds east of Amathus, the survey work presented here suggests several interpretations of the growth of power relations and control. With future investigations, these may substantiate top-down impositions of land use and labor and the deliberate oversight of valued resources in the Vasilikos and Maroni valleys within its growing political economy. Future work may also reveal more complex, rural formations of hierarchies that developed agropastoral wealth and then sought access to, allegiance with, or competitive status within the margins of the Amathusian polity. Arguably, available evidence suggests that a spectrum of these different political associations was developing, given the indications of "high-status" individuals with access to imports and the orientation of local objects toward Amathusian workshops (e.g., Georgiadou 2016: 104–105) but also regional patterns of land use, maintenance of landscape modifications, separate mortuary and sacred places, and use of nearby harbors.

How then did a potential increase in precipitation affect land use practices and create avenues for agropastoral wealth for some, like those buried in wealthy tombs around the two valleys? Does the manipulation of terrace systems indicate a shift in technological choice toward new forms of cultivation, requiring community labor or authoritative supervision? Alternatively, do they reflect a more organic system of reuse and reinvestment on the parts of smaller, competing groups? An integrated methodological approach to these questions can begin to elucidate how ancient environments on Cyprus were (and are) not always restrictive and immutable. Their sudden shifts mediated human practice and ingenuity, from habits of settlement and metal production to the creation of governing authorities of trade or symbolic inclusion in elite circles, not only during the Iron Age but also throughout the island's long and rich history.

More concretely, discerning social and environmental change during the transformations of the Iron Age on Cyprus can reveal the problems with our field's traditional focus on the king, his city, and his iconography that dominates most scholarship on the transition to historical polities (e.g., Satraki 2012). Looking outside the excavated cities such as Kition and Paphos reveals a messy countryside (*sensu* Hritz 2013), where local groups around the ninth to eighth centuries BCE began intensifying certain parts of the landscape to enter or gain control of new economic networks and to establish settlement zones and their interrelationships that could connect growing communities with places considered sacred and culturally salient. An integrated methodology offers a counternarrative to the hypothesized centripetal power projected from the would-be city-kingdoms over dependent hinterlands and instead underscores the heterogeneity and accumulation of local practices in relation to preceding landscape modifications or to novel attempts at place-making. I would suggest that an approach that privileges neither environmental nor archaeological data and avoids reductive causal and temporal relationships by taking seriously the social lives of environments offers a more nuanced and robust examination of historical change and landscapes in the making.

Acknowledgments

I would like to thank Sturt Manning and Jeff Leon for their help in organizing this conference and A. Bernard Knapp and the two anonymous reviewers for providing insightful comments. Brita Lorentzen aided the charcoal identification and dendroclimatological analysis, Akio Enders and Johannes Lehmann helped with the carbonization study, and Kim Sparks and the Cornell Isotope Lab helped run the isotopic analysis. Funding for this research was provided by a Fulbright grant from the U.S. State Department and the Cyprus Fulbright Commission as well as by a Mellon fellowship at Stanford, the Society of Humanities at Cornell, and the Loeb Foundation. I especially thank Ian Todd and Alison South, Anna Georgiadou, Zomenia Zomeni and the Geological Survey Department, and the Department of Antiquities of Cyprus for providing data and support. Sabine Fourrier, Sophocles Hadjisavvas, Andrew Sneddon, Aurelie Carbillet, and Pamela Gaber kindly provided charcoal samples. All errors or omissions are my own.

References

Alcock, S.E. 1993. *Graecia Capta: The Landscapes of Roman Greece*. Cambridge: Cambridge University Press.

Alcock, S.E., and J.F. Cherry. (eds.) 2004. *Side-By-Side Survey: Comparative Regional Studies in the Mediterranean World*. Oxford: Oxbow Books.

Andreou, G.M., R. Opitz, S.W. Manning, K.D. Fisher, D.A. Sewell, A. Georgiou, and T. Urban. 2017. Integrated methods for understanding and monitoring the loss of coastal archaeological sites: The case of Tochni *Lakkia*, south-central Cyprus. *Journal of Archaeological Science: Reports* 12: 197–208.

Appadurai, A. 2015. Mediants, materiality, normativity. *Public Culture* 27.2: 221–237.

Aupert, P. (ed.) 1996. *Guide D'Amathonte*. Paris: École Française d'Athènes—Fondation A.G. Leventis.

Bar-Matthews, M., A. Ayalon, and A. Kaufman. 1998. Middle to late Holocene (6500 yr. period) paleoclimate in the eastern Mediterranean region from stable isotopic composition of speleothems from Soreq Cave, Israel. In A.S. Issar and N. Brown (eds.), *Water, Environment, and Society in Times of Climate Change*, 203–214. Boston, MA: Kluwer Academic Publishers.

Barnes, J., and M.R. Dove. (eds.) 2015. *Climate Cultures: Anthropological Perspectives on Climate Change*. New Haven: Yale University Press.

Bauer, A.M., and S. Kosiba. 2016. How things act: An archaeology of materials in political life. *Journal of Social Archaeology* 16.2: 1–27.

Bekker-Nielsen, T. 2004. *The Roads of Ancient Cyprus*. Copenhagen: Museum Tusculaneum.

Bevan, A. 2002. The rural landscape of neopalatial Kythera: A GIS perspective. *Journal of Mediterranean Archaeology* 15.2: 217–256.

Blackwell, N. 2010. Mortuary variability at Salamis (Cyprus): Relationships between and within the Royal Necropolis and the Cellarka Cemetery. *Journal of Mediterranean Archaeology* 23.2: 143–167.

Bolger, D. 1989. Regionalism, cultural variation, and the culture-area concept in later prehistoric Cypriot studies. In E.J. Peltenburg (ed.), *Early Society in Cyprus*, 142–152. Edinburgh: Edinburgh University Press.

Bond, G., B. Kromer, R. Muscheler, M.N. Evans, W. Showers, S. Hoffman, R. Lotti-Bond, I. Hadjas, and G. Bonani. 2001. Persistent solar influence on North Atlantic climate during the Holocene. *Science* 294: 2130–2136.

Braudel, F. 1980. *On History*. Trans. S. Matthews. Chicago: University of Chicago Press.

Butzer, K.W. 2012. Climate, environment, society. *Proceedings of the National Academy of Sciences of the United States of America* 109.10: 3632–3639.

Butzer, K.W., and S.E. Harris. 2007. Geoarchaeological approaches to the environmental history of Cyprus: Explication and critical evaluation. *Journal of Archaeological Science* 34: 1932–1952.

Cadogan, G. 1983. Maroni I. *Report of the Department of Antiquities, Cyprus*: 154–157.

Catling, H. 1962. Patterns of settlement in Bronze Age Cyprus. *Opuscula Atheniensia* 4: 129–169.

Chambers, F.M., D. Mauquoy, S.A. Brain, M. Blaauw, and J.R.G. Daniell. 2007. Globally synchronous climate change 2800 years ago: Proxy data from peat in South America. *Earth and Planetary Science* 253: 439–444.

Christodoulou, D. 1959. *The Evolution of Rural Land Use Pattern in Cyprus*. The World Land Use Survey, Regional Monograph No. 2. London: Geographical Publications Ltd.

Christodoulou, A. 1972. A Cypro-Archaic I tomb-group from Maroni. *Report of the Department of Antiquities, Cyprus*: 156–160.

Coombes, P., and K. Barber. 2005. Environmental determinism in Holocene research: Causality or coincidence? *Area* 37.3: 303–311.

Crumley, C.L. 1994. Historical ecology: A multidimensional ecological orientation. In C.L. Crumley (ed.), *Historical Ecology: Cultural Knowledge and Changing Landscapes*, 1–16. Santa Fe: SAR Press.

Crumley, C., S. Laparidou, M. Ramsey, and A.M. Rosen. 2015. A view from the past to the future: Concluding remarks on the "The Anthropocene in the Longue Durée." *The Holocene* 25.10: 1721–1723.

Czimczik, C.I., C.M. Preston, and M.W.I. Schmidt. 2002. Effects of charring on mass, organic carbon, and stable carbon isotope composition of wood. *Organic Geochemistry* 33: 1207–1223.

Devillers, B., M. Brown, and C. Morhange. 2015. Paleo-environmental evolution of the Larnaca Salt Lakes (Cyprus) and the relationship to second millennium BC settlement. *Journal of Archaeological Science: Reports* 1: 73–80.

Diacopoulos, L. 2004. Investigating social complexity through regional survey: "Second-generation" analysis of Bronze Age data from the Canadian Palaipaphos Survey Project, southwestern Cyprus. *Journal of Mediterranean Archaeology* 17.1: 59–85.

Diamond, J. 2005. *Collapse: How Societies Choose to Fail or Succeed*. New York: Viking Press.

Drake, B.L. 2012. The influence of climatic change on the Late Bronze Age collapse and the Greek Dark Ages. *Journal of Archaeological Science* 39: 1862–1870.

Emeis, K.-C., U. Struck, H.-M. Schulz, R. Rosenberg, S. Bernasconi, H. Erlenkeuser, T. Sakamoto, and F. Martinez-Ruiz. 2000. Temperature and salinity variations of Mediterranean Sea surface waters over the last 16,000 years from records of planktonic stable oxygen isotopes and alkenone unsaturation ratios. *Palaeogeography, Palaeoclimatology, Palaeoecology* 158: 259–280.

Fall, P.L., S.E. Falconer, C.S. Galletti, T. Shirmang, E. Ridder, and J. Klinge. 2012. Long-term agrarian landscapes in the Troodos foothills, Cyprus. *Journal of Archaeological Science* 39.7: 2335–2347.

Farquhar, G.D., J.R. Ehleringer, and K.T. Hubick. 1989. Carbon isotope discrimination and photosynthesis. *Annual Review of Plant Physiology and Plant Molecular Biology* 40: 5035–5037.

Ferrio, J.P., N. Alonso, J.B. Lopez, J.L Araus, and J. Voltas. 2006. Carbon isotope composition of fossil charcoal reveals aridity changes in the NW Mediterranean Basin. *Global Change Biology* 12: 1253–1266.

Flourentzos, P. 1985. An Archaic tomb from Khirokitia. *Report of the Department of Antiquities, Cyprus*: 222–231.

Flourentzos, P. 2008. *Annual Report of the Department of Antiquities for the Year 2006*. Nicosia: Department of Antiquities.

Fourrier, S. 2002. Les territoires des royaumes Chypriotes archaïques: Une esquisse de géographie historique. *Cahiers du Centre d'Études Chypriotes* 32: 135–146.

Frankel, D., J.M. Webb, and S. Lawrence. (eds.) 2013. *Archaeology in Environment and Technology: Intersections and Transformations*. New York: Routledge.

Gagen, M., D. McCarroll, I. Robertson, N.J. Loader and R. Jalkanen. 2008. Do tree ring $\delta^{13}C$ series from *Pinus sylvestris* in northern Fennoscandia contain long-term non-climatic trends? *Chemical Geology* 252: 42–51.

Georgiadou, A. 2016. Geometric-Archaic. In I. Todd (ed.), *The Vasilikos Valley Project 10: The Field Survey of the Vasilikos Valley Vol II, Artefacts Recovered by the Field Survey*, 95–128. Studies in Mediterranean Archaeology 71.11. Sävedalen, Sweden: Åströms Förlag.

Gifford, J.A. 1985. Paleogeography of ancient harbor sites of the Larnaca lowlands, southeastern Cyprus. In A. Raban (ed.), *Harbor Archaeology*, 45–48. British Archaeological Reports, International Series 257. Oxford: Oxbow Books.

Given, M., and A.B. Knapp. (eds.) 2003. *The Sydney Cyprus Survey Project: Social Approaches to Regional Archaeological Survey*. Monumenta Archaeologica 21. Los Angeles: UCLA Institute of Archaeology.

Given, M., and J. Smith. 2003. Geometric to Classical landscapes. In M. Given and A.B. Knapp (eds.), *The Sydney Cyprus Survey Project: Social Approaches to Regional Archaeological Survey (Monumenta Archaeologica 21)*, 270–277. Los Angeles: UCLA Institute of Archaeology.

Given, M., A.B. Knapp, J. Noller, L. Sollars, and V. Kassiandou. 2013. *Landscape and Interaction: The Troodos Archaeological and Environmental Survey Project, Cyprus. Volume 1: Methodology, Analysis and Interpretation*. Levant Supplementary Series 14. London: Council for British Research in the Levant.

Gjerstad, E. 1926. *Studies on Prehistoric Cyprus*. Stockholm: Uppsala University.

Greene, E.S., J. Leidwanger, and H. Ozdas. 2013. Expanding contacts and collapsing distances in early Cypro-Archaic trade: Three case studies of shipwrecks off the Turkish Coast. In M.L. Lawall and J. Lund (eds.), *Transport Amphorae and Trade of Cyprus*, 21–34. Aarhus: Aarhus University Press.

Gomez, B. 1987. The alluvial terraces and fills of the lower Vasilikos Valley, in the vicinity of Kalavasos, Cyprus. *Institute of British Geographers, Transactions* N.S. 12: 345–359.

Griggs, C.B., C.L. Pearson, S.W. Manning, and B. Lorentzen. 2014. A 250-year annual precipitation reconstruction and drought assessment for Cyprus from *Pinus brutia* Ten. tree-rings. *International Journal of Climatology* 34.8: 2702–2714.

Hadjicosti, M. 1997. The family tomb of a warrior of the Cypro-Archaic period at Mari. *Report of the Department of Antiquities, Cyprus*: 251–266.

Haldon, J., M. Cassis, O. Doonan, W. Eastwood, H. Elton, D. Fleitmann, A. Izdebski, S. Ladstätter, M. McCormick, S.W. Manning, J. Newhard, K. Nichol, N. Roberts, I. Telelis, and E. Xoplaki. 2014. Byzantine Anatolia: A "laboratory" for the study of climate impacts and socioenvironmental relations in the past. *Journal of Interdisciplinary History* 45: 113–161.

Halstead, P., and J. O'Shea. (eds.) 1989. *Bad Year Economics: Cultural Responses to Risk and Uncertainty*. Cambridge: Cambridge University Press.

Hamilakis, Y., and S. Sherratt. 2012. Feasting and the consuming body in Bronze Age Crete and Early Iron Age Cyprus. In G. Cadogan, M. Iacovou, K. Kopaka, and J. Whitley (eds.), *Parallel Lives: Ancient Island Societies in Crete and Cyprus. Proceedings of the Conference in Nicosia Organized by the British School at Athens, the University of Crete and the University of Cyprus in November–December 2006*, 187–209. Athens: British School at Athens.

Harris, W.V. 2013. What kind of environmental history for antiquity? In W.V. Harris (ed.), *The Ancient Mediterranean Environment between Science and History*, 1–10. Leiden: Brill.

Hassan, F.A. 1997. The dynamics of a riverine civilization: A geoarchaeological perspective on the Nile Valley, Egypt. *World Archaeology* 29: 51–74.

Held, S.O. n.d. Contributions to the early prehistoric archaeology of Cyprus: Environmental and chronological background studies. Unpublished manuscript.

Hermary, A. 1992. Les limites du royaume d'Amathonte. *Cahier Centre d'Études Chypriotes* 17: 25–26.

Horden, P., and N. Purcell. 2000. *The Corrupting Sea: A Study of Mediterranean History*. Malden, MA: Blackwell Publishing.

Hoskins, W.G. 1955. *The Making of the English Landscape*. London: Hodder.

Hritz, C. 2013. Urbanocentric models and "rural messiness": A case study in the Balikh River valley, Syria. *American Journal of Archaeology* 117.2: 141–161.

Hulme, M. 2011. Reducing the future to climate: A story of climate determinism and reductionism. *Osiris* 26.1: 245–266.

Hulme, M. 2015. Climate and its changes: A cultural appraisal. *Geo: Geography and Environment* 2.1: 1–11.

Hulme, M. 2016. *Weathered: Cultures of Climate*. Thousand Oaks, CA: SAGE Publications.

Iacovou, M. 2008. Cultural and political configurations in Iron Age Cyprus: The sequel to the protohistoric episode. *American Journal of Archaeology* 112.4: 625–657.

Iacovou, M. 2012. From regional gateway to Cypriot kingdom: Copper deposits and copper routes in the chora of Paphos. In V. Kassianidou and G. Papasavvas (eds.), *Eastern Mediterranean Metallurgy and Metalwork in the Second Millennium BC: A Conference in Honor of James D. Muhly, Nicosia, 10th–11th October 2009*, 58–69. Oxford: Oxbow Books.

Iacovou, M. 2013. Historically elusive and internally fragile island polities: The intricacies of Cyprus's political geography in the Iron Age. *Bulletin of the American Schools of Oriental Research* 370: 15–47.

Iacovou, M. 2014a. Cyprus during the Iron Age through the Persian period: From the 11th century BC to the abolition of the city-kingdoms (c. 300 BC). In A.E. Killebrew and M. Steiner (eds.), *The Oxford Handbook of the Archaeology of the Levant: c. 8000–332 BCE*, 795–824. Oxford: Oxford University Press.

Iacovou, M. 2014b. Political economies and landscape transformations: The case of ancient Paphos. In J. Webb (ed.), *Structure, Measurement, and Meaning: Studies on Prehistoric Cyprus in Honour of David Frankel*, 161–174. Studies in Mediterranean Archaeology 143. Uppsala, Sweden: Åströms Förlag.

Iacovou, M. (ed.) 2004. *Archaeological Field Survey in Cyprus: Past History, Future Potentials. Proceedings of a Conference Held by the Archaeological Research Unit of the University of Cyprus, 1–2 December 2000*. London: The British School at Athens.

Janes, S. 2013. Death and burial in the age of the Cypriot city-kingdoms: Social complexity based on the mortuary evidence. *Bulletin of American Schools of Oriental Research* 370: 145–168.

Janes, S., and K. Winther-Jacobsen. 2013. Iron Age pottery. In M. Given, A.B. Knapp, J. Noller, L. Sollars, and V. Kassianidou (eds.), *Landscape and Interaction: The Troodos Archaeological and Environmental Survey Project, Cyprus. Volume 1: Methodology, Analysis and Interpretation*, 62–63. Levant Supplementary Series 14. London: Council for British Research in the Levant.

Johnson, J. 1980. *Maroni de Chypre*. Studies in Mediterranean Archaeology 59. Göteborg, Sweden: Paul Åströms Förlag.

Kaniewski, D., E. Van Campo, J. Guiot, S. Le Burel, T. Otto, and C. Bateman. 2013. Environmental roots of the Late Bronze Age crisis. *PLOS One* 8.8: e71004. https://doi.org/10.1371/journal.pone.0071004.

Karageorghis, V. 1972. Chronique des fouilles et découvertes archéologiques à Chypre en 1971. *Bulletin de Correspondance Hellénique* 96.2: 1005–1088.

Karageorghis, V. 1978. Chronique des fouilles et découvertes archéologiques à Chypre en 1977. *Bulletin de Correspondance Hellénique* 102.2: 879–938.

Karageorghis, V. 1984. Chronique des fouilles et découvertes archéologiques à Chypre en 1983. *Bulletin de Correspondance Hellénique* 108.2: 893–966.

Kassianidou, V. 2013. The exploitation of the landscape: Metal resources and the copper trade during the age of the Cypriot city-kingdoms. *Bulletin of American Schools of Oriental Research* 370: 49–82.

Kassianidou, V. 2014. Cypriot copper for the Iron Age world of the eastern Mediterranean. In J. Webb (ed.), *Structure, Measurement, and Meaning: Studies on Prehistoric Cyprus in Honour of David Frankel*, 261–271. Studies in Mediterranean Archaeology 143. Uppsala, Sweden: Åströms Förlag.

Kearns, C. 2013. "On a clear day the Taurus Mountains hang like a cloud": On environmental thought in Cypriot archaeology. In A.B. Knapp, J.M. Webb, and A. McCarthy (eds.) *J.R.B. Stewart—An Archaeological Legacy*, 121–132. Studies in Mediterranean Archaeology 139. Uppsala, Sweden: Åströms Förlag.

Kearns, C. 2015. Unruly landscapes: Making 1st-millennium BCE political landscapes on Cyprus. Unpublished PhD dissertation, Cornell University.

Kearns, C. 2016. Re-survey and spatial analysis of landscape developments during the first millennium BCE on Cyprus. *Antiquity Project Gallery* 90.353: https://doi.org/10.15184/aqy.2016.164.

Kearns, C. 2017. Mediterranean archaeology and environmental histories in the spotlight of the Anthropocene. *History Compass* 15:e12371. https://doi.org/10.1111/hic3.12371.

Kintigh, K.W. *et al.* 2014. Grand challenges for archaeology. *American Antiquity* 79.1: 5–24.

Knapp, A.B., and S.W. Manning. 2016. Crisis in context: The end of the Late Bronze Age in the eastern Mediterranean. *American Journal of Archaeology* 120.1: 99–149.

Kotsonas, A. 2016. Politics of periodization and the archaeology of early Greece. *American Journal of Archaeology* 120.2: 239–270.

Kouki, P. 2013. Problems of relating environmental history to human settlement in the classical and late classical periods: The example of southern Jordan. In W.V. Harris (ed.), *The Ancient Mediterranean Environment Between Science and History*, 197–211. Leiden: Brill.

Langgut, D., I. Finkelstein, and T. Litt. 2013. Climate and the Late Bronze Age collapse: New evidence from the southern Levant. *Tel Aviv* 40: 149–175.

Leon, J.F. 2016. More than "counting sheep": Isotopic approaches to Minoan and Late Cypriot wool production economies. Unpublished PhD dissertation, Cornell University.

Manning, S.W. 2010. Radiocarbon dating and climate change. In A.B. Mainwaring, R. Giegengack, and C. Vita-Finzi (eds.), *Climate Change in Human History*, 25–59. Philadelphia: American Philosophical Society.

Manning, S.W. 2013a. The Roman world and climate: Context, relevance of climate change, and some issues. In W.V. Harris (ed.), *The Ancient Mediterranean Environment between Science and History*, 103–172. Leiden: Brill.

Manning, S.W. 2013b. Appendix: A new radiocarbon chronology for prehistoric and protohistoric Cyprus, ca. 11,000–1050 Cal BC. In A.B. Knapp, *The Archaeology of Cyprus: From Earliest Prehistory through the Bronze Age*, 485–533. Cambridge: Cambridge University Press.

Manning, S.W., D.L. Bolger, A. Swinton, and M.J. Ponting. 1994. Maroni Valley Archaeological Survey Project: Preliminary report on the 1990–1991 seasons. *Report of the Department of Antiquities, Cyprus*: 271–284.

Mayewski, P.A., E.E. Rohling, J.C. Stager, W. Karlen, K.A. Maascha, L.D. Meekler, E.A. Meyerson, F. Gasse, S. van Kreveld, K. Holmgren, J. Lee-Thorp, G. Rosqvist, F. Rack, M. Staubwasser, R.R. Schneider, and E.J. Steig. 2004. Holocene climate variability. *Quaternary Research* 62: 243–255.

McCarroll, D., and N.J. Loader. 2004. Stable isotopes in tree rings. *Quaternary Science Reviews* 23: 771–801.

Middleton, G.D. 2012. Nothing lasts forever: Environmental discourses on the collapse of past societies. *Journal of Archaeological Research* 20: 247–307.

Morden, M.E., and I.A. Todd. 1994. Vavla *Kapsalaes*: An Archaic sanctuary site. *Archaeologia Cypria* 3: 53–63.

Morhange, C. 2000. Recent Holocene paleo-environmental evolution and coastline changes of Kition, Larnaca, Cyprus, Mediterranean Sea. *Marine Geology* 170.1–2: 20–30.

Morris, I. 2009. The eighth-century revolution. In K.A. Raaflaub and H. van Wees (eds.), *A Companion to Archaic Greece*, 64–80. Malden, MA: Wiley-Blackwell.

Morrison, K.D. 2014. Capital-esque landscapes: Long-term histories of enduring landscape modifications. In N. Thomas Hakansson and M. Widgren (eds.), *Landesque Capital: The Historical Ecology of Enduring Landscape Modifications*, 49–74. Walnut Creek, CA: Left Coast Press.

Noller, J. 2010. *The Geomorphology of Cyprus*. Cyprus Geological Survey, Open File Report, 269 pp.

Papantoniou, G., N. Kyriakou, A. Sarris, and M. Iacovou. 2015. Sacred topography in Iron Age Cyprus: The case of Vavla-*Kapsalaes*. In C. Papadopoulos, E. Paliou, A. Chrysanthi, E. Kotoula, and A. Sarris (eds.), *Archaeological Research in the Digital Age*, 70–75. Rethymno, Greece: IMS-FORTH.

Pederson, N., A.E. Hessl, N. Baatarbileg, K.J. Anchukiatis, and N. di Cosmo. 2014. Pluvials, droughts, the Mongol Empire, and modern Mongolia. *Proceedings of the National Academy of Sciences of the United States of America* 111.12: 4375–4379.

Petit, C. 1996. Amathonte et son territoire à traverse les âges. In P. Aupert (ed.), *Guide D'Amathonte*, 173–182. Paris: École Française d'Athènes—Fondation A.G. Leventis.

Petit, T. 2001. The first palace of Amathus and the Cypriot poleogenesis. In I. Nielsen (ed.), *The Royal Palace Institution in the First Millennium BC: Regional Development and Cultural Interchange between East and West*, 53–75. Athens: Danish Institute at Athens.

Pettegrew, D. 2001. Chasing the classical farmstead: Assessing the formation and signature of rural settlement in Greek landscape archaeology. *Journal of Mediterranean Archaeology* 14.2: 189–209.

Pollard, A.M., and P. Bray. 2014. The archaeological bazaar: Scientific methods for sale? Or: Putting the "arch-" back into archaeometry. In R. Chapman and A. Wylie (eds.), *Material Evidence: Learning from Archaeological Practice*, 113–127. Abingdon and New York: Routledge.

Rautman, M. 2000. The busy countryside of Late Roman Cyprus. *Report of the Department of Antiquities, Cyprus*: 317–331.

Resco, V., J.P. Ferrio, J.A. Carreira, L. Calvo, P. Casals, A. Ferrero-Serrano, E. Marcos, J.M. Moreno, D.A. Ramirez, M.T. Sebastià, F. Valladares, and D.G. Williams. 2011. The stable isotope ecology of terrestrial plant succession. *Plant Ecology and Diversity* 4.2–3: 117–130.

Riehl, S., R. Bryson, and K. Pustovoytov. 2008. Changing growing conditions for crops during the Near Eastern Bronze Age (3000–1200 BC): The stable carbon isotope evidence. *Journal of Archaeological Science* 35: 1–12.

Roberts, N., W.J. Eastwood, C. Kuzucuoglu, G. Fiorentino, and V. Caracuta. 2011. Climatic, vegetation and cultural change in the eastern Mediterranean during the mid-Holocene environmental transition. *The Holocene* 21: 147–162.

Roberts, N., A. Moreno, B.L. Valero-Garcés, J.P. Corella, M. Jones, S. Allcock, J. Woodbridge, M. Morellón, J. Luterbacher, E. Xoplaki, and M. Türkes. 2012. Palaeolimnological evidence for an east-west climate see-saw in the Mediterranean since AD 900. *Global and Planetary Change*, 84: 23–34.

Rohling, E.J., A. Hayes, P.A. Mayewski, and M. Kucera. 2009. Holocene climatic variability in the eastern Mediterranean, at the end of the Bronze Age. In C. Bachhuber and R.G. Roberts (eds.), *Forces of Transformation: The End of the Bronze Age in the Mediterranean*, 2–5. Themes from the Ancient Near East, BANEA Publication Series 1. Oxford: Oxbow Boks.

Rosen, A.M. 2007. *Civilizing Climate: Social Responses to Climate Change in the Ancient Near East*. Lanham, MD: Altamira Press.

Rosen, A.M., and S.A. Rosen. 2001. Determinist or not determinist? Climate, environment, and archaeological explanation in the Levant. In S.R. Wolff (ed.), *Studies in the Archaeology of Israel and Neighboring Lands in Memory of Douglas L. Esse*, 535–549. Chicago: The Oriental Institute of the University of Chicago.

Rupp, D. 1987. Vive le roi: The emergence of the state in Iron Age Cyprus. In D.W. Rupp (ed.), *Western Cyprus Connections: An Archaeological Symposium*, 147–168. Studies in Mediterranean Archaeology 77. Göteborg, Sweden: Paul Åströms Förlag.

Rupp, D. 1997. Constructing the Cypriot Iron Age: Present praxis, future possibilities. *Bulletin of the American Schools of Oriental Research* 308: 69–75.

Satraki, A. 2012. Από τον Κοσμάσσος στο Νικοκρέοντα: η πολιτειακή οργάνωση της αρχαίας Κύπρου από την Ύστερη Εποχή του Χαλκού μέχρι το τέλος της Κυπροκλασικής περιόδου με βάση τα αρχαιολογικά δεδομένα. Nicosia: University of Cyprus.

Sherratt, S., and A. Sherratt. 1993. The growth of the Mediterranean economy in the early first millennium BC. *World Archaeology* 24: 361–378.

Shirley, R. 2001. *Kitchener's Survey of Cyprus 1878–1883: The First Full Triangulated Survey and Mapping of the Island.* Nicosia: The Bank of Cyprus Cultural Foundation.

Smith, A.T. 2003. *The Political Landscape: Constellations of Authority in Early Complex Polities.* Berkeley: University of California Press.

Sørensen, L.W., and K. Winther-Jacobsen. (eds.) 2006. *Panayia Ematousa I: A Rural Site in South-Eastern Cyprus.* Monographs of the DIA 6. Athens: Danish Institute at Athens.

South, A. 2002. Late Bronze Age settlement patterns in southern Cyprus: The first kingdoms? *Cahiers du Centre d'Études Chypriotes* 32: 59–72.

Stanley Price, N.P. 1979. *Early Prehistoric Settlement in Cyprus: A Review and Gazetteer of Sites, c. 6500–3000 B.C.* British Archaeological Reports International Series 65. Oxford: British Archaeological Reports.

Stewart, J., and E. Stewart. 1950. *Vounous 1937–1938: Field Report on the Excavations Sponsored by the British School of Archaeology at Athens.* Lund, Sweden: British School of Archaeology at Athens.

Swindles, G.T., G. Plunkett, and H.M. Roe. 2007. A delayed climatic response to solar forcing at 2800 cal. BP: Multiproxy evidence from three Irish peatlands. *The Holocene* 17.2: 177–182.

Taylor, J. Du Plat. 1952. A Late Bronze Age settlement at Apliki, Cyprus. *The Antiquaries Journal* 32: 133–167.

Thompson, S. 2004. Side-by-side and front-to-back: Exploring intra-regional latitudinal and longitudinal comparability in survey data. Three case studies from Metaponto, southern Italy. In S.E. Alcock and J.F. Cherry (eds.), *Side-By-Side Survey: Comparative Regional Studies in the Mediterranean World,* 65–85. Oxford: Oxbow Books.

Todd, I.A. 2004. *Vasilikos Valley Project 9: The Field Survey of the Vasilikos Valley Vol. I.* Studies in Mediterranean Archaeology 71.9. Sävedalen, Sweden: Paul Åströms Förlag.

Todd, I.A. 2013. *Vasilikos Valley Project 12: The Field Survey of the Vasilikos Valley Vol. III, Human Settlement in the Vasilikos Valley.* Studies in Mediterranean Archaeology 71.12. Uppsala, Sweden: Åströms Förlag.

Todd, I.A. 2016. *Vasilikos Valley Project 11: The Field Survey of the Vasilikos Valley Vol. II, Artefacts Recovered by the Field Survey.* Studies in Mediterranean Archaeology 71.11. Uppsala, Sweden: Åströms Förlag.

Toumazou, M.K., P.N. Kardulias, and D.B. Counts. (eds.) 2011. *Crossroads and Boundaries: The Archaeology of Past and Present in the Malloura Valley, Cyprus.* Boston: American Schools of Oriental Research.

Turney, C.S.M., D. Wheeler, and A.R. Chivas. 2006. Carbon isotope fractionation in wood during carbonization. *Geochimica et Cosmochimica Acta* 70: 960–964.

Ulbrich, A. 2012. Cult and iconography: Votive sculptures from the Archaic to early Hellenistic sanctuary at Maroni-*Vournes*. In A. Georgiou (ed.), *An Island Culture: Society and Social Relations from the Bronze Age to the Venetian Period,* 177–195. Oxford: Oxbow Books.

Ulbrich, A. 2013. Hellenistic evidence from the sanctuary at Maroni *Vournes. Keryx* 2: 31–61.

van Geel, B., C.J. Heusser, H. Renssen, and C.J.E. Schuurmans. 2000. Climatic change in Chile at around 2700 BP and global evidence for solar forcing: A hypothesis. *The Holocene* 10.5: 659–664.

van Geel, B., N.A. Bokovenko, N.D. Burova, K.V. Chugunov, V. Dergachev, V.G. Dirksen, M. Kulkova, A. Nagler, H. Parzinger, J. van der Plicht, S.S. Vasiliev, and G.I. Zaitseva. 2004. Climate change and the expansion of the Scythian culture after 850 BC: A hypothesis. *Journal of Archaeological Science* 31: 1735–1742.

Wagstaff, J.M. 1978. Geographical contribution to the Vasilikos Valley Project, 1977. In I.A. Todd, Vasilikos Valley Project: Second Preliminary Report, 1977. *Journal of Field Archaeology* 5: 161–195.

Wagstaff, J.M. 1992. Agricultural terraces: The Vasilikos Valley, Cyprus. In M. Bell and J. Boardman (eds.), *Past and Present Soil Erosion: Archaeological and Geographical Perspectives,* 155–161. Oxford: Oxbow Books.

Wasse, A. 2007. Climate, economy, and change: Cyprus and the Levant during the Late Pleistocene to Mid-Holocene. In J. Clarke (ed.), *On the Margins of Southwest Asia: Cyprus during the 6th to 4th Millennia BC*, 43–62. Oxford: Oxbow Books.

Wallace, M., G. Jones, M. Charles, R. Fraser, and P. Halstead. 2013. Stable carbon isotope analysis as a direct means of inferring crop water status and water management practices. *World Archaeology* 45: 388–409.

Webb, J.M., and D. Frankel. 2013. Cultural regionalism and divergent social trajectories in Early Bronze Age Cyprus. *American Journal of Archaeology* 117.1: 59–81.

Weiss, H., and R.S. Bradley. 2001. What drives societal collapse? *Science* 291: 609–610.

Wilkinson, T.J. 2003. *Archaeological Landscapes of the Near East*. Tucson: University of Arizona Press.

Zwicker, U. 1986. Ancient metallurgical methods for copper production in Cyprus. Part 2: Sulphide ores and copper-arsenic-alloy production. *Bulletin of the Cyprus Association of Geologists and Mining Engineers* 3: 92–111.

Index

Page references in *italics* refer to maps, graphs and figures.